Fodor's   W9-BRH-744

ROCK & ROLL TRAVELER USA

THE ULTIMATE GUIDE TO JUKE JOINTS,

STREET CORNERS, WHISKEY BARS AND HOTEL

ROOMS WHERE MUSIC HISTORY WAS MADE

BY TIM PERRY & ED GLINERT

FODOR'S TRAVEL PUBLICATIONS, INC.
NEW YORK * TORONTO * LONDON * SYDNEY * AUCKLAND
VISIT US ON THE WEB AT HTTP://WWW.FODORS.COM/

Rock & Roll Traveler USA

Editor: Chelsea Mauldin
Photo Editor: Kelly Duane
Text and Cover Design: Guido Caroti
Special Projects Editor: Nancy van Itallie
Production Editor: Linda K. Schmidt
Map Editor: Robert P. Blake

Copyright

Special Sales

Fodor's Travel Publications are available at special discounts for bulk purchases for sales promotions or premiums. Special editions, including personalized covers, excerpts of existing guides, and corporate imprints, can be created in large quantities for special needs. For more information, contact your local bookseller or write to Special Markets, Fodor's Travel Publications, 201 East 50th Street, New York, NY 10022. Inquiries from Canada should be directed to your local Canadian bookseller or sent to Random House of Canada, Ltd., Marketing Department, 1265 Aerowood Drive, Mississauga, Ontario L4W 1B9. Inquiries from the United Kingdom should be sent to Fodor's Travel Publications, 20 Vauxhall Bridge Road, London, England SW1V 2SA.

PRINTED IN THE UNITED STATES OF AMERICA

10 9 8 7 6 5 4 3 2 1

CONTENTS

A NOTE FROM THE AUTHORS

More than a million people have already passed through the Rock and Roll Hall of Fame in Cleveland, Ohio, and thousands fill Austin's hotel rooms each weekend for a taste of live music. We all know people who go on vacation and come back with tales not of the major tourist sights, but of some obscure neighborhood that was mentioned in a song or of a great spot where their favorite band used to hang out. Yet when it comes to travel guides and brochures, rock and other popular music is largely ignored—which is why it seemed obvious that we should write this book.

Our aim was to provide a fun read—something that's as enjoyable while you're lazing on the sofa as it is useful in the glove compartment on a road trip. That's why we've provided a grounding on all the country's famous venues, from D.C.'s 9:30 Club to San Francisco's Fillmore. We include the histories of many groundbreaking studios, from Boston's indie-hits factory, Fort Apache, to the heart of soul in Muscle Shoals and the Memphis studios where rock & roll first bloomed. We've also unearthed great second-hand-record stores like Pittsburgh's Jerry's and the Great Escape in Nashville, and provided listings of top bars, clubs, and places to grab a bite to eat nationwide. We've included many former homes of the stars and other privately owned places (so please don't give us a bad name by hanging around too much).

Inevitably we had conflicts of space, trying to combine practical, contemporary information and historical facts about where the great songs were written and where those who wrote them were born, got married, got out of their heads, or even died. We also tried to give a nod to important local bands and highlight the current scene in cities. There's no way everything can go in. Fans of particular genres or artists will undoubtedly question our choices on occasion. Bear in mind that this book is focused on *destinations*: If a band hasn't written about a particular place, or done something of note at specific locations, then they're not going to get as much attention as a Springsteen (who mentions towns at any convenience), Led Zeppelin (whose '70s tours left a catalog of chaos), or Nirvana (whose brief history is both one of this decade's most influential musical episodes and directly linked to a particular city's sound).

We hope you grab a friend, compile some tapes, do the road trip, and let us know how you get on. We'd be happy to get letters and cards care of Fodor's Travel Publications, 201 East 50th Street, New York, NY 10022, or email us at tim@tperry.demon.co.uk.

Tim Perry and Ed Glinert
July 1996

ACKNOWLEDGMENTS

We figured that we would get all kinds of help along the way for this book, but the response from people in cities across the USA was really great, to say the very least. The list of names below is as comprehensive as our memories could make it, but if you helped out and you're not here, give us a hard time and we'll give you a mention in the next edition.

TIM WOULD LIKE TO THANK: Hope Dreyfuss, Wendy Shlensky, Gary Smith, and Dave Snow (Boston); Ric Addy, Jim DeRogatis, John Hardman, Joe Shanahan, and Bill Wyman (Chicago); Joseph Gorman and Dan Lincoln (Cincy); Cindy Barber, Jeff Hagan, John Habat, Jim Hencke, and Mike Shea (Cleveland); Jeff Wignall (Connecticut); G. Brown and Lisa Bringardner (Denver); Karen Yakovac (Indianapolis); Ciaran at the House of Blues, Carol Martinez, and Mike McHugh (L.A. area); Hiawatha Bailey and the Cult Heroes, Stephen Bergman, Michelle Cavanaugh, Don Davis, Chris Karwowski, Scott Morgan, Linda Siglin, and Ron Swope (Michigan); Christine Kieser (Minneapolis); the staff at the Bienville House Hotel, Jerry Brock, Jan V. Ramsey, Mike West, and John Sinclair (New Orleans); Todd Erkel, Manny Theiner, and Matt Wrbican (Pittsburgh); Jill Abrahamson, Chip Conley and all at the Phoenix Hotel, Jerry Pompili, Dawn Stranne, and Ada Vassilovski (San Francisco); Jo Rae DiMenno, Bill Griggs, Eric Hartman, Bob Myers, Scott Owings, and Eddie Wilson (Texas); Doug Barker and David Blandford (Washington); Gus at the 9:30 Club (Washington, D.C.); and Susan Dean and Al Hoffman (Woodstock, NY).

Particular thanks must go to **CHARLES ANDREW** in L.A., **DAVE GOODRICH** in Pittsburgh, **DAVID PRINCE** in Chicago, and **JOEL SELVIN** in San Francisco for really going out of their way to help. Much appreciated, guys—I owe you sometime. Thanks to Northwest Airlines for a top flight to Cleveland to check out the Rock and Roll Hall of Fame and to Alamo Car Rental for making big road trips possible with the best rates.

Back home, thanks to John Breslin, Chris Charlesworth (Omnibus Press), Suzie Corrigan, Magnus Mills, Pat and Linda Richardson, David Thomas, Mick Wall, and Slim for advice and sorting out key queries, and to **ROS BELFORD** and **SARAH CHAMPION** for encouraging words and professional advice when this was book was still in its barroom stage. E grazie mille, Silvia.

ED WOULD LIKE TO THANK: **RUTH BIRCH SYKES** from the Macon-Bibb County CVB for her indefatigable help and enthusiasm, plus all the others in Macon—Alan Walden, Zelma Redding, Kirsten West, Hamp Swain, Rob Blount, Mama Louise Hudson, and the staff at the 1842 College Inn—and **GEORGE BEECROFT** for such wonderful hospitality at the Lillagaard Hotel in Ocean Grove, New Jersey. And thanks again to Stanley Goldstein, Ted Allen, Stanley Bard at the Chelsea Hotel, Stephanie Oxley, Le Bar Bat, and Manny's Music (New York); Ellen Kornfield and Hotel Atop The Belle Vue (Philadelphia); Dennis Greenia and Ort from Flagpole, Frank at the Georgia Theater, and Weaver Dexter (Athens, GA); Jim O'Neal, the Blues Archive (Oxford, MS); Kimmie McNeil at the Memphis CVB, Arcade Restaurant, Center for Southern Folklore, W.C. Handy House, Sun Records, Rum Boogie Cafe, and B.B. King's Blues Club (Memphis); the Hall family at FAME Studios (Muscle Shoals); Terry Clements and Jack's Tracks (Nashville); the Andrew Johnson Hotel (Knoxville); and Alamo Car Rental.

In the U.K., thanks to Marian Walsh for driving in New Jersey and Pennsylvania and for all her time and encouragement; to Lucy Richmond, for driving around the South; and to Celia Boggis, John Nicholson, Doug Mackay, Jonathan Hamp, Lisa Chamberlain, and Barbara Bailey.

Both authors would like to say a big thanks to the people at Fodor's, particularly to Chelsea Mauldin for coping with a way-too-big manuscript, to Nancy van Itallie for picking up on the idea, to Guido Caroti for the design, and to Kelly Duane, who gathered an amazing collection of photos through dedication and charm alone.

The editors wish to extend particular thanks to photographers **MURRAY BOWLES, PAT GRAHAM, DENNIS KLEIMAN,** and **BROOKE WILLIAMS**—their generosity and remarkable pictures made it possible to illustrate this book—and to **JUDY PEISER** at the Center for Southern Folklore for her kind help with archival images.

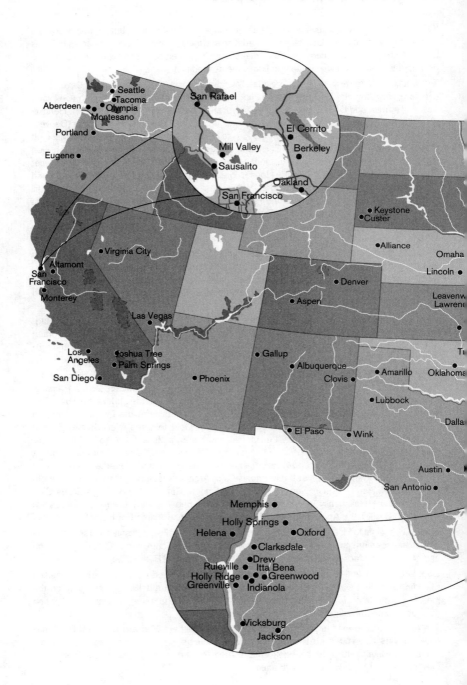

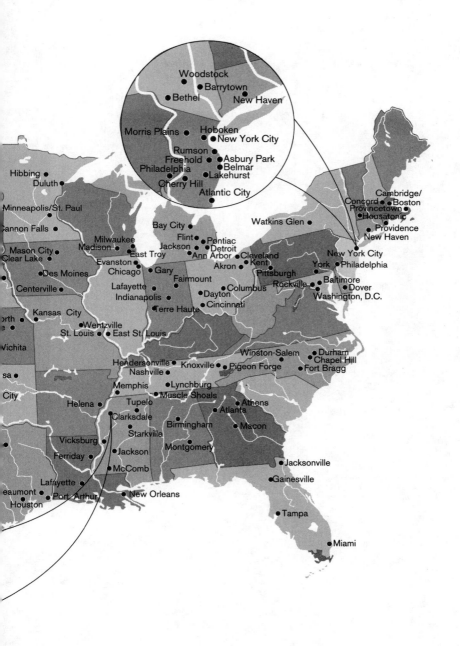

Woodstock
Barrytown
Bethel
New Haven
Morris Plains
Hoboken
New York City
Rumson
Freehold
Asbury Park
Philadelphia
Belmar
Cherry Hill
Lakehurst
Atlantic City

Hibbing
Duluth
Minneapolis/St. Paul
Cannon Falls
Mason City
Clear Lake
Des Moines
Centerville
Watkins Glen
Cambridge/
Concord
Boston
Provincetown
Housatonic
Providence
New Haven
Bay City
Milwaukee
Flint
Pontiac
Madison
Jackson
Detroit
East Troy
Ann Arbor
Cleveland
Evanston
Akron
Kent
New York City
Chicago
Gary
Pittsburgh
York
Philadelphia
Lafayette
Fairmount
Columbus
Rockville
Baltimore
Indianapolis
Dayton
Dover
Terre Haute
Cincinnati
Washington, D.C.
Kansas City
orth
Wentzville
St. Louis
East St. Louis
Wichita
Winston-Salem
Durham
Chapel Hill
Hendersonville
Knoxville
Pigeon Forge
Fort Bragg
sa
Nashville
City
Memphis
Lynchburg
Helena
Muscle Shoals
Tupelo
Athens
Clarksdale
Atlanta
Vicksburg
Birmingham
Macon
Starkville
Ferriday
Jackson
Montgomery
McComb
Lafayette
Jacksonville
eaumont
Port Arthur
New Orleans
Gainesville
Houston
Tampa
Miami

THE
EAST

New Haven

When the Five Satins recorded "In the Still of the Night" here in 1956, little did anyone know that New Haven was already guaranteed a place in rock history as the birthplace of Richard and Karen Carpenter (born in 1946 and 1950, respectively).

*EATING*DRINKINGDANCINGSHOPPINGPLAYINGSLEEPING

New Haven, Connecticut's largest city, suffers from a particularly virulent strain of urban blight. Only the city center, enlivened by the presence of Yale University, is worth visiting. Near the campus, check out **CUTLER'S** (33 Broadway, tel. 203/777−6271), which has the state's largest selection of new and used CDs.

NEW HAVEN ARENA

Jim Morrison had one of his infamous run-ins with the law at a Doors gig at the New Haven Arena on December 9, 1967. Before the show, Morrison was in the shower necking with a woman when a cop walked in and, failing to recognize Morrison, tried to kick the couple out. Words were exchanged—the singer diplomatically asked if the cop would like to eat his crotch—and the cop maced him. Later, while performing "Back Door Man" from behind a line of police stationed at the edge of the stage, Morrison recounted the event to the audience. The house lights were flipped on, and a lieutenant arrested the singer, who was subsequently charged with "indecent and immoral exhibition." The arrest

POLICE DEPT
NEW HAVEN CONN
23750
12·10·67

New Haven P. D./courtesy of Jeff Wignall

Public Enemy and Lizard King

was featured in Oliver Stone's biopic *The Doors,* but as the venue (State and Grove Sts.) had by that time been replaced by a parking lot, the director shot the relevant scenes at the Palace Performing Arts Center (248 College St.).

[TOAD'S PLACE]

Despite a capacity of just 700, this club on the edge of the Yale campus has managed to book its fair share of superstars. The Rolling Stones kicked off their Steel Wheels tour here in January 1990. Around the same time, Bob Dylan played a 6½-hour set, reputedly his longest ever. Johnny Cash, David Bowie, U2, Radiohead, Matthew Sweet, and the Goo Goo Dolls have also appeared here. *300 York St., tel. 203/624–TOAD.*

DELAWARE

Delaware may have been the first state to ratify the U.S. Constitution, but in terms of popular-music history, it's a nonstarter. In 1966 Bob Marley lived briefly at his mom's in Newark and worked at the local Chrysler plant, but he returned to Jamaica the following year to sign a deal with Johnny Nash's Cayman Music. So the state's unfortunate claim to musical fame is Perry Como's jaunty 1960 novelty hit, "Delaware," which contains the unforgettable line "What did Della wear, boy?...she wore a brand new jersey."

Dover

The Victrola, an early phonograph, was invented at the turn of the 20th century by a local engineer, Eldridge Johnson. The image of his dog Nipper with an ear cocked to a Victrola speaker has long been used as the logo for RCA Victor in the United States and for HMV Records and shops in the United Kingdom.

Courtesy of Delaware State Museums, Dover

Victrola inventor and Nipper's owner, Eldridge Johnson

CARL PERKINS
CRASH SITE

In March 1956 Carl Perkins, en route to New York City to do a TV show, was involved in a car wreck in Dover. His vehicle hit the back of a truck, killing the truck driver and Perkins's brother. Perkins was a star on the rise, having composed the chart-busting "Blue Suede Shoes," but while he recovered from his injuries, his original was overshadowed by Elvis Presley's cover, and Perkins's career never regained momentum. The Beatles felt a debt to the rockabilly singer and covered three of his songs—"Everybody's Trying to Be My Baby," "Honey Don't," and "Matchbox"—on early records. *Rte. 13, 4 mi south of Dover, near Woodside.*

Baltimore

OH BALTIMORE, MAN IT'S HARD JUST TO LIVE—RANDY NEWMAN, "BALTIMORE"

A no-crap blue-collar city, Baltimore has enjoyed celluloid exposure thanks to native sons John Waters (*Hairspray*) and Barry Levinson (*Diner*). Its best-known musical documentation, however, was written by Randy Newman, who'd never set foot in the city when he wrote his despairing lyrics to "Baltimore" back in 1977.

Baltimore was the birthplace of '50s songwriter Jerry Lieber (born April 25, 1933) and Frank Zappa (December 21, 1940), as well as avant-garde composer Philip Glass (January 3, 1937), who has written a symphony based on David Bowie's album *Low*. Chief Talking Head David Byrne was born in Scotland but spent his early teens in Baltimore; details of his humdrum suburban existence can be found on his "And She Was."

Two pioneering jazz musicians were also locals. Billie ("Lady Sings the Blues") Holiday was born here on April 7, 1915, and a statue in her honor stands on Pennsylvania Avenue between Lanvale and Lafayette Streets. Cab Calloway, whose rock credits

John H. Murphy III/courtesy of Cab Calloway Museum, Coppin State College

Cab Calloway

include an appearance in *The Blues Brothers*, spent his youth in the city and is commemorated by a collection of his effects on the Coppin State College campus.

EATINGDRINKINGDANCINGSHOPPINGPLAYINGSLEEPING

The city has a healthy number of live-music venues. One of the best is the cramped **EIGHT BY TEN** (10 E. Cross St., tel. 410/625—2000), which offers a good range of reggae, hip-hop, and indie music. Emerging alternative and punk bands, both national and local, play **MEMORY LANE** (1433 W. Hamburg St., tel. 410/837—5070). **HAMMERJACKS** (1101 S. Howard St., tel. 410/752—3302) serves the metal market.

FRANK ZAPPA BOYHOOD HOME
During the '40s Frank Zappa lived in an army housing project in Edgewood, near Baltimore, when his father worked as a meteorologist at the local weapons plant. Mustard gas was among the items manufactured, so area residents were issued gas masks—the seeds of Frank's alienation? The family moved to Monterey in 1951. *15 Dexter St., Edgewood.*

Baltimore Five

Scott Walker, "The Lady Came from Baltimore" (1967)
Gram Parsons, "Streets of Baltimore" (1973)
Randy Newman, "Baltimore" (1977)
Nils Lofgren, "Baltimore" (1979)
Counting Crows, "Raining in Baltimore" (1994)

Rockville

It was this college town that R.E.M. had in mind when they sang "(Don't Go Back to) Rockville" on 1984's *Reckoning.* One reason to disregard that advice is **YESTERDAY AND TODAY RECORDS** (1327 Rockville Pike #J, tel. 301/279–7007), which has one of the D.C. area's best selections of new and alternative music, including plenty of vinyl.

The Damned make an instore appearance at Yesterday and Today

Bert Queiroz/courtesy of Yesterday and Today Records

MASSACHUSETTS

New England's liveliest state has generated plenty of musical interest over the years, a fact owing in no small part to its vibrant student population. The twin cities of Boston and Cambridge have been the source of some of the leading alternative bands of the past decade, while Amherst and Northampton, college towns in the west of the state, are where Dinosaur Jr and Buffalo Tom emerged before making their names in Boston in the mid-'80s. Massachusetts's college towns are also generally notable for a welcoming mix of bars, cafés, and offbeat stores.

Boston

WELL I LOVE THAT DIRTY WATER/BOSTON YOU'RE MY HOME—THE STANDELLS, "DIRTY WATER"

Rock & roll had a hard time getting off the ground in Boston, largely due to opposition from the Catholic Church and from local Irish-American politicos who took their lead from that body. In the '50s, authorities stopped a road show organized by early rock DJ Alan Freed and did their best to ban new sounds from the airwaves. The city was barely involved when the first wave of American guitar groups began emulating the British sound, and the song most associated with '60s Boston, "Dirty Water," was recorded by the L.A.-based Standells.

Then up stepped the MGM. Having missed out on West Coast psychedelia, the label desperately tried to concoct a Boston scene in 1968. In a big *Newsweek* spread in January 1969, Hallucinations's singer Peter Wolf (later of the J. Geils Band) said the town was buzzing with clubs like the Catacombs (a preferred hangout of Van Morrison), the

Aerosmith, Boston's best-known rockers

Psychedelic Supermarket (where Boston-born Donna Summer sang in a rock band), and the famous Boston Tea Party (now the Avalon). Unfortunately, the so-called "Bosstown Sound" depended on the work of no-hope groups like Ultimate Spinach, Phluph, and Beacon Street Union. The hype was a complete flop, MGM lost some $20 million, and the local scene was dead for years to come.

Boston bounced back in the mid-'70s. The Tom Scholtz supergroup named for the city dominated the airwaves with its megahit "More Than a Feeling," and notable albums were released by the J. Geils Band, the Cars, Jonathan Richman and the Modern Lovers, and Aerosmith (in their first run at fame). The city's student masses have continued to support a healthy independent scene, and Boston is now a leading indie center. In recent years, the city has produced the Pixies, the Lemonheads, Come, Buffalo Tom, Throwing Muses, Belly, Sebadoh, Gigolo Aunts, the Mighty Mighty Bosstones, and Letters to Cleo. A particularly rich crop of female performers has also come out of Boston in recent years, including solo acts Jennifer Trynin, Tracy Bonham, Juliana Hatfield (ex–Blake Babies), Aimee Mann (ex–'Til Tuesday), and Mary Lou Lord. The metro area has also produced embryonic soul supergroup New Edition and, lest we forget, NKOTB.

EATINGDRINKINGDANCINGSHOPPINGPLAYINGSLEEPING

Lansdowne Street, a row of nightclubs and bars in the shade of Fenway Park, includes the Avalon and Mama Kin (*see below*), as well as **BILL'S BAR** (7 Lansdowne St., tel. 617/421–9678), whose CD jukebox is one of the best-stocked in the city. A few minutes away is the legendary Rathskeller, better known as the Rat (*see below*).

Tiny Boylston Place, commonly known as the Alley, runs off the south side of Boston Common. It's home to a number of popular joints, the pick of which are **STICKY MIKE'S** (21 Boylston Pl., tel. 617/251–2583) for blues, **SWEETWATER CAFÉ** (3 Boylston Pl., tel. 617/351–2515) for Southwestern music and cuisine, and the **ALLEY CAT** (1 Boylston Pl., tel. 617/351–2510), a lounge bar and great hangout.

Newbury Street runs from the west side of Boston Common toward Fenway; it's full of designer stores at the Common end, but it blurs agreeably into a more alternative scene of coffee shops and record stores—including Newbury Comics (*see below*) and a huge Tower branch—at its Massachusetts Avenue end.

To bone up on the local rock scene, pick up the free monthly music paper *Boston Rock*, available from bins, cafés, and venues. For more comprehensive listings, there's the weekly *Boston Phoenix*, which costs a buck and a half.

AEROSMITH APARTMENT

The band lived here in the early '70s before signing with CBS. The apartment building was featured in the 1991 video for "Sweet Emotion." *1325 Commonwealth Ave., Apt. 2B.*

BOSTON ARENA

In May 1958, an Alan Freed–organized concert was about to start when a phalanx of Boston's finest stormed to the stage and turned to face the crowd, nightsticks drawn. Freed, the show's emcee, was informed that the show would not be allowed to go on until everyone in the audience sat down. Freed instead egged on the crowd, got himself arrested, and caused the gig to be canceled. Meanwhile, backstage, two of the performers on Freed's package tour had finally had enough of each other's company. The story goes that while Freed was arguing with the cops out front, Jerry Lee Lewis's father had a gun trained on Chuck Berry, who was in turn holding a knife to Jerry Lee's neck. It was smoother sailing for the first Motown Revue, held here in November 1962 with Mary Wells, the Supremes, and Marvin Gaye. The arena is now an ice rink. *238 St. Botolph St.*

Courtesy of the Boston Globe

Freed's rock & roll riot makes the papers

BOSTON GARDEN

Fans in line on January 6, 1975, for tickets to a Led Zeppelin gig caused nearly $50,000 of damage to the lobby of this downtown venue. The show, scheduled for February 4, was subsequently canceled. The auditorium, renowned both for its parquet basketball floor and its terrible sightlines, was demolished in 1996; the floor was moved next door to the new **FLEETCENTER** (tel. 617/624–1000), home of the Celtics and Bruins.

[BOSTON TEA PARTY (THE AVALON)]

A former synagogue at 53 Berkeley Street became the first sizable rock venue on the East Coast when the Boston Tea Party opened in January 1967. It quickly became one of the top psychedelic showplaces in the country, up there with the Fillmore ballrooms.

The Velvet Underground played the city regularly. (Local Jonathan Richman, who claims to have seen every one of the Velvets' Boston shows, once joked that he saw the group more times than any individual member played with them.) It was at the Tea Party in September 1968 that John Cale gave his last performance with the band for over two decades. (The band found a replacement backstage after the gig when bassist Doug Yule got to chatting with the remaining bandmembers and joined up.) A farcical December 1968 gig by the Velvets and MC5 was crashed by a group of violent pseudoradical politicos known as the East Village Motherfuckers. At the end of the show, some Motherfuckers got on stage and urged the crowd to burn down the venue, much to the displeasure of Lou Reed, who took the mike and calmly suggested that that just might be a stupid idea.

In the spring of 1969, Led Zeppelin did four nights at the Tea Party; at the last show, the crowd called them back for so many encores that they were onstage for over four hours and ran out of material. They ended up playing their set twice and spent the last hour doing Stones, Who, and Beatles numbers. Later that year the Tea Party moved from its original location to Lansdowne Street. Operating under the name Avalon since the early '90s, the venue now sells out its 1,500 seats for such top names as the Stone Roses, who played here in May 1995, their first U.S. gig after a half-decade layoff. *15 Lansdowne St, tel. 617/262–2424.*

THE ESPLANADE

The ever-popular Boston Pops Fourth of July bash and other free summer concerts are held at this public park on the banks of the Charles River. When Green Day played gratis in August 1994, the kids and the cops had a misunderstanding, and the ensuing "riot" was national news.

HARD ROCK CAFE

Kay Hanley, lead singer of Boston popsters Letters to Cleo, was until recently a staff member at this HRC branch, where the decorative memorabilia includes platinum discs and old clothes representing locals Aerosmith, the Cars, and Boston. On Friday and Saturday, two New England bands play in the small downstairs Cavern Club (yes, it's dressed up with Beatles stuff). *131 Clarendon St., tel. 617/424-7625.*

MAMA KIN

Members of Aerosmith are part-owners of this club, the only one on the Lansdowne Street strip with a particularly phallic microphone above the front door. The band opened the joint in December 1994 with the last gig of their 30-month world tour. The main room is a cozy gigging space that holds 300, but additional rooms can boost the club's capacity to 1,250. Established names have played—from Tom Jones to the Cramps to Throwing Muses—but Mama Kin was planned as a nurturing ground for new bands and provides in-house digital recording and video filming at cost. *36 Lansdowne St., tel. 617/536-2100 or 617/351-2525 (24 hours).*

MUSEUM OF FINE ARTS

Jonathan Richman sang about looking among the Cézannes here for a girlfriend—"G-I-R-L-F-R-E-N"—in the song of the same name from the Modern Lovers' 1976 debut album. *465 Huntington Ave., tel. 617/267-9300.*

Outside Mama Kin

NEWBURY COMICS

In 1978 Mike Dreese and John Brusger, two students at the Massachusetts Institute of Technology in Cambridge, used $2,000 and a big comic-book collection to open the first branch of this hip local chain at 268 Newbury Street, a few doors down from the current flagship location. It wasn't long before records—particularly indie imports—became an important part of their stock. In the early '80s, the pair started the Modern Method punk label and also launched *Boston Rock* magazine (which they've since sold); the Wicked Disc label is also part of the Newbury Comics setup. Nowadays there are around a dozen branches in the Boston area, stocking a great range of alternative sounds, as well as comics and T-shirts. *332 Newbury St., tel. 617/236-4930.*

THE PARADISE

This club opened its doors in 1977 and has maintained a consistent policy of booking bands on their first national tours, particularly European bands making their U.S. debuts. At a December 1980 gig, during their first short tour of the States, U2 discovered a strong following in this heavily Celtic city—150 fans turned up, and about 100 of them left before headliner Barooga came on. When Bono and friends came back three months later, they sold out the venue's 500 tickets two nights running and recorded the live version of "11 O'Clock Tick Tock" that appears on the B side of the 1981 single

"Fire." The press conference shown in U2's *Rattle and Hum* was also filmed here. *967 Commonwealth Ave., tel. 617/562–8804.*

PARK STREET "T" STATION

In the early '90s, before her involvement with Kurt Cobain and her subsequent run-ins with Courtney Love made her a hot topic in the indie-music press, folk-rocker Mary Lou Lord was making a more low-key impression as a busker in the underground stations of Boston's subway system (known locally as the "T"). James Taylor and Shawn Colvin were among those who descended to this stop on the northeast edge of Boston Common to check her out. *Park and Tremont Sts.*

[THE RAT]

This pioneering rock club, under the same ownership now for over a quarter century, may have a sign out front that says the Rathskeller, but it's been known as the Rat since Willie Alexander rewrote Danny and the Juniors' "At the Hop" as "At the Rat."

Thanks in part to a close working relationship with New York's CBGBs, the Rat has attracted many of the best breaking bands to Boston. The Cars started out here with regular gigs in 1977 and were soon followed by such top names in new wave as the Police, Blondie, the Jam, and Squeeze. Recently it's been an early gigging ground for some of the city's finest, including the Pixies, the Lemonheads, and Buffalo Tom; members of the Del Fuegos were on the club's dishwashing crew. Alternative rock, punk, and rockabilly continue to be prominent on the schedule.

The three-level club, in Kenmore Square in the heart of Boston's college land, is always humming with a lively crowd. The downstairs bar, which adds sidewalk seating in summer, has a well-stocked jukebox; the Belfry, upstairs, has pool tables and showcases paintings by young local artists. Hundreds of papier-mâché rats decorate the music room—they're grafted onto columns, attached to the walls, huddled in a grotto that gleams with their bright red eyes—making it no place to experiment with mood-altering substances for the first time. *528 Commonwealth Ave., tel. 617/536–2750 or 617/536–6508 (24 hours), http://xensei.com/users/therat.*

At the Rat

SPIT 13 (AXIS)

Starting in 1978, this club was a key punk venue that developed a reputation for booking such emerging Brit bands as the Buzzcocks, the Police, and Flock of Seagulls. Now called AXIS, the club holds 800 and showcases local acts, but out-of-towners sometimes occupy the bottom of the bill; in 1991, a band called Pearl Jam opened for headliners Buffalo Tom. *13 Lansdowne St., tel. 617/262-2437.*

NOT MUCH OF A COLLEGE TOWN

"Don't worry about Boston, it's not much of a college town," claimed the manager in *This Is Spinal Tap* when a Boston gig on the celluloid band's ill-fated U.S. tour was canceled. The irony is that Boston is *the* college town: Dozens of educational institutions make their home along the Boston and Cambridge sides of the Charles River. Joan Baez spent a term or two as a drama student at Boston University. Gram Parsons and Modern Lover–cum–Talking Head Jerry Harrison had spells at Harvard, as did Dean Wareham of Galaxie 500 and Luna. Tracy Chapman went to Tufts, and Bonnie Raitt studied at Radcliffe. The Berklee College of Music counts among its alumni Quincy Jones, Donald Fagen, Steve Vai, Aimee Mann, Melissa Etheridge, Bruce Hornsby, Ed Roland of Collective Soul, and Juliana Hatfield.

Cambridge

The hub of activity in Cambridge is Harvard Square, which sprawls out from the front gates of the university. The square is always full of street musicians, many of whom attract large crowds, and the immediate area is a good place to drop some dollars, not just in cafés and bars but in over 20 bookstores and a dozen record stores. One T-stop southeast is Central Square, a less studenty, more bohemian zone with a slight edge to it.

EATING DRINKING DANCING SHOPPING PLAYING SLEEPING

Harvard Square is home to several music chains, including a branch of Newbury Comics. Some smaller stores have secondhand selections, including SECOND COMING (1105 Massachusetts Ave., tel. 617/576-6400) and MYSTERY TRAIN (1208 Massachusetts Ave., tel. 617/497-4024). The world's largest cybercafé, CYBERSMITH (42 Church St., tel. 617/492-5857), has nearly 50 computer terminals for surfing or trying out CD-ROMs (they have a fair selection of music titles). The main music venue in this part of town is the House of Blues (*see below*).

Crammed together in Central Square are three popular venues: the Middle East (*see below*); the often crowded and superbly atmospheric TT THE BEAR'S PLACE (10 Brookline St., tel. 617/492-0082), which specializes in up-and-coming alternative bands; and MAN RAY (21 Brookline St., tel. 617/864-0400), with a wide spectrum of dance music, from industrial to goth.

Two T-stops north of Harvard Square is JOHNNY D'S (17 Holland St., at Davis Sq., tel. 617/776-9667), a nationally known blues club offering a wide range of top-drawer roots music.

CLUB 47 (PASSIM)

This coffeehouse opened in 1958 at 47 Mt. Auburn Street, and during the early '60s it became one of the premier venues on the national folk circuit; Bob Dylan, Joan Baez, and Arlo Guthrie played here regularly. In 1964 Club 47 relocated to its present address, and while it was eventually renamed Passim, it continued to expose its predominantly white, academic audience to such musicians as Howlin' Wolf, Muddy Waters, and Buddy

Guy. Blues, roots, and folk are still the club's focus; recent performers have included Tom Waits, Tracy Chapman, and Suzanne Vega. *47 Palmer St., tel. 617/492–7679.*

[FORT APACHE STUDIOS]

Alison Dyer/courtesy of Fort Apache Studios

What started in 1986 as a humble eight-track studio has grown into an alternative-music empire with two full-size studios, its own record label, and a management company that looks after Juliana Hatfield and Belly, among others. Fort Apache Studios functions around a core of resident producers/engineers—Paul Kolderie, Sean Slade, Tim O'Heir, Lou Giordano, Gary Smith (who co-owns the joint with Brit folk-rocker Billy Bragg), and most recently Wally Gaggle—who have built up a stellar portfolio of alternative names. The Pixies made their debut EP, *Come on Pilgrim,* at the Fort, and were followed by Dinosaur Jr, Throwing Muses, the Lemonheads, Sebadoh, Buffalo Tom, Come, Radiohead, Superchunk, and many more.

The studio's first location was on the edge of Roxbury, one of Boston's toughest neighborhoods, and it resembled a rehearsal space more than today's high-tech setup. The resident producers set out not to record anything fancy but, as Tim O'Heir has said, "to make the band sound like they do in a club on a good

Fort Apache's Julianna Hatfield

night." The little studio had problems, however: In winter it got so cold that the musicians had to keep their gloves on while playing, and in summer the lack of air-conditioning dictated that they wear little more than shorts. And there was always the problem of cars and equipment being stolen—not for nothing had the studio been named Fort Apache.

In 1990 the partners jumped at a cheap lease in the Rounder Records building (*see below*); they operated the two facilities simultaneously for a year or so, but when a band was held up at gunpoint at the Roxbury studio, they realized the time to move out had come. In 1994 the Fort acquired a new location across Massachusetts Avenue on Edmund Street. This space has hosted concerts and may also mount film screenings, spoken-word performances, and so on.

The Fort Apache label, distributed by MCA, got off the ground in 1995 with a compilation album of the best of the bands that have recorded at the studio. Among the new groups to be signed have been locals Coldwater Flat, Minnesota's Shatterproof, and New York City's Speedball Baby. *1 Camp St., Suite 2, tel. 617/868–2242.*

HARVARD SQUARE THEATER

After a May 1974 gig, rock journalist Jon Landau single-handedly created the Springsteen hype by writing in a local mag, *The Real Paper,* "Last Thursday at Harvard Square Theater I saw my rock & roll past flash before my eyes. And I saw something else. I saw rock & roll's future, and its name is Bruce Springsteen. And on a night when I needed to feel young, he made me feel like I was listening to music for the first time." The Boss must have been pleased—he later tapped Landau as his producer. The venue has since been replaced by a movie multiplex. *10 Church St.*

HARVARD UNIVERSITY

Gram Parsons formed the International Submarine Band while studying theology here in 1965. He went on to use a great deal of religious imagery in his songs and covered the Louvin Brothers' "The Christian Life" on the Byrds' *Sweetheart of the Rodeo* album. In 1971 Jonathan Richman and the Modern Lovers played at a student dance, recordings of which appear on the live album *Precise Modern Lovers Order*, not released until 1994; the front cover pictures the band outside the university. One of the bandmembers, Jerry Harrison, studied architecture here but left both school and the Modern Lovers to join up with Talking Heads. *Harvard Sq.*

The House of Blues

HOUSE OF BLUES

The first in the House of Blues chain opened in this blue-and-white 19th-century clapboard home off Harvard Square in 1992. Although much smaller than the branches that followed, and not nearly as glitzy, it still attracts top names from the blues circuit on weekends; local artists take the stage during the week. There's a gift store, decent down-home food, and a very popular gospel Sunday brunch (served in three sittings). *96 Winthrop St., tel. 617/491–2583.*

MIDDLE EAST RESTAURANT

Since this Middle Eastern restaurant in Central Square began booking bands in 1988, it's hosted most of the major players on the Massachusetts rock scene, including Juliana Hatfield, Morphine, Dinosaur Jr, Come, and the Lemonheads. Many nights there are three different performances going on: In the "Bakery"—a makeshift stage at the end of one of the dining rooms—you can expect anything from belly dancing (every Wednesday night, Beavis) to jazz guitarists or local bands. "Upstairs," a small room at the back of the restaurant, puts on mostly regional bands. "Downstairs" is the major room, where an enlightened booking policy guarantees the best new music in a nice space that holds around 500. The Middle East produces a handy monthly broadsheet with good bios on the bands coming up in the next few weeks. Should you care to eat, portions are big and inexpensive. *472–480 Massachusetts Ave., tel. 617/497–0576.*

NAMELESS COFFEE HOUSE

One of the first places Tracy Chapman played was this coffee shop near Tufts University, where she was a student. *3 Church St., tel. 617/864–1630.*

ROUNDER RECORDS

Rounder, based in Boston since 1970, is a major independent distributor of American roots, blues, and folk music. It has scored major successes with George Thorogood (whose first two LPs on the label went gold), Nanci Griffith, Burning Spear, and Professor Longhair and has a most eclectic and huge back catalog. *1 Camp St., tel. 617/354–0700.*

Concord

WALDEN POND

Twenty miles northwest of Boston, just beyond the Minute Man National Historic Park, is the body of water made famous by Henry David Thoreau in his 1854 *Walden*. In the early '90s, ex-Eagle Don Henley organized a successful campaign to keep Walden Pond from being filled in and replaced by an office block and parking lot. A gaggle of celebrities played benefit gigs and even churned out a book, *Heaven Is Under Our Feet*, with literary contributions from Henley, Paula Abdul, Jimmy Buffett, Arlo Guthrie, rock critic Dave Marsh, E. L. Doctorow, and Jimmy Carter, among others. *Rte. 126, tel. 508/369–3254.*

Housatonic

ALICE'S CHURCH

"Alice's Restaurant," Arlo Guthrie's antidraft anthem (among other things), was named for Alice Brock, who lived in this converted church and ran the restaurant featured in the song and related movie. Details of Guthrie's attempt to take out Alice's trash—which precipitated his 1965 littering arrest, his encounter with the draft board, and the song—are available. Guthrie bought the building in the early '90s, and it now houses his record company and the charitable organization he runs. *4 Van Deusenville Rd., tel. 413/623–8925.*

Provincetown

The state's hippest summertime resort, Provincetown lies on the farthest point of Cape Cod, 120 miles from Boston. A Beat hangout in the '50s, it's now a vacation favorite of gays and lesbians. The stores along Commercial Street are full of trendy alternative gear, and its clubs are hopping all summer with music. Members of Belly and Throwing Muses live here when not on the road.

WOMR-FM RADIO

Before making the rebel-DJ movie *Pump Up the Volume,* Christian Slater is said to have popped into this community station, 92.1 FM, to get some pointers from his Uncle Bill. *14 Center St., tel. 508/487–2619.*

Belly on the beach

NEW JERSEY

For rock fans, the Garden State has been synonymous with Bruce Springsteen since the release of his first album, *Greetings from Asbury Park, N.J.,* in 1973. For a new artist, such a dedication was a bold move: The state and its bands had long been the butt of jokes from those who considered New Jersey little more than a grimy landscape of smokestack industries and overcrowded highways.

Twenty years after Springsteen's debut, the state's tourism people push the singer's vanishing New Jersey as an unlikely tourist draw. As former Springsteen guitarist Miami Steve Van Zandt told the magazine *Backstreets,* "What Bruce and I did for New Jersey has given hope to all the Des Moines in the world."

There's more to the state than Springsteen, however. Bon Jovi formed in anonymous Sayreville in 1983, but apart from the title of their 1988 No. 1 album, *New Jersey,* the band has made little mention of their home state. Glenn Danzig and the new wave Feelies have also called New Jersey home. The Jersey sound of the '90s has come from the depressed towns across the Hudson River from New York City, via the jackhammer hip-hop of Naughty by Nature (from Dionne Warwick's birthplace, East Orange, a.k.a. Illtown, and Jersey City, a.k.a. Chilltown) and Newark's Ice-T and Redman.

Asbury Park

Despite bringing greetings from this once-popular resort town on his first album, Bruce Springsteen never came closer to here than crashing on the beach after gigs with short-lived turn-of-the-'60s bands like Steel Mill, Child, and Earth. By then Asbury Park was already filled with run-down hotels and decaying blocks, having failed to pick itself up after a spate of riots at the beginning of the decade. For Springsteen, however, Asbury Park is a never-ending source of imagery, and fans will be familiar with such landmarks as the Tunnel of Love and Madam Marie's.

With the hype that surrounded Springsteen after the release of *Born to Run,* journalists and A&R chiefs swept into town looking for a bandwagon to jump on. Instead they found a declining club scene and a handful of bands like the Shakes and Lord Gunner and the Cahoots playing mostly Top 40 stuff; Southside Johnny and the Asbury Jukes got a recording contract with Epic but barely dented the *Billboard* 100. The only major find from the area came in the early '80s with the Rest, featuring singer John Bongiovi, who soon changed his name and that of his band to Bon Jovi. The Jersey Shore continues to produce new bands with attitude—Mars Needs Women, Rotator Cuff, Monster Magnet, and Mothersound in the mid-'90s—but so far none has made inroads into Springsteen's or Bon Jovi's market.

ASBURY PARK BEACH

John Bongiovi slept on the beach in the summer during the early '80s, and on "99 in the Shade" from the *New Jersey* LP, he sings about the shoreline being temporarily closed because of the number of hypodermic needles washing up. Bruce Springsteen also claims to have slept here. He remembers trying to "walk like a man" on the beach behind his father on the *Tunnel of Love* track of the same name.

THE CASINO

Bruce Springsteen sang about "the boys from the Casino dancing with their shirts open," on "Fourth of July, Asbury Park (Sandy)," remembering the days when he used to hang out here until dawn with the E Street Band. The owners allowed him access to the long-closed venue to shoot part of the video for 1987's "Tunnel of Love." The building still stands vacant. *Ocean Ave. at Asbury Ave.*

KINGSLEY AVENUE

Springsteen sang about "driving down Kingsley, figuring I'll get a drink," in "Something in the Night" on *Darkness on the Edge of Town.* Kingsley Avenue was part of the shore-area cruising circuit (mentioned on the *Born to Run* track "Night"), but its popularity decreased after traffic lights were added in the '80s.

MADAME MARIE'S

Madame Marie is a fortune teller who was romanticized by Springsteen on the 1974 track "Fourth of July, Asbury Park (Sandy)." She still gazes into her crystal ball from her boardwalk hut. *Boardwalk at 4th Ave.*

Pam Springsteen/courtesy of Columbia

Bruce Springsteen, the man who put Asbury Park on the map

THE STONE PONY

The club most associated with Bruce Springsteen and the Jersey Shore scene actually opened as late as 1974, after Springsteen had recorded his first album, but it quickly became one of the most popular venues in the state. Springsteen played regularly in the mid-'70s and has returned occasionally since, often with Nils Lofgren, to jam with whoever happened to be onstage, including David Johansen (March 1980), former Band drummer Levon Helm (August 1980), Jon Bon Jovi (April 1987), and the Pretenders—on the adjacent vacant lot—for 1994's Fourth of July celebrations. *913 Ocean Ave., tel. 908/775–5700.*

THE STUDENT PRINCE

The Asbury Park scene shifted here when the Upstage closed in 1971. Springsteen played the club every weekend that summer and first met saxophonist Clarence Clemons here. It's now a strip joint called Seduction. *911 Kingsley St.*

TUNNEL OF LOVE

Part of the Palace Amusement Arcade, long closed now, the Tunnel of Love provided Springsteen with the name of his 1987 album. On its release he returned to shoot the video for the title track, using images of the then functioning twister, merry-go-round, and fun house. For a few years after it closed, the arcade housed Asbury Park's rock

& roll museum—mostly a collection of Springsteen memorabilia—which may soon reopen at an as yet unknown venue. The arcade was featured in "Born to Run" with the line "Beyond the Palace, hemi-powered drones scream down the boulevard." *Asbury Ave. at Kingsley St.*

THE UPSTAGE

Though short-lived, this alcohol-free, second-floor club had a big hand in boosting the Asbury Park scene in the '60s . Anyone could get up and jam—the management even provided guitars. Springsteen hung out here in 1969 and 1970 with future E Street Band members, and in the liner notes for Southside Johnny's first album, *I Don't Wanna Go Home,* he remembers the Upstage as a place where "you could work it so you never have to go home." The club closed in 1971; downstairs is now a shoe store. *702 Cookman Ave.*

GREETINGS FROM ASBURY PARK

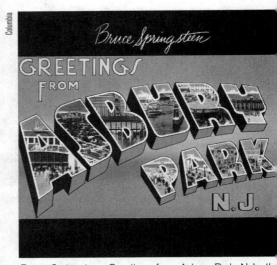

Bruce Springsteen, Greetings from Asbury Park, N.J.—th 1973 debut

The letters on the flap-away sleeve of Bruce Springsteen's *Greetings from Asbury Park, N.J.* debut album contain a series of shots of the town's lively postwar days as a popular resort.

"A" shows crowds entering the Convention Hall.

"S" has an aerial shot of the Berkeley-Cartaret Hotel.

"B" pictures the vestibule inside the Convention Hall.

"U" frames Wesley Lake between Asbury Park and Ocean Grove, the township immediately to the south.

"R" shows the now demolished carousel on the boardwalk.

"Y" encloses the Fishing Pier in Ocean Grove.

"P" depicts a crowded Asbury Park boardwalk.

"A" features sun worshipers hanging out on the Ocean Grove boardwalk.

"R" contains an outside shot of the Casino.

"K" shows the Paramount Theater, on 5th Avenue at Broadway.

Atlantic City

PUT YOUR MAKEUP ON, FIX YOUR HAIR UP PRETTY AND MEET ME TONIGHT IN ATLANTIC CITY—BRUCE SPRINGSTEEN, "ATLANTIC CITY"

Atlantic City was once a major resort and, as such, has left a cultural legacy: The picture postcard and the Miss America pageant both originated here, and the streets on a Monopoly board take their names from the city's thoroughfares. Since the '70s, however, casinos have been Atlantic City's main draw. Gambling has brought an upturn in the local economy and nightlife—the biggest lounge acts and plenty of championship boxing matches come here—but the millions raised in taxes have barely filtered down to the crime-ridden projects of the South Inlet area.

The Miss America Pageant

ATLANTIC CITY BOARDWALK AND BEACH

Atlantic City built the world's first elevated boardwalk in 1870, and such was its recognition among Americans that Atlantic Records came here to promote the Drifters' 1963 single "Under the Boardwalk." The Beach Boys played to 200,000 people at the town beach on July 5, 1983, after a scheduled Fourth of July appearance at the White House was aborted (*see* Washington, D.C., *below*).

HERMAN'S BAR (HERMAN'S PLACE)

Screamin' Jay Hawkins wrote "I Put a Spell on You" in 1954 after a run-in with his girl-friend at this club. While he was performing, she pushed her way to the front of the auditorium, fished through her purse, and threw his keys onto the stage. He rushed through the final two songs, made his way to their locked room upstairs, broke in, and found the message "Goodbye my love" scrawled on the mirror in lipstick. Hawkins then reputedly sat down and wrote the famous song, noted for its distinctive agonizing screams and grunts. *2 S. New York Ave., tel. 609/344–1800.*

Belmar

E Street, in the middle of this small shore town a few miles south of Asbury Park, gave its name to Bruce Springsteen's backing outfit and second album. Keyboard player David Sancious lived on E Street, and the band rehearsed at his house in the early '70s. At its western end, E Street meets 10th Avenue, inspiration for the *Born to Run* track "Tenth Avenue Freeze Out." The signpost for the two roads has been embedded in concrete to stymie souvenir-hunting Springsteen fans.

Cherry Hill

THE LATIN CASINO

In September 1975 Jackie Wilson suffered a heart attack onstage at this club while singing the line "My heart is crying" from "Lonely Teardrops." Wilson bumped his head as he fell, went into a coma from which he never recovered, and died 8½ years later in the Cherry Hill Medical Center. The club closed in October 1981 and was demolished soon after. *2235 Marlton Pike.*

Freehold

This community of some 10,000 citizens, 25 miles inland from Asbury Park, was where Bruce Springsteen's family lived in the '50s and '60s. Freehold—dubbed "Texas" by locals for the large influx of post–World War II settlers from the South—was featured in "My Hometown," the song that closes 1984's *Born in the U.S.A.* Apart from its romantic images of a young Brucie sitting on his pop's lap as they drive around town in a "big old Buick," the song also mentions "fights between black and white," empty stores, and shut-down factories. In Dave Marsh's biography, *Born to Run,* Springsteen describes the place as "a small town, just a small, narrow-minded town."

MY FATHER'S HOUSE

87 RANDOLPH STREET. The home where Bruce Springsteen lived until 1957, when he was eight, with his paternal grandparents, his legal-secretary mom, Adele, and his taxi-driving dad, Douglas, no longer stands. The site is now a driveway for the St. Rosa of Lima Church, mentioned on Springsteen's 1987 song "Walk Like a Man" in the line "By Our Lady of the Roses, we lived in the shadow of the elms."

39½ INSTITUTE STREET. The Springsteens lived in this white house, with its porch and neat front garden, from 1958 to 1961. Edward and Joan Kress, next door at the larger No. 39, have welcomed curious Springsteen devotees and even started keeping a register. In the early '80s, Springsteen himself turned up unannounced and was photographed leaning against the sycamore tree in front of the house for the underlay of *Born in the U.S.A.*'s lyric sheet.

68 SOUTH STREET. The family moved to this large villa in 1961. On summer nights Bruce would lie on the flat roof and teach himself to play guitar. In the late '60s, Adele and Douglas moved to California, and Springsteen left Freehold.

A&M KARAGHEUSIAN RUG MILL

The closure of this factory in the mid-'60s and its relocation to North Carolina meant lay-offs for hundreds of Freehold workers. The story was recalled in Springsteen's "My Hometown" with the line "they're closing down the textile mill across the railroad tracks." *Jackson St. at Center St.*

FREEHOLD HIGH SCHOOL

While attending this school in 1965, Springsteen formed his first band, the Castiles. He graduated two years later but did not attend ceremonies after teachers declared that his hair was too long and asked classmates to keep away from him. *Broadway at Robertsville Rd.*

ROUTE 33 AND SOUTH STREET

The *Born in the U.S.A.* closer, "My Hometown," briefly refers to the riots and looting—"troubled times had come to my hometown"—that followed an incident at this junction in May 1969. A carload of whites pulled up alongside a vehicle of black workers and started shooting indiscriminately.

Hoboken

The *New Yorker* called Hoboken the Liverpool of the '80s after scores of jangly guitar groups like the dB's began appearing at Maxwell's. The city is still mainly

Michael Lavine/courtesy of Matador

Hoboken's own Yo La Tengo

known for rearing Frank Sinatra, the erstwhile "kid from Hoboken," but in recent years locals Yo La Tengo have become a cult favorite.

MAXWELL'S

This indie club near the Maxwell House coffee plant spawned an exciting, if brief, power-pop scene in the late '70s around Chris Stamey and the dB's and the Bongos. The club was run by Steve Fallon, who also owned the Pier Platters record store and a label, Coyote, which released the Feelies. In September 1980, New Order made their U.S. debut here, and Fallon soon began booking a new wave of guitar-thrash bands like the Replacements and Hüsker Dü. He has since set up the Singles Only Label (strictly vinyl) with the latter's Bob Mould. The club, which holds 200, remains one of the premier small venues on the indie touring circuit. In other news, director John Sayles shot Springsteen's "Glory Days" video here in May 1985; in keeping with the singer's image, the club was converted into a sweaty blue-collar dive for the occasion. *1039 Washington St., at 11th St., tel. 201/798–4064.*

Lakehurst

On May 6, 1937, the *Hindenburg* caught fire and exploded, killing 33 people, as it tried to land near Lakehurst, 15 miles inland in the middle of the state. A photo of the burning airship was used by Led Zeppelin for the front cover of the band's self-titled debut album in 1969.

Morris Plains

GREYSTONE PARK PSYCHIATRIC HOSPITAL

Woody Guthrie suffered from Huntington's disease and was hospitalized at Greystone for much of the last 15 years of his life, until he died in 1967. A reverential visitor in January 1961 was Bob Dylan, who wanted to pick up some tips while working on *Bob Dylan,* his heavily Guthrie-influenced debut album. *W. Hanover Ave., Exit 42 off Rte. 80.*

THE NEW JERSEY TURNPIKE

When Jack Kerouac headed off across the country in *On the Road,* it was on the New Jersey Turnpike, which starts in the morass of highways north of Newark and zooms southeast through the belly of the state into Delaware. It has also popped up in a fair number of songs. Paul Simon counted the cars on it in "America." Chuck Berry's "You Can't Catch Me" tells the story of a late-night race on the turnpike that he wins, only to be pulled over and ticked off by the cops. In "State Trooper," on *Nebraska,* Springsteen sings of riding the "New Jersey Turnpike on a wet night," while "Jungleland," on *Born to Run,* casually dismisses "the opera out on the turnpike."

Rumson

BRUCE SPRINGSTEEN AND JON BON JOVI HOUSES

In a relatively modest suburban villa, shielded from passersby by discreet landscaping at the front, Bruce Springsteen wrote and recorded the *Tunnel of Love* LP. When he played a benefit for a local school on Bellevue Avenue in October 1987, he told his backing musicians, the Fabulous Grease Band, to keep the noise down because his wife was asleep across the road. Although he now spends most of his time in L.A., Springsteen still keeps his Rumson address, as does near neighbor Jon Bon Jovi. The two houses are easily distinguishable—there will usually be a gaggle of girls hanging outside Bon Jovi's and maybe just a couple of cars outside Bruce's. *Bellevue Ave. at Ridge Rd.*

New York City vies only with Los Angeles for the title of America's leading rock & roll center. The city has contributed to rock's development in all sorts of unexpected ways— as the home of doo-wop harmony groups in the '50s, Greenwich Village folkies in the early '60s, '70s punk rockers, rap and hip-hop artists in the '80s, and indie bands in the '90s. For nearly 50 years, new acts have built their reputations at Manhattan's nightspots, while the biggest names in rock have come to tap the energy of one of the world's most exciting cities.

Upstate from the Big Apple, the rural hamlets of this huge state have provided more notable rock moments than its midsize cities. Buffalo, the second-largest town, hasn't much to show but the Goo Goo Dolls. The village of Woodstock, however, has been a favorite retreat of musicians, although it may be more renowned for lending its name to the most famous music festival of all time, actually held in Bethel, some 60 miles away.

Bethel

[**WOODSTOCK FESTIVAL SITE**]

The most famous outdoor event in rock history was held August 15–17, 1969, at Max Yasgur's farm in Bethel, some 60 miles southwest of the town of Woodstock. Bethel was the third choice for the festival: The event was originally slated for Woodstock itself, but the town board refused to grant permission. By the time Bethel was settled on, it was too late to change the name, and so the event went ahead as the Woodstock Music and Art Fair.

Perhaps as many as half a million people braved rain, mud, bad dope, junk food, and terrible toilets to watch Jimi Hendrix, the Who, Santana, Sly and the Family Stone, Janis Joplin, Country Joe and the Fish, Joe Cocker, the Band, Ten Years After, Sha Na Na, and many others. These "three days of peace and music" have come to be considered the apotheosis of the hippie era, but at the time the festival was better known for being declared a national disaster thanks to the lousy facilities. The site is marked by a memorial stone bearing the event's dove-and-guitar symbol on a red background.

3 days of peace & music

From the cover of the Woodstock event program

In 1994 a second Woodstock festival was held in Saugerties, a few miles from Bethel, but several thousand people shunned the event, deeming it too commercial, and instead gathered here at the original site. Among those to perform from the back of a flatbed truck were Soul Asylum's Dave Pirner and girlfriend Winona Ryder. *Hurd and W. Shore Rds. off Hwy. 17B.*

- Although Joni Mitchell sings "By the time we got to Woodstock" in her hit song about the festival, she actually never got there—she was stuck in traffic.

- Three deaths, two births, and four miscarriages took place during Woodstock. Of the deaths, one person OD'd, another died from a burst appendix, and a third was run over by a tractor.

- Few now remember that the Grateful Dead, the Incredible String Band, the Band (who lived in Woodstock itself), and Creedence Clearwater Revival (the biggest-selling band in America by the turn of the '70s) were on the bill: Their record companies wouldn't allow their performances to appear on Atlantic Records' triple LP or in the *Woodstock* movie.

- At the end of the event, farm owner Max Yasgur emotionally told the crowd, "You've proved to the world that half a million kids can get together for fun and music and have nothing but fun and music."

Barrytown

Donald Fagen and Walter Becker of Steely Dan depicted this Hudson River hamlet as the embodiment of tiny-minded, small-town life in "Barrytown" on 1974's *Pretzel Logic* album. A decade later Roddy Doyle borrowed the name for the fictional Dublin suburb where he set such novels as *The Commitments*. Steely Dan fan and cy-fi novelist William Gibson mentioned Barrytown in *Count Zero,* and also included a character called Becker in *Mona Lisa Overdrive*. About 4 miles away is Annandale-on-Hudson, which appears in *Countdown to Ecstasy*'s "My Old School," a song inspired by Becker and Fagen's time there at Bard College; Bard is also the alma mater of the Beastie Boys and members of the rock/rap crossover act AD.

New York City

WELL NEW YORK CITY REALLY HAS IT ALL—THE RAMONES, "SHEENA IS A PUNK ROCKER"

New York City has a venerable rock & roll tradition. In the '50s, the city was a melting pot of black R&B and white pop traditions. Harlem's Apollo Theater began booking big R&B acts, many of whom cut their most famous discs on the city's Atlantic record label. Doo-wop hits on local labels—songs like the Orioles' "Crying in the Chapel" and the Five Satins' "In the Still of the Night"—inspired such local teenagers as Lou Reed and Paul Simon. Cleveland DJ Alan Freed moved his successful format of black music for white listeners to New York radio station WINS and began staging sold-out shows at the Brooklyn Paramount.

By the late '50s, music-biz people headquartered on midtown Broadway, most famously at the Brill Building, were churning out pop hits inspired equally by teenage angst and the sophisticated Tin Pan Alley songwriting tradition. Working under assembly-line conditions, the songwriting partnerships of Barry Mann and Cynthia Weill, Gerry Goffin and Carole King, and Jerry Leiber and Mike Stoller turned out such massive-selling anthems of teen romance as "Will You Still Love Me Tomorrow?" and "On Broadway." Eventually, however, the teen stars and girl groups of the early '60s were eclipsed by a wave of British bands, the Brill Building sound faded, and New York's musical center of gravity shifted south. A harder-edged aesthetic, nurtured in the divey clubs and artsy lofts below 14th Street, was to dominate the city's next decade.

The possibility of a downtown sound first appeared with the protest singers of the Greenwich Village coffee-bar folk scene, a genre epitomized by pre–*Bringing It All Back Home* Bob Dylan. Folk's promise faded after 1965, however, when Dylan shocked his early fans by adding electric guitars and drums and dropping his overtly political songs.

New York's musical future belonged thenceforth to loud guitars and nihilism, a development attributable almost entirely to the Velvet Underground, biting art-rockers whose heavily amplified drone owed as much to avant-garde jazz as to pop or R&B. In the public imagination, the Velvets may be most associated with New York because of their relationship with impresario Andy Warhol, but the group's lasting legacy to the city was as the inspiration to a whole generation of New York bands.

In the early '70s, New York's music scene was dominated by big-name out-of-town bands that played such large venues as the Fillmore East and Madison Square Garden. On the local level, a vacuum was waiting to be filled—as it turned out, by bands that came to be known as "punk" or "new wave." The New York Dolls, done up to look something like transvestites from hell, startled audiences at downtown dives like Max's Kansas City and the Mercer Arts Center with their debauched show and stripped-down musical approach. Other homegrown acts—Patti Smith, Television, Blondie, the Ramones, Richard Hell (the first rocker known to have performed in a ripped T-shirt)—

Blondie's Debbie Harry and Chris Stein at CBGBs with the Ramones' road manager

tried to recapture the spirit of early rock & roll at a new center of activity: CBGBs, a deliberately seedy Hell Angels hangout in the East Village. The scene stayed underground until late 1976 and then exploded on both sides of the Atlantic.

At the opposite end of the spectrum, disco became the music of choice for the city's large nightclubbing audience, especially at glitterati-studded Manhattan venues like Studio 54. The disco movement reached critical mass in 1977 with the release of *Saturday Night Fever,* set in Brooklyn, and the formation of Chic, disco's most successful group, by two Apollo house-band players, Bernard Edwards and Nile Rodgers.

But perhaps the most far-reaching musical moment in New York in the '70s went largely ignored at the time: In 1978 Joseph Saddler set up two record decks in his South Bronx apartment and began switching channels to mix snatches of two songs. Saddler, a.k.a. Grandmaster Flash, and his group, the Furious Five, developed a cool, fast-paced slang that was captured on their 1979 single "Superrapping." Another uptown group, the Sugarhill Gang, soon popularized the new rap sound on "Rapper's Delight," a sequence of macho boasts set against the barely disguised music of Chic's "Good Times." Grandmaster Flash and the Furious Five responded by incorporating bits of their favorite records and brief samples of turntable noise or "scratching" on their 1981 single "Adventures on the Wheels of Steel."

Bronx-born Afrika Bambaataa moved the genre into a new direction with 1982's "Planet Rock," which borrowed heavily from European computer-generated electropop. This record led to an explosion of new groups that borrowed snatches of not just funk but anything they could find. This new genre, combining rap vocals with electronic bleeps, sampled noises, and bits of other songs, was renamed hip-hop, a term taken from the first line of "Rapper's Delight." Although the ensuing decade saw New Yorkers overshadowed by the gangsta rappers of the West Coast, the city continued to nurture successful new groups—the hedonistic Beastie Boys and Run-D.M.C. and the more ideological Public Enemy, for example, as well as such more recent successes as 3rd Bass, Wu-Tang Clan, and Shootyz Groove.

Since the birth of rap, the downtown scene has not been idle. After new wave came the guitar-driven white noise of "no wave," a sound typified by the Theoretical Girls, DNA, the Contortions, and New York's most successful noiseniks, Sonic Youth. In their footsteps, more uncompromising indie bands have appeared—Das Damen, Helmet, the Band of Susans, Pussy Galore (renowned for the glorious title of their 1989 LP, *Dial M for Motherfucker*), and mosh-pit–friendly metal outfits like Cannibal Corpse—but these groups have made little of the commercial impression of West Coast grunge and punk bands. Nonetheless, New York continues to be one of America's main gigging cities, with downtown clubs featuring the latest batch of hopefuls from the city and beyond.

Greenwich Village and Chelsea

After a drunken binge in 1917, Dadaist painter Marcel Duchamp and radical writer John (*Ten Days That Shook the World*) Reed declared Greenwich Village's Washington Square Park "the new and separate city of the new Bohemia." The neighborhood does have a long-standing reputation for attracting bohemian writers, artists, and musicians. During the '50s, while much of the country fell prey to red-baiting and a bland suburban mentality, the Village gave birth to a radical cultural and musical scene. Jack Kerouac, Allen Ginsberg, and other beats hung out in the coffee bars around MacDougal Street. By day young folksingers busked in the park, and at night they dropped into Gerde's Folk City or Cafe Wha? to hear the young Bob Dylan or old masters like Pete Seeger. Dylan's conversion to an electric sound in 1965 saw many Village clubs, particularly the Night Owl and Café Bizarre, dump folk and become the first to put on heavily amplified rock groups like the Lovin' Spoonful and the Velvet Underground.

When bigger venues elsewhere in Manhattan began putting on rock shows in the late '60s, the Village scene collapsed, though its reputation as the nerve center of America's political underground remained intact. A June 1969 police raid on Christopher Street's Stonewall Inn led to riots that galvanized the gay-rights movement, and the following year the Weathermen—revolutionaries or terrorists, depending on whom you talk to—accidentally blew up their hitherto secret headquarters at 18 West 11th Street (coincidentally next door to where Dustin Hoffman was living at the time).

The Village experienced a brief revival in the '70s when the Mercer Arts Center put on early punk acts, but since then the Bottom Line has been the area's only consistently popular venue. Nowadays the neighborhood maintains its reputation for hipness but with a markedly upscale bent.

Just north of the Village, across 14th Street, is Chelsea. Now a largely unremarkable residential neighborhood popular with the gay community, it had its moments as an enclave of bohemia in the '60s when Leonard Cohen and Joni Mitchell lived at the area's best-known rock & roll landmark, the Chelsea Hotel.

Greenwich Village has many decent bars. **THE LION'S HEAD** (59 Christopher St., tel. 212/929–0670) is a former beat hangout. As befits a former speakeasy, **CHUMLEY'S** (86 Bedford St., tel. 212/675–4449) has no sign. Chelsea's sprawling **LIMELIGHT** (6th Ave. at W. 20th St, tel. 212/807–7850), a nightclub in an old gothic-style church, puts on occasional gigs—Hawkwind and Moby played here in 1995—but is also notable for such decor as women swinging in cages overhead.

Dennis Kleiman

Gwen Mars at the Limelight

Some of New York's best record shops (many of which don't open until noon) stand in the heart of the Village, including the pricey but well-stocked **BLEECKER BOB'S** (118 W. 3rd St., tel. 212/475–9677) and a branch of **TOWER RECORDS** (692 Broadway, tel. 212/505–1500).

THE BITTER END

Curtis Mayfield recorded *Curtis Live* at this upscale Village club in 1971. Bob Dylan chose to make his 1974 Manhattan comeback here—playing a series of informal gigs alongside old folk buddy Ramblin' Jack Elliott, former sidekick Bobby Neuwirth, and Patti Smith—and a number of songs on his romantic 1976 album *Desire* were road tested here. The club now puts on new bands most nights of the week. *147 Bleecker St., between LaGuardia Pl. and Thompson St., tel. 212/673–7030.*

[THE BOTTOM LINE]

One of New York's most popular small venues, the 450-seat Bottom Line opened in February 1974 with a show by Dr. John, who got some help from Johnny Winter, Stevie Wonder, and Mick Jagger. In August 1975 Bruce Springsteen got his big break here after a five-night run where he premiered material from *Born to Run*. The club has good acoustics and is popular with industry movers and shakers, so several live albums have been recorded here over the years, including Lou Reed's *Take No Prisoners*, Todd Rundgren's *Back to the Bars*, and Richard Thompson's *Small Town Romance*. Big names of that era still make frequent appearances, and their celebrated friends sometimes help out on a song or two. When Lou Reed played a Songwriters' Night in February 1994, he was joined onstage by Kris Kristofferson, who tried to accompany him on harmonica during "Sweet Jane"; Reed told him to stop, but Kristofferson persisted, so Reed stopped singing and his uninvited guest had to slink off. The club is also a favorite haunt of David Johansen's lounge-lizard alter ego, Buster Poindexter. If you want a good table for the shows—usually two a night, at 7:30 and 10:30—it's best to show up early. Tickets usually run from $15 to $25 and must be purchased from the box office. *15 W. 4th St, tel. 212/228–6300.*

CAFÉ WHA?

In 1961 club owner Manny Roth let Bob Dylan, newly arrived from Minnesota, play a few Woody Guthrie songs to a small audience, an experience Dylan later recounted in the song "Talkin' New York." A regular audience member at the club's mid-'60s folk nights was a young Bruce Springsteen; this is where he met his future guitarist "Miami" Steve Van Zandt. That was not Café Wha?'s most famous find, however: Animals bassist Chas Chandler "discovered" Jimi Hendrix here in July 1966. Hendrix's finger trickery and confident swagger astonished Chandler, but what would become one of the most celebrated manager/producer–performer partnerships in rock was put on hold for a few months while the Animals went back out on tour. Chandler returned in September and, with the promise of an introduction to Eric Clapton, persuaded Hendrix to accompany him to Britain. The club now offers dance nights and a house band. *115 MacDougal St., tel. 212/254–3706.*

Marian Walsh

Café Wha?

[CHELSEA HOTEL]

Rock & roll's most famous hotel, seediness incarnate, was built in 1884 as a cooperative apartment block and was then the tallest building in Manhattan. The Chelsea became a hotel in 1905 and since 1940 has been owned by the Bard family, who have enthusiastically courted the bohemian fringes of literature and rock & roll. Writers such as Mark Twain and Eugene O'Neill were drawn by the hotel's cheap rates and its proximity to both the Village and the publishing offices of midtown. Welsh poet Dylan Thomas, allegedly the inspiration for Robert Zimmerman's name change to Bob Dylan, checked in during a lecture tour in 1953 and went into a fatal coma in Room 206 after a drinking binge at the White Horse Tavern on Hudson Street. William S. Burroughs came here to write *Naked Lunch* (1959), and Arthur C. Clarke stayed here while turning out the screenplay for *2001: A Space Odyssey.*

Kelly Duane

In the '60s the hotel began to attract members of rock's more intellectual wing, who knew that at the Chelsea they could do more or less whatever they liked, uninterrupted. While staying here, Janis Joplin told the rest of Big Brother and the Holding Company she was going solo. Here she also met Leonard Cohen, who recalled Joplin's "giving [him] head on an unmade bed" in "Chelsea Hotel No 2." Jefferson Airplane recalled their stay on the *Bark* track "Third Week in Chelsea." Jimi Hendrix was mistaken for a janitor by an old lady but modestly fetched her bag before quickly checking out. Joni Mitchell's waking moments were the basis for "Chelsea Morn-

The Chelsea Hotel

ing," supposedly the song that inspired Bill and Hillary Clinton's daughter's name. Other regulars were Andy Warhol and many of his outré followers, including three named in Lou Reed's "Walk on the Wild Side": actors Candy Darlin' and Joe Dallesandro ("Little Joe") and transvestite Holly Woodlawn (who "came from Miami F-L-A"). Another Reed song, "Chelsea Girls," introduced other unusual guests: "Room 506, it's enough to make you sick, Bridget's all wrapped in foil…room 115 filled with S&M queens."

Bob Dylan was another famous guest. "Sara," which closes his 1976 album *Desire* and is dedicated to his ex-wife of that name, reveals that he stayed "up for days in the Chelsea Hotel [in Room A17] writing 'Sad-Eyed Lady of the Lowlands' " for her. This was disputed, however, by the late rock critic Lester Bangs. He claimed that Dylan actually wrote the song, which occupies an entire side of *Blonde on Blonde,* not in the Chelsea but in Columbia Records' Nashville studio while bored session musicians waited around for him to get his act together.

More conflicting stories were to come: Sid Vicious and girlfriend Nancy Spungen were staying in Room 100 when, on October 12, 1978, Spungen was found stabbed to death. Vicious claimed that he woke up and found Nancy in the bathroom with the knife sticking out of her. He was nonetheless subsequently charged with her murder, but before he could come to trial, he died from a heroin overdose while out on bail. Some reports later claimed that a dealer killed Spungen after an argument over drug prices or that she was accidentally murdered during a robbery—she had $3,000 in door takings from Sid's shows at Max's Kansas City in the room. Over the next few years a steady trickle of morbid curiosity seekers made the pilgrimage to the scene of the crime, disturbing those who had the misfortune of staying there, until the manager finally had the walls of the room knocked down. The space was subsumed into other rooms.

Among the bigger acts who have dropped in during the '90s are the Red Hot Chili Peppers, Sinead O'Connor, and Madonna, who came here to shoot her video for *Sex.* Although the rooms are too spartan for most stars and record-company execs—no MTV or minibars—the Chelsea continues to draw a rock crowd, particularly among new bands looking for immersion in New York's rock heritage. In March 1995 a British band called the Wildhearts had only been in the hotel for a few hours when, after messing about with some candles, they fell asleep and their room burnt down. As one bandmember told the *New Musical Express,* "there've only been two fires there before, started by Sid Vicious and Andy Warhol…both dead now, spookily enough. I'm not sure what that means." *222 W. 23rd St., between 7th and 8th Aves., tel. 212/243–3700. Suites start at $100; singles are less.*

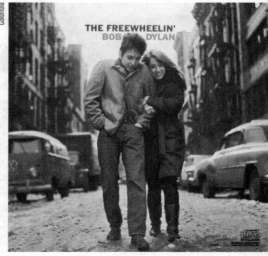

Bob Dylan, The Freewheelin' Bob Dylan—*Bob and Suze Rotolo on West 4th Street*

BOB DYLAN
RESIDENCE, 1961–65

In December 1961, after spending most of the year sleeping on friends' floors, Bob Dylan moved into an apartment on West 4th Street, his first permanent address in New York City. Girlfriend Suze Rotolo soon joined him, and the two were pictured walking arm in arm down the snow-covered street for the front cover of 1963's *Freewheelin' Bob Dylan*. Their brief affair inspired several Dylan love songs, including "Don't Think Twice, It's All Right" and "Tomorrow Is a Long Time," popularized a decade later by Rod Stewart. Dylan later used the street as a metaphor for betrayal on the 1965 single "Positively 4th Street," in which he savaged those who attacked him for dropping political songs and taking up the electric guitar. *161 W. 4th St.*

ELECTRIC LADY SOUND STUDIOS

Having forked out $300,000 to record at the Record Plant in 1968, Jimi Hendrix started looking for a site for a studio of his own. He found this four-story brownstone, previously the Generation club, where Sly and the Family Stone played their first gig. Hendrix pumped a million bucks into converting the building—designing a guitar-shaped ground floor, soundproofing it to keep out noise from the nearby subway, and sealing it from a flood-prone small creek—then died in September 1970, only three months after the studio opened. During that short time, however, Hendrix was not idle. The hundreds of hours of demos and unfinished pieces he had taped were edited after his death, new backing musicians were brought in to replace Hendrix's band, and the results were released as a series of "lost" Hendrix albums. *52 W. 8th St., tel. 212/677–4700.*

FOLKLORE CENTER

Mail-order book publisher Izzy Young turned his office into a daytime meeting place for Village folkies in the early '60s. Regular visitors were Bob Gibson (who pioneered the 12-string guitar sound popularized by the Byrds) and Bob Dylan, who would often stroll in to test out guitars, play records, and dabble with half-written songs. Dylan was wont to weave a web of mystique around his Midwest upbringing. One of his fanciful stories was about how he'd run away from home at 13 and met Mississippi blues singer Big Joe Williams on a boxcar. Naturally no one believed him, until one day Williams turned up at the center before a gig, strode over to Dylan, and exclaimed, "My, I haven't seen you, Bob, since that boxcar trip to Mexico." The center closed after the Village folk scene died in the mid-'60s, and the site is now occupied by a kebab house. *110 Mac-Dougal St.*

GASLIGHT (SCRAP BAR)

When it opened in 1958, the Gaslight featured such beat poets as Allen Ginsberg, but it shifted to folk in 1960 and then to rock. Bob Dylan banged out "A Hard Rain's A-Gonna Fall" on an old typewriter while lodged above the smoky coffeehouse in the early '60s. Jimi Hendrix jammed regularly with Eric Clapton in July 1967, and five years later Bruce Springsteen auditioned here for Columbia in front of label boss and legendary blues impresario John Hammond. Since becoming the Scrap Bar, the club has been a favorite haunt of metal bands—Axl Rose insisted on being interviewed here when MTV wanted to talk with him. *116 MacDougal St., no phone.*

GERDE'S FOLK CITY, 1956–69

For over 20 years, Gerde's Folk City was one of the biggest names in the Village. Owner Mike Porco began booking folksingers and in 1960 was charging $1.50 to see the likes of Pete Seeger, Ireland's Clancy Brothers, and an acoustic John Lee Hooker. In February 1961 a 19-year-old Bob Dylan made the first of several appearances at the Monday-night hootenannies.

Dylan's first-ever paid gig was on April 11, opening for Hooker. Porco thought Dylan was too young to play in a licensed bar and, wary of the authorities, asked him to bring proof of age when they visited the union before the gig. The union official told Dylan that since he was under 21, he needed his mother or father to countersign. With his typical disregard for bureaucratic mundanities, Dylan denied having a father or mother, so

Porco ended up offering himself as guardian. Wearing one of Woody Guthrie's suits (Guthrie was then dying from Huntington's disease in a New Jersey hospital), Dylan performed "House of the Rising Sun" and "Song to Woody" (both of which appeared on his subsequent first album) and ".Talking Hava Nagilah Blues" (a hilarious rendition of the old Jewish song). After the gig, word about the singer began to spread around the Village, leading to a visit from Columbia's John Hammond, who signed him after an impressive performance on September 26, 1961. For his first album, Bob Dylan received $402, the union rate. *11 W. 4th St.*

GERDE'S FOLK CITY, 1969–86 (KETTLE OF FISH)

By the end of the '60s, the folk scene was over, and Folk City moved to a former strip club on 3rd Street. In 1975 a thankful Dylan returned to play at Porco's birthday party, along with Patti Smith, Bette Midler, and Phil Ochs. (It was Ochs's last show before he hanged himself in his sister's flat in Queens.) By the mid-'80s, the club had broadened its brief to include rock bands; Sonic Youth played here shortly before the venue closed in 1986. The site is now occupied by the Kettle of Fish bar. *130 W. 3rd St.*

Lisa Kristal

Patti Smith

MERCER ARTS CENTER

Before the decrepit Broadway Central Hotel fell down in 1973, it housed the Mercer Arts Center, New York's leading art workshop, which had 10 rooms featuring avant-garde films, cabaret, experimental theater, and left-field rock bands. A very raw New York Dolls began a 17-week Tuesday residency in June 1972 in the Oscar Wilde room. Dressed in Lurex pants and stacked heels, their faces caked with makeup, the Dolls initially played R&B covers but quickly added their own debauched originals and began to attract such notables as Lou Reed (who hated them), Bette Midler (who loved them), and Todd Rundgren (who produced their first album).

The front of the building collapsed in August 1973 while Eric Emerson and the Magic Tramps were rehearsing inside. Used to earthquakes in their native L.A., the band carried on jamming until it was pointed out that the building was literally crumbling around them. The site is now an empty lot. *240 Mercer St.*

STRAND BOOKS

New York's largest used-book store, which stocks over 2 million volumes on 8 miles of shelving, numbers among its past employees Tom Miller (later Tom Verlaine) and

Richard Meyers (Richard Hell), who both worked here in 1969, and Patti Smith. *828 Broadway, tel. 212/473–1452. Open Mon.–Sat. 9:30–9:30, Sun. 11–9:30.*

DEF JAM

NYU film student Rick Rubin started Def Jam records with Russell Simmons in 1984 while living in Room 203 of the Weinstein residence hall (5-11 University Pl.). Rubin's favorite groups were Troublefunk and AC/DC, so he tried to bring the two styles together when producing three breakthrough hip-hop records that year: L.L. Cool J's "I Need a Beat," the Beastie Boys' "Rock Hard," and Jazzy Jay and TLA Rock's "It's Yours." A year later Columbia paid Rubin more than half a million dollars for a distribution deal. He now runs the eclectic American Recordings label—featuring Johnny Cash, the Black Crowes, and Danzig—while Simmons went on to manage Public Enemy and De La Soul and to produce movies (Abel Ferrara's *The Addiction*, Eddie Murphy's remake of *The Nutty Professor*).

Danny Clinch/Def Jam Music Group, Inc.

Ladies Love Cool James

SoHo and TriBeCa

Over the past two decades, the face of the west-downtown area has changed. As Greenwich Village was taken over by touristy shops, high rents drove artists south into the cast-iron warehouses of nearby SoHo (*south of Houston Street*) and then, when SoHo became too expensive, a few blocks farther south to TriBeCa (the *triangle below Canal Street*).

EATINGDRINKINGDANCINGSHOPPINGPLAYINGSLEEPING

With the escalation of property prices in SoHo and TriBeCa during the '90s, many artists continued their migration and left Manhattan entirely, leaving the warehouses to sport trendy restaurants, such as Robert De Niro's **TRIBECA GRILL** (375 Greenwich St., tel. 212/941–3900). Sought-out local nightclubs include the **BEAVHER** (511 Greenwich St., tel. 212/219–2850), which by the mid-'90s had established itself as the place to pose, and the techno-playing **NASA** (157 Hudson St., tel. 212/330–8233).

East of TriBeCa is Little Italy, a small stretch of delis and restaurants around Mulberry Street. Mafia boss Joey Gallo, whom Bob Dylan commemorated on the *Desire* track "Joey," was murdered in a 1972 gangland shooting while eating at **UMBERTO'S CLAM HOUSE** (129 Mulberry St., tel. 212/431–7545).

BOB DYLAN RESIDENCE, 1969–72

By the end of the '60s, Bob Dylan's Woodstock home had been besieged by fans and freaks and he was back in Manhattan, living in this four-story SoHo town house and looking for some peace and quiet. Things didn't go according to plan, however. Returning home one day in 1970, he was shocked to find a group of 30 or so people sifting through his garbage. At their helm was the eccentric A. J. Weberman, who lectured on Dylan's music at the Alternative University on 14th Street and regularly brought his students to this address to peer through the windows and search trash cans for clues to the meaning of Dylan's work. Weberman also styled himself leader of the "Dylan Liberation Front," which urged the singer to return to his radical-folk days. Eventually a truce was declared, and Dylan even invited members of the Front inside…but not Weberman. *94 MacDougal St.*

[KNITTING FACTORY, 1994–PRESENT]

With a policy of booking challenging acts in rock, jazz, and classical avant-garde, Michael Dorf's Knitting Factory has become one of New York's most popular venues since opening in 1987. Arto Lindsay, James Blood Ulmer, and John Zorn, as well as lots of cutting-edge jazz acts, have played regularly. When Sonic Youth played the original East Village venue, at 47 East Houston Street, in 1987, the people who lived upstairs promptly moved out, and the landlord persuaded Dorf to take over the space as no tenant would want to live there. In fall 1994 the Knitting Factory moved to TriBeCa after a six-night farewell stint by jazz saxophonist Anthony Braxton, making his debut on piano. The original space still books jazz bands under the name the Old Knit. Many of the Factory's best gigs have been captured on a series of *Live at the Knitting Factory* albums, recorded at both venues and featuring the above acts as well as Defunkt and Lee Ranaldo. *74 Leonard St., tel. 212/219–3006.*

Velocity Girl at the Knitting Factory

OK HARRIS GALLERY

This pioneering Pop Art gallery hosted a number of sculpture exhibitions by Alan Vega in the late '60s and early '70s. Vega soon got bored with sculpting and in 1970 decided to join up with keyboardist Martin Rev to play a rock & roll stripped of excess baggage (i.e., the drums, bass, and lead guitar). At first the twosome had no name, but emblazoned on the back of Vega's black leather jacket—in the days before it was de rigueur rock & roll mufti—was the legend SUICIDE. Suicide became a leading exponent of the mid-'70s CBGBs punk scene, and the band's hypnotic electronic beats had a significant influence on hip-hop and '80s electronic pop. *383 W. Broadway, tel. 212/431–3600.*

LOU REED AND STERLING MORRISON RESIDENCE, 1965

Lou Reed and Sterling Morrison moved into underground filmmaker Piero Heliczer's fifth-floor loft in 1965. One winter's day they and a fellow member of the fledgling Velvet Underground, John Cale, were visited by journalist Al Aronowitz, who wanted to check out Reed's claim that he was the fastest guitarist in the world. Waiting outside in Aronowitz's limo was Rolling Stone Brian Jones. The then-unknown Cale rushed down to meet his hero, but according to Velvet Underground biographer Victor Bockris, Jones sped off to score some acid in this seedy part of Little Italy. *450 Grand St.*

WHITE COLUMNS

Sonic Youth played their first gig under that name at this alternative gallery during Noise-fest, a nine-day festival held in June 1981 and co-organized by the group's guitarist, Thurston Moore. On June 18, halfway through the event, Moore decided to name the group Sonic Youth out of reverence for the MC5's Fred "Sonic" Smith and Jamaican dub artist Big Youth. Among those meant to perform was the late, legendary rock critic Lester Bangs, who missed his chance by turning up drunk after the festivities had finished. Three years later, over five days in May 1984, Homestead Records recorded the *Speed Trials* LP here with Sonic Youth, the Fall, the Swans, and the Beastie Boys (who were making their stage debut). White Columns moved to 154 Christopher Street in 1992. *325 Spring St.*

East Village and Nearby

The lively East Village—more youthful in outlook than Greenwich Village and considerably more low-rent—centers on St. Marks Place (East 8th Street), site of poky bookshops, junk stores, offbeat theaters, and the community center where Andy Warhol put on the Velvet Underground. The entire neighborhood is a nightlife mecca, with an impressive number of bars that range from divey to conceptual. South of Houston Street the East Village becomes the seedy Lower East Side, while north of 14th Street is Gramercy, the mainly residential neighborhood based around the private, gated park of the same name.

East Village locals play outside McSorley's

EATINGDRINKINGDANCINGSHOPPINGPLAYINGSLEEPING

On St. Marks Place, flick through rare vinyl discs at **SOUNDS** (16 St. Marks Pl., tel. 212/677–2727), or join the circle of coffee drinkers watching the folksingers at tiny **CAFE SIN É** (122 St. Marks Pl., tel. 212/982–0370). **MCSORLEY'S OLD ALE HOUSE** (15

E. 7th St., tel. 212/473–9148) opened in 1854—although it didn't admit women until 1970—and claims to be the oldest bar in New York; local musicians sometimes jam out front on weekends. The **Kiev** (117 2nd Ave., at E. 7th St., tel. 212/674–4040), a 24-hour coffee bar–cum–Ukrainian restaurant, has fed many a bleary-eyed club kid and in the early '90s was a favorite hangout of a teenage Beck ("Loser") Hansen. East 6th Street is famed for its dense concentration of cheap Indian restaurants.

Head west, and before Broadway you hit the desolate Bowery, a strip of abandoned stores and long-stay hotels that some New Yorkers view as a no-go zone. It's also home to the fashionable **Bowery Bar** (358 Bowery, at 4th St., tel. 212/475–2220), haunt of supermodels and the people who love them.

The East Village has a good selection of nightclubs. **Grand** (76 E. 13th St., tel. 212/777–0600) hosts a Friday hip-hop night. Funk and soul can be heard at the **Den of Thieves** (145 E. Houston St., at Eldridge St., tel. 212/477–5005).

JOHN CALE RESIDENCE, 1964–65

In fall 1964 a classically trained Welsh viola player, John Cale, arrived in New York from London to work with avant-garde composer John Cage on an 18-hour piano marathon that involved playing an Erik Satie song 888 times. His roommate at 56 Ludlow Street, a dank flat without heat or hot water, was Tony Conrad, who introduced Cale to rock & roll via the collected works of Hank Williams, Sr. At a party that Christmas, Conrad and Cale met executives from the cheapo compilation label Pickwick, who recruited them for a rock group being assembled to tour promoting "The Ostrich," a novelty song written by an embarrassed Pickwick staffer—Lou Reed. After touring around the East Coast, the group returned to Manhattan and eventually began calling itself the Velvet Underground, a name taken from a Michael Leigh S&M novel Cale found lying in a Broadway gutter. The Velvets made their first demo at the Ludlow Street apartment, a recording that included "Heroin," "Venus in Furs," and "Black Angel's Death Song," all of which can be found on *The Velvet Underground and Nico*, the group's first album. *56 Ludlow St.*

[CBGB & OMFUG]

It was behind the graffiti-splattered shutters of this former Hells Angels' hangout that American punk got its first airing. When Hilly Kristal decided to book bands in his no-

Television and Paul Simon at CBGBs

Lou Reed at CBGBs with the Tom Tom Club

frills dive bar in 1973, he gave the club the unwieldy name Country Blue Grass Blues & Other Music for Urban Gourmets (or, according to some versions, Uplifting Gourmandizers)—but CBGB & OMFUG for short. Within days, Television's Tom Verlaine and Richard Hell wandered in, told Kristal they could play that kind of stuff, and got a booking. In fact, they could barely play at all; an early review in the *SoHo Weekly News* claimed they had no musically or socially redeeming characteristics, although the stage set made of stacked televisions got the okay.

From the start CBGBs (as it was soon universally known) was popular with artists; the acoustics were great, and the narrowness of the long room made even a small crowd look like a full house. Among the early acts were the Stilettos (who became Blondie), Patti Smith (doing poetry readings backed by rock journalist Lenny Kaye on electric guitar), and Suicide (whose vocalist, Alan Vega, would block off the exit to prevent anyone from escaping and would occasionally wield a chain that he'd smash into the wall). Regular headliners in those days were the Ramones, who would introduce each of their breakneck-speed two-minute numbers with a rushed "1-2-3-4" before a guitar string would invariably break and the band would walk offstage, returning a few moments later to repeat the farce. A press handout for an early Ramones gig described their sound as "not unlike a fast drill on a rear molar."

By mid-1975 CBGBs had established itself as New York's hippest rock venue and was attracting enthusiastic press in the local underground papers and in Britain—especially after a July 1975 festival for the world's "best unsigned bands," with performances by the Ramones, Television, and Talking Heads (who later mentioned the club in 1979's "Life During Wartime"). The event was also attended by hip rock journalists and New York Dolls impresario Malcolm McLaren, who was managing the Sex Pistols and looking to sign a similar act.

Once the Ramones and Television had recorded their debut albums and gone off to headline European tours (leaving the club for good), the next wave took over. Teenage Jesus and the Jerks, DNA, and the Theoretical Girls (who played at a packed audition night in late 1979), were dubbed by Brian Eno as "no wave." Although these bands had short-lived careers and made no dent on the charts, they did lay the groundwork for bands like Sonic Youth and Pussy Galore.

In the '80s CBGBs was one of the few permanent venues to give new bands a helping hand, one that the Swans, They Might Be Giants, and Living Colour gladly took. Living Colour was particularly fortunate: A 1987 set was witnessed by Mick Jagger, who subsequently took time off from his solo album *Primitive Cool* to produce demos for the band. During the 1990 New Music Seminar, Scottish power-poppers Teenage Fanclub played a triumphant set and were hailed by the *Village Voice* as "band of the seminar."

CBGBs still sticks to its alternative roots by hosting guitar-thrash bands like NY Loose, Chainsaw Kittens, Eugenius (about whom Kurt Cobain raved), and Piss Factory (an all-girl band named after the Patti Smith song). Next door is the smaller CB's Gallery, which puts on experimental bands and theater. *315 Bowery, at Bleecker St., tel. 212/982–4052.*

THE DOM/ELECTRIC CIRCUS

Andy Warhol introduced his Exploding Plastic Inevitable shows—an East Coast version of Ken Kesey's Trips Festivals—in April 1966 at this former Polish National Hall, then known as the Dom. While the Velvet Underground (billed as Ultra Sound Music, Multiple Film and Food, No Minimum) cranked up the feedback, Warhol movies (*Harlot, The Shoplifter, Blow Job*) played in the background, and a troupe of sexually explicit dancers (among them Beck Hansen's mother) gyrated under the psychedelic lights using hypodermic needles and wooden crosses as props. When Lou Reed sang "kiss the boot of shiny shiny leather" during the "Venus in Furs," Gerard Malanga would kiss Mary Woronov's black leather boots while she whipped him. Reopening as the Electric Circus in May 1967 with the Alternative Legal Entertainment Experiment (a show of acrobats, astrologers, and clowns), the venue began booking such big-name bands as the Doors. It closed in September 1971 after a bomb went off, injuring 17 people. The building is now occupied by a community center. *23 St. Marks Pl.*

[FILLMORE EAST]

During its three-year existence, from 1968 to 1971, the Fillmore East was one of New York's most prestigious live venues. Rock promoter Bill Graham opened the ballroom as the New York sibling of his famous San Francisco operation and imported such popular West Coast bands as Big Brother and the Holding Company (who opened the hall), the Grateful Dead, and Crosby, Stills and Nash, joined by Neil Young when they made their stage debut here in 1969.

Thanks to the Fillmore's fine P.A. system and enthusiastic crowds, leading bands of the day flocked to the ballroom to cut live albums. One of the first was Jimi Hendrix, who premiered his new outfit Band of Gypsys on New Year's Eve 1969. Humble Pie's *Performance—Rockin' the Fillmore* and the Mothers of Invention's *Mothers/Fillmore East* were both released in 1971. More commercially successful was the Allman Brothers' *At Fillmore East*, recorded at a March 1971 gig; when the bandmembers tried to leave the stage at quarter to five in the morning, they were repeatedly called back by the crowd and ended up playing encores until 7 AM.

All was not so rosy, however. Graham had to contend with the dynamics of a neighborhood even seamier than it is now. The Hells Angels, to whom an entrance fee was an alien concept, had their New York headquarters around the corner, while anarchic underground political groups like the Motherfuckers tried to use the place as a launching pad for changing the world. The MC5, who rolled into the Fillmore advertised as the "people's revolutionary band," had all their gear ripped off. Graham recalled the incident with an ironic chuckle in his autobiography: "The people's band had all their equipment stolen. By the *other* people, I guess."

The reissued At Fillmore East, *by the Allman Brothers Band*

Other mishaps included Led Zeppelin bassist John Paul Jones being turned away from his own gig in May 1969 by a security-conscious steward—Jones threatened to bring gargantuan manager Peter Grant's wrath down on the guy's head—and the firebombing of the grocery store next door during a packed Who concert. As the blaze threatened to spread, an undercover cop in full hippie gear rushed onto the stage to try to clear the building; not aware that there was a fire or that the stage crasher was a cop, guitarist Pete Townshend knocked him off the stage with a well-aimed kick to the nads. Graham eventually got to the mike and organized a peaceful exit as the Who slunk out the side door. The next day Townshend and Roger Daltrey, who had also shown some tasty brawling skills, gave themselves up to the police.

Graham—frustrated by bands who found they could make as much money by playing one night at Madison Square Garden as from several shows at this 2,000-seat ballroom—surprised the rock world by closing the Fillmore East on June 2, 1971, a few days before he also closed San Francisco's Fillmore West. For the New York hall's final show, the Allmans were back, accompanied by the J. Geils Band, the Beach Boys, and Albert King. The building soon reopened as the Saint, a gay disco, but closed in the early '80s. It's currently boarded up, awaiting redevelopment. *105 2nd Ave., at E. 6th St.*

LOU REED'S NEW YORK

After the Velvet Underground's dissolution, Lou Reed continued to make music in and about New York. The certifiable hit of his otherwise erratic solo career is 1972's "Walk on the Wild Side," based largely on characters he met while hanging out with the Warhol crowd at the Chelsea Hotel. In the '80s Reed cleaned up his act and launched a successful comeback, culminating in 1989's *New York*: a fierce portrait in which Manhattan is said to be "sinking like a rock into the filthy Hudson" and the Statue of Liberty is denounced as the "Statue of Bigotry." *Magic and Loss,* Reed's 1991 tribute album to Brill Building songwriter Doc Pomus, premiered at a lyrics-only open-air recital in Central Park. Two years later Reed opened the Guggenheim Museum's Robert Mapplethorpe Room with an acoustic set.

GRAMERCY PARK HOTEL

A midpriced 1920s hotel, the Gramercy Park was popular with touring bands, and especially the Byrds, until a 1969 incident: When bassist John York tried to take his mother to dinner in the hotel's restaurant, he was turned away for wearing a leather jacket. Drummer Gene Parsons wrote up the incident on "Gunga Din," a track from *The Ballad of Easy Rider*. Actor and Dinosaur Jr video director Matt Dillon lived here in the early '90s. *2 Lexington Ave., at E. 21st St., tel. 212/475–4320. Rooms: $150.*

MAX'S KANSAS CITY

Best known as one of New York's hippest punk-era clubs, Max's began attracting an artsy crowd soon after opening in the late '60s. The Velvet Underground played a 10-week stint in the summer of 1970, and the last of these gigs (the band's last with Lou Reed) was captured on *Live at Max's Kansas City,* an album released in 1972. In March 1973 Columbia A&R chief John Hammond suffered a heart attack during an energetic set by Bruce Springsteen—who, oddly enough, was opening for Bob Marley—but recovered in time to get Bruce's signature on a long-term contract.

Max's became a key punk hangout in the mid-'70s. Iggy Pop met David Bowie for the first time at an RCA party in 1972; Richard Hell, Johnny Thunders, and Alan Vega could often be found drinking away until five in the morning; Debbie Harry worked as a waitress; and records were spun by Wayne (later Jayne) County, who was wont to turn up in a baby-doll nightie, black wig, and feather hat. County soon began opening for punk acts, using a gigantic dildo as a prop and eating dog food—which the audience assumed to be feces—out of a toilet bowl during the song "Shit." He would also dress up in Patti Smith's trademark black-and-white garb and perform a parody of her song "Land"; in the revised version, Smith chases Jim Morrison's pubic hairs through Paris, singing "Horseshit, horseshit, horseshit." County later released a single, dedicated to Lou Reed, called "Max's Kansas City" that roll-called such local punk acts as Mink De Ville, Cherry Vanilla, Blondie, and the New York Dolls.

With "My Way" in the English charts (but failing to catch on in America), Sid Vicious played here in September 1978, backed by ex-Dolls Arthur Kane and Jerry Nolan. Max's closed on New Year's Eve 1981 after playing a decisive role in the emergence of New York's grungish no-wave movement and providing Aerosmith with its big New York break. A deli now marks the spot. *213 Park Ave. S.*

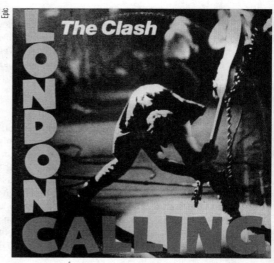

NUYORICAN POETS CAFÉ

Bob Holman, co-owner of this performance space and bar, has appeared with Henry Rollins on the MTV Unplugged's spoken-word show, and Rollins himself has also played here. Poetry slams and open-mike nights are common, but the real fun is the raucous audience. *236 E. 3rd St., tel. 212/505–8183.*

THE PALLADIUM

The Band recorded *Rock of Ages* at this former opera house on Christmas 1972, when the venue

The Clash, London Calling—cover shot at the Palladium

was still known as the Academy of Music; the group was joined onstage by jazzmen from the Count Basie band, and Allen Toussaint and Dr. John arranged the horns. Three years later, the Band came back to inaugurate the venue's new incarnation as the Palladium. The Clash kicked off its Pearl Harbor '79 tour here, opening the set provocatively with "I'm So Bored with the USA"; a photo of bassist Paul Simonon onstage made the front cover of *London Calling*, which *Rolling Stone* named the top album of the '80s. Frank Zappa wore full evening dress when here to introduce a 1981 tribute to his favorite classical composer, French electronic music pioneer Edgard Varèse. Varèse's widow was impressed and described Zappa to journalists as a "lovely person." Here on a late-night drinking binge in 1986, the Beastie Boys wrote "Fight for Your Right to Party." Elvis Costello turned up to play in 1989 but was upset at seeing a banner proclaiming BURGER KING PRESENTS ELVIS COSTELLO; a strict vegetarian, he insisted it be pulled down or he would go home. The venue now draws crowds for its hip-hop nights with Funkmaster Flex. *126 E. 14th St., between 3rd and 4th Aves., tel. 212/473–7171.*

PHYSICAL GRAFFITI COVER SITE

Led Zeppelin fans will recognize these tenements from the front cover of *Physical Graffiti*. The basement of one houses a clothing shop named after the album. The Rolling Stones used the same location for the video of "Waiting for a Friend." *96–98 St. Marks Pl., between Ave. A and 1st Ave.*

Midtown

Heading north from downtown, New York's landmark skyscrapers—the Empire State Building and the Chrysler Building—signal the arrival of midtown Manhattan, with its big department stores, corporate office blocks, and elegant boutiques. Dividing the east and west sides is busy 5th Avenue, along which the Rolling Stones played live on a flatbed truck to announce their 1975 U.S. tour.

In stark contrast to the swank air of much of midtown, the area just north of Madison Square Garden is rather unsavory—according to the Clash, 42nd Street is where "hustlers hustle and pimps pimp the beat." Adjoining 42nd Street is Times Square, the neon-bedecked intersection of Broadway and 7th Avenue. North of Times Square is Broadway theaterland. Although more associated with showy musicals than rock & roll, this part of Broadway was home to many '50s independent record labels and music-biz offices, the most famous being the Brill Building.

EATINGDRINKINGDANCINGSHOPPINGPLAYINGSLEEPING

Times Square is home to the Marriott Marquis Hotel, where you can sip a cocktail in the revolving **BROADWAY BAR** (1535 Broadway, at W. 45th St., 8th floor, tel. 212/704–8756), overlooking the square. Farther north is the Paramount Hotel's chic **WHISKEY BAR** (235 W. 46th St., tel. 212/819–0404). Next door to the Brill Building is **COLONY RECORDS** (Broadway and W. 49th St., tel. 212/265–2050), excellent for all types of sheet music; Jimi Hendrix used to shop here for his LPs. On the other end of the spectrum is the Times Square **VIRGIN MEGASTORE** (1540 Broadway, tel. 212/921–1020), the world's largest record store, which opened amid much hoopla in April 1996.

ATLANTIC RECORDS

Although it's now part of the Warner Elektra Atlantic corporate empire, Atlantic was one of the pioneering independent rock & roll record companies. Founded in 1947 by jazz buffs Herb Abramson and Ahmet Ertegun, it was initially based in the latter's hotel room—not really a hardship, considering that Ertegun, the well-heeled son of a Turkish diplomat, had elegant quarters at the Ritz overlooking Central Park. The label had its first hit in 1949 with Stick McGhee's R&B classic "Drinkin' Wine Spo-Dee-O-Dee," and soon Ertegun was scouring the country for black singers to cut hits in what was then called the "race" market. In 1954 one Atlantic race record, "Shake, Rattle and Roll," was touched up for mass consumption by Decca Records' Bill Haley; it sold a million copies and was one of the first records to be described as "rock & roll."

The 1953 arrival of *Billboard* journalist Jerry Wexler as vice president catalyzed the label. At *Billboard* Wexler had begun calling race records "rhythm 'n' blues," and on joining Atlantic, he began producing some of the most successful artists in the genre—the Drifters, Ruth Brown, and Ray Charles—as well as signing up rock & roll acts like the Coasters and Bobby Darin.

In the early '60s, with Atlantic now based at 157 West 57th Street, near Carnegie Hall, the run of success continued on both the pop and R&B charts with Ben E. King's "Spanish Harlem" and "Stand By Me" and the Drifters' "On Broadway." But Wexler felt that the label had lost touch with its blues roots, and he began trekking down to the South. He consolidated a distribution deal with Memphis's Stax Records, where Wexler supervised Wilson Pickett's "In the Midnight Hour" in 1965 and signed up the rights for Percy Sledge's "When a Man Loves a Woman" (the first soul record to top the pop charts). He took Aretha Franklin to Muscle Shoals, Alabama, where she relaunched her career with 1967's "I Never Loved a Man (the Way I Love You)." That year Atlantic had 18 of the year's 100 top-selling soul records and was bought out by Warner Bros. for $17.5 million.

After the assassination of Dr. Martin Luther King, Jr., in 1968, the mixed-race recording sessions common in Memphis and Muscle Shoals became tense affairs, and Atlantic eased away from its southern studio work. Ertegun built up the label's roster of white rock groups by acquiring the distribution rights to the Rolling Stones and by signing Yes, ELP, King Crimson, and Crosby, Stills, Nash and Young. He also signed Led Zeppelin, who brought the label more income than the Stones but was in turn outsold by a radio-friendly band of British expatriates, Foreigner.

Flush with success, Atlantic moved into ever more luxurious offices—first 1841 Broadway, then 75 Rockefeller Center, the current address. But the label was also getting careless, letting Willie Nelson go to Columbia after one unsuccessful album (his next sold a million) and passing up an option on Michael Jackson. Atlantic also missed out on rap even though it had recorded Chic, one of the genre's prime influences. Despite successes with such mainstream acts as INXS, En Vogue, and Phil Collins, the label no longer has any particular musical identity. *75 Rockefeller Center.*

BLOOMINGDALE'S

It was at this world-famous department store that Sonic Youth's Kim Gordon recorded the video for "Addicted to Love" in a do-it-yourself photo booth. The track was released on *The White(y) Album,* which the group recorded under the name Ciccone Youth in honor of Madonna. *1000 3rd Ave., at E. 59th St., tel. 212/355–5900.*

BRILL BUILDING

Early in this century, the area around the vaudeville theaters and publishers' offices of West 27th Street was nicknamed Tin Pan Alley. By the '40s this music-and-theater district had moved north 20 or so blocks, and by the early '60s many record labels and publishers' offices were based on a stretch of Broadway in the heart of theaterland. One of the area's unremarkable high-rises, the Brill Building, became the driving force behind pop music during the period between Elvis's entry into the army and the Beatles' landing.

In the Brill Building's windowless cubicles, which were often furnished with nothing more than a piano, teams of songwriters worked almost literally cheek by jowl under assembly-line conditions to turn out as many as three songs a day. They nevertheless produced hits: Jerry Leiber and Mike Stoller, who had written "Hound Dog," moved in with their then little-known assistant Phil Spector and penned "Spanish Harlem," a huge

1961 hit for Ben E. King. Barry Mann and Cynthia Weill wrote the Crystals' "Uptown" and the Drifters' Top 10 hit "On Broadway." The most consistently successful writers, however, were a husband-and-wife team, Gerry Goffin and Carole King, who scored No. 1's with "The Loco-Motion," sung by King's maid, Little Eva; Bobby Vee's "Take Good Care of My Baby"; and the Shirelles' "Will You Still Love Me Tomorrow?"

In the Brill's heyday, the success of its songs attracted hundreds of hopefuls—a young and loitering Paul Simon was ejected from the offices—but after British groups swept the U.S. charts in 1964, the Brill Building's girl-group sound quickly went out of fashion. The publishers remained, but the songwriters moved out and on to other things. Nowadays the building still houses music-biz offices, ironically including Paul Simon's headquarters. In 1995 director Alison Anders began work on the movie *Grace of My Heart,* which focuses on the songwriters of the Brill's heyday and includes appearances by the Red Hot Chili Peppers and J. Mascis of Dinosaur Jr. *1619 Broadway.*

[CARNEGIE HALL]

This prestigious concert hall, which opened its inaugural season in 1891 with Tchaikovsky conducting, has a long history of hosting popular music. Back in 1938, impresario John Hammond booked legendary Delta bluesman Robert Johnson to play a "From Spirituals to Swing" concert alongside Count Basie and Benny Goodman. Trying to track Johnson down, Hammond searched his regular Delta haunts, only to find that a few weeks previously the guitarist had died in Greenwood, Mississippi, reputedly from bad whiskey poisoned by a jealous love rival.

The hall first hosted rock & roll in May 1955 with a performance by Bill Haley and the Comets. When Bob Dylan appeared in November 1961—his first professional show outside Greenwich Village—he had to make do with the small Recital Hall and 60 paying customers. Two years later, after a performance in the main auditorium, his car was mobbed by screaming fans, a rare example of Dylanmania. In 1968 he ended his post–motorcycle-crash layoff by playing here, supported by the Band.

Carnegie Hall also hosted the Beatles' 1964 New York debuts. With "I Want to Hold Your Hand" topping the U.S. charts, they played two 35-minute sets on Lincoln's birthday, shortly after their triumphant February 9 appearance on *The Ed Sullivan Show.* Because of a ticket mix-up, 200 fans—including Lauren Bacall—ended up sitting on the stage. Tours of the hall are held regularly. *154 W. 57th St., tel. 212/247–7800.*

COLUMBIA STUDIOS

Up through *Highway 61 Revisited,* Bob Dylan cut his albums in Studio A. Miles Davis recorded the breakthrough jazz-rock fusion album *Bitches Brew* upstairs in Studio B in August 1969. The building now houses the label's archives. *49 E. 52nd St.*

DRAKE SWISSÔTEL

A double room will cost visitors a couple hundred bucks these days, but Led Zeppelin was even more out of pocket in 1973. Just before the last of three gigs at nearby Madison Square Garden, $200,000 worth of gate receipts went missing from the hotel's safe deposit box. Although the police searched the hotel while a desperate John Bonham relocated the band's drug stash, the money was never found. Typically, some journalists thought it was a publicity stunt. Back in April 1968, Jimi Hendrix stayed here for most of the month after being thrown out of the Warwick on West 54th; he recorded a handful of (unreleased) songs in his room, including "Cherokee Mist" and "Angel." *440 Park Ave., at E. 56th St., tel. 212/421–0900. Rooms: $200.*

ED SULLIVAN THEATER

The Ed Sullivan Show was broadcast from this Broadway studio until it went off the air in 1971. When Elvis Presley performed in 1956, he was shot from the waist up—

Sullivan claimed he wanted to protect the sensibilities of the large number of good Christian folk watching. No such bodily restraints were placed on the Beatles when they played in February 1964. There were more than 50,000 applications for the 730-odd seats, and 70 million people tuned in, causing what police claimed was a relatively juvenile-crime–free night across the nation. The group played a 13-minute set, in the midst of which a congratulatory telegram from Elvis's manager, Colonel Tom Parker, was read on air. While they played "Till There Was You," the Beatles' first names were flashed on the screen, with the caption SORRY GIRLS, HE'S MARRIED underneath John's.

Before appearing on the show in August 1967, the Doors were told that CBS television objected to the line "Girl we couldn't get much higher" in "Light My Fire," then No. 1 on the U.S. charts. Jim Morrison agreed to change the lyric but then sang it anyway during the live broadcast. In the console room, the show's director went purple with rage, screaming at the monitors and promising that the Doors would never appear again. Sullivan died in 1974, but the theater retains his name and is now used for *The Late Show with David Letterman,* which occasionally hosts a rock band. *1697 Broadway, at W. 53rd St, tel. 212/975–4321.*

THE FACTORY

Andy Warhol's loft studio was housed on the fifth floor of a former hat factory that lay in the shadow of the Empire State Building. Everything in the Factory, as it was called, was painted silver—supposedly the space-age color of the future. After taking the Velvet Underground under his wing, Warhol brought the band here in 1966 and—deciding they needed a more glamorous singer than Lou Reed—introduced the players to the German actress Nico, who took some of the lead vocals on the first album. A group rehearsal in 1966, shot on black-and-white film as *The Velvet Underground and Nico: A Symphony of Sound,* was so loud that the cops came and broke it up. In June 1968, Valerie Solanas, self-styled leader of SCUM (Society for Cutting Up Men) and star of Warhol's movie *I, a Man,* followed Warhol into the building and shot him in the liver and stomach with a .32 automatic. He survived. The building didn't and was demolished at the end of the '60s. A parking lot stands on the site. *231 E. 47th St.*

Andy Warhol

ZEP AT THE GARDEN

Led Zeppelin ended up on the receiving end of a miniriot in summer 1972 when the air-conditioning at Madison Square Garden failed. Fans tried to storm the stage during "Whole Lotta Love," damaging the platform and sending speakers crashing; the group encored unplugged. A triumphant three-day return engagement the following year was recorded for the film and album *The Song Remains the Same.* The band's 1975 Garden gig was reviewed for *Crawdaddy* by William S. Burroughs, who watched them from the 13th row and refused offers of cotton wool to protect his ears from the decibel overload. The group sold out six nights in June 1977 with Plant electronically backing himself on harmony. In 1988—with the late John Bonham replaced on drums by his son Jason—Led Zeppelin emerged from retirement to play Atlantic Records' 40th-birthday party.

[MADISON SQUARE GARDEN]

This 20,000-capacity arena—equally famous in the music and sport worlds—has just about seen it all since it started hosting bands in the late '60s: celebrity mishaps, live albums, benefit gigs, and hyped reunions. At the Winter Festival for Peace in January 1970, Jimi Hendrix, playing with his new outfit, Band of Gypsys, walked off during the second number, humbly telling the audience, "We can't get it together." He subsequently broke up the band. In October 1971 at a rock & roll revival show, early-'60s teen star Ricky Nelson was booed for refusing to stick to oldies; he managed to write the hit single "Garden Party" about the experience. In July 1974 Sly Stone married Kathy Silva onstage in a televised service. Sly, who was once arrested on West 45th Street before a gig for allegedly threatening to shoot an elderly woman, became notorious in the '70s for starting performances late. He was only two minutes behind schedule for his wedding, but three months later Silva filed for divorce.

One of rock's first live albums, the Rolling Stones' *Get Yer Ya-Ya's Out!*, was recorded at a four-day Garden stint in November 1969, just before Altamont. In June 1972 Elvis Presley made his very first stage appearance in New York; as he came onstage, the theme from *2001: A Space Odyssey* was played. The show became *Elvis Is Recorded at Madison Square Garden*, which stalled at No. 11 on the U.S. charts. More successful was Led Zeppelin's No. 2 *The Song Remains the Same*, culled from three July 1973 shows.

The Rolling Stones, Get Yer Ya-Ya's Out!—*recorded live at the Garden*

The Garden staged one of rock's first big benefit shows: the August 1971 Concert for Bangladesh. Organized by George Harrison, it starred the former Beatle, along with Eric Clapton, Leon Russell, and Bob Dylan (making a surprise appearance during one of his reclusive phases); the triple album and spin-off film raised $15 million for the war-torn Asian country. Another major benefit that spawned a movie and album set, the No Nukes Concert (officially Musicians United for Safe Energy), was staged in September 1979, with Bruce Springsteen, Jackson Browne, Bonnie Raitt, and the Doobie Brothers appearing. John Lennon, backed by Elephant's Memory, played two shows on August 30, 1972, in aid of disabled children; these performances turned out to be his last full-length gigs. His next live appearance at the Garden, in November 1974, was to join Elton John in performing their recent U.S. No. 1 song, "Whatever Gets You Thru the Night." The rusty guitarist was relieved to receive a standing ovation, and he proceeded to tackle "Lucy in the Sky with Diamonds" and then, surprisingly, the McCartney-written "I Saw Her Standing There." The first song on the Beatles' first album, it also turned out to be the last song Lennon ever performed before a live audience.

Bob Dylan celebrated 30 years as a recording artist here in 1992 with such star-studded back-up help as the Band, Johnny Cash, Eric Clapton, George Harrison, Roger McGuinn, Eddie Vedder, and Neil Young. When Sinead O'Connor came onstage, the

The Beasties play b-ball with some other Garden regulars, members of the Knicks

crowd reaction was split between cheers and jeers as the singer had been in the news for dissing the national anthem and ripping up a picture of Pope John Paul II during a performance on *Saturday Night Live.* Major acts still play the Garden—the Beastie Boys staged a triumphant gig in June 1995. *4 Pennsylvania Plaza (8th Ave. and W. 33rd St.), tel. 212/465–6741.*

MANNY'S MUSIC

Although half a dozen musical-instrument shops are grouped together along West 48th Street, the most celebrated is Manny's, which claims to be the best-stocked instrument store in the United States. Hundreds of pictures of famous customers cover every available bit of wall space. Bob Dylan's bears the suitably cryptic message KEEP ONE EYE CLOSED AT ALL COST, while Ronnie Wood, pictured grinning alongside a twisted guitar, jokes I'LL NEVER FALL FOR ONE OF THESE AGAIN. Other signed photos are of Madonna, Bob Marley, Bon Jovi, Lou Reed, and Jethro Tull, while Eddie Van Halen left an autographed guitar.

The store was opened by Manny Goldrich in 1935, but it is Manny's son Henry who has courted many of rock's most famous guitarists. Jimi Hendrix would buy three or four guitars a week, often giving them to friends, and he furnished his Electric Lady studio with Manny's equipment. Hendrix was such a valued customer that Manny would personally deliver new gear or open up after hours to let Hendrix wander around unhassled. A couple of less technically proficient musicians dropped in from Forest Hills in January 1974; John Cummings went for a blue Mosrite guitar, Doug Colvin got a Dan Electro Bass— and the Ramones were born. Cummings adopted the pseudonym Johnny Ramone, Colvin became Dee Dee Ramone, and they teamed up with Jeffrey Hyman (Joey Ramone) and Tommy Erdelyi (Tommy Ramone). *156 W. 48th St., tel. 212/819–0576.*

MEDIA SOUND (LE BAR BAT)

Le Bar Bat, a restaurant that occupies a former Baptist church, was once the Media Sound studio. The walls are lined with gold records recorded here, including Aerosmith's *Night in the Ruts,* the Stones' *Tattoo You,* and Lennon's *Walls and Bridges.* Media Sound albums that didn't go gold include Lou Reed's *New York* and T Rex's *Electric Warrior. 311 W. 57th St., tel. 212/307–7228.*

MUSEUM OF TELEVISION AND RADIO

More than 50,000 TV and radio broadcasts, including much rare footage, are available here at the flick of a switch. The most requested program is *The Ed Sullivan Show* with the Beatles. Visitors simply request an item from the index, and when it arrives, they can play it in cubicles equipped with individual screens and headphones. *25 W. 52nd St., tel. 212/621–6800. Admission: $5 suggested. Open Tues.–Sun. noon–6.*

NBC STUDIOS

Saturday Night Live has been broadcast from NBC's Studio 8H since 1975. Hour-long tours of the studio are available daily from 9 to 4:30 (but the $8 tickets are often sold out by lunchtime). Tickets for the show are sent out by lottery each August, although some standbys are handed out at 9 on Saturday mornings; people start lining up at 4 or 5 AM. Those who lose out on the standbys often wait around to get a space at the rehearsal, which is often looser and occasionally funnier than the televised version. *GE Building, 30 Rockefeller Plaza, W. 49th St. at 6th Ave., tel. 212/664–7174.*

[RADIO CITY MUSIC HALL]

New York's ultimate example of Art Deco chic, with its elegant chandeliers and grand staircases, has hosted several rock concerts over the years. Fans, such as those at a lively 1984 U2 gig for Amnesty International, have not always been respectful of the hall's 6,000 comfy seats, so these days the music roster is filled mainly with the likes of Amy Grant, Jon Secada, and the Allman Brothers Band, who in 1995 were still able to sell out six consecutive nights.

Steely Dan sang about "stomping on the avenue by Radio City" on "Bad Sneakers" from 1975's *Katy Lied*. The Ramones recorded their self-named debut album in February 1976 downstairs in the Plaza Sound recording studio, and soon after Blondie recorded its first album in the Stravinsky Room. Tours of the hall—said to be the largest purpose-built indoor theater in the world—start at 10 each morning. *1260 6th Ave., at W. 50th St., tel. 212/247–4777.*

RECORD PLANT

Hendrix recorded *Electric Ladyland* at this studio in 1968, rounding up musicians who happened to be hanging out at the Scene, Steve Paul's nearby nightclub. Among those roped in were Jefferson Airplane bassist Jack Casady and Steve Winwood, who played organ on the sprawling version of "Voodoo Chile" that closes the album's first side. The Stooges recorded their first album here in June 1969, and Bruce Springsteen cut "Born to Run" in 1975 at a time when Tommy Erdelyi worked here as an assistant engineer (the future Ramone didn't take part in the Boss's sessions, however). A few hours before he was murdered, in December 1980, John Lennon was here mixing tracks for *Milk and Honey*, which was released posthumously. The building still stands, but the Record Plant no longer flourishes. *321 W. 44th St.*

ROSELAND

Despite Kurt Cobain's request that the audience "have patience, we're one of the biggest rock & roll bands in history," Nirvana's acoustic versions of "Polly" and "Dumb," unveiled here during the 1993 New Music Seminar, were booed—reminding journalists of the treatment Dylan received when he used an electric guitar for the first time, at the 1965 Newport Folk Festival. The first part of the gig—Nirvana's first New York appearance since hitting the big time—had been much more enthusiastically received, with three-quarters of the crowd moshing and fans continually clambering up onto the stage to dive into the crowd.

When Roseland was around the corner at 1658 Broadway, it was the city's premier dance hall, with the likes of Count Basie, Bix Biederbecke, and Louis Armstrong playing

Oasis at Roseland

Dennis Kleiman

before segregated audiences in the '30s and '40s. There's still ballroom dancing on the polished wooden boards of the current location, but it's usually confined to the afternoons. At night bands like Belly and Weezer pull in the crowds. *239 W. 52nd St., tel. 212/249–8870.*

(STEVE PAUL'S) THE SCENE

Led Zeppelin's favorite New York hangout, set among some of the city's harder-core sex stores, The Scene is long gone, but it was once the hippest joint in town. The Doors' first New York gigs took place here during a successful three-week residency in 1967. Returning the following March, they were joined onstage by Jimi Hendrix, who was inclined to jam with whomever was playing. During "Sunshine of Your Love," Morrison faked fellatio on Hendrix as the two wrestled to the floor.

Zep's devotion should not be underestimated: One night in 1969, the band had a gig in Philadelphia with Jethro Tull opening. The headliners insisted they had to go on first because a sickly Jimmy Page was on the verge of passing out. Naturally, Page was fine except for a bad thirst, and the band turned out a stellar set (much to Tull's disappointment) before speeding back to Manhattan to party here. *301 W. 46th St.*

STUDIO 54

Studio 54 was New York's most glamorous disco-era nightclub. Gucci-wearing rock stars, models, starlets, and society types came to pose under the mirrored ceilings and occasionally bop on the spotlit dance floor to Chic, Odyssey, and Kool and the Gang. After closing in the early '80s, it reopened as the Ritz, an exciting place that booked James Brown, Bow Wow Wow, the Pixies, and 2 Live Crew, among others. An April 1990 gig by the Boo-Yaa T.R.I.B.E., a sextet of Samoan heavyweights–cum–former L.A. gang members, came to an inglorious end when one of the group's onstage dancers twisted a mike stand around his own neck. The space is now empty. *254 W. 54th St.*

WALDORF-ASTORIA

After their triumphant performance at the Monterey Pop Festival, the Jimi Hendrix Experience returned to New York in July 1967 and checked into the glamorous Waldorf-

Astoria. A tour with the Monkees had been arranged, but Hendrix and company wanted out, so they made up a story about a religious sect complaining that Hendrix was corrupting the Monkees' teen audience. *American Bandstand* host Dick Clark, who was in charge of the Monkees tour, allowed the Experience to leave the bill.

At the 1987 Grammy awards, held at the Waldorf, Frank Zappa and the Mothers of Invention were asked to perform as a sop to those who claimed the show was too staid; while the Woody Herman jazz band played "Satin Doll," the Mothers, clad in freaky gear, ambled onto the stage and began taking dolls apart, offering the limbs to the executives in the front row. The hotel experienced a rare punk moment in 1973 when the New York Dolls played a Halloween do; the highlight of the night was a costume competition in which the first prize was a night out on the town with the band and a weekend for two at a luxury motel near Newark Airport. *301 Park Ave., tel. 800/ 932–3322. Rooms: $260.*

The Upper East and Upper West Sides

Central Park—where Simon and Garfunkel, Jefferson Starship, and many others have given open-air concerts—splits Manhattan into the Upper East and the Upper West sides. The West Side is popular with intellectuals and artists, boasting such exclusive apartment buildings as the Dakota, outside of which John Lennon was murdered in 1980. The East Side is Manhattan's old-money area, with designer boutiques, multimillion-dollar town houses, and world-class museums. The nightclubs are mostly snooty and can't compete for excitement with downtown venues. An exception is the Latin-flavored Copacabana, once a leading MOR concert venue, where Sam Cooke cut a celebrated live album.

EATING DRINKING DANCING SHOPPING PLAYING SLEEPING

Two of Manhattan's biggest record shops are on the Upper West Side: **TOWER RECORDS** (1965 Broadway, near the southwest edge of Central Park, tel. 212/799-2500) and **HMV** (2081 Broadway, near W. 72nd St., tel. 212/721–5900).

CENTRAL PARK

Manhattan's biggest open space, 840 acres that stretch the 2½ miles between 59th and 110th Streets, has hosted many rock events, as well as the May 1984 wedding of Chrissie Hynde and Jim Kerr. In 1970 rock promoter Bill Graham wanted to stage a free concert but was refused by the city on the grounds that it would generate too much garbage. Graham responded by buying New York City 160 new trash cans. He was then allowed to put on Jefferson Airplane. Fifteen years later the group's latest incarnation, Jefferson Starship, gave a free show for 60,000 fans and was saddled with a $14,000 clean-up bill.

Simon and Garfunkel drew a crowd of 400,000 for a free concert in September 1981, their first joint appearance since a 1972 benefit performance at Madison Square Garden for George McGovern's presidential campaign. In June 1982 a million people came to see Jackson Browne, Joan Baez, Linda Ronstadt, and Gary U.S. Bonds. A free Diana Ross concert the following summer was abandoned due to heavy rain after only a few songs; rescheduled for the next night, it was marred by an invasion of well-organized teams of muggers.

Steely Dan used a shot of one of the park's many pretzel sellers for the album cover of *Pretzel Logic*. The band's record label asked the vendor's permission to use the photo but were refused. When the legal team found out that he didn't have a vendor's license, they let the shot be used, and there were no legal repercussions. The Dan weren't the first band to use the park for an album-cover photo shoot. In August 1968 the Jimi Hendrix Experience booked photographer Linda Eastman (now McCartney) to take shots of the band beside the Alice in Wonderland statue for the cover of *Electric Ladyland*. The photos were ditched in favor of a picture of 21 naked women, but the Eastman shots later found their way onto the inside cover of the U.S. release.

After John Lennon was murdered at the nearby Dakota in 1980, thousands of mourning fans gravitated toward the park. The bandstand (just south of 72nd Street) was filled with flowers, and Beatles songs were played over a P.A. Soon after, Yoko Ono asked the city if she could landscape a plot of parkland in Lennon's memory;

Steely Dan, Pretzel Logic—*a cover found in Central Park*

although she ran into opposition from a group of politicians who wanted to honor Bing Crosby, the city council voted to allow the memorial. Ono paid $1 million to landscape three acres, which she named after the Beatles' 1967 song "Strawberry Fields Forever." The patch contains 161 plant species—one for each of the world's countries at the time of Lennon's death—and a stone monument that reads: STRAWBERRY FIELDS. IMAGINE ALL THE PEOPLE LIVING LIFE IN PEACE.

COPACABANA

New York's leading '50s nightclub, a favorite spot for singers like Tony Bennett and Ella Fitzgerald, was where Sam Cooke recorded his sophisticated live album, *Live at the Copa,* in July 1964. A sober contrast to James Brown's *Live at the Apollo,* recorded in Harlem in 1962, Cooke's album reached only No. 29 on the U.S. charts; Brown's had made No. 2. Cooke had previously played the club in 1958, opening for Jewish comedian Myron Cohen; he did a tap dance wearing top hat and tails and was the butt of Cohen's jokes. In 1965, during their debut appearance at the Copa, the Supremes recorded a live album featuring a medley of Cooke numbers—a tribute to the singer, who had been murdered in L.A. the previous December. The Copacabana was closed in 1973 after owner Frank Costello's death. It reopened as a disco three years later and now features salsa music. *10 E. 60th St., tel. 212/582–2672.*

THE DAKOTA

This late-19th-century, pseudo-Gothic apartment block of yellow brick and terra-cotta witnessed rock & roll's most infamous assassination. On December 8, 1980, John Lennon was gunned down near the 72nd Street entrance of the building that had been his home since April 1973. Killer Mark Chapman had been wait-

The Dakota

ing for him on and off for three days and, a few hours before shooting him, had even gotten Lennon to autograph a record sleeve. For more than a week after the murder, hundreds of fans kept vigil outside and festooned the building with photos and record sleeves. More or less directly east in Central Park is Strawberry Fields, Yoko Ono's memorial garden to John. Ono still lives on the Dakota's sixth floor and has retained Lennon's all-white room, as well as the white piano on which he composed "Imagine."

Lennon was not the Dakota's first brush with the rich and famous. The building opened in the 1880s—it received its name shortly thereafter when a cynical New Yorker suggested that it was as far from the center of town as the Dakotas—and has housed celebrities throughout its history. Boris Karloff, Leonard Bernstein, Judy Garland, Lauren Bacall, and Roberta Flack have lived here, and Roman Polanski used the building to film parts of *Rosemary's Baby*. *1 W. 72nd St.*

GUGGENHEIM MUSEUM

The Guggenheim's brash concrete swirls were designed by architect Frank Lloyd Wright, who inspired Simon and Garfunkel's "So Long Frank Lloyd Wright," included on the *Bridge over Troubled Water* album. Inside is a room dedicated to the late Robert Mapplethorpe, Patti Smith's photographer and onetime companion; the exhibit opened in November 1993 with a short acoustic set by Lou Reed. *1071 5th Ave., at 89th St., tel. 212/360–3500.*

METROPOLITAN OPERA HOUSE

The Who performed *Tommy* at this prestigious opera house for two nights in June 1970. It was the first time a rock group had been allowed to play the venue, but Pete Townshend wasn't fazed: He smashed his guitar at the end of the shows as usual. The Met is part of the eight-block Lincoln Center performing-arts complex, built in the 1960s to replace the tenement-ridden ghetto where *West Side Story* was filmed. *Lincoln Center, Broadway at W. 64th St., tel. 212/362–6000.*

QUEENSBORO (59TH STREET) BRIDGE

In the mid-'60s Paul Simon lived on the Upper East Side, and this bridge was his route back to Forest Hills, the Queens suburb where he grew up. In March 1967 he and Art Garfunkel released the single "At the Zoo"; the B side, "The 59th Street Bridge Song (Feelin' Groovy)," quickly established itself on radio playlists at the expense of "At the Zoo" and later reappeared on the duo's megaselling *Greatest Hits* album.

WHITNEY MUSEUM OF AMERICAN ART

In the late '80s, Pavement's Steve Malkmus and Steve West worked briefly in this Bauhaus structure, where the permanent collection includes works by such 20th-century artists as Roy Lichtenstein, Jackson Pollock, and Edward Hopper. *945 Madison Ave., at 75th St., tel. 212/570–3676.*

Harlem

North of Central Park, above 110th Street, Harlem takes over. The most famous black neighborhood in the United States, perhaps in the world, Harlem has been a mecca for African-American culture for nearly a century. Many of the area's greatest musical moments have taken place on lively Martin Luther King, Jr. Boulevard (West 125th Street) at the world-famous Apollo Theater.

Not so welcoming is East 125th Street's decrepit junction with Lexington Avenue, where Lou Reed waits for his drug dealer with "$26 in my hand" in the Velvet Underground's "I'm Waiting for the Man"; when Reed wrote the song in 1967, this spot already had a reputation for being a junkie's hangout where a rare white visitor could only be looking to score. While much of Harlem reeks of poverty, neighborhoods such as Sugar

Hill (around West 145th Street and St. Nicholas Avenue), as in rap's pioneering record label, have lovely, historic blocks of restored brownstones.

[APOLLO THEATRE]

After temporarily closing in the late '70s and early '80s, America's most celebrated black concert hall is again putting on big-name soul, R&B, and rap acts. Even the Wednesday Amateur Night at the Apollo (won in the '60s by the Ronettes, Jimi Hendrix, Dionne Warwick, and the Jackson Five) are back.

Completed in 1914, the building began operating in 1919 as Hurtig and Seamon's New Burlesque Theater, a whites-only venue, even though Harlem was then a vibrant, integrated area. Both its stars and its liquor made it a popular destination during Prohibition, but when the Depression began to bite, white audiences trailed off. The theater was renamed the Apollo in 1932 and began to but on black vaudeville and jazz acts. After World War II, it cemented its place as the key nightspot on the exploitative R&B chitlin' circuit, as the black-only theaters necessitated by Jim Crow laws were called. (The club's management got a shock in 1957 when Buddy Holly and the Crickets turned up to play and were discovered to be white, but the bespectacled Texan and his band were welcomed nonetheless.)

The Apollo in the '70s

The Apollo's place in rock & roll mythology was sealed with the release of James Brown's *Live at the Apollo,* recorded in December 1962. Brown had won the Amateur Night contest in 1956 and made his professional debut opening for Little Willie John in September 1958, but in October 1962 he returned for six nights over the protests of Syd Nathan, his boss at King Records, who thought a live album would never work. *Live at the Apollo* proved Nathan wrong by becoming the first R&B album to make the pop charts, reaching No. 2, and it sealed Brown's position as one of the most exciting acts in showbiz. The emcee introduced the singer with a breathless "So now ladies and gentlemen, it's star time, are you ready for star time?" and Brown groaned, moaned, wept, wailed, whispered, and screamed his way through a succession of his hits, including "I'll Go Crazy," "Think," and "Please Please Please." Other headlining acts of the period included Sam Cooke, Aretha Franklin, and the Miracles, whose Smokey Robinson wrote "My Girl" backstage.

After suffering closures and bankruptcy in the '70s, The Apollo was sold and reopened in 1983, designated an official landmark by the city, state, and federal government. A couple of years later, Darryl Hall and John Oates cut a Top 30 live album here with the help of the Temptations' Eddie Kendricks and David Ruffin. Nowadays the venue is operated by a nonprofit organization and books rap acts like L.L. Cool J, as well as such blues legends as B.B. King and Bobby Bland. The original Wednesday amateur nights continue to be a popular showcase for new talent, and *It's Showtime at the Apollo,* a syndicated program run by an independent production company, brings performances at the Apollo to a national TV audience. *253 Martin Luther King, Jr., Blvd. (W. 125th St.), tel. 212/749–5838.*

SUGARHILL RECORDS

Harlem's Sugar Hill neighborhood has for decades attracted middle-class blacks. In the late '70s Sylvia and Joe Robinson, then one of the music industry's rare black owner teams, founded Sugarhill Records. Sylvia Robinson's rock & roll associations went back far. As part of Mickey and Sylvia she had recorded the well-known 1956 hit "Love Is Strange," and in the early '70s she enjoyed her second success, "Pillowtalk." The fledgling label quickly hit gold with one of the first rap records, the Sugarhill Gang's "Rapper's Delight." No sooner had "Rapper's Delight" charted than the Robinsons moved the label out of Manhattan to new offices in Englewood, New Jersey.

In 1981 Sugarhill released Grandmaster Flash and the Furious Five's "Adventures on the Wheels of Steel," little more than rearranged snippets of their favorite contemporary disco records (including its B side, "The Birthday Party") but also the first record to use the sound of turntable manipulation that came to be known as "scratching." The song failed to chart in the States or in Britain, but scratching became one of the dominant sounds of the '80s. With two big social-commentary hits, "The Message" and the antidrug "White Lines (Don't Do It)," Flash also showed that rap need not concern itself solely with sexual braggadocio.

BOBBY'S HAPPYHOUSE RECORD STORE

Bobby Robinson has run a record store in the shadow of the Apollo Theatre since 1946 (it was based nearby at 301 West 125th Street until the '90s). He also set up one of America's first black-owned record labels, Red Robin, which released the '50s doo-wop songs of the Orioles. In the '80s Robinson helped kick-start the career of Grandmaster Flash and the Furious Five—the group's Spoonie Gee is his nephew. *2347 Frederick Douglass Blvd. (8th Ave.), tel. 212/864–8910.*

HOTEL THERESA

Now an office building, the Theresa was once Harlem's biggest hotel. As such, it hosted many jazz and R&B musicians—and, in 1960, Cuban president Fidel Castro. Jimi Hendrix moved in when he first arrived in New York City, in January 1964. That February Hendrix entered the Apollo's weekly amateur contest and won, his first big break. His guitar prowess came to the attention of the Isley Brothers, with whom he toured and cut a single for Atlantic, "Testify," later that year. Hendrix returned to the hotel in May 1965, moving into Room 416 while playing the Apollo with Little Richard's band under the name Maurice James. When Richard fired him for persistent lateness, Hendrix could no longer afford the hotel's rent and was forced to seek cheaper accommodation downtown and pawn his guitar. *2090 Adam Clayton Powell, Jr., Blvd., at 125th St.*

The Bronx

Some of hip-hop's best-known DJs—Afrika Bambaataa, Grandmaster Flash, and Scott La Rock—were raised in the area. La Rock also died here, gunned down while trying to settle an argument outside the Highbridge Gardens Homes in 1987 just after recording the *Criminal Minded* album with Laurence "KRS-1" Parker. In an earlier generation, doo-wop singer Dion Di Mucci named his backing group the Belmonts after the area where they lived around East 183rd Street.

RIKER'S ISLAND DETENTION CENTER

Set on a island in the East River, but officially a part of the Bronx, this prison has attracted an interesting range of inmates. Folk pioneer Huddie Ledbetter, better known as Leadbelly, served a year for assault in 1939. Nearly 40 years later, in 1978, Sid Vicious was remanded here while awaiting trial for allegedly murdering Nancy Spungen at Manhattan's Chelsea Hotel. Sid tried unsuccessfully to commit suicide during his stay; after being released, he returned to Manhattan, where he fatally OD'd the same year. In October '95 rapper Tupac Shakur spent some time at Riker's before being released on bail pending his eventually sucessful appeal of a conviction for sexual assault.

Queens

The largely uneventful residential neighborhoods that make up Queens are better known for the interesting people they produced than for interesting events. Paul Simon and Art Garfunkel grew up in the wealthy enclave of Forest Hills. They met at school when they were nine but had moved out of the borough by the time they began record-ing together in the mid-'60s. In 1975 they took a swipe at the place on the single "My Little Town." Other well-known Forest Hills natives include Steely Dan's Walter Becker and the Ramones. Rappers Run-D.M.C. were more sympathetic to their Queens 'hood, Hollis, 5 miles east of Forest Hills, on the 1987 single "Christmas in Hollis."

JOHN F. KENNEDY AIRPORT

Ten thousand screaming teens greeted the Beatles when they got off PanAm Flight 101 on February 4, 1964. The group had spent much of the flight—their first to Amer-ica—being hassled by English businessmen trying to entice the group into merchandis-ing deals. On arriving, the Beatles were ushered into a press conference and subjected to the usual round of dumb questions: "Will you be getting a haircut" (Paul: "No"); "How do you find America?" (Ringo: "We went to Greenland and made a left turn"). That June the Rolling Stones followed but were met by only a few hundred fans after a stormy trip, later recounted on the *Aftermath* track "Flight 505." When the Sex Pistols touched down 14 years later, the only welcoming party was an ambulance to take Sid Vicious to the hospital—he'd OD'd on the plane on booze and barbiturates.

SHEA STADIUM

The Beatles set an attendance record for a stadium concert when they played the Mets' baseball stadium before 55,600 fans on August 15, 1965. (The record stood until '70s supergroup Grand Funk Railroad pulled in just over a thousand more in 1971.) Although gate receipts totaled $304,000—the group took $150,000—the huge security and insurance costs left promoter Sid Bernstein with a profit of just $6,500. When the Bea-tles returned in August 1966 to play one of their last live dates, 12,000 seats went unsold. A benefit gig held in 1970 to commemorate the 25th anniversary of the Hiroshima bombing fell flat when fewer than 20,000 turned up to see John Sebastian, Janis Joplin, Paul Simon, and Johnny Winter. The Rolling Stones gave one of Shea's last rock concerts in 1989. *126th St. at Roosevelt Ave., Flushing Meadows Park, tel. 718/507-8499.*

Brooklyn

Brooklyn, where DJ Alan Freed promoted some of the earliest rock & roll shows in 1956, was a separate city until the beginning of the 20th century. In the '50s Coney Island, now a faded seaside neighborhood on Brooklyn's Atlantic shoreline, attracted

100,000 revelers a day. Lou Reed used the resort as a metaphor for decay on his 1976 album, "Coney Island Baby," the title track of which was dedicated to his then partner, a transsexual named Rachel. The Ramones sang about riding Coney Island's roller-coaster in 1976's "Oh Oh I Love Her So."

BROOKLYN ACADEMY OF MUSIC

In 1995 Hole kept an invited audience waiting for two hours before performing a Valentine's Day MTV Unplugged set at this concert venue, known for its avant-garde programming. In an effort to inject some rock & roll revelry into the staged format, Love and company ended the show by smashing their acoustic guitars. *30 Lafayette St., tel. 718/636–4100.*

BROOKLYN PARAMOUNT

Alan Freed promoted many raucous rock & roll shows in the '50s at this long-closed concert hall, now part of Long Island University. The first, a 10-day Christmas 1956 residency with Fats Domino and Frankie Lymon, was so successful that Freed soon became a millionaire: He had wisely arranged to take a large cut of the door takings rather than a fixed fee. The big stars of the day—Buddy Holly and the Crickets, Little Richard, and so on—played over the next two years, but the shows were stopped in 1958 after a riot at a Freed-sponsored gig in Boston (*see* Boston Arena *in* Boston, Massachusetts, *above*). At one of Freed's last Paramount shows, the never-very-chummy Chuck Berry and Jerry Lee Lewis had a furious argument over who should top the bill. Berry claimed seniority, and so Lewis went on first and ended by setting fire to the piano with gasoline while still playing it. The crowd went wild. Off went Lewis, who turned to Berry and jeered, "Follow that, nigger." *University Plaza, Flatbush and DeKalb Aves.*

Courtesy of Center for Southern Folklore

Jerry Lee Lewis

ST. ANNE'S (PACKER COLLEGIATE INSTITUTE)

In February 1990 John Cale and Lou Reed debuted *Songs for Drella,* a tribute to the then recently deceased Andy Warhol, at this Gothic former Episcopal church (now the Packer Collegiate Institute). That May, former Band organist Garth Hudson and friends played a concert of Romanian folk tunes, jazz numbers, and Appalachian songs staged by Marianne Faithfull's producer, Hal Willner. A few months later, Faithfull returned to record parts of her live album, *Blazing Away. Clinton St. at Livingston St., Brooklyn Heights.*

Staten Island

Staten Island, birthplace of Joan Baez, is notably lacking in interesting rock landmarks. Not connected to Manhattan by road or rail, it is best reached by ferry from Battery Park, a trip that offers a glimpse of the Statue of Liberty and one that Bob Dylan sang about on "Hard Times in New York Town."

New York City Jukebox—50 Songs Sung by 50 Artists

Ben E. King, "Spanish Harlem" (1961)
The Drifters, "On Broadway" (1963)
Bob Dylan, "Spanish Harlem Incident" (1964)
The Ad Libs, "The Boy from New York City" (1965)
Bob and Earl, "Harlem Shuffle" (1965)
Trade Winds, "New York's a Lonely Town" (1965)
Lovin' Spoonful, "Night Owl Blues" (1966)
Simon and Garfunkel, "The 59th Street Bridge Song (Feelin' Groovy)" (1966)
The Velvet Underground, "I'm Waiting for the Man" (1967)
Joni Mitchell, "Chelsea Morning" (1969)
Laura Nyro, "New York Tendaberry" (1970)
John Lennon, "New York City" (1972)
Steely Dan, "Brooklyn Owes the Charmer Under Me" (1972)
Bobby Womack, "Across 110th Street" (1973)
Leonard Cohen, "Chelsea Hotel No. 2" (1974)
Genesis, "The Lamb Lies Down on Broadway" (1974)
Bruce Springsteen, "New York City Serenade" (1974)
10cc, "Wall Street Shuffle" (1974)
Thunderthighs, "Central Park Arrest" (1974)
Hello, "New York Groove" (1975)
Steeleye Span, "New York Girls" (1975)
T Rex, "New York City" (1975)
Lou Reed, "Coney Island Baby" (1976)
Wayne County, "Max's Kansas City" (1976)
Graham Parker and the Rumour, "New York Shuffle" (1977)
Mink De Ville, "Venus of Avenue D" (1977)
Odyssey, "Native New Yorker" (1977)
The Ramones, "Rockaway Beach" (1977)
Sex Pistols, "New York" (1977)
Candi Staton, "Nights on Broadway" (1977)
Talking Heads, "Life During Wartime" (1979)
Tom Browne, "Funkin' for Jamaica (NY)" (1980)
Suicide, "Harlem" (1980)
Marianne Faithfull, "Times Square" (1983)
Prince, "All the Critics Love U in New York" (1983)
Orange Juice, "Salmon Fishing in New York" (1984)
The Beastie Boys, "No Sleep 'Til Brooklyn" (1986)

The Pogues, "Fairytale of New York" (1987)
Run-D.M.C., "Christmas in Hollis" (1987)
Tom Waits, "I'll Take New York" (1987)
Jennifer Warnes, "First We Take Manhattan" (1987)
U2, "Angel of Harlem" (1988)
Dion DiMucci, "King of the New York Street" (1989)
Don Henley, "New York Minute" (1989)
Kirsty MacColl, "Walking Down Madison" (1991)
Public Enemy, "A Letter to the New York Post" (1991)
Charles and Eddie, "NYC (Can You Believe This City?)" (1993)
Luscious Jackson, "City Song" (1994)
Ol' Dirty Bastard, "Brooklyn Zoo" (1995)
Scott Walker, "Manhattan" (1995)

Watkins Glen

WATKINS GLEN RACEWAY

Six hundred thousand people, believed to be the largest crowd ever to attend a rock event, saw just three bands—the Grateful Dead, the Allman Brothers, and the Band—play this NASCAR racetrack in July 1973. The Band, which headlined, claimed they agreed to play only because Watkins Glen was "up the road," at the southern tip of upstate's Lake Seneca. Because of rain, the musicians had to abandon the stage after eight numbers, but they soon returned—fortified by a bottle of Glenfiddich—and enjoyed themselves so much that they decided to return to live performance, making plans for what became the well-received 1974 *Before the Flood* "comeback" tour with Bob Dylan. Their Watkins Glen performance was released as a live album by Capitol 22 years later. *Rte. 16 and Meads Hill Rd., about 25 mi east of Ithaca.*

From the collection of Stacey Wixson

The Watkins Glen Summer Jam

Woodstock and Environs

Nestling in a cool setting in the Catskill mountains, Woodstock has been a haven for artists and bohemians for much of the 20th century, beginning in 1902 with the arrival of Ralph Radcliffe Whitehead and his wife, Emily Byrd. During World War II the painter Manuel Bromberg, German author Thomas Mann, and classical composers Aaron Copland and John Cage moved in. In 1964 Albert Grossman, Bob Dylan's manager, and his wife, Sally, bought a large estate from the artist John Striebel and opened up the Bearsville Arts Complex. Dylan began dropping by regularly and later recuperated from his 1966 motorcycle crash in town. By 1968 the growing music community included the Band, installed in a big pink house near Overlook Mountain; Scottish folksinger John Martyn; and Van Morrison, who moved into a house on Ohayo Mountain in February 1969.

The presence of these stars attracted scores of followers, and soon the sleepy town was not so sleepy, what with curious visitors looking for Dylan, and Janis Joplin and Jimi Hendrix jamming at local clubs like Rose's Cantina and the Joyous Lake. Woodstock was seen as the ideal setting for an August 1969 music and art festival, but by then the locals had had enough. Fearful of being overrun by a quarter of a million hippies, the town rejected the event, and the Bethel site was chosen. By the beginning of the '70s, most of the rock crowd had left, and Woodstock has since settled down somewhat. The surrounding hills do still hold some top studios (such as Bearsville and Applehead), and current rock residents include Donald Fagen and Graham Parker.

Many rock visitors have celebrated Woodstock on vinyl. John Martyn extolled the town's beauty on the 1970 song "Woodstock," Van Morrison sang of "Old Old Woodstock" on 1971's *Tupelo Honey,* and the Band decried the way the town's innocence had been spoiled by the arty media crowd in their 1970 song "The Rumor."

EATING DRINKING DANCING SHOPPING PLAYING SLEEPING

These days a quick visit to Woodstock will reveal little, bar a few New Age gift shops, but a couple of nights spent at the **TWIN GABLES GUEST HOUSE** (73 Tinker St., tel. 914/679–2487) or camping in the woods allows time to sample the rough and ready Woodstock nightlife. At the Tinker Street Cafe (*see below*) or the **JOYOUS LAKE** (42 Mill Hill Rd., tel. 914/679–1234), you can meet people who've been here since the '60s and others who've come to work in studios away from the big city. **WDST** (100.1 FM) pumps out alternative sounds from a house on Tinker Street, having taken over the wavelength from a woolly throwback format; each Friday the station broadcasts a live gig from a local venue.

BEARSVILLE ARTS COMPLEX AND STUDIOS

In 1964 Albert Grossman, then managing Bob Dylan, bought this massive plot of land on an unmarked dirt track atop a wooded hill and built an arts complex, with a small theater, a restaurant, and a bar. He died of a heart attack on a plane to England in 1986 and is buried by the stream behind the Little Bear restaurant under a hard-to-find flat headstone. His widow, Sally, who was on the front cover of Dylan's *Bringing It All Back Home,* now owns and runs the complex.

Bearsville's studios opened as a state-of-the-art venture in 1971 and gave a name to the record label set up soon after by knobs-and-wires whiz kid Todd Rundgren. Besides recording his own works—particularly 1973's *A Wizard/A True Star*—Rundgren has mixed LPs here for the New York Dolls, Jesse Winchester, Grand Funk, and Meatloaf. Others who have used the studio include the Band (*Cahoots*), R.E.M. (*Green*), the Butthole Surfers, and Phish. The studio is in a secret wooded location on a private drive at the top of a hill off Speare Road. In the woods behind the studios, off Striebel Road, Dylan and three unknown locals were photographed for the cover of *John Wesley Harding*; if you look closely at the left side of the image, the ghostly outline of the Beatles' faces can be made out between the branches. *Hwy. 212, 2 mi west of Woodstock, just past Striebel Rd.*

In 1967, members of what became the Band began renting this pink clapboard four-bedroom house in West Saugerties, a few miles northwest of Woodstock, for $125 a month. A regular visitor was Bob Dylan, recuperating from his motorcycle crash (*see below*). They jammed daily, recording some 150 new songs—including "The Mighty Quinn," "You Ain't Goin' Nowhere," and "This Wheel's on Fire"—compositions that reflected the rustic charm the area held for musicians winding down after years of hectic touring schedules.

The Band, Music from Big Pink

Over the next two years, some of these songs were passed to friends like Manfred Mann and the Byrds, and the cover versions only increased the mystique that grew around Dylan and company's activities. Many of the songs began appearing on various bootlegs, the most famous of which was known as *The Great White Wonder,* an official collection of 24 tracks, a third of them not featuring Dylan, was belatedly released by Columbia in 1975 as *The Basement Tapes.* Meanwhile, the Band was busy working on a debut album, which appeared in August 1968 to glowing reviews. The original U.S. gatefold sleeve of the album, *Music from Big Pink,* depicted the musicians and their families gathered by the side of the house; the cover art was by Dylan. In fall 1995 the house, one of the most famous in rock history, was back on the market, priced at $179,000. *2188 Stoll Rd., West Saugerties.*

BOB DYLAN CRASH SITE

On July 29, 1966, Bob Dylan hit an oil slick on Zena Road and fell off his Triumph motorbike en route to a garage in Bearsville. Or did he? The myth persists that Dylan fabricated the crash so he could get out of the public eye and chill out in peace (in his Woodstock cabin and at Big Pink), away from tour managers, inquisitive journalists, demanding fans, groupies, and other rock & roll pressures. There are even two different stories about where the crash took place: The most commonly quoted crash site is on a very sharp bend about a mile up Zena Road near an old barn, although some maintain it was on the other side of Woodstock on a downhill stretch of Streibel Road. *Zena Rd., 1 mi south of Rte. 212.*

[THE ESPRESSO (TINKER STREET CAFE)]

Bob Dylan wrote songs for two albums, 1964's *Another Side of Bob Dylan* and the following year's *Bringing It All Back Home,* while living in a room above this café, then known as the Espresso. The sleeve of the earlier work is dedicated to proprietors Bernard and Marylou "for use of their house"; they had no idea who their lodger was until Tom Paxton played one night and dedicated "Blowin' in the Wind" to Dylan, who was sitting in the audience.

Among those who regularly drank, dined, and performed in the café at this time were Janis Joplin, Jimi Hendrix, and Van Morrison. Although it barely holds 150 people, as varied a bunch as Mick Ronson, the Del Fuegos, R.E.M., the Band, Burning Spear, and

10,000 Maniacs have made surprise appearances onstage. Living Color played three nights here in the early '90s to test out some material they were recording up the road, and Ozzy Osbourne wrote "Mr. Tinker Train" while sitting in the café.

The Espresso was renamed the Tinker Street Cafe in 1988, and in 1994 the owners released a compilation album—*Where Woodstock Lives*—featuring groups from New York state that have played here, including the local band 3, which played Woodstock '94 and is featured in the movie of that event. Unchanged in appearance since the '60s, the café is the center of Woodstock nightlife; it rocks well into the night and is open for breakfast. *59 Tinker St, tel. 914/679–2487.*

WOODSTOCK '94 SITE

A crowd of 300,000—mostly collegiate types who could afford the $130 ticket, rather than unreconstituted heads—attended Woodstock '94, held to celebrate the 25th anniversary of the August 1969 festival. The Woodstock townsfolk had rejected the 1969 festival, held 60 miles away in Bethel; this time the organizers were able to get permission to hold the show closer to the village, in Saugerties, some 10 miles away. Nonetheless, local sheriffs felt obliged to knock on doors, warning residents that it was illegal to shoot somebody for inadvertently treading on their property.

Veterans of the first festival—Santana, the Band, Joe Cocker, and Crosby, Stills and Nash (without Young)—turned up, joined by others from the Woodstock era (the Allman Brothers, Traffic). Contemporary names on the slate ranged from the Rollins Band, Cypress Hill, and Metallica to Sheryl Crow, Del Amitri, and Brian May. On the final night the festival closed with Bob Dylan, the Red Hot Chili Peppers (who had the bright idea of wearing lightbulbs on their heads), and Peter Gabriel (who, typically, made everyone light a candle for Rwanda).

Heavy-handed organization put a ban on almost everything other than music, including food, children, alcohol, and cameras. Purchases could be made only with "Woodstock Money," which was handed out in exchange for real cash. Unfortunately the organizers failed to take into account the possibility of rain, and when it rains in the Catskills, Mother Nature doesn't mess around. When the downpour came, the site rapidly became a fetid swamp. The crowd took it in stride, however, and as at the original festival, started playing in the mud, egged on by Green Day and Nine Inch Nails. The Nails stepped out of their bus in makeup and tight leather but, after a friendly intraband wrestle, appeared onstage to play their set caked in mud—much to the appreciation of the masses. *Winston Park, Saugerties, 10 mi north of Woodstock.*

Philadelphia

THEY'LL BE ROCKING ON BANDSTAND, IN PHILADELPHIA, PA—CHUCK BERRY, "SWEET LITTLE SIXTEEN"

The nation's first capital and now its fifth-largest metropolis, Philadelphia has made three significant contributions to popular music: the teen idol, the twist, and Philly Soul. During the early days of rock & roll, the city had scores of independent labels; two of the most successful were Jamie, which signed Duane Eddy, and Cameo, which released Chubby Checker's million-selling 1960 version of "The Twist."

The twist was just one of many new dances featured on the Philadelphia-based *American Bandstand* in the early '60s. The nationally televised show was also a breeding ground for a new brand of mildly rock & rolling teenage heartthrobs: Singers like Fabian, Frankie Avalon, and Bobby Rydell were often chosen by program boss Dick Clark more for their looks and miming talent than for their ability to cut a well-crafted song.

The British invasion dampened America's enthusiasm for dance crazes and cute singers. Philadelphia, however, stuck to what it knew. Even at the height of psychedelia, dance numbers like Cliff Nobles's "The Horse" continued to pour out of Philly's studios, while rock groups were few and far between—Todd Rundgren's Nazz didn't have much company.

By the early '70s, when a new generation of upwardly mobile soul fans were looking for an alternative to Motown and Stax, local producers Kenny Gamble and Leon Huff had developed a powerful new sound. Philly Soul exploded onto the charts and into clubs but was killed off by funk and disco at the end of the decade. Since then homegrown talent has amounted to little more than Jazzy Jeff and the Fresh Prince, Boyz II Men, and the Goats.

EATINGDRINKINGDANCINGSHOPPINGPLAYINGSLEEPING

Although Philly was sent up as "a great rock & roll city" in *This Is Spinal Tap,* it nevertheless has some good places to catch a band, many of the best of which are downtown along South Street; try J.C. Dobbs (*see below*) and the **THEATER OF THE LIVING ARTS** (334 South St., tel. 215/922−1011). While you're in the neighborhood, stop by **PHILADELPHIA RECORD EXCHANGE** (608 S. 5th St., between South and Bainbridge Sts., tel. 215/925−7892), a great spot to buy or sell indie albums. The adjacent Old City area has such popular clubs as the **MIDDLE EAST** (126 Chestnut St., tel. 215/922−1003) and **KHYBER PASS** (54 S. 2nd St., tel. 215/440−9683).

Downtown

Downtown Philadelphia is big enough to contain several distinctive areas. Center City, the area around City Hall, is thick with corporate skyscrapers, smart hotels, and shopping malls. To the west, between lively Chinatown and the redeveloping waterfront, is Independence National Historic Park, encompassing numerous sites relating to the Revolutionary War. At downtown's southern edge is South Street; described by the Orlons as "the hippest street in town" on their 1963 "South Street" single, it once rivaled Memphis's Beale Street as a center of black social life. Now Philly's equivalent of the

Haight or Greenwich Village, South is where tourists mingle with nipple-pierced locals in myriad clothing stores, secondhand outlets, lounges, cafés, clubs, and record stores. The area just south of it, around 9th Street, is dominated by the sprawling Italian Market, where Chubby Checker once worked; it's still a great place to load up on inexpensive edibles. The empty lots and burned-out blocks a little farther west were used by Bruce Springsteen in the video for "Streets of Philadelphia," showing yet again his all-around blue-collarness.

THE SOUND OF PHILADELPHIA

Philly Soul was created by Jamaican-born songwriter Kenny Gamble and Philadelphian session musician Leon Huff. After meeting in 1964, they assembled a session group, Kenny and the Romeos, featuring Thom Bell (who wrote "Tighten Up") and Van "The Hustle" McCoy; as writers and producers, they hit the charts in 1967 with the Soul Survivors' million-selling "Expressway to Your Heart" and relaunched Wilson Pickett's career with "International Playboy" three years later.

In 1971 the duo formed Philadelphia International Records (PIR) and came up with the "Philly Sound"—an update of '50s doo-wop and '60s Bacharach–David sophistication—expressed through the O'Jays, Harold Melvin and the Blue Notes, and Billy Paul. Instrumental backup was provided by MFSB (Mother Father Sister Brother), basically a revamped Kenny and the Romeos. PIR's musicians began leaving for new ventures at the end of the '70s, and once CBS scrapped the label's distribution deal, PIR went into decline.

CAMEO/PHILADELPHIA INTERNATIONAL

Cameo, along with its Parkway subsidiary, was Philadelphia's most successful record label in the '50s and '60s, releasing hits like Charlie Gracie's "Butterfly" and the Rays' double-sider "Silhouettes"/"Daddy Cool." The label's biggest coup was Chubby Checker's massively successful "The Twist." Cameo diversified in the '60s, recording the garage band ? and the Mysterians (of "96 Tears" fame) and an early Bob Seger, but made a big mistake when it rejected future producer Kenny Gamble. Gamble got the last laugh—he moved his Philadelphia International Records label into the building after Cameo folded in 1968. The building is now an art supply store. *309 S. Broad St.*

HENRY COLT'S POULTRY STORE

In the '50s Ernest Evans used to sing the hits of the day while working as a chicken plucker in the heart of Philadelphia's Italian Market. His singing so impressed store owner Henry Colt that Colt got him a deal with Cameo, where he recorded under the stage name Chubby Checker, inspired by his musical hero, Fats Domino. The store is now an Italian deli. *S. 9th St. at Washington Ave.*

J.C. DOBBS

This little no-frills venue opened in 1975 and was where George Thorogood made his name, playing three times on Saturday nights and sleeping upstairs. A few years later the Stray Cats appeared on Sundays as the Tom Cats, and club bartender Tony Bidgood became their manager. Today J.C. Dobbs presents up-

J.C. Dobbs

and-coming alternative bands; a virtually unknown Nirvana appeared in the early '90s, and five years later former MC5 guitarist Wayne Kramer gave the debut performance of his *The Hard Stuff* material to a packed house. *304 South St., tel. 215/925–4053.*

WALK OF FAME

More than 30 plaques commemorating Philly greats (locals and those who established themselves here) are set into the pavement outside the Academy of Music at Broad and Locust streets. Look for tributes to John Coltrane, Dizzy Gillespie, Todd Rundgren, Teddy Pendergrass, Bill Haley, and Jim Croce. *West side of S. Broad St. between Spruce and Walnut Sts.*

Beyond Downtown and Suburbs

JFK STADIUM

The American leg of Live Aid, produced by Fillmore founder Bill Graham, took place at the now-demolished JFK Stadium on July 13, 1985. Divided into 20-minute segments, the bill starred the Beach Boys; Neil Young; Tina Turner; Joan Baez; the Four Tops; Crosby, Stills and Nash; Led Zeppelin; and Bob Dylan. Phil Collins had a particularly busy day, speeding across the Atlantic on the Concorde right after playing the London Live Aid gig to do a spot of drumming for Led Zeppelin, which was playing for the first time since John Bonham's death. *Broad St. near Pattison Ave.*

MOUNT LAWN CEMETERY

After a lavish funeral here in 1937, Bessie Smith lay in an unmarked grave—her insurance policy didn't cover a headstone—until August 1970, when Janis Joplin helped pay for a tribute shortly before her own death. *84th St. and Hook Rd., Sharon Hill, tel. 215/586–8220.*

SCHUYLKILL EXPRESSWAY

The Schuylkill Expressway, as the stretch of I–76 west of downtown Philadelphia is known, was the inspiration for the Soul Survivors' 1967 hit "Expressway to Your Heart." Gamble and Huff's first success, it featured highway noises and car horns recorded on the Schuylkill. Sonic Youth gave a nod to the song with 1986's "Expressway to Yr. Skull," the closing track on the band's *EVOL.*

SIGMA SOUND

Sigma had contributed little to rock & roll besides a few teen hits for Bobby Rydell before1968, but then engineer Joe Tarsia joined the staff. His touch was instrumental in creating the Philly Soul sound, and most of the early-'70s hits of that genre were cut here. At the height of its success, Sigma also attracted plenty of big-name rock acts looking for a sleek upmarket sound: Todd Rundgren recorded "Hello It's Me" here, Robert Palmer did *Double Fun,* and Bowie came for *Young Americans.* More recently, the studio has been used by Eric Clapton and Bon Jovi. *212 N. 12th St., tel. 215/561–3660.*

TOWER THEATER

David Bowie recorded *David Live* at this 3,000-seat venue on the western edges of the city in July 1974. As the sleeve took pains to explain, "No studio overdubs or re-recording of voices, instruments or audience have been added, with the exception of several backing vocals due to loss of mike contact." U2 played the Tower in May 1983 after the release of *War,* and again on the Zoo TV tour 11 years later. *69th St. and Ludlow, West Darby, tel. 610/352–0313.*

[WFIL STUDIOS (AMERICAN BANDSTAND)]

American Bandstand, one of the pioneering rock & roll TV shows, was broadcast from this warehouse for 12 years. When the show began, in October 1952, it was just called

American Bandstand *in its heyday*

Bandstand and went on at 2:45 P.M. so that kids could get home from school in time to watch. In 1956 a former DJ, Dick Clark, took over as host and the program, renamed *American Bandstand,* began being broadcast nationally on ABC.

Clark devised what was then a fresh format—artists miming their songs while surrounded by enthusiastic dancers, most of them schoolkids. The cynical view was that the singers had to mime because they could never reproduce their studio-contrived sound live; another kind of disingenuousness decreed that although the dances had been developed in Philly's black clubs, the dancers be mostly white. Nevertheless, *American Bandstand* was phenomenally popular, and the dances that aired on the show—most famously the twist, but also the Bristol stomp, mashed potato, watusi, pony, monkey, and fly (there was a thing about animals)—each accompanied by its own catchy dance tune, became national crazes.

Clark also booked a new breed of rocking crooners who became instant (albeit short-lived) teen idols. That Clark had a financial stake in the careers of many of the singers who appeared on his show got him hauled into the House of Representatives' 1959 hearings on payola. It was found that between October 1957 and October 1959 the charts often contained three or four records in which Clark had a financial interest, but he denied all allegations of favoritism and was cleared (unlike Alan Freed; *see* Washington, D.C., *below*). Clark continued hosting *American Bandstand* from here until 1964, when the show moved to California. The building is now used as a warehouse by Philadelphia's public-television station. *46th St. at Market St.*

Philadelphia Songs

Hall and Oates, "Fall in Philadelphia" (1972)
MFSB, "TSOP (The Sound of Philadelphia)" (1974)
Elton John, "Philadelphia Freedom" (1975)
Magazine, "Philadelphia" (1980)
George Thorogood and the Destroyers, "Kids from Philly" (1980)

Boyz II Men, "Motownphilly" (1991)
Bruce Springsteen, "Streets of Philadelphia" (1994)
Neil Young, "Philadelphia" (1994)

Pittsburgh

Pittsburgh has been a better consumer than producer of rock. In the '40s it was a hot jazz city—Art Blakey, Kenny Clarke, Stanley Turrentine, and Billy Eckstine come from here—and toward the end of the decade, a four-year-old George Benson began singing on street corners in the Hill district. The city's hills blocked it from receiving radio signals from Cleveland or Philadelphia and so developed its own little scene in the '50s and '60s. The Del-Vikings, the first integrated doo-wop group, formed in 1955 at Pittsburgh Air Force Base and went on to record the popular "Come Go with Me." Other groups soon followed, including the Skyliners, the Marcels (who did the best-known version of "Blue Moon"), Lou Christie, Bobby Vinton, and the Jaggers, who had a big hit with "The Rapper." The '60s saw the city consumed with the Brit invasion, and the '70s and '80s were quiet, too—things might have been different if visa problems hadn't caused the Sex Pistols to call off all the northern concerts on their 1978 tour.

Today Pittsburgh has a healthy number of local alternative bands—Speaking Canaries, Don Caballero, and Blunderbuss, to name but three. A significant amount of coverage has also gone to two acts that served their time in the city's clubs: Rusted Root, once the house band at the Graffiti Club, provided support on 1995 summer tours by the Grateful Dead and a reunited Plant and Page, while Joe Grushesky, a mainstay of the local Iron City Rockers, released a solo album that same year produced by one Bruce Springsteen. Pittsburgh's best-known export, however (unless you count Perry Como), remains Andy Warhol; a massive museum dedicated to his work and pastimes opened in 1994.

Downtown and North

Downtown, known as the Golden Triangle because it's surrounded by the city's three rivers—the Ohio, Allegheny, and Monongahela—is an appealing place, especially considering that it was a polluted hellhole three decades ago. Follow the Allegheny River east from downtown for a dozen or so blocks and you'll get to the emerging Strip District, which has great ethnic food and a couple of good venues. Directly across the Allegheny is the North Side, home of the Warhol Museum.

EATINGDRINKINGDANCINGSHOPPINGPLAYINGSLEEPING

The Strip District's **METROPOL** (1600 Smallman St., tel. 412/261–2232) attracts most of the best touring bands; the adjacent **ROSEBUD CAFÉ** (1600 Smallman St., tel. 412/261–2232) serves decent food by day and live acoustic and roots music by night. **EIDE'S** (1111 Penn Ave., tel. 412/261–0900), between downtown and the Strip, sells records but is much better for mags and comics.

CIVIC ARENA

Elvis Presley's last New Year's Eve show took place here, in 1976, with pop Vernon and daughter Lisa Marie watching. The 18,000-seat arena opened in 1961 was soon playing host to the British invasion. First up, in 1964, was the Dave Clark Five, whose show was stopped prematurely by cops who thought that screaming girls constituted a riot. Perhaps the most popular Brit act among Pittsburghers were Herman's Hermits, who played here several times with the Who and the Animals as support.

Although the liner notes don't credit the venue, at least three tracks from the Doors' 1970 album *Absolutely Live* were recorded here. The silver-domed arena—known locally as the Igloo—still puts on gigs when the NHL's Penguins aren't playing. *Auditorium Pl. between Bedford and Center Aves., tel. 412/462–1800.*

STANLEY THEATRE (BENEDUM CENTER FOR THE PERFORMING ARTS)

Bob Marley's last concert appearance took place here, on October 8, 1980. He collapsed onstage and was taken to Memorial Sloan–Kettering Hospital in New York City, then to a specialist in Germany and on to Florida, where he died of a brain tumor eight months later. *719 Liberty Ave., tel. 412/471–6930.*

WARHOL AROUND PITTSBURGH

Andy Warhol—celebrated painter, filmmaker, and Velvet Underground producer—was born Andrew Warhola on August 6, 1928, the youngest of three sons of Carpatho-Russian immigrants who lived in a two-room row house at 73 Orr Street in the Soho district, about a mile east of downtown. This was an area of cheap housing for steelworkers, and fumes from the mills along the Monongahela River would waft over the houses. The Warhol house is now an empty lot, but next door is a grim little house that shows just how basic things were back then.

The family eventually moved to 3252 Dawson Street in the more verdant Oakland area, and young Andy attended Holmes Elementary School (now demolished) across the street. The Warholas were deeply religious—Andy kept faith in his Catholicism right up to his death, just before which he met Pope John Paul II—and attended the St. John Chrysostom Byzantine Rite Church a couple of miles away in the "Russian Valley" area of Greenfield.

In 1945 Warhol enrolled in a painting-and-design course at Carnegie Mellon University (then known as the Carnegie Institute of Technology) in Oakland. Four years later, at 21, he left for New York. After his death, on February 22, 1987, from complications following gallbladder surgery, a private funeral service was held at the Holy Ghost Byzantine Catholic church on Superior Avenue on the city's North Side. He is buried at Castle Sharon in Bethel Park, just south of the city.

[ANDY WARHOL MUSEUM]

The museum, which opened in May 1994, occupies the eight floors of a Victorian warehouse just over the Seventh Street Bridge from downtown. Although the majority of Warhol's most famous works have been bought by private collectors, the museum has been able to accumulate an impressive selection of his work: Over 500 items from all periods of his career are on display at any one time, and his musical associations also receive good coverage.

After establishing himself as one of America's most in-demand commercial artists in the late '50s, Warhol turned his attention to Pop Art. To complement his visual work, he expanded into other media—film, books, performances—all under the umbrella of Andy Warhol Productions. Since his empire-building plans required the acquisition of a rock band, he took on the Velvet Underground and fine-tuned the group with the addition of German singer and model Nico. Warhol became the band's manager and "executive producer" of their first album, *The Velvet Underground and Nico,* whose cover features that famous banana. The Velvets also joined the Exploding Plastic Inevitable, a traveling psychedelic extravaganza incorporating Warhol's movies, lighting effects, live music, and suggestive dancers.

Warhol later became one of the world's best-known socialites, celebrated in song by artists as diverse as David Bowie and Crowded House. Former Velvets Lou Reed and John Cale got together in 1990 to record a tribute album, *Songs for Drella,* on which they reveal Warhol's fears about having been born in Pittsburgh ("Small-town…where nobody famous came from").

The five main gallery floors show archival material and his artworks side by side. Music pops up everywhere—including a draft album cover for Billie Holiday in the '50s section—but most of his rock stuff is in a cabinet on the fourth floor, where you can find the Velvet Underground's 1966 contract with MGM, early posters, the Rolling Stones' record-label logo, covers of the Warhol-designed *Sticky Fingers* and *Love You Live* albums, and a platinum record for his video for the Cars' 1984 single "Hello

The Andy Warhol Museum

Again," in which he made a cameo appearance. Elsewhere are a bar stool and a trunk from the Factory, his virtually all-silver studio and performance space in New York, as well as the *Eleven Elvis's* screen print and portraits of Mick Jagger.

The museum pays equal attention to such archival material as Warhol's 608 "time capsules"—chronological collections of everyday things, including party invites, letters, news clippings, toys, shoes, and anything else he felt like throwing in a box. Serious Warhol students can sometimes get access to these through the museum's excellent Archives Department. Other arms of the enterprise include a theater showing films and videos (included in admission), a well-stocked gift store, and a great hangout café. *117 Sandusky St, tel. 412/237–8300. Admission: $5. Open Thurs.–Sat. 11–8, Wed. and Sun. 11–6.*

Oakland and South

Pittsburgh, spread like a blanket over hills, knobs, and valleys, is truly what many towns claim to be—a city of neighborhoods. Of most interest to rock fans is Oakland, two miles east of downtown and the home of massive Carnegie Mellon University.

EATING DRINKING DANCING SHOPPING PLAYING SLEEPING

Though pockets of Oakland can get rough at night, this is where you'll find some of the best small venues, record stores, bars, cafés, and hangouts. Clubs include the Decade and the Electric Banana (*see below*) and **GRAFFITI SHOWCASE CAFÉ** (4615 Baum Blvd., tel. 412/682−4210), an excellent venue with good sight lines, excellent sound, and a roster of touring bands that often fill it to its 800-person capacity. The city excels in record stores, which for the most part sell well-priced merchandise. Go to Jerry's (*see below*) for vinyl, but for local bands and alternative music, try **PAUL'S COMPACT DISCS** (4526 Liberty Ave., just across Liberty Bridge from Oakland, tel. 412/621−3256). Over on the South Side, **GROOVY** (1304 E. Carson St., tel. 412/381−8010) has all sorts of '70s kitsch, including Devo suits.

ELECTRIC BANANA

Locals have fond memories of the days when this compact little club on the edge of Oakland had a family of raccoons in the ceiling, and punks used to spear hot dogs on pool cues and feed them. Opened in May 1970, the club hosted go-go dancers and disco until one day in 1979 when Carl Mullen of the local punk band Car Sickness walked in and convinced owner John Zarra that it should be an alternative-music club. Other key local bands—the Five and the Cynics—got their start here, and in the '80s it was a popular port of call for Cali punk bands like the Circle Jerks, the Minutemen, and fIREHOSE. Black Flag played here several times, and the Banana was one of the first places the Rollins Band played on tour; Hank mentions it affectionately in his book *Get in the Van.* Of late the club has failed to get the best regional bands, as these things tend to be cyclical, the Banana could be a hot scene again soon. *3887 Bigelow Blvd., tel. 412/682−8296.*

[JERRY'S RECORDS]

Pittsburghers will tell you that Jerry's, a five-minute drive from Oakland in the old Jewish neighborhood of Squirrel Hill, is the biggest store of its kind. Although it's difficult to verify such things, it's hard to disagree after a visit to the store, which covers the entire second story of a strip mall. Every type of music from alternative to Broadway to Christmas albums is covered, and there are plenty of big old heavy 78s. Best of all, like most other places in Pittsburgh, the prices are very nice indeed. There's also a Jerry's Music Market and Dollar Store in Oakland with two floors of CDs and tapes, plus a huge section of slow-moving items sold for a buck apiece. *2136 Murray Ave., Squirrel Hill, tel. 800/95− VINYL or 412/421−4533, fax 412/421−2728; 3710 Forbes Ave., Oakland, tel. 412/687−1234. Both open weekdays 10−8, Sat. 10−6, Sun. noon−5.*

At York's Harley plant: Ride to live, live to ride

TOBACCO ROADHOUSE

Since opening in 1973, when it was called the Decade, this little bar has put on scores of name acts in a cramped performance space at the rear—as a gig history painted on slate and copper plates attests. The list takes some time to read, so for the less anal, the club's major coups have helpfully been highlighted: U2 (1981), Springsteen (1984), Bon Jovi (three times in 1987), and Aerosmith (1990). Alternative, rock, and blues bands still play six nights a week. *223 Atwood St., tel. 412/682—7707.*

York

Pennsylvania's most successful band of late, Live, whose *Throwing Copper* was one of the big successes of 1995, hails from this small, blue-collar town in the south-central part of the state. Hitherto, York was best known as the site of **HARLEY-DAVIDSON PLANT AND MUSEUM** (1425 Eden Rd., U.S. 30, tel. 717/848—1177), which has free tours; it's open Monday—Saturday 10—3.

Newport

America's yachting capital is famed for the remarkable "summer cottages" (read: mansions) commissioned by various Astors, Vanderbilts, Kennedys, and other Social Register families, but it is best known in rock circles for its summer music festivals. The Jazz Festival, which began in 1954, takes place over three days in mid-August. The Folk Festival, first staged in 1959, was promoted by Albert Grossman, who later managed Bob Dylan and founded the Bearsville Arts Complex in Woodstock; the festival is held early August. A third bash, the Newport R&B Festival, was inaugurated in 1995 with performances by Bonnie Raitt and a healthy number of old Stax hands; it's scheduled to take place at the end of each July. For details on all three events, held on the green waterside acres of Fort Adams State Park, call the city's **FESTIVAL HOTLINE** (tel. 401/847–3700).

FREEBODY PARK

Until the early '70s, this downtown green was home to Newport's annual musical events, including the infamous July 1965 folk fest where Bob Dylan first plugged in. Two years after a sterling acoustic performance during which he, Joan Baez, and Phil Ochs were dubbed "Woody's children" by Pete Seeger, Dylan returned high on speed; wearing black jeans, an orange shirt, and Cuban heels; and backed by a rock band. The audience, anticipating Dylan-the-radical-folk-poet, was surprised and unimpressed by the electric numbers ("Like a Rolling Stone," "It Takes a Lot to Laugh It Takes a Train to Cry," and

R.I.S.D. alum David Byrne playing with John Cale in 1977

"Maggie's Farm") and booed him off the stage. He returned on his own to do an acoustic set, including a pointedly insulting "It's All Over Now Baby Blue." Witnesses now claim that, as with later concerts in England, the crowd was bothered less by the electric instruments than by the sloppiness of the performance. The jazz fest went through a similar evolution: Beginning in 1958, when the inclusion of Ray Charles upset some, the lineup became increasingly nontraditional, until in 1969 headliners included Jeff Beck, Jethro Tull, and Led Zeppelin. *Freebody St. near Memorial Blvd. and Tennis Hall of Fame.*

Providence

Providence is home to the Ivy League's Brown University and the Rhode Island School of Design, one of the country's top art schools. Recent alternative bands to come out of the college scene include Six Finger Satellite and Scarce.

RHODE ISLAND SCHOOL OF DESIGN

David Byrne, Chris Frantz, and Tina Weymouth met while studying here in 1974. Along with various short-term collaborators, they formed the Artistics and played '60s garage-rock covers and an original ditty called "Psycho Killer," which they performed for the first time at a Valentine's Day masquerade ball. After graduation, the trio went to Manhattan and changed the band's name to Talking Heads. *2 College St., tel. 401/454−6100.*

WASHINGTON, D.C.

The nation's capital has always been a great clubbing city—the landmark 9:30 Club and newer Black Cat are as good an excuse as any to visit—but it established a meager recording tradition in the first decades of rock & roll history. Homegrown stars like Marvin Gaye had to move away to make it. The last 20 years, however, have seen two distinct musical movements come out of the D.C. area.

At the back end of the '70s, a heavy thumping dance hybrid called go-go emerged from the southeast part of town, where it provided the sound track for all-night dance marathons. The scene's biggest star was onetime boxer Chuck Brown (with his band, the Soul Searchers), who enjoyed national success with "Bustin' Loose" (1978) and "We Need Money" (1984), huge club favorites. Local Me'Shell Ndegéocello has also been influenced by the go-go sound.

Meanwhile, the city's disaffected white kids turned punk (harDCore, they like to say here) but with a straightedge ethic—no drugs, no smokes, no meat, no booze, and no stagediving—that never would have flown with Iggy Pop. An enduring figure on the local scene has been Ian MacKaye, who went from one of the first hardcore bands, the Teen Idles, to seminal D.C. noise-makers Minor Threat, who split in 1983; today he is the force behind Fugazi and the Dischord record label. MacKaye's childhood friend Henry Rollins (whose debut 1987 solo album MacKaye produced)

Fugazi at the Washington Monument

was part of the early hardcore scene before leaving the city in 1981 to join L.A.'s Black Flag. Former Nirvana drummer and leading Foo Fighter Dave Grohl is also a D.C. native; in 1986, at 17, he was drumming with hardcore favorites Scream and Dain Bramage.

Power pop is the genre of choice of such recent D.C. groups as Chisel, Shudder to Think, Jawbox, Mother May I, and Tuscadero. Hardcore vets Edsel are more popular than ever, and Velocity Girl has scored some success now that it's on Sub Pop and has dropped its original name, Gotter Democrat.

Downtown, The Mall, and Capitol Hill

THEY'RE PASSING ALL KINDS OF BILLS DOWN ON CAPITOL HILL—THE VALENTINE BROTHERS, "MONEY'S TOO TIGHT TO MENTION"

Politics and music have on occasion collided in D.C.'s heady landscape of monumental buildings, cultural institutions, and closed-door wheeling and dealing. This convergence has produced moments both serious (Stevie Wonder lobbying for a Martin Luther King, Jr., holiday) and surreal (Elvis receiving his narc badge from Richard Nixon).

THE CAPITOL

In 1959, on the heels of the TV quiz-show scandals recalled in the 1994 movie *Quiz Show,* the House of Representatives set up a subcommittee to investigate the music-industry practice of paying DJs to play certain records. Everyone knew that many of the big DJs took payola (as the practice was called), but one name kept coming up: that of DJ Alan Freed, who had helped to launch the whole rock & roll movement when he was in Cleveland. Those with conspiratorial minds will recall that Freed, an indefatigable promoter of black music, was turning millions of white kids on to independently produced R&B at the expense of sanitized major-label pop. This was costing the white music establishment money, so industry shakers were in no hurry to keep Freed from taking a fall. The cannier and more clean-cut Dick Clark was also dragged before the hearings, but whereas Clark escaped prosecution, Freed was indicted by a grand jury in New York and in 1962 pleaded guilty on two counts of commercial bribery. His career was effectively destroyed, and he died in 1965 of cirrhosis of the liver at the age of 42 just before a second trial, on tax-evasion charges, was due to begin.

In fall 1985 the Parents Music Resource Center (*see box below*), a lobbying group composed mainly of politicians' wives, took center stage in the Senate Commerce Committee's hearings on pornography in music. The PMRC had a shopping list of demands—that lyrics be printed on outer sleeves, controversial artists be dropped from labels, and so on. Standing up for the defense were Frank Zappa (whose next album would be called *Frank Zappa Meets the Mothers of Prevention*), John Denver, and Twisted Sister's Dee Snider, whom one congressman referred to during the hearing as "Mr. Sister." In the end the PMRC had to settle for an out-of-Senate compromise with the Recording Industry Association of America (RIAA) that called for voluntary EXPLICIT LYRICS—PARENTAL ADVISORY stickers on recordings. These warnings have since been placed on 2 Live Crew's *As Nasty as They Wanna Be* and Guns N' Roses' *Use Your Illusion* albums. *1st St. between Constitution and Independence Aves.*

MOTHERS OF PREVENTION

The Parents Music Resource Center was organized in the mid-'80s to force record companies to put warning stickers on discs with violent or sexual content. Leading the group were Tipper Gore (wife of then-Senator Al Gore), Susan Baker (wife of Reagan's Treasury Secretary), and several other congressional spouses; donations came from Beach Boy Mike Love, among others. The campaign started after one of the Gore daughters brought home Prince's *Purple Rain* LP, which disgusted and shocked Mrs. Gore with its graphic references to masturbation and other unsavory topics. In 1987 Gore was sued by the heavy-metal band WASP ("We Are Sexual Perverts"), who claimed she used the cover of their

single "Animal—Fuck Like a Beast" without permission in her book *Raising PG Kids in an X-Rated Society*.

D.C. SPACE

This shabby little gallery was instrumental in nursing the city's hardcore scene. Of particular note were such early multiband, all-day events as 1980's Unheard Music Festival, whose roster of 10 bands included the Nurses, SOA, and Teen Idles, Ian MacKaye's first band. Throughout the '80s, d.c. space saw a string of great names, from local favorites Bad Brains and Fugazi to touring bands like Helmet, Hole, and Jesus Lizard. For a number of years in the late '80s, Henry Rollins did a spoken-word night here each February, when he came to town to see his mom on his birthday (2.13.61, like his publishing company). The venue closed in 1991 but still maintains a presence in the city by booking local bands for an occasional "d.c. space night out" at **PLANET FRED** (1221 Connecticut Ave. NW, tel. 202/331—FRED). *443 7th St. NW, at E St. NW.*

appearing at d.c. space...

Courtesy of Cynthia Connolly

THE MALL

This long grassy parkway runs some 30 blocks between the Capitol and the Lincoln Memorial, passing Smithsonian museums, the Washington Monument, and the reflecting pool along the way. In 1981, on what would have been the 53rd birthday of Dr. Martin Luther King, Jr., 50,000 people assembled here to demand a public holiday dedicated to the assassinated civil-rights leader. At the head of the march was Stevie Wonder, who had written "Happy Birthday" in praise of King; Diana Ross and Gil Scott-Heron also attended.

In 1983 Interior Secretary James Watt scratched the Beach Boys from the Mall's annual Fourth of July celebration, fearing that they would attract "the wrong element." President and Mrs. Reagan—apparently big fans ever since the band broke in southern California in the early '60s—apologized and invited them to return the following year. The Beach Boys became fixtures at the event for much of the '80s.

Rollins at the old 9:30

9:30 CLUB, 1970–1995

Beginning in 1970, an alternative band hadn't played D.C. until they'd played the 9:30 Club. Besides having a major role in the local hardcore scene—Minor Threat, Fugazi, and Scream had early outings here and continued to play the joint after they became established—the 9:30 built its reputation by hosting a virtual who's who of the past two decades' alternative bands, including R.E.M., Sonic Youth, Nirvana, the Red Hot Chili Peppers, and Oasis (who played here on their first U.S. tour).

What made the 9:30 so remarkable was that it was such an inadequate dump. Until the end of 1995, it was located in a down-at-heel building behind Ford's Theater. The sight lines were appalling, sweat dripped off the walls, and it was such a tight squeeze that the official capacity of 350 seemed crazy. Naturally, everyone mourned the end of an era when the club moved in 1995 to the Shaw district (*see below*). *930 F St. NW.*

[THE WHITE HOUSE]

THE ONLY WAY I'M GOING INTO THE WHITE HOUSE IS WITH A FLASHLIGHT AND A SKI-MASK"—ICE T

Being president of the United States of America places its demands on a person's time, so rather than head out to gigs, most of the nation's leaders have invited their favorite bands back to the house. The following is an abridged list of those who have played or visited D.C.'s most prestigious venue:

NIXON ADMINISTRATION: Johnny Cash performed on April 17, 1970, and played Tricky Dick's special request, "A Boy Named Sue," but refused to do "Okie from Muskogee." Jefferson Airplane's Grace Slick, invited here in 1970 by Tricia Nixon, brought along Abbie Hoffman, then on trial for conspiring to cause a riot at the 1968 Democratic convention in Chicago. Hoffman was refused entry and Slick left with him, unable to carry out her threat of lacing the presidential cup with the finest San Francisco acid. In 1973 the Carpenters played for Nixon, who called them "young America at its very best." Another fine young American to play here was Tad Doyle—then in a jazz ensemble—who went on to head the Sub Pop bad-asses TAD.

FORD ADMINISTRATION: In September 1976 Peter Frampton was invited to the White House by Gerald Ford's son, Steven. Frampton, his girlfriend, and his manager spent most of the time watching TV with the president.

CARTER ADMINISTRATION: Jimmy Carter was the first rocking president—he had even been a financial backer of Macon's Capricorn label. His inaugural ball in January 1977 featured the southern boogie stylings of the Marshall Tucker and Charlie Daniels bands; the latter did a well-received rendition of "The South's Gonna Rise Again." Willie Nelson gave a private performance the following year, as did Muddy Waters, who played at a picnic on the White House lawn. Chuck Berry performed for Carter and friends on the lawn on June 7, 1979, a week before he was sentenced to four months in jail for tax evasion.

REAGAN ADMINISTRATION: On July 17, 1983, after Interior Secretary Watt banned the Beach Boys from an Independence Day celebration, Reagan called Watt in and presented him with a plaster foot with a hole in it. In 1984 Michael Jackson posed with Reagan as part of a campaign against drunk-driving; Billy Joel, a Democrat, declined the invite.

CLINTON ADMINISTRATION: Being a democrat didn't stop Billy Joel from turning down an invitation to join in a jam session with the president during the first family's first Martha's Vineyard summer vacation; Joel was quoted as saying "How good would it have been?" Aretha Franklin performed for the Clintons in 1994, and a "Women in Country" night in May 1995 included Grammy-winners Kathy Mattea and Alison Krauss.

One visit easily wins out as the greatest rock-star-meets-president moment: In the Oval Office on December 21, 1970, Elvis Presley, attired in a bold purple jumpsuit, managed to get President Nixon to swear him in as a federal narcotics officer. *1600 Pennsylvania Ave. NW, tel. 202/456-7041.*

Dupont Circle, the U District, and Shaw

The Shaw neighborhood, north of downtown, is the traditional hub of D.C.'s African-American nightlife. Until desegregation began in earnest in the '60s, the area's main thoroughfare, U Street, was known as the Black Broadway. Today, U Street's environs—often called the U District or U Street Corridor—are undergoing a revitalization and provide cheap space for some of D.C.'s best clubs and bars. To the west is Dupont Circle, a yupped-out haven of restaurants, shops, leafy residential streets, embassies, and hip clubs.

EATINGDRINKINGDANCINGSHOPPINGPLAYINGSLEEPING

The Shaw area is not too handsome at night and car theft remains a problem, but it's worth the trouble to hang out at the increasing number of inexpensive eateries and bars. **THE ANDALUSIAN DOG** (1344 U St. NW, tel. 202/986-6364) serves up reasonable Spanish food and live acoustic music amid cranky Dalí-inspired decor. The noisy **ASYLUM IN EXILE** (1210 U St. NW, tel. 202/319-9353) always seems to have good beer specials. **REPUBLIC GARDENS** (1355 U St. NW, tel. 202/232-2710), its facade dominated by Lenin and hammer-and-sickle images, has live local alternative bands. **STATE OF THE UNION** (1357 U St. NW, tel. 202/588-8810) puts on acid jazz and progressive dance sounds. A major black theater from the '20s through '50s, the **LINCOLN THEATER** (1215 U St. NW, tel. 202/328-6000) received an impressive restoration and reopened in 1994; it now hosts soul acts from time to time.

Not far from the U Street Corridor, the excellent and unpretentious **15 MINUTES CLUB** (1030 15th St. NW, tel. 202/408-1855), a sandwich bar by day, books some of the best local alternative bands or has DJs playing progressive dance music. The laid-back and bluesy **NEW VEGAS LOUNGE** (1415 P St. NW, tel. 202/483-3971) is a favorite of Stephen Stills, who has jammed here on several occasions.

Eggs at the Black Cat

BLACK CAT

D.C. native and Foo Fighter Dave Grohl has a stake in this venue, and it is one of the first places the Foos played when they took off on a national tour of small clubs with Hovercraft (the strange side project of Eddie Vedder and his wife, Beth) and Mike Watt. The Black Cat opened in mid-1993 and had a few difficult years trying to establish itself as something different from the 9:30 Club. By 1995, however, the Cat was attracting a wide range of independent and alternative bands, particularly such Brit imports as Elastica and Blur (supposedly streetwise types who found out what street life means in D.C. when someone pulled a gun on lead singer Damon Albarn on his way to a gig here in fall 1995). Morphine, Pavement, and 7 Year Bitch have also made appearances. *1831 14th St. NW, tel. 202/667–7960.*

MARVIN GAYE MURAL

This massive mural, entitled *Movin' on Down the Line,* is dedicated to the Shaw neighborhood's musical tradition; local Cardozo High School student Marvin Gaye is its centerpiece. Unfortunately, two years after the mural's completion in 1993, a new building rose up right next door, obscuring much of it. Gaye is also remembered by an April street festival that commemorates his birth (April 2, 1939) and death (April 1, 1984). *U St. NW between 13th and 14th Sts.*

HILTON HOTEL

After years of trying to see her estranged son, Clara Morrison turned up as a surprise member of the audience at a 1967 Doors gig in the ballroom here. Jim's younger brother, Andy, smuggled her into the gig, but when the singer spotted his mother in the crowd, he went into "The End" and serenaded her with the song's infamously oedipal lyric, "Mother...I want to fuck you." *1919 Connecticut Ave. NW, tel. 202/483–3000.*

HOWARD THEATER

One of the oldest black venues in the country, the Howard opened its doors in 1915 and was one of the preeminent theaters on the chitlin' circuit. A regular visitor during the '40s was Ahmet Ertegun, founder of the then fledgling Atlantic label. In 1948 he signed 21-

year-old Ruth Brown, whom he'd seen here and at the nearby Crystal Caverns bar many times. On her way to New York to record, she was injured in a car crash, but the little indie label stood by her, paying her hospital bills. They were rewarded with a series of R&B hits like "(Mama) He Treats Your Daughter Mean." The Shaw area was wracked by unemployment and riots in the late '60s, and the Howard declined and then finally closed. In the '80s there was talk of renovating the theater, but today it lies in ruins. *620 T St. NW.*

9:30 CLUB, 1996—PRESENT

After several decades in an dank downtown space, the 9:30 moved into the restored WUST Radio Hall, a space that holds 1,000. The glitzy new surrounds include multiple bars, a balcony, and a moveable stage that slides forward so smaller and local acts can play in a cozy atmosphere.

The new 9:30 opened on January 5, 1996, with a two-night stand by the Smashing Pumpkins. Since then an impressive list of top alternative names have played, including Cypress Hill, Radiohead, and Primus. The club has also broadened its roster by putting on Tony Bennett, the Cowboy Junkies, the Rev. Al Green, and Joan Osbourne. Midweek shows, many of which cost a mere five bucks, finish before midnight so concertgoers can make the last train home; on weekends doors open at 9:30, the headliners go on at midnight, and the show is over by 2. *815 V St. NW, near U St./Cardozo subway, tel. 202/265–0930.*

THE EDUCATION OF AHMET ERTEGUN

Ahmet Ertegun lived at the Turkish Embassy on Massachusetts Avenue from 1934 (when he was 11) until 1944, during his father's tenure as Turkish ambassador to the United States. In these years Ahmet and his brother Nesuhi collected some 15,000 jazz and blues records. It gave them the idea of setting up a jazz label, which developed into Atlantic Records.

The embassy's janitor, Cleo Payne, was the one who introduced young Ahmet to soul food and encouraged his appetite for jazz. Payne refused to take him to Harlem, however, chauffeured limo or no, so when Ertegun was 13, he went on his own and stayed out all night visiting the Plantation club, cops on his tail, since his family was convinced he had been abducted. Eventually he began inviting big-name black jazz musicians to jam sessions at the embassy, which as sovereign Turkish territory was not subject to the laws that otherwise restricted black musicians to juke joints.

Georgetown and North

On the west side of the city is Georgetown, D.C.'s oldest neighborhood. A mix of students, diplomats, and tourists frequent the sidewalks of this enclave on the Potomac, which has the city's greatest concentration of restaurants and bars. (It was also on one of these sidewalks that Stevie Wonder was arrested in the mid-'80s while singing at an antiapartheid protest outside the South African embassy—and charged with disturbing the peace. Wonder followed up on the incident by writing "It's Wrong," a condemnation of the apartheid system, which appears on his 1985 album *In Square Circle*.)

EATINGDRINKINGDANCINGSHOPPINGPLAYINGSLEEPING

On Wisconsin Avenue NW, alongside some decent record stores, is the basic little **GROG AND TANKARD** (2408 Wisconsin Ave. NW, tel. 202/333–3114), which thuds to the sounds of local punks. The **PARK HYATT WASHINGTON HOTEL** (1201 24th St. NW, tel. 202/789–1234) has been favored by rock stars from Tom Petty and Meatloaf to the Red Hot Chili Peppers and Spinal Tap.

THE BAYOU

R.E.M. and U2 have played this long-established club in a brick warehouse by the river. College-circuit rock acts are the staple entertainment, though Todd Rundgren and other well-knowns still pop in. The weekly Grateful Mondays night features a local Dead-covers band, the Next Step. *3135 K St. NW, at Wisconsin Ave. NW, tel. 202/333–2897.*

Minor Threat

DISCHORD HOUSE

When Ian MacKaye and Jeff Nelson of Minor Threat founded Dischord Records in 1981 to provide a vinyl outlet for the emerging hardcore scene, they ran it out of MacKaye's childhood home. Dischord has since moved, but the house remains the label's mailing address.

MacKaye had an attack of hardcore conscience in 1987 and declared that his new band, Fugazi, would only play all-ages shows with low admission charges. By 1995 the band had released five albums on Dischord Records, and the last CD, *Red Medicine,* hit the racks at the admirably low price of $10. Others on the label include Shudder to Think, Circus Lupus, Autoclave, and the short-lived Nation of Ulysses, remembered for its *Thirteen Point Program to Destroy America* album.

Dischord avoids industry schmoozing, refuses to issue press releases, and rarely grants interviews. So far there seem to be no plans to slip into the indie commercialism of labels like Sub Pop and SST by opening an outlet/souvenir store. This antimarketing style of marketing gets results—industry analysts reckon that Fugazi sells as many as 250,000 albums worldwide. *3819 Beecher St. NW.*

THE
SOUTH

ALABAMA

God-fearing Alabama, scene of several key battles during the civil rights years, was an easy target for radical artists in the '60s and '70s. Neil Young's vilifying "Southern Man" prompted a sharp rebuttal from good ole (Florida) boys Lynyrd Skynyrd in "Sweet Home Alabama" ("Well, I hope Neil Young will remember/A southern man don't need him around anyhow"). Touchingly, Young and the Skynyrds who survived their 1977 plane crash became the best of friends. Alabama's substantive rock & roll contributions come from Muscle Shoals, the collective name given to four small towns in the north of the state, which are home to two of America's most successful small-town studios.

Alabama Songs

The Charlatans, "Alabama Bound" (1966)
The Doors, "Alabama Song (Whiskey Bar)" (1967)
Janis Ian, "Alabama" (1971)
Neil Young, "Alabama" (1972)
Jim Croce, "Alabama Rain" (1973)
Lynyrd Skynyrd, "Sweet Home Alabama" (1976)

Birmingham

The hometown of Emmylou Harris and Jimmy Jones made its mark on popular music in less than enviable ways. In 1956 Nat King Cole was badly beaten up onstage by half a dozen members of the White Citizens Council, an organization which aimed to eradicate all "bop and Negro music," claiming it had been introduced by the NAACP to subvert America. Five years later Otis Redding received bomb threats when he played the Jewish Community Center.

Folksinger Richard Farina was one of the first songwriters to take Alabama's largest city to task over its civil rights record: His "Birmingham Sunday" (popularized by Joan Baez) tells the story of four young girls killed by a bomb planted by white supremacists in a church in September 1963. Talking Heads were more cryptic on *Fear of Music*'s "Cities," where they sang of "a lot of rich people in Birmingham, a lot of ghosts, a lot of houses."

The Birmingham Six

Joan Baez, "Birmingham Sunday" (1965)
Phil Ochs, "Talking Birmingham Jam" (1965)
Randy Newman, "Birmingham" (1974)
Charlie Daniels Band, "Birmingham Blues" (1975)
Emmylou Harris, "Boulder to Birmingham" (1975)
John Cougar Mellencamp, "When Jesus Left Birmingham" (1993)

Montgomery

When Dr. Martin Luther King, Jr., led one of many marches through glum Montgomery in 1967, also along were Tony Bennett—who that year refused to play South Africa, turning down big money—and Sammy Davis, Jr. The duo performed an impromptu concert on a makeshift stage made out of coffins donated by a funeral parlor. On a lighter note,

Man or Astro-man? from Planet Auburn

surf punks Man or Astro-man? came out of the city's Auburn University in the late '80s; their gigs are noted for rambling references to space flight, including quips like "If you came from Alabama/you'd know what space was all about."

HANK WILLIAMS, SR., GRAVE

A country singer who lived a rock & roll lifestyle, Hank Williams, Sr., lies under an impressive white marble headstone etched with notes from "Your Cheatin' Heart." Thousands of mourners attended Williams's funeral, held at the City Auditorium in January 1953. Among the country stars paying tribute were the straight-laced Roy Acuff, who performed the singer's evangelical "I Saw the Light." A statue of Hank is in Lister Hall Plaza on North Perry Street. *Oakwood Cemetery Annex, 1305 Upper Wetumpka Rd., near downtown, tel. 334/264–4938.*

Muscle Shoals

At first glance it's hard to believe that the adjoining blue-collar towns of Florence, Sheffield, Tuscumbia, and Muscle Shoals (whose name is generally used to refer to all four) have contributed so much to rock & roll. Because of the area's proximity to Nashville, Memphis, and the Delta, however, local musicians developed an eclectic sound that has successfully backed singers from Wilson Pickett and Aretha Franklin to Paul Simon and Rod Stewart.

The area has also produced thousands of so-called "deep soul" records. Though hits in this genre, like Percy Sledge's "When a Man Loves a Woman," are few and far between, tracks like Tony Borders's "Cheaters Never Win" and Sam and Bill's "I Feel Like Cryin' " have become dance-floor favorites and cult items on collectible soul compilations.

ALABAMA MUSIC HALL OF FAME

A diverse mix of music memorabilia is housed in what looks like an aircraft hangar, 2 miles from Tuscumbia. Open since 1990, the Hall of Fame has inducted Tammy Wynette, Emmylou Harris, Percy Sledge, and Hank Williams, Sr., among others. Check out the informative section on the history of the Muscle Shoals scene. The costume displays include the Commodores' matching three-piece white brocade suits and the blue embroidered gown worn by Muscle Shoals native Donna Godchaux, an occasional Grateful Dead singer, at the band's 1978 gig at the Great Pyramid in Egypt. Also on display are the contract Elvis Presley signed when leaving Sun Records for RCA in 1956, courtesy of Florence-born Sun boss Sam Phillips, and the country group Alabama's tour bus, conspicuously parked inside the building. *Hwy. 72, Tuscumbia, tel. 205/381– 4417 or 800/239–AMHF. Admission: $6. Open Mon.–Sat. 10–6, Sun. 1–5.*

[FAME RECORDING STUDIOS]

Florence Alabama Music Enterprises—responsible for more than 20 Top 10 hits, 10 country No. 1's, and nine U.S. pop No. 1's—was opened in 1958 by country fiddler Rick Hall with the help of producer Billy Sherrill and movie-theater manager Tom Stafford. Its first location, above Florence's only drugstore, at 123½ Tennessee Street (now demolished), had walls hung with plaster casts of people's feet—its previous tenant had been a podiatrist.

In 1960 Sherrill headed to Nashville to work at Sun (and later to produce Tammy Wynette and Elvis Costello), while Hall moved FAME to an old tobacco warehouse on the Wilson Dam Highway in Florence, just north of the Tennessee River. The studio's first hit—"You Better Move On," by local bellhop Arthur Alexander, later covered by the Rolling Stones on their first EP—wasn't long in coming. With the profits, Hall moved the studio to the current location, where in 1962 FAME achieved its first Top 10 hit, Jimmy Hughes's "Steal Away," a favorite of British bands of the era.

Rick Hall, Little Richard's manager, Little Richard, and Mickey Buckins at FAME

In 1966 FAME struck a lucrative deal with Atlantic Records that resulted in Atlantic VP Jerry Wexler bringing Wilson Pickett down to cut a version of Chris Kenner's "Land of 1000 Dances." Pickett wasn't initially impressed: When he got off the plane, he assumed the approaching Hall was a cop; he wasn't reassured when he saw black workers picking cotton in the surrounding fields. Nevertheless, "Land of 1000 Dances" was a huge dance-floor hit (reintroduced to punk fans when Patti Smith reworked it as the track "Land" on *Horses*). Pickett cut additional soul standards here, "Funky Broadway" and "Mustang Sally" among them.

In 1967 Wexler applied the same successful strategy to Aretha Franklin, bringing the then run-of-the-mill pop singer down to Muscle Shoals, where she recorded "I Never Loved a Man (the Way I Love You)"—the song that revitalized her career. On finishing the track, the musicians began drinking champagne in copious amounts, and the party got out of hand when one of the session men pinched La Franklin's butt. This pleased neither the singer nor her husband/manager, Ted White, and the couple packed up and left town. Atlantic, with a hot track but no B side, waited for the dust to settle and then, at much expense, flew the entire Muscle Shoals team up to New York. There they rounded off the B side, "Do Right Woman—Do Right Man," cut the single's chart-topping follow-up, "Respect," and finished the rest of the album. So one of the best examples of the Southern groove was cut not in Alabama but in the Big Apple.

Hits continued to pour out of FAME, among them James and Bobby Purify's "I'm Your Puppet," Wilson Pickett's "Hey Jude" (with regular session hand Duane Allman on slide guitar), and Clarence Carter's maudlin "Patches," the studio's first pop No. 1. But after Dr. Martin Luther King, Jr., was assassinated in Memphis in 1968, it became harder to find black soul singers willing to work with white musicians. Then the rhythm section left to open their own studio, Muscle Shoals Sound (*see below*).

FAME went pop. When MGM phoned to see if the studio could knock out a Jackson 5 sound for a new group of singing brothers, Rick Hall duly obliged. The record was "One Bad Apple," and the singing brothers were the Osmonds. The Utah-based Mormons crooned their way through massive-selling teenybopper anthems at FAME, with the lush orchestration added in L.A. Hall also recorded Paul Anka ("You're Having My Baby," another No. 1), Liza Minnelli, and Sammy Davis, Jr. In 1971 *Billboard* named him Producer of the Year.

Beginning in the '80s, the studio turned its hand to country—where the money was— striking gold with Marie Osmond and Shenandoah, as well as publishing megaselling hits for Reba McEntire and John Michael Montgomery. The studio is still open; if you drive by, look for the building displaying the sign WHERE IT ALL STARTED. *603 E. Avalon Ave., Muscle Shoals, tel. 205/381–0801, http://www.fame2.clever.net.*

OUT OF LEFT FIELD

Few of the people behind the Muscle Shoals sound have become public figures. Photos are rarely seen of the session musicians who backed the Picketts and Franklins of this world. The same is true of songwriters, including Dan Penn, who was responsible for turning out scores of now-standard Southern soul songs. He wrote "The Dark End of the Street," originally cut by James Carr and later covered by Aretha Franklin, the Flying Burrito Brothers, and Diamanda Galas; Aretha Franklin's "Do Right Woman—Do Right Man"; Percy Sledge's "Out of Left Field"; the hard-to-find Otis Redding number "You Left the Water Running"; Janis Joplin's "A Woman Left Lonely"; and James and Bobby Purify's smoochy "I'm Your Puppet." Penn, described by some critics as the world's greatest white soul singer, has made only two albums; 1994's *Do Right Man* is a compilation of some of his best-known songs.

MUSCLE SHOALS SOUND STUDIO, 1969—78

Founded by a group of frustrated session musicians from FAME studios, Muscle Shoals Sound opened in 1969 in a former coffin factory. The team, which included Roger

Hawkins on drums and Jimmy Johnson on guitar, had little trouble attracting big names—Atlantic Records boss Jerry Wexler quickly transferred his Southern interest from FAME to the new studio. Hawkins and company were astute enough to realize that they wouldn't sell many records if they relied solely on soul, however, and they began courting white rock acts who wanted to add a Southern groove. One of their first clients was Cher, who cut *3614 Jackson Highway,* named after the studio address, in spring 1969. She was followed by the Rolling Stones, who recorded three songs for their *Sticky Fingers* album—"Brown Sugar," "You Gotta Move," and "Wild Horses."

While their former employers were producing the Osmonds, the Muscle Shoals Sound crew worked with Paul Simon (*There Goes Rhymin' Simon*), Bob Seger (*Night Moves*), and Rod Stewart (*Atlantic Crossing*). One session regular was slide guitarist Duane Allman, who played on many Muscle Shoals recordings in the late '60s. Allman recorded his much-copied solo on Boz Scaggs's "Loan Me a Dime" (coproduced by *Rolling Stone* editor Jann Wenner) while sitting on the john, too stoned to get off. Muscle Shoals Sound moved to a new studio in 1978 (*see below*); the original building is now used to sell secondhand fridges and ovens. *3614 Jackson Hwy., Sheffield.*

MUSCLE SHOALS SOUND STUDIO, 1978–PRESENT

A state-of-the-art two-studio complex on a picturesque stretch of the Tennessee River became Muscle Shoals Sound's new HQ in 1978. It was once the main local power plant and was used as a navy depot before hosting high-school hops in the '50s. Big-selling albums recorded here include Bob Dylan's *Slow Train Coming,* Glenn Frey's *No Fun Aloud,* and Bob Seger's *Against the Wind.* Although little R&B comes out of Muscle Shoals these days, Atlantic Records chief Jerry Wexler arranged for aspiring soul shouter Beth Bosheers to cut her debut album here in spring 1995. Tours of the studio are available by appointment. *Old Naval Reserve Bldg., 1000 Alabama Ave., Sheffield, tel. 205/381–2060.*

ARKANSAS

TELL YOUR MA, TELL YOUR PA/GONNA SEND YOU BACK TO ARKANSAS—RAY CHARLES, "WHAT'D I SAY"

When a sax-wielding Arkansan hit the White House in 1993, this state suddenly vaulted into the public consciousness. As to what you'll find, besides the Ozark Mountains in the north and a slab of the Mississippi Delta in the east, the answer is relatively little—save for the birthplaces of a handful of notable musicians. An Arkansas Music Hall of Fame would include Johnny Cash (born in 1932 in Kingsland), Glen Campbell (1938, Delight), "Fever" songwriter Little Willie John (1937, as William Edward John in Lafayette), Al Green (1946, Forrest City), and Junior Walker (1942, as Autry DeWalt II in Blythesville). All these places have one thing in common with Clinton's birthplace, Hope: They're not worth visiting unless you're the most devoted of devotees.

Fans of the Band looking for the "mission hall, down in Modock, Arkansas," that crops up on *Music from Big Pink* are in for a disappointment: Neither the building nor the town exist. There are some real Band landmarks in Arkansas, however. Ronnie Hawkins—the rockabilly singer who gave the future Band members their big break when he asked them to become his backing band, the Hawks—was born in Huntsville in 1935, and drummer Levon Helm, the only non-Canadian member of the Band, was born in Marvell in 1942. Helm's father, the town's deputy sheriff, often led family sing-alongs around the campfire. It wasn't all good times, however—any time it rained for more than a few hours, the Helm home became so flooded that the family needed a boat to get out.

Songs of Arkansas

Black Oak Arkansas, "The Hills of Arkansas" (1971)
Black Oak Arkansas, "When Electricity Came to Arkansas" (1971)
Bruce Springsteen, "Mary Queen of Arkansas" (1973)
Michelle Shocked, "Arkansas Traveler" (1992)

Helena

The small port of Helena, 50 miles south of Memphis and described by Mark Twain as being in "one of the prettiest situations on the Mississippi," was one of the main gathering places for Delta blues artists during the '30s and '40s. Robert Johnson, Howlin' Wolf, and Honeyboy Edwards busked during the day before moving on to the local juke joints at night. A 70-year-old Sonny Boy Williamson II returned to Helena in 1965 suffering from TB; despite spending most of his time spitting blood into a can, he found time to jam with the Hawks (the prototype Band) and tell anyone who would listen wild tales about touring Europe with the Animals and the Yardbirds.

Helena's blues heritage is celebrated by the annual **KING BISCUIT TIME BLUES FESTIVAL** (tel. 501/338–9144), one of the south's biggest musical events, which takes over the tiny downtown for much of the second week of October. A useful source of information on gigs around town, as well as a place to pick up rare records, is **BUBBA SULLIVAN'S BLUES CORNER** (105 Cherry St., tel. 501/338–3501).

DELTA CULTURAL CENTER

First stop for blues enthusiasts should be this museum, based in the 1912 rail depot. Crammed with exhibits focusing on all aspects of Delta life, from cotton gathering to the Ku Klux Klan, it also devotes a fair bit of floor space to the region's musical heritage. Displays cover all major players, from the two Sonny Boy Williamsons to Al Green and Levon Helm. *95 Missouri St., tel. 501/338–8919. Admission free. Open Mon.–Sat. 10–5, Sun. 1–5.*

KING BISCUIT TIME

The legendary *King Biscuit Time* blues program is broadcast most weekday afternoons between 12:15 and 12:45 from the Delta Cultural Center on station KFFA, 1360 AM (the station is actually based outside town on Highway 185). It began in 1941, when Rice Miller, the harmonica player who adopted the name Sonny Boy Williamson when the original artist bearing that name was fatally stabbed in Chicago, asked the station's owner, Sam Anderson, if he could have a show. Anderson agreed on the condition that Miller could get a sponsor. The Interstate Grocery Company took up Miller's offer to advertise its King Biscuit Flour, and so the show began with the jingle "Pass the biscuits, because it's King Biscuit Time," after which he got to play the blues on the air. Today visitors are welcome to drop by the center to watch the program being taped.

Al Green, Arkansan soul man

FLORIDA

While the Sunshine State is comparatively short on rock history, it is the home ground of a couple of huge bands—Tom Petty and Lynyrd Skynyrd—and of the sun-soaked Miami disco sound of the '70s and '80s. Jim Morrison was also a Florida native; born in Melbourne in 1943 while his father was serving at a nearby naval base, he attended St. Petersburg Junior College, then briefly Florida State University in Tallahassee before going to L.A. to become a rock star. Nowadays Florida is big on death metal, a gloomy underground movement led by the band Deicide, whose Glen Benton heats up a silver cross every morning and brands it upside down on his forehead to keep the Holy Spirit away.

Gainesville

Gainesville is the birthplace of Tom Petty, who is said to have received his early rock inspiration after seeing Elvis Presley film some scenes for *Follow That Dream* nearby. On leaving high school in the early '70s, Petty joined Mudcrutch and began playing local bars, including spots on North West 13th Street. This road, also known as Highway 441, features on Petty's 1977 debut single, "American Girl."

Jacksonville

The Allman Brothers left their native city to form their band in Macon, but Jacksonville went on to develop a lively Southern-boogie scene in the '70s. The two homegrown standouts were Lynyrd Skynyrd and .38 Special (formed by Donnie Van Zant, brother of Lynyrd Skynyrd's Ronnie). Jacksonville was also the birthplace of Gary U.S. Bonds, born Gary Anderson on June 6, 1939.

EATINGDRINKING**DANCING**SHOPPING**PLAYING**SLEEPING

Since the mid-'80s, the city's leading alternative-music venue has been **EINSTEIN A-GO-GO** (327 1st St. N, tel. 904/249–4646), which books bands from southeastern college towns like Athens and Chapel Hill, as well as such touring acts as the early Nirvana and Pixies.

Einstein A-Go-Go

ROBERT E. LEE HIGH SCHOOL

While the future members of Lynyrd Skynyrd were going to school here in the early '70s, they joined a band called My Backyard and grew their hair, which pissed off their gym teacher, Leonard Skinner. Getting punished by Skinner was called, in the school slang, getting "Leonard Skinner'd." Ronnie Van Zant wanted to use this spelling as the band's name but was talked into a subtle alteration. *1200 S. McDuff Ave.*

The two Lynyrd Skynyrd band members who died in an October 1977 plane crash—Ronnie Van Zant and Steve Gaines—are buried at Jacksonville Memory Gardens, as is Gaines's sister Cassie, who was on tour with the band as a backing vocalist. Van Zant has his own mausoleum, decorated with inscriptions from "Free Bird." *111 Blanding Blvd., Orange Park, south of town off I–295, tel. 904/272–2435.*

Miami

Perhaps because of its geographical remove from the centers of America's musical tradition, Miami is, for a city of its size and importance, short on rock & roll credentials. In the '50s the Overtown Square area was filled with R&B joints like the Harlem Square Club, where Sam Cooke recorded a famous live LP in 1963, but during the '60s the scene moved to the discos of Collins Avenue. By the '70s Miami had become a leading center for disco, its studios pumping out the salsa-splashed sound of George McCrae and KC & the Sunshine Band and the revitalized Bee Gees' massive-selling *Saturday Night Fever* soundtrack. Today Miami struggles to reprise the success of those days, although the city's biggest act, Gloria Estefan, manages to populate the dance floors just as well as the Bee Gees did in their heyday.

EATINGDRINKINGDANCINGSHOPPINGPLAYINGSLEEPING

Caribbean sounds dominate the live-music scene in Miami. The **HUNGRY SAILOR** (3064 Grand Ave., tel. 305/444–9359) provides a good taste of Latin, Haitian, and reggae styles. **CHURCHILLS, A SORT OF ENGLISH PUB** (5501 N.E. 2nd Ave., tel. 305/757–1807), hosts alternative bands. **STEPHEN TALKHOUSE** (616 Collins Ave., Miami Beach, tel. 305/531–7557) puts on everything from rock to blues icons. The cramped surrounds of **TOBACCO ROAD** (626 S. Miami Ave., tel. 305/374–1198), a

Courtesy of Tobacco Road

Tobacco Road, downtown Miami's oldest bar

venerable downtown tavern now approaching its 90th year, have welcomed all the biggest names in the blues and R&B world, from B.B. King to Taj Mahal.

Este-fans can visit the singer's restaurant, **LARIO'S ON THE BEACH** (820 Ocean Dr., tel. 305/532–9577). Miami's **HARD ROCK CAFE** (Bayside Marketplace, 401 Biscayne Blvd., tel. 305/377–3110) does better at incorporating local flavor than most in the chain; a stained-glass window in the main dining area features Jim Morrison, Eric Clapton, and Duane Allman.

Miami Five

James Gang, "Miami Two-Step" (1974)
Billy Joel, "Miami 2017" (1976)
Randy Newman, "Miami" (1983)
Jan Hammer, "*Miami Vice* Theme" (1985)
Bob Seger, "Miami" (1986)

CEDARS MEDICAL CENTER

Bob Marley died at this hospital on May 11, 1981. He had known of his cancer since the amputation of a toe two years before, but he had refused further medication and the disease spread, finally causing the brain tumor that ended his life at age 36. Marley had chosen to be treated in Miami because it was where his mother lived. *1400 N.W. 12th Ave., tel. 305/325–5511.*

CLUB FUTURA

Three members of 2 Live Crew were arrested in June 1990 for allegedly performing obscene lyrics and having obscene dancers onstage at this club in Hollywood, 30 miles north of Miami. Sales of the group's LP *As Nasty As They Wanna Be* subsequently soared, though many record chains refused to stock it. The accused were later acquitted, but a hapless record-store owner in Broward County got a $1,000 fine for selling the LP. The club's notoriety was short-lived—it closed at the end of the year. *Hollywood Blvd. and Dixie Hwy.*

[CRITERIA STUDIOS]

With more than 150 gold and platinum records to its credit, Criteria is by far the most successful studio in the Southeast. In 1969 Atlantic Records boss Jerry Wexler, looking to get out of New York for the winter and spend it fishing in the Florida Keys, bought the studio and enlisted Tom Dowd, rock's most celebrated recording engineer, to install an eight-track deck. Under this new management, Criteria had runaway successes with soul hits like Aretha Franklin's "Spanish Harlem" and Brook Benton's "Rainy Night in Georgia," and with big-name rock albums—Bob Seger's *Stranger in Town,* Dr. John's *In the Right Place,* and the Eagles' *Hotel California.*

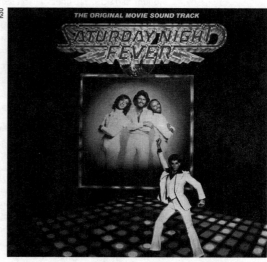

THE ORIGINAL MOVIE SOUND TRACK

SATURDAY NIGHT FEVER

While the Allman Brothers were working on *Idlewild South* in 1970, Eric Clapton turned up with his new group, Derek and the Dominos, to record *Layla and Other Assorted Love Songs.* He enlisted Duane Allman on slide guitar, and it was Duane, lounging around the Criteria studio, who composed the famous guitar intro to "Layla." Criteria's biggest financial success came a few years later when producer Arif Mardin came up with disco treatments for the Bee Gees songs that appeared on the *Saturday Night Fever* soundtrack. *1755 N.E. 149th St., tel. 305/947– 5611.*

The Bee Gees' finest—Saturday Night Fever *soundtrack*

DINNER KEY AUDITORIUM

Jim Morrison was famously arrested for exposing himself onstage here at a March 1969 Doors gig. It was a bad night all around. The singer turned up over an hour late and the worse for drink. The band was then obliged to play the opening number, "Break on Through," for 10 minutes while Morrison chatted with the audience. Eventually he clambered onto the stage, did a long monologue about partying in L.A., and asked if anyone was from Tallahassee. From there it went downhill. During "Back Door Man," Morrison suddenly stopped singing and declared his "need for love." During "Touch Me" he threw his shirt into the audience and attempted to expose himself. Though he was stopped from going all the way by sound manager Vince Treanor, the gig inevitably fell apart.

Morrison, it seems, was fired up to do something outrageous after witnessing an avant-garde theater performance in L.A. the week before. Soon after the Dinner Key show, however, he was arrested for "lewdly and lasciviously exposing his penis"; three weeks later, after much media attention, he was charged with "open profanity and drunkenness." The Miami courts fined the singer $500 and sentenced him to eight months hard labor. He never served time, however: The case was still on appeal when he died in 1971. The auditorium is now part of the massive Coconut Grove Exhibition Center. *2700 S. Bayshore Dr., at Pan American Way., tel. 305/579–3310.*

461 OCEAN BOULEVARD

This waterfront house in a wealthy residential neighborhood was where Eric Clapton and backing musicians, including ex-Domino Carl Radle, hung out while recording his 1974 "comeback" album at the nearby Criteria Studios. Clapton loved the place so much he rejected suggested album titles like *When Pinky Gets the Blues* or *Feed the Cook* and simply went with the address. Although you can get a good view from the beach, be warned that the house is on private property, and people with money tend not to like trespassers. *461 Ocean Blvd. (Hwy. A1A), Golden Beach, 20 mi N of downtown.*

ORANGE BOWL

Some 30,000 young Americans rallied in this stadium to support a "teenagers' crusade for decency in entertainment," organized after Jim Morrison exposed himself at the Dinner Key Auditorium in 1969. President Nixon sent the organizers a letter that said, in part, "I was extremely interested to learn about the admirable initiative taken by you and the 30,000 other young people last Sunday...it strengthens my belief that the younger generation is our greatest natural resource and therefore of tremendous hope for the future." The local Catholic diocese and the mayor of Miami objected to a Prince gig scheduled for the Bowl on Easter Sunday 1985, claiming that the singer was known to simulate sex with a boy onstage, but 70,000 fans attended nonetheless—a new house record. *1400 N.W. 4th St., tel. 305/643–7100.*

SUNNY ISLES BRIDGE

The clunking sound made by their car wheels as the Bee Gees drove across this bridge, shuttling between their home and Criteria Studios, inspired their 1975 disco departure, "Jive Talkin'." *Hwy. 826 between North Miami Beach and Sunny Isles Beach.*

TK RECORDS

Record distributor and former Chess Records producer Henry Stone ran several labels—Alston, Cat, Marlin, Glades, Stone Dog—under the TK banner in '70s Miami. The TK sound borrowed heavily from late-'60s funk but also incorporated sounds from the nearby West Indies, such as Bahamian Junkanoo. The corporation's first big international hit, Timmy Thomas's 1973 "Why Can't We Live Together?," offered the unusual trio of Timmy, his organ, and a drum machine. A succession of jaunty '70s disco hits followed: Betty Wright's "Clean Up Woman," George McCrae's "Rock Your Baby," KC & the Sunshine Band's "Get Down Tonight," and Anita Ward's "Ring My Bell." James Brown was so impressed he joined up for one record, the successful "Rapp Payback." TK crashed in the early '80s, and the building is now a warehouse. *495 S.E. 10th Ct., Hialeah, NW of downtown, between Miami International and Opalocka airports.*

Tampa

Gram Parsons often played in lively Tampa, on Florida's west coast, in the early '60s; his several bands included the Legends, with Jim "Spiders and Snakes" Stafford. These days the city is probably better known as the place where the top death-metal bands—

Sepultura, Morbid Angel, and Obituary—record at high-tech **MORRISOUND RECORDING** (1211 56th St. N, tel. 813/989–2108) on the city's north side.

GRAM'S PLACE

This B&B in the heart of Tampa is run by the secretary of the Gram Parsons Fan Club and is stuffed with mementos and rare recordings of the late singer. However, the music policy in the guest house is "everyone from Buck Owens to Metallica," and guests are encouraged to bring their own CDs and cassettes. *3109 N. Ola Ave., tel. 813/221–0596. Rooms: $60.*

GEORGIA

Atlanta has produced few major performers, but the smaller towns of Athens and Macon, each just over an hour's drive from Atlanta, can boast a sizable rock influence. The B-52's and R.E.M. emerged from the university scene that dominates Athens, and they have been followed by scores of lesser-known but equally quirky acts. From Macon came three of R&B's great legends—Little Richard, Otis Redding, and James Brown—and there's still much evidence locally of the town's most successful rock export, the Allman Brothers Band.

Georgia in Song

Ray Charles, "Georgia on My Mind" (1960)
Jerry Reed, "Georgia Sunshine" (1970)
The Crusaders, "Georgia Cottonfield" (1972)
Gladys Knight and the Pips, "Midnight Train to Georgia" (1973)
Vicki Lawrence, "The Night the Lights Went Out in Georgia" (1973)
Tony Joe White, "Rainy Night in Georgia" (1975)
Boz Scaggs, "Georgia" (1976)
Charlie Daniels Band, "The Devil Went Down to Georgia" (1979)
Al Green, "Georgia Boy" (1979)
Jason and the Scorchers, "Hot Nights in Georgia" (1983)

Athens

The tag "from Athens, Georgia" means something on the gig circuit. This small, friendly college town, setting for the University of Georgia, produced a bumper crop of bands in the '80s, including Pylon, the Method Actors, and Love Tractor. The thriving local scene has since given rise to Dreams So Real (occasionally produced by Peter Buck), the Chickasaw Mudd Puppies, hardcore noise merchants Jack O'Nuts, the Capricorn signings Vigilantes of Love, country rocker John Berry, and the cultish folkie Vic Chesnutt. All this local talent keeps 15 area studios busy, and there are various independent labels like Zontar (which records the Woggles and Southern Culture on the Skids) and Planned Obsolescence (with Mercyland and Daisy).

Athens is best known, however, as R.E.M.'s hometown. Lead singer Michael Stipe, who studied painting and photography at the university in the late '70s, met Peter Buck at a local record store and Mike Mills and Bill Berry at a party. The foursome formed the band in

Howie Oakes

The Woggles

1980 and quickly latched on to Athens's close-knit party circuit (out of which the B-52's had emerged a few years earlier). Despite going big-time, the band continues to be based here.

EATINGDRINKINGDANCINGSHOPPINGPLAYINGSLEEPING

Sidewalk cafés, offbeat stores, lively bars, and packed clubs make Athens buzz day and night. College authorities admit that R.E.M.'s decision to live and work in town has boosted student numbers and in turn led to a livelier scene, and some Athenian ventures have even been propped up by R.E.M. dollars. Michael Stipe is involved with two vegetarian restaurants, **THE GRIT** (199 Prince Ave., tel. 706/543–6592) and **GUARANTEED** (167 E. Broad St., tel. 706/208–0962). Grab an English ale at the popular **GLOBE** (199 N. Lumpkin St., tel. 706/353–4721) or try the **GEORGIA BAR** (159 W. Clayton St., tel. 706/546–9884), an R.E.M. hangout.

Everything that's happening in Athens can be discovered in the pages of the excellent free listings magazine *FLAGPOLE,* (online at http://www.flagpole.com), for which Sugar bassist Dave Barbe wrote record reviews in the '80s. Sugar later rehearsed in Athens for its convenient situation midway between drummer Malcolm Travis's New York home and Bob Mould's base in Austin.

Flagpole *covers the Athens scene*

ATOMIC MUSIC HALL

In February 1985, when this venue was known as the Uptown Lounge, R.E.M. appeared under the name Hornets Attack Victor Mature, a title inspired by a tabloid article. Now there's live music nightly from bands like Prozac or the Sugardaddies, and if the moshing gets too sweaty, you can escape to the pleasant courtyard out front. *140 E. Washington St., tel. 706/369–7315.*

BARBER STREET

Members of some of Athens's best-known bands lived in this street's generously proportioned villas in the early '80s. Michael Stipe moved into No. 169 when he was a student at the university; his journey "up the stairs into the hall" inspired the lyric for the song "We Walk" on *Murmur.* R.E.M. rehearsed in Stipe's bedroom, which was convenient for bassist Mike Mills, who lived next door (at No. 167), and drummer Bill Berry (No. 181). Members of Pylon and Love Tractor also then lived in this leafy neighborhood a mile northwest of downtown.

[40 WATT CLUB]

Athens's most famous music venue now puts on touring and local bands, such as the Grifters, John Osborne, Magna Pop, and Better Than Ezra—what *Flagpole* publisher Dennis Greenia calls "tomorrow's legends today." The 40 Watt has never quite managed to settle in one spot, however, popping up in several downtown locations over the years.

In 1978 Curtis Crowe opened the club at 171 College Avenue; one tiny bulb lit the huge room—hence the name 40 Watt. Without an alcohol license, Crowe couldn't charge an entrance fee, so admission was through a $2 "donation." During the day Bill Berry used the club as an office for his booking agency. The site is now partly occupied by the Grill, a 24-hour burger bar.

Sugar at the 40 Watt

Two years later the 40 Watt moved to 100 College Avenue for a few months, above what is now Yudy's Philly Steaks. R.E.M. members regularly worked the door or behind the bar. In 1981 the club moved to 256 West Clayton Street; it was at this location that Michael Stipe did a solo performance, billed as 1066 Gaggle O'Sound, in which he doodled on a Farfisa organ to prerecorded tracks while slides were projected onto the walls. (Stipe chose "1066" because it was his favorite year in history.)

In 1983 there was another move, to 382 East Broad Street, where in January 1984 the Hindu Love Gods (featuring Warren Zevon) made a rare live performance. In 1987 the club returned to 256 West Clayton Street, where it stayed for four years. R.E.M., too big to headline under their own name, would occasionally perform ad hoc sets to showcase new material. A regular performer was eccentric Athens songwriter Vic Chesnutt, who has used a wheelchair since a car crash in the early '80s. Michael Stipe produced Chesnutt's debut LP, *Little,* even though Chesnutt had called him a "dick" when they first met. The building is now a T-shirt factory two doors down from the band's offices.

Since 1991, the year that R.E.M. played a surprise unplugged gig as William, the club has occupied its current site, formerly the Potter's House junk store, where local musicians came looking for cheap threads. *285 W. Washington St., tel. 706/549–7871.*

MORTON THEATER

Built in 1910 as a vaudeville theater, the 550-seat Morton was Athens's leading venue for black artists in the '30s, booking Duke Ellington and other big names. By the '50s the building had fallen into disrepair and was abandoned, save for the El Dorado restaurant in the basement, where the B-52's first rehearsed. The Morton has since been restored and occasionally puts on bands; one recent gig was by Jack Logan and Liquid Cabinet, the group named for the artist of a comic book featuring Peter Buck as its main character. *199 W. Washington St., tel. 706/613–3770.*

ROCK LOBSTERS

In 1976, over a Chinese meal at the Hu Nan (2139 W. Broad St.; now the Mexicali), Kate Pierson, Cindy Wilson, her brother Ricky, Keith Strickland, and former forestry student Fred Schneider III decided to form what would become

Athens's first major band as a kitsch '50s-parody outfit. The B-52's took their name from the slang term for the bouffant hairdo (itself named for the World War II bomber) sported by Pierson and Cindy Wilson. The group didn't stay around Athens for long, opting for the New York new-wave scene, but Pierson later teamed up with R.E.M. to do vocals for "Shiny Happy People" on *Out of Time*.

R.E.M. CHURCH

Only the steeple remains of the former church, converted into inexpensive student apartments, where Peter Buck and Michael Stipe lived in the late '70s. The then-unnamed R.E.M. also made their debut here, at a friend's birthday party on April 5, 1980. Five hundred revelers witnessed this first set, beefed up with covers of "Honky Tonk Women," "God Save the Queen," and "Roadrunner." A promoter from a local club, Tyrone's, was impressed and offered them $100 to play that May—provided they came up with a name. The band members wrote some ideas on the apartment building's notice board and invited other residents to do likewise. Among the suggestions were Slut Bank, Twisted Kites, and R.E.M., which narrowly beat out Cans of Piss as first choice. Nearby is the railway trestle bridge featured on the back cover of *Murmur. 394 Oconee St.*

Curt Doughty

WEAVER D'S

Automatic for the People, R.E.M.'s quintuple-platinum 1992 album, took its name from the slogan of this down-home soul-food café—fried chicken and collards a specialty—about a mile east of downtown. Owner Weaver Dexter, who catered Stipe's sister's wedding in the late '80s, has long used *automatic* as his personal buzzword. Nowadays Weaver D's is full of tourists hoping to spot a lunch-

Mike Mills and Michael Stipe of R.E.M.

ing band member, and Dexter is able to cash in with AUTOMATIC T-shirts, posters, and mugs. *1016 E. Broad St., tel. 706/353–7797.*

WUXTRY RECORDS

In 1979 store assistant Peter Buck got to chatting with student Michael Stipe and decided to form the band that became R.E.M. Eight years later, after the release of *Document*, Buck tried to reinsert some normalcy into his life by coming back to work at Wuxtry but was forced to quit after a few weeks because of the number of fans asking him to sign records.

Apart from the racks of CDs, Wuxtry has an excellent collection of reasonably priced vinyl and is particularly good for '80s indie bands. Upstairs, in the smaller Bizarro Wuxtry store, there's more emphasis on '60s and '70s stuff and loads of comics. Bizarro Wuxtry sells vinyl by weight at $1.99 per pound. *197 E. Clayton St., tel. 706/353–9303.*

Atlanta

Atlanta, the South's largest metropolis (population 2.5 million), provides an attractive home base for Coca-Cola, the Turner Broadcasting Company, and a variety of music superstars from Curtis Mayfield to Bobby Brown and Elton John. In rock or even R&B terms, however, Atlanta has surprisingly few sites of much historical interest. Gladys Knight had to move to Detroit to make it. James Brown came to Atlanta to join the

Gospel Starlighters in 1949 but had left for Macon by the time his first single, "Please Please Please," was released in 1956. A few years later, Jimi Hendrix lived downtown for a short time before joining Little Richard's tour as his valet.

Atlanta's musicians have recently begun to make waves, though. The Georgia Satellites and the Black Crowes have carried the torch for old-style Southern rock, and the boho-folkie Indigo Girls moved here from nearby Decatur at the beginning of the '90s. Another local band, a heavy-metal outfit called Jackyl, is best known for its track on the Beavis and Butt-Head compilation and for organizing a crowd chant of "What have you got? No beer, no pot!" at Woodstock '94. Toenut recently became the first U.S. band to be signed by leading British indie label Mute. And Atlanta's busy hip-hop and dance scene has produced Arrested Development, TLC, Kriss Kross, and Antonio Reid's LaFace Records, home of the multimillion-selling Toni Braxton.

EATINGDRINKINGDANCINGSHOPPINGPLAYINGSLEEPING

Atlanta is a major nightlife center, with a strong selection of clubs. The **STAR BAR** (437 Morland Ave., tel. 404/681–9018), the hippest joint in town, calls itself the birthplace of the "redneck underground." The **MASQUERADE** (695 North Ave., tel. 404/577–8178) promotes top indie bands. The **VARIETY PLAYHOUSE** (1099 Euclid Ave., Little Five Points, tel. 404/521–1786) offers a more eclectic roster, recently putting on a Richard Thompson/Roger McGuinn bill. One of the best for R&B is **BLIND WILLIE'S** (828 N. Highland Ave. NE, tel. 404/873–2583), named after Georgia blues artist Blind Willie McTell, whose work has been covered by the Allmans and Taj Mahal. Lynyrd Skynyrd was discovered at **BACKSTREET ATLANTA** (845 Peachtree St. NE, tel. 404/873–1986), when the club was known as Funochio's, by Al Kooper, who played the organ on Bob Dylan's "Like a Rolling Stone"; it's now a popular gay bar and dance club, open 24 hours on weekends. **CRIMINAL RECORDS** (466 Morland Ave., tel. 404/215–9511) specializes in local and hard-to-find CDs and LPs; the incredibly helpful staff is a font of local club info.

FOX THEATER

This extravagant '20s Art Deco movie theater, just north of downtown, was where the Marshall Tucker Band headlined a presidential-campaign benefit for Jimmy Carter in October 1975. The following year Lynyrd Skynyrd came here to record the live version of "Freebird," and in fall 1978 a Bruce Springsteen set from the Fox was broadcast live on TV. The 3,000-seat venue now puts on musicals and occasional supper-club concerts. *600 Peachtree St. NE, tel. 404/881–2110.*

GOVERNOR'S MANSION

Governor Jimmy Carter entertained Bob Dylan and the Band at a postgig party here during their 1974 comeback tour. In the early hours, Gregg Allman turned up the worse for wear, only to find the party already over. He left a message with the security guard thanking the governor for the invitation, but just as he was leaving, a shirtless, shoeless, Levi's-clad Carter called him back for a chat about fund-raising. *391 W. Paces Ferry Rd., tel. 404/261–1776.*

GREAT SOUTHEAST MUSIC HALL AND EMPORIUM

Most foreign bands visiting the States for the first time play New York. The Sex Pistols came to Atlanta. In early 1978, at the start of the band's first American tour, U.S. immigration officials—objecting to Johnny Rotten's and Steve Jones's criminal pasts (mostly drug offences and petty theft)—threatened to refuse the group entry and delayed their visas. The northern dates had to be scrapped, and the tour was hastily rearranged for the South. The Atlanta opener on January 5 attracted almost as many curious media types as punks. Peter Buck, R.E.M.'s guitarist, was thrown out for not having a ticket. The hall was later demolished. *3871 Peachtree Rd. NE.*

Macon

Famed for its cherry trees and antebellum mansions, Macon—a tidy city of 100,000, 75 miles southeast of Atlanta—has contributed much to rock & roll. Little Richard and Otis Redding grew up in the city's Pleasant Hill area, and James Brown came to Macon to start his career. R.E.M.'s Mike Mills and Bill Berry were born locally, as were the Connells (Mike and David), whose single "74−75" hit the upper levels of the charts in 1995.

The city's most famous export, however, was a pair of Nashville-born brothers. Gregg and Duane Allman were living in Macon in 1969 when they formed the Allman Brothers Band, which successfully fused black R&B with longhair rock & roll. Before the band broke up in 1976, after the deaths of guitarist Duane and bassist Berry Oakley in downtown-Macon motorcycle crashes, it spawned a host of imitators. Wet Willie, the Marshall Tucker Band, and others recorded for the city's Capricorn label, *the* Southern-rock label of the '70s; one of the label's founders, Alan Walden, now manages the Outlaws from his downtown Macon office.

EATINGDRINKINGDANCINGSHOPPINGPLAYINGSLEEPING

ELIZABETH REED'S MUSIC HALL (557 Cherry St., tel. 912/741−9792), named after the Allman Brothers song, often features teen slide guitarist Derek Trucks, nephew of Allmans drummer Butch. Maps of the local rock & roll landmarks are available from the **CONVENTION AND VISITORS BUREAU** (200 Cherry St., tel. 800/768−3401).

OTIS BLUE

Otis Redding, born in Dawson, Georgia, came to Macon when he was three. After dropping out of school, he took a variety of dead-end jobs, such as well digger and gas-station attendant. At the same time, he was on the road to stardom: He sang in church, played with Little Richard's old band, the Upsetters, and won talent contests at the Douglass Theater. Macon has commemorated the singer, who died in a Wisconsin plane crash in December 1967, with the Otis Redding Memorial Bridge, which spans the Ocmulgee River at 5th Street. Redding's widow, Zelma, runs a shoe store at 603 Cherry Street with daughter Karla and still lives on the outskirts of the city at the 500-acre Big 'O' estate (pictured on the cover of the *History of Otis Redding*), where Otis is buried.

Otis Redding

BEALL'S 1860 RESTAURANT

The Allman Brothers were photographed in 1969 lounging on the veranda of this white-columned mansion, now a swanky restaurant, for the cover of their first album, *The Allman Brothers Band*. Members of the group lived next door at No. 309 at the time, and one of the entourage carved the band's distinctive mushroom logo into the sidewalk, where it can still be seen outside the restaurant. *315 College Ave., tel. 912/745–3663.*

The Allman Brothers Band on the veranda of 315 College Avenue

Courtesy of the Big House

THE BIG HOUSE

In the early '70s, Allmans Greg and Duane, plus bassist Berry Oakley, lived and rehearsed in this large suburban home, now owned by the band's road manager, Kirk West, and his wife, Kirsten. The Wests have spent around $100,000 on this museum-cum-B&B. Their collection of Allmans memorabilia is immense—hundreds of videos, thousands of photos, and 4,000 tapes. Tours can be arranged by appointment, or you can spend the night in one of three bedrooms, named after Duane, Gregg, and Berry. *2321 Vineville Ave., tel. 912/742–5005. Rooms: $80.*

CAPRICORN RECORDS

The label most associated with the '70s Southern boogie scene was cooked up by former Otis Redding manager Phil Walden, his brother Alan, and Atlantic Records A&R chief Jerry Wexler (like Phil Walden, a Capricorn) after a companionable fishing trip. The label concentrated on country soul—Sam and Bill, Arthur Conley, Swamp Dogg—at first but shifted toward rock with the signing of the Allman Brothers. Imitators who had a more conscious Southern image, like Wet Willie and Marshall Tucker, quickly followed. In 1978 the whole team pulled together behind Georgian Jimmy Carter's presidential campaign, bankrolling him to the tune of $3 million. Carter responded by taking an interest in Southern rock & roll. Turning up at the Capricorn studio during the recording of Dicky Betts's *Highway Call* album, Carter was thanked by the musicians for downgrading pot smoking to misdemeanor status during his time as governor. The label went bust in the late '70s but has since been re-formed in Nashville, where it records Widespread Panic and Dixie Dreggs. The Macon building, at one time a slaughterhouse, is empty, but the goat's-head logo is still in place on the glass panel above the door. *535 Cotton Ave.*

DOUGLASS THEATER

Built in the '20s by entrepreneur Charles Douglass as a blacks-only vaudeville hall and cinema, this theater put on Bessie Smith and Ida Cox before World War II and turned to rock & roll in the '50s with weekly talent shows held by radio WIBB. The contests, regularly won by the teenage Otis Redding, were emceed by DJs King Bee and Satellite Poppa, who would be lowered from the ceiling in space suits to announce, "We're bringing you a taste from outer space." With the end of segregation, whites began using the venue, and many regulars left for more upmarket locations. The Douglass closed in the early '70s but is now being renovated as part of the Georgia Music Hall of Fame project (*see below*). *355 Broadway.*

DUANE ALLMAN DEATH SITE

While swerving to avoid a truck, 24-year-old Duane Allman fell off his motorcycle at this junction on October 29, 1971. He was taken to the Middle Georgia Medical Center, where he died within a few hours. The following year, on November 11, Allmans bassist Berry Oakley was also killed in a motorbike accident when he crashed into a bus at Napier and Inverness, just a few blocks away. He was also 24. *Hillcrest Ave. and Bartlett St.*

GEORGIA MUSIC HALL OF FAME

Macon lobbied hard to secure the just-completed Georgia Hall of Fame—most people expected it to go to Atlanta—and its opening is part of a Macon musical revival linked with the planned reopening of the Douglass Theater and other sites. On display are posters, photos, unusual memorabilia like the Stax Records recording console, and plenty of information on Georgia-associated rock & rollers, including Ray Charles (the first performer inducted into the Hall), James Brown, Lynyrd Skynyrd, R.E.M., Otis Redding, Little Richard, and the Allman Brothers. Theme rooms—country café, gospel chapel, '50s soda fountain, R&B club—allow visitors to tune in to the sounds of an era or select videos featuring local artists. *305 Coliseum Dr., tel. 912/738–0017. Admission: $6.50. Open Mon.–Sat. 9–6, Sun. 1–6.*

H & H

The members of the Allman Brothers Band were so poor when they first ate here in the late '60s that they had the money for only one dinner; owner Mama Louise Hudson took pity on them and laid on extra soul food. The band later repaid her generosity by enlisting her as tour cook for their U.S. shows. H&H still serves Southern home cooking, and its rock history is documented on a wall set aside as a shrine to the band, complete with drawings of two winged angels in the image of the late Duane Allman and Berry Oakley. *807 Forsyth St., tel. 912/742–5237.*

The H&H kitchen—that's Mama Louise in back

[ROSE HILL CEMETERY]

Duane Allman and Berry Oakley are buried in adjacent plots in the Carnation Ridge area of this small cemetery, bounded by the Ocmulgee River and a railroad. Allman's headstone is inscribed with one of his love poems; Oakley's carries the legend HELP THY

BROTHER'S BOAT ACROSS/AND LO! THINE OWN HAS REACHED THE SHORE. Both stones also bear the band's motto, The road goes on forever—a line taken from their best-known song, "Midnight Rider."

In their early days the band members came to Rose Hill regularly to smoke dope and look for inspiration. They found it in two graves: that of Elizabeth Jones Reed (1845–1936), a servicewoman buried in the north part of the grounds, to whom "In Memory of Elizabeth Reed" was dedicated; and that of 12-year-old Martha Ellis (born 1924), buried on the west side of the cemetery, who was commemorated on the *Eat a Peach* track "Little Martha." The Allmans were photographed here, by the Overlook Monument, for the back cover of their 1969 debut album. *Riverside Dr., east of I–75, tel. 912/751–9119.*

WIBB RADIO

In 1955 WIBB, 1280 AM, helped break James Brown when they allowed the 22-year-old singer to cut a demo of what became his first single, "Please Please Please." DJ Hamp Swain played the track regularly, and it was soon picked up by Cincinnati's King records, which went on to release many of Brown's biggest hits. (Swain, now a Macon car dealer, continued to DJ at WIBB until 1979; he played gospel as Deacon Swain and R&B under the name King Bee—the two markets attracted different audiences, so few realized Deacon and Bee were the same person.) WIBB is now a talk station based at 369 2nd Street, and this building is an insurance office. *830 Mulberry St.*

TRY ME

James Brown was born in 1933 in South Carolina but spent his adolescence—some of it in trouble with the law—in neighboring Georgia. In the late '40s he was caught stealing and sent to the Alto Reform School in Toccoa, where as pitcher for the prison baseball team he met Bobby Byrd, who later played the organ in the Famous Flames. On his release Brown drifted around Georgia. In Augusta he swept up, washed cars, and shined shoes on the steps of WRDW, the radio station he later owned. By the end of the '50s, he was in trouble again, this time in Columbus, where he was taken into police custody after inviting a woman onstage during a show and hunching over her in a "situation of sexual intercourse"; he was fined $652.

CATCHING AN ALL-NIGHT STATION/SOMEWHERE IN LOUISIANA/SOUNDS LIKE 1963/BUT FOR NOW IT SOUNDS LIKE HEAVEN—SON VOLT, "WINDFALL"

Louisiana's rich musical history takes in Dixieland jazz, early rock & roll, R&B, Cajun, zydeco, swamp pop, and country. New Orleans, a 24-hour city with significant Creole and Cajun traditions and a reputation for partying, is the obvious place to hear live music, while Cajun-country towns provide the best setting for seeing pumped-up zydeco bands.

Cajun music, characteristically accordion- and fiddle-heavy, is the legacy of the French-speaking settlers who came to Louisiana in the 18th century after the British expelled them en masse from eastern Canada, then called Acadia (*Cajun* is a corruption of *Acadian*). That journey south was sympathetically recounted by the Band on "Acadian Driftwood." While many bands continue to play traditional ballads, Steve Riley and the Mamou Playboys and the very poppy Wayne Toups have a more modern sound.

Zydeco is the label usually stuck on black Louisianan music, a kind of Cajun with balls, fusing R&B guitar sounds with accordions and washboards. The term is often said to be a corruption of the French *les haricots*, from the Cajun dance tune "*Les Haricots Sont Pas Salés*" ("The Beans Aren't Salted"). Until his death, in 1987, Clifton Chenier personified the sound; his son C. J. Chenier, Buckwheat Zydeco, and Willis Prudhomme are prominent practitioners today.

Cajun-country zydeco fave Nathan Williams

Swamp pop—Cajun-spiced rock & roll—saw success with Tommy McLain's "Sweet Dreams" (Top 10 in 1966) and Tony Joe White's "Polk Salad Annie," though the disc that's had the most lasting recognition is Johnnie Allan's energetic reworking of Chuck Berry's "Promised Land." In the early '70s, Allan thought his music career was over and was teaching in a Lafayette public school; then English musicologist Charlie Gillett rereleased "Promised Land" on his Oval label and turned Allan into an overnight hero. Current swamp-pop names include Zachary Richard and Charles Mann, who scored a big local hit with his cover of Dire Straits' "Walk of Life."

Louisiana Lucky 7

Muddy Waters, "Louisiana Blues" (1950)
Paul Revere and the Raiders, "Louisiana Redbone" (1969)
Charlie Daniels Band, "Sweet Louisiana" (1976)
Emmylou Harris, "Leaving Louisiana in the Broad Daylight" (1978)
Gil Scott Heron, "Angola, Louisiana" (1978)
Dr. John, "Louisiana Lullabye" (1979)
Tom Petty and the Heartbreakers, "Louisiana Rain" (1979)

Ferriday

Jerry Lee Lewis was born in this unassuming Mississippi River town, 190 miles northwest of New Orleans, on September 29, 1935, and spent his youth here with his cousins Mickey Gilley (a kitsch country star) and Jimmy Swaggart (the god-fearing, flesh-loving preacher). Jerry and Jimmy are said to have hung around a black club called Haney's Big House, where they saw Ray Charles, Muddy Waters, and other big names perform.

Lafayette and Cajun Country

Louisiana's Cajun country centers on the sprawling oil and college town of Lafayette, 130 miles northwest of New Orleans. Smaller and more enjoyable surrounding towns include Opelousas, New Iberia, Breaux Bridge, and Eunice. On the weekend the region's bars swing to the sounds of Cajun and zydeco bands, although the best venues are usually hard-to-find little dance halls up unpaved roads. Try the places below, but also listen to local radio and ask around for news of the community gatherings and regular weekly blowouts where you can hear and dance to authentic regional music.

EATING DRINKING DANCING SHOPPING PLAYING SLEEPING

Top clubs for live zydeco include **EL SID O'S** (1523 Dr. Martin Luther King, Jr. Dr., Lafayette, tel. 318/235–0647), **GILTON'S CLUB** (Hwy. 190, Eunice, tel. 318/457–1241), **HAMILTON'S** (1808 Verot School Rd., Lafayette, tel. 318/984–5583), **RICHARD'S** (Hwy. 190, Lawtell, tel. 318/543–8233), **SLIM'S Y KI KI BAR** (Hwy. 167, Opelousas, tel. 318/942–9980). If you've had your fill of swamp sounds, try the **METROPOLIS CLUB** (425 Jefferson St., Lafayette, tel. 318/233–6320), which puts on local experimental music and the occasional touring act.

New Orleans

I'M GOING DOWN TO NEW ORLEANS/GET ME A MOJO HAND—MUDDY WATERS, "LOUISIANA BLUES"

The Big Easy has exerted a more powerful and mystical hold on modern American music than any other city, with the possible exception of Memphis. First and foremost, it is the birthplace of jazz, whose roots go back to the early 19th century, when Congo Square was one of few public places in the South where slaves were allowed to congregate to dance and sing each Sunday. This area is now part of Louis Armstrong Park, named for the jazz pioneer, born in 1900, who spent his adolescence in the city's Colored Waifs' Home.

In his teens Armstrong played trumpet with such early greats as King Oliver in the bordellos of fabled Storyville, a legalized red-light district just north of the French Quarter. By 1917, when Storyville was closed down, a distinctive "Dixieland" jazz sound had emerged, exemplified by Jelly Roll Morton, the innovative piano player who later claimed that he (and he alone) created jazz. Morton was just the first of many pianists—Professor Longhair, Fats Domino, James Booker—to have a crucial impact on the city's music scene.

King Oliver's Jazz Band, early stars of the New Orleans sound

By the '50s New Orleans was no longer a major force in jazz (New York and the West Coast were then drawing the innovators), but unlike St. Louis and Kansas City, other early jazz centers whose stars had faded, New Orleans played a significant role in the development of rock & roll. Bandleader Dave Bartholomew was almost single-handedly responsible for devising the characteristic New Orleans R&B sound—heavy on piano and saxes, light on guitars and vocal harmonies—exemplified by Fats Domino and Little Richard. In the first few years of the '60s, more than 50 New Orleans records hit the *Billboard* Hot 100. Allen Toussaint, who produced hits for Lee Dorsey, Ernie K. Doe, Irma Thomas, and Chris Kenner, took over Bartholomew's position as the city's lynchpin in the mid-'60s. The British invasion and Motown soon put an end to New Orleans's musical preeminence, however.

The city failed to produce any major white guitar groups, but local session pianist Mac Rebennack reworked the New Orleans sound into a psychedelic concoction administered by his alter ego, Dr. John Creaux, the Night Tripper, a frog-throated, voodoo-spouting, spell-casting witch doctor. In 1968 he recorded *Gris-Gris,* now revered as the archetypal stoned-out psychedelic trip, part of which was sampled by Beck Hansen on "Loser." Since then, the Meters, LaBelle, and the Neville Brothers have caused ripples in the charts, but the city has often relied on endless peddling of its musical heritage. It also introduced Harry Connick, Jr., to the world.

Lately, however, things are stirring: In this decade an assortment of big names have relocated to the city, from Alex Chilton and John Sinclair to Trent Reznor (who set up a studio in the Garden District) and Courtney Love. Cool alternative groups play on the same bills as jazzy brass bands, and influences rub off. Since Better Than Ezra broke in the mid-'90s, local bands, most of whom defy easy categorization, are enjoying exposure. Look out for Evil Nurse Sheila!, Burnversion, Nut, and the punk-jazz Lump.

Most cities of this size boast free music papers, but few offer anything as comprehensive as New Orleans's monthly *OFFBEAT MAGAZINE*, a virtual encyclopedia of the local scene; it's also available online at http://www.neosoft.com/~offbeat.

Professor Longhair, "Mardi Gras in New Orleans" (c.1950)
Freddy Cannon, "Way Down Yonder in New Orleans" (1957)
Elvis Presley, "New Orleans" (1958)
Johnny Horton, "Battle of New Orleans" (1959)
Gary U.S. Bonds, "New Orleans" (1960)
Fats Domino, "Walking to New Orleans" (1960)
Redbone, "Witch Queen of New Orleans" (1971)
Led Zeppelin, "Royal Orleans" (1976)
Tom Waits, "I Wish I Was in New Orleans" (1977)
John Kay, "Down in New Orleans" (1978)
Dr. John, "I Thought I Heard New Orleans Say" (1979)
Gillan, "New Orleans" (1981)
R.E.M., "New Orleans Instrumental No. 1" (1992)
Silver Jews, "New Orleans" (1994)
The Tractors, "Trying to Get to New Orleans" (1995)

The French Quarter, Faubourg-Marigny, and East

Tourists make a beeline for the French Quarter, the riverside area, six blocks by 12, where the French established the city in 1718. A mix of businesses, bars, and residences, the Quarter contains boozy Bourbon Street (named after French royals, not the drink). Decatur Street, better than Bourbon for bars, merges on its eastern end into Frenchman Street, which leads to the bohemian Faubourg-Marigny area and some of the city's best live-music venues.

EATINGDRINKINGDANCINGSHOPPINGPLAYINGSLEEPING

Bourbon Street may be the most celebrated seven blocks in the city, but with more and more tacky places opening, it doesn't make for a great night out. Zep fans might want to stop in at the Absinthe (*see below*), but the best place is the ancient LAFITTE'S BLACKSMITH SHOP (941 Bourbon St., tel. 504/523–0066) at the quieter, eastern end of the street. Otherwise it's best to ignore Bourbon, if only because it's pricey.

CHECKPOINT CHARLIE'S (501 Esplanade Ave., tel. 504/947–0979), at the punk end of Decatur, is the loudest rock club in the French Quarter; it's open late, charges no cover, and has a laundromat and game room. Parts of *The Pelican Brief* were filmed here. DONNA'S (800 N. Rampart St., tel. 504/596–6914) is one of the best clubs for brass bands; gigs start around 8 every night. DRAGON'S DEN (435 Esplanade Ave., tel. 504/949–1750), a tiny bar above a Thai restaurant, feels like an opium den that just happens to put on a good range of acoustic rock, blues, and country. It's great in the early hours of the morning.

SNUG HARBOR (626 Frenchman St., tel. 504/949–0696) is the top modern-jazz venue in town; cover is between $5 and $15, and Ellis Marsalis plays most Saturdays. VAUGHAN'S (800 Lesseps St., tel. 504/947–5562), a bar east of the French Quarter in the Ninth Ward, serves dollar beers, free beans and rice, and good barbecue; Kermit Ruffins plays top jazz every Thursday.

To satisfy the city's massive number of music fans, New Orleans offers a number of interesting record stores. There's a big branch of **TOWER RECORDS** (408 N. Peters St., tel. 504/529–4411); a couple of blocks away is the Louisiana Music Factory (*see below*), specializing in all things local. **MAGIC BUS** (527 Conti St., tel. 504/522–0530) has a well-priced range of used rock on vinyl and CD. The founder and namesake of **RECORD RON** (1129 Decatur St., tel. 504/524–9444) died recently, but his long-running store remains filled with well-cataloged vinyl. **ROCK 'N' ROLL RECORDS AND COLLECTIBLES** (1214 Decatur St., tel. 504/561–5683) is a small store stacked high with vinyl jazz, R&B, and rock, as well as with many rare limited-edition singles.

Rooms can be had for an affordable $50 a night at **ST. PETER GUEST HOUSE** (1005 St. Peter St., tel. 504/524–9232) a small French Quarter hotel that saw the death of former New York Doll Johnny Thunders in April 1991.

The A Bar

ABSINTHE BAR

This Bourbon Street joint was a regular hangout for Led Zeppelin. The band had the place—with thousands of yellowed business cards and signed dollar bills behind the bar—faithfully re-created in England's Shepperton Film Studios for the cover of their last studio album, *In Through the Out Door*. Jimmy Page met his wife here, and a signed photo of the guitarist hangs on a wall. The A Bar, as it's known locally, has a good blues house band in Bryan Lee and the Jump Street Five, but ultimately it's now more of a tourist magnet than a decent hangout. *400 Bourbon St., tel. 504/525–8108.*

CAFÉ BRASIL

Lyle Lovett and Julia Roberts had their first public date watching the Klezmer All-Stars at this conservatory-like venue on the eastern border of the French Quarter. The Brasil has one of the most diverse programs in the city, with reggae, gospel, spoken word, brass bands, and innovative genre-blurring acts. *2100 Chartres St., tel. 504/947–9386.*

CALDONIA INN (WWOZ-FM)

R&B legend Professor Longhair got his major break at the Caldonia in 1948 when he went to see local trumpet-playing supremo Dave Bartholomew (by then an important A&R scout, songwriter, and producer for Imperial records) and got the chance to sit in on piano. The club owner liked him so much that he sacked Bartholomew and recruited Longhair, who put together his own band, the Shuffling Hungarians.

The current occupant of the building is WWOZ (90.7 FM), the official station of the city's spring Jazz and Heritage Festival (*see box below*). The station's roster centers on jazz, blues, and R&B on weekdays, diversifying on weekends to include traditional Irish music and Afro-pop. At festival time the station broadcasts more than 100 hours of live performances direct from the Fairgrounds Racetrack. *1201 St. Phillip St., at St. Claude Ave., tel. 504/568–1234 (request line), http:/www.gnofn.org/~wwoz.*

ERNIE K. DOE'S MOTHER-IN-LAW LOUNGE

Ernest Kador, Jr., born in the city's Charity Hospital on February 22, 1936, adopted the snappy name change in 1960 and hit paydirt the following year with "Mother-in-Law," a No. 1 *Billboard* R&B smash. He remains one of New Orleans' most energetic performers and recently opened this club, where he plays every Sunday night. *1500 N. Clairborne, just north of French Quarter by I–10, tel. 504/947–1078.*

HOUSE OF BLUES

When the second in the House of Blues chain—part stylish rock and blues venues, part restaurants, part folk-art museums—opened in January 1994 in an old French Quarter shoe warehouse, New Orleans musicos decried the intrusion of corporate interests into the city's free-and-easy 24-hour music scene. However, the House of Rules (as a local artist dubbed it) has since generated widespread respect with a quality program of music running from Cash, Dylan, and Baez to Motörhead, Seven Mary Three, and Sebadoh; all the blues and R&B greats appear, and there's an ever-popular Sunday gospel brunch. Vision lines and acoustics are superb in the showroom, and in the restaurant, which dishes up Southern and Cajun-style food, video monitors allow diners to see the gig without leaving their tables (or buying a ticket).

There have been a few embarrassing moments: When Eric Clapton played in 1994, his tour staff turned away Clarence "Gatemouth" Brown. Venue staff intervened, and the Brit crooner-guitarist invited the Texas blues legend onstage to jam. The chance meeting led to Brown joining Clapton on his European tour, including an appearance at Clapton's annual Royal Albert Hall gig in London. Meanwhile, back at the House of Blues, a booth near the kitchen has been dedicated to Gatemouth, complete with a folk-art portrait and a steer-horn hat rack, and there's a gig in his honor held on his birthday each April. *225 Decatur St., tel. 504/529–BLUE, 504/529–1421 (concert line), or 540/529–3480 (ticket office), http://www.hob.com.*

J&M STUDIOS, 1945–55

Cosimo "Coz" Matassa, the central figure in recording New Orleans rock & roll, opened his first tiny studio in the back of an old grocery store around the end of World War II. Despite the underwhelming facilities, some top independent labels booked time, eager to record and distribute the city's emerging R&B sound. The first big break came from L.A.'s Imperial, which paid for Fats Domino's first session, in which he recorded the Top 10 R&B hit "The Fat Man" in 1949. Frequent visitors before the studio moved to new quarters included Ahmet Ertegun and Jerry Wexler from the then little-known New York–based Atlantic label. *838 N. Rampart St.*

J&M STUDIOS, 1955–66

After outgrowing his Rampart Street studio, Matassa leased a warehouse for a few months before moving next door into bigger premises in 1955. It was here that many of R&B's most celebrated New Orleans tracks were laid down, including Little Richard's "Tutti Frutti" and most of Fats Domino's hits. During the '60s Allen Toussaint used the studio as a base, producing hundreds of records, including Lee Dorsey's "Working in a Coalmine." Cosimo's was also where Mac Rebennack (Dr. John) started sessioning at 15. After a dozen years, Matassa was once again on the move, to the Central Business District (*see below*); apartments now occupy the site. *521–525 Gov. Nicholls St.*

Courtesy of Kaldi's Coffeehouse and Coffee Museum

Kaldi's Coffeehouse

KALDI'S COFFEEHOUSE

One of the city's best hangouts began life as a bank in 1907. Now decked out with dark-wood tables, stools, and chairs, this spacious joint has become known for its contemporary-jazz jams. Here, in September 1994, John Sinclair and His Blues Scholars cut *Full Moon Night,* which includes a 30-minute homage to John Coltrane; an accompanying 10" disc features a joint effort with Wayne Kramer, ex-guitarist in MC5, of which Sinclair had been manager. Although Sinclair had been involved in rock and blues since the early '60s as a songwriter, critic, band manager, and broadcaster, this was his first foray into the recording side of things. *941 Decatur St., tel. 504/586–8989.*

LOUISIANA MUSIC FACTORY

This French Quarter shop, known for its lively in-store appearances, is crammed with bins of vinyl LPs of all the local genres—R&B, swamp pop, zydeco, and jazz. Every May since 1993 it has held the Brass Band Blowout, with live music all day long; all the best brass bands—Dirty Dozen, ReBirth, Chosen Few, and Little Rascals—have taken part. The shop has also hosted a couple of official Professor Longhair birthday parties, and most weekends there's an in-store appearance with R&B names like Chuck Cabo. LMS also features a big selection of T-shirts and staff who'll tell you all you need to know about local live roots music. *225 N. Peters St., tel. 504/523–1094.*

MARGARITAVILLE CAFE

Country-'n'-cheeseburger artist Jimmy Buffett opened this surprisingly down-to-earth joint in the mid-'90s. Locals view the place as one of the top venues in town, but serious Buffet fans, known as Parrotheads, may be disappointed by the lack of lurid decor (that's saved for the adjacent gift shop and restaurant).

Every day from 2 to 11 PM, some of New Orleans' best musicians (from all of the city's genres) squeeze into the smallish bar to play , and there's no cover charge. The not-to-be-missed show is R&B piano veteran Eddie Bo, who does a three-hour set, starting at 5 PM, Thursday through Sunday. Bo, who's been around New Orleans clubs since 1955, had a *Billboard* R&B Top 20 hit in 1969 with "Hook and Sling (Part 1)" and in the '60s had production credits for such artists as Johnny Adams and Irma Thomas. During the Jazz and Heritage Festival, big names and Buffett himself often drop in. *1104 Decatur St., tel. 504/592–2565.*

MUNICIPAL AUDITORIUM

Country star Hank Williams married Billie Jean Eshlimar here twice on the same October 1952 day in front of sellout crowds. Tickets cost $1.50, and Hank and wife ended up some $25,000 richer. In May 1995 the building was renovated to provide a temporary home for Harrah's, the city's first land-based casino, which made headlines by going bust a few months later. *Louis Armstrong Park, off N. Rampart and St. Peter Sts.*

SEA-SAINT STUDIOS

After producing thousands of tracks at J&M Studios, Allen Toussaint opened this state-of-the-art facility in August 1973. When Wings recorded *Venus and Mars* here in, Paul McCartney got turned on to the piano skills of Professor Longhair and invited the veteran player to perform at a private party. Longhair agreed but wondered what the fuss was about—he had never heard of the Beatles, let alone McCartney. Albert King, the Pointer Sisters, the Neville Brothers, and Dr. John were other big names who came during the '70s, and LaBelle recorded its New Orleans tribute, "Lady Marmalade," here. The studio had to scale down operations in the early '80s after Warner Bros. failed to renew its contract, but recent visitors have included Michelle Shocked and Lenny Kravitz. *3809 Clematis Ave., Gentilly District, tel. 504/949–8386.*

SON OF THE NINTH WARD

New Orleans's most successful rock & roller was born Antoine Domino on May 10, 1929, one of a family of nine who lived in a tiny house at 2407 Jourdain Avenue in the Ninth Ward. He got the nickname "Fats" at an early age from other neighborhood kids, who included Lee Dorsey.

Domino was discovered in 1949 by producer Dave Bartholomew at the Hideaway, a Ninth Ward club (now long gone) at 2900 Desire Street. The two went on to collaborate on such '50s smash hits as "Blueberry Hill" and "Ain't That a Shame," as well as the much-covered "Land of 1000 Dances." (The song actually names only 16: the pony, mashed potato, alligator, twist, ya ya, sweet pea, Watusi, fly, hand jive, slop, chicken, bop, fish, slow twist, tango, and Popeye.)

Despite having sold some 70 million records, Fats Domino still lives in the Ninth Ward, one of the city's poorer neighborhoods. His current homestead, at Marais Street and Caffin Avenue, is rather magnificent compared with those around it. Surrounded by a white wrought-iron fence with painted flower decals, it has surveillance cameras on the roof for good measure.

The CBD, Warehouse District, Uptown, and West

West of the Quarter, across lurid Canal Street, is the Central Business District, often referred to as the CBD. Just beyond this is the Warehouse District, home of the city's best galleries. Upriver (northwest) from the CBD are the antebellum mansions of the Garden District, the lushest residential part of a city where few places are considered absolutely safe. Beyond here is Uptown, a mix of studenty and down-at-the-heels neighborhoods.

EATINGDRINKINGDANCINGSHOPPINGPLAYINGSLEEPING

CARROLLTON STATION (8140 Willow St., tel. 504/865−9190) is a neighborhood bar with a great beer selection; Peter Holsapple (formerly of the dBs, featured on R.E.M!'s *Green* tour, and now in the Continental Drifters) plays acoustic most Sundays with no cover. **JIMMY'S** (200 Willow St., tel. 504/861-8200) is good for up-and-coming rock bands, as well as national ska bands and the local ska act Kelly's Heroes. **LITTLE PEOPLE'S PLACE** (3334 Washington St., no phone) is a crazy little bar in the Treme district—one of the city's longest-established African-American neighborhoods—so small that you can whack one of the musicians if you open the door too fast. Jazz and brass bands squeeze in. Irma Thomas, the "Soul Queen of New Orleans," performs most Friday and Saturday nights at the **LION'S DEN** (2655 Gravier St., at Broad, tel. 504/822−4693), a neighborhood club (in a fairly rough area) that she part owns.

The **HUMMINGBIRD HOTEL AND GRILL** (804 St. Charles Ave., tel. 504/561−9229), a 24-hour café with a sketchy clientele and sketchier food, is so awful it's good. There's no live music, but it's a key postgig hangout for the city's musicians. **SNAKE AND JAKE'S CHRISTMAS CLUB LOUNGE** (7612 Oak St., tel. 504/861−2802) is a neighborhood hangout with year-round yuletide decor.

In the recorded-music department, check out **MUSHROOM** (1037 Broadway, tel. 504/866−6065), a student-oriented store near Tulane University that stocks general rock, alternative bands, and local sounds; you'll also find lots of posters, T-shirts, and Grateful Dead paraphernalia. **UNDERGROUND SOUNDS** (735 Octavia St., tel. 504/897−9030) has a good selection of new rock music and is particularly strong on local bands.

JAZZ AND HERITAGE FESTIVAL

New Orleans likes to say that its annual Jazz and Heritage Festival, held since 1968, is the leading music fest in the nation. Given that the events take place over seven days between 11 AM and 7 PM on 10 stages, with the action then moving into dozens of bars and clubs, it's no idle boast. The city's staples of R&B and jazz are well-represented, but with 4,000 musicians invited, the range of sounds

Krewe dancers at Jazz Fest

covers everything from Mardi Gras through zydeco and country to alternative bands. The 1996 lineup included artists as diverse as B.B. King, Van Morrison, Wynton Marsalis, Phish, and Joan Osborne. The festival—which also features dozens of stalls serving regional dishes and selling traditional crafts—takes place from the last weekend of April through the first weekend of May on the Fair Grounds Racetrack, near the southeast corner of City Park. Over 400,000 visitors flock to the city, so book a room well in advance. For details, contact the New Orleans Jazz and Heritage Foundation (Box 53407, New Orleans, LA 70153, tel. 504/522–4786); there are also several sites online.

DEW DROP INN

The city's leading '50s R&B club was noted for its wild female impersonators and for such regular headliners as Dinah Washington and Little Richard, who premiered "Tutti Frutti" here in the summer of 1955. Two years later the piano skills of a teenage Allen Toussaint impressed Imperial Records producer Dave Bartholomew, who immediately gave him a start as a session player. Other regulars were New Orleans R&B artist Guitar Slim, before his death in 1959 at 32, and Lee Dorsey, who had some of his earliest gigs here. The Dew Drop closed in 1972 after owner Frank Pania died, and it now stands boarded up in a tough area opposite a housing project. Each October, however, it's dusted down for the Dew Drop Inn Revisited gig, and there are promotions under that name at various venues during Jazz Fest. *2836 La Salle St.*

THE HOWLIN' WOLF

New Orleans resident Alex Chilton regularly plays '60s covers at this neat club, which also has the best touring alternative bands and a Monday open-mike session where Jimmy Page has jammed several times. The Howlin' Wolf (check out the comical lupine logo) began life in December 1988 in nearby Metairie before moving, three years later, to an old coffee warehouse with lots of wooden beams and a low-slung roof. Although its capacity is around the 1,000 mark, the Wolf manages to get some more prestigious acts: Recent visitors have included Sonic Youth, Alanis Morissette, and John Cale, while the local band Better Than Ezra played here for years before hitting MTV. You can catch gigs live on Tulane's WTUL (91.5 FM) on Wednesday nights. *828 S. Peters St., tel. 504/523-2551 or 504/523-2341.*

J&M STUDIOS, 1966-69

Although the New Orleans recording scene took a nosedive with the advent of Motown and British Beat bands, Cosimo Matassa expanded his operations in late 1966, moving his studio to a warehouse in the CBD. Beyond recording, he ran the Dover label and distribution company from here, and although he scored a massive strike with Aaron Neville's 1966 breakthrough, "Tell It Like It Is," the business soon failed, and the IRS swiped all the recording equipment. Matassa then went on to help found Sea-Saint Studios (*see above*). *748 Camp St.*

SHANNON HOON DEATH SITE

The 28-year-old lead singer of Blind Melon, Shannon Hoon, was found dead in his tour bus by fellow Hoosier Axl Rose on October 21, 1995. The bus had been parked in a lot next to the Hotel Inter-Continental. The probable cause of death was a drug overdose. *440 St. Charles Ave.*

[MAPLE LEAF BAR]

Regarded as one of the city's best down-home venues, the long-running Maple Leaf started out with a twin focus on chess and music; there are still a couple of chess tables in the back room, but an eclectic mix of roots music has taken over. These days the hot ticket is the ReBirth Brass Band, whose sounds boom out most Tuesday nights. Cajun, zydeco, and blues dominate the rest of the week. With a pleasant outdoor patio, walls of pressed tin, and hardworking ceiling fans, the Maple Leaf is a good hangout, but its neighborhood is not so welcoming. It's only a few blocks from the Oak and Carrollton stop of the St. Charles streetcar, but most locals advise taking a taxi at night rather than wandering around on foot. *8316 Oak St., tel. 504/866-9359.*

MERMAID LOUNGE

Although it opened only in early 1995, this basic little performance space has achieved national recognition thanks to sugary compliments in *Rolling Stone* and shows by Man or Astro-man?, Throwing Muses, the Dirty 3, and others who have chosen to play here rather than at larger and better-equipped venues. The Mermaid features a small art gallery, but since there's no stage, alternative and experimental acts like AGB or Myshkin Impossible are shunted into a corner. Behind the bar is a small recording room; the owners brought out a live CD in 1996 with songs by Evil Nurse Sheila, FSQ, Weedeater, Burn Version, the Gas Tank Orchestra (who play...gas tanks), and other local bands. Although the place is on the fringe of the Warehouse District in the shade of I-10, it's best to call for directions before setting out. Things usually don't get going until 10. *1102 Constance St., at J. C. Chase, tel. 504/524-4747.*

MID CITY LANES ROCK N' BOWL

One of the best places in New Orleans to catch top blues or to dance to the best zydeco sounds is a pastel blue-and-pink bowling alley that boasts 18 lanes—and two stages. You could say this weird and wonderful joint came about through divine providence. Owner John Blancher (who seems to always be in the club, willing to give dance lessons) was in a bit of a financial pickle in 1988 but scraped together enough cash to go on a pilgrimage to Medjugorje, a town in the former Yugoslavia that was experiencing what were reportedly apparitions of the Virgin Mary. Blancher didn't get to see Mary, but he did ask for good luck at the shrine. A few days after getting home, he heard about a '40s bowling alley on the market for a ridiculously low price and bought it. A friend suggested he put a band on one night, and the business took off from there. Thursday is the key zydeco dance night; the Iguanas, Snooks Eaglin, and Johnny Adams have also

Mid City Lanes Rock n' Bowl

been regular fixtures. "The Home of Rock 'n Bowl" also does a neat line of T-shirts and bowling shirts. *4133 S. Carrollton Ave., tel. 504/482–3133.*

[TIPITINA'S]

New Orleans's most celebrated current-day club was opened in 1977 by a dedicated gang of Professor Longhair fans, who got the club's name from one of the rhumba-boogie pianist's songs and installed a bust of him in the entrance. Longhair himself was a regular fixture here until his death, in 1980, and despite his age was said to put in some of the best shows of his career.

Tipitina's

The club has two dance floors and three bars. It occupies premises that have been hosting live music since the early '40s and was the setting for several scenes in *The Big Easy*. Tip's has put on R&B legends and funk, rock, and Cajun bands, as well as all the big New Orleans names. The Meters, the Radiators, and Cowboy Mouth have played; the Neville Brothers had their first gig here in late '77 and recorded a live album in the '80s.

In 1995 there was much speculation in the local press about Tipitina's ability to survive the arrival of the House of Blues. However, the club began booking younger bands—including Hootie and the Blowfish, PJ Harvey, and Better Than Ezra—and management recently took out an ad in *Offbeat* claiming that "legends don't die...they continue to grow." *501 Napoleon Ave., tel. 504/895-8477 (tickets) or 504/895-3943 (concert info).*

THE WAREHOUSE

The Grateful Dead played the first show at this venue, a barely renovated former coffee warehouse, in front of a crowd of 6,000 in January 1970. When the band members returned to their hotel after the gig, most of them and the touring party were busted for cannabis possession. The next night Fleetwood Mac supported the Dead in a benefit at the venue to raise money for legal fees. On November 12, 1970, the Doors played what turned out to be their last gig with Jim Morrison. Morrison was his usual petulant self, bashing a microphone stand against the wooden stage until the floorboards broke; soon after he left for Paris, where he died. The venue closed in the early '80s. *1820 Tchoupitoulas St.*

MISSISSIPPI

THE MISSISSIPPI DELTA WAS SHINING LIKE A NATIONAL GUITAR—PAUL SIMON, "GRACELAND"

The dark, fertile soil of the Mississippi Delta has produced more than cotton—it's also the birthplace of the blues. Around the turn of the century, field workers on the plantations began adapting old slave songs and spirituals to the guitar. But it wasn't until the '20s and '30s, when musicologists from the Library of Congress journeyed south to record local folk music and "discovered" the blues, that the music of the Delta took off as a marketable form. Many of the best-known blues performers, Muddy Waters among them, were first recorded by such folklorists as the father-and-son team of John and Alan Lomax.

Blues music was soon to become more than a local phenomenon, however. With the mechanization of cotton picking in the '40s, the slow trickle of black Southerners to the big cities of the North became a deluge—more than 5 million moved in the three decades following 1940. Chicago, on a direct train line from the Delta, was a particular beneficiary of this migration. Along with the migrants (among them Muddy Waters, John Lee Hooker, and B.B. King) came the acoustic-guitar blues that would become one of the prime sources of rock & roll.

The Mississippi Delta itself is really no delta at all, but a 120-mile-long alluvial flood plain that stretches from the confluence of the Mississippi and Yazoo rivers near Vicksburg, some 150 miles inland from the Gulf of Mexico, north to Memphis. It takes up the northwestern corner of the state, with I–55 acting as an approximate eastern border. Tiny hamlets dot the flat, sun-scorched plain, and big towns are few and far between. It's a landscape that brings home the sense of loneliness and oppression that Robert Johnson and other early blues masters tried to convey.

The area looks daunting, but with a good road map it's not too difficult to explore, starting at Clarksdale, home of the Delta Blues Museum, and heading south to sites like Dockery Farms or either of Robert Johnson's two graves. Clarksdale and Greenville are two of the best places to catch live music. Although the blues has made little stylistic progress in this part of Mississippi since the big migrations of the '40s and '50s, it's is still the most popular live sound. On Saturday night, clubs and bars all over the Delta jump to the sound of blues bands.

Not that getting to blues gigs in the Delta is always easy. Most juke joints are basic little affairs; many don't have phones, and there's often a laissez-faire attitude as to whether or not the event goes on. In major centers, there's usually some live music each weekend, but you should also be prepared to travel 50 miles down lonely roads. Talk with locals, such as the excellent staff at Stackhouse Records in Clarksdale, before you set out and you'll avoid a lot of hassle.

Mississippi is more than just the Delta, however. It also gave the world Elvis Presley, who was born in 1935 in Tupelo, a sleepy town in the northeast of the state. Fifty miles west is the genteel university town of Oxford, which holds a massive scholarly archive on the Delta blues. Farther south is Jackson, the state capital, connected to Tupelo by the Natchez Trace, one of the nation's loveliest drives.

Papa Freddie, "Low Down Mississippi Bottom Man" (1928)
Charley Patton, "Mississippi Boll Weevil Blues" (1929)
Muddy Waters, "Mississippi Blues" (1956)
Ray Charles, "Mississippi Mud" (1960)
Bo Diddley, "Mississippi" (1964)
Phil Ochs, "Here's to the State of Mississippi" (1965)
Mountain, "Mississippi Queen" (1970)
Jerry Reed, "Tupelo Mississippi Flash" (1973)
Jerry Garcia, "Mississippi Moon" (1974)
Lynyrd Skynyrd, "Mississippi Kid" (1974)
Jimi Hendrix, "Peace in Mississippi" (1975)
Chicago, "Mississippi Delta Queen Blues" (1977)
Charlie Daniels Band, "Mississippi" (1979)
Ry Cooder, "Down in Mississippi" (1986)
Jim Croce, "Mississippi Lady" (1986)
ZZ Top, "My Head's in Mississippi" (1990)

Clarksdale

The nerve center of Delta blues, Clarksdale is the birthplace of Junior Parker, Bukka White, Son House, and John Lee Hooker, as well as the rock & roll era's Ike Turner and Sam Cooke. Before World War II, Muddy Waters and Howlin' Wolf gravitated here to play juke joints and busk on street corners. Visitors come to see Tennessee Williams's home and the Delta Blues Museum, but Clarksdale, 75 miles southwest of Memphis, is far from being a smaller cousin of touristy Beale Street. It's still a vital performing center with lively, homegrown venues.

EATING DRINKING DANCING SHOPPING PLAYING SLEEPING

Contemporary singers Lonnie Pitchford (who often busks on 4th Street) and Frank Frost play no-frills venues like SMITTY'S RED TOP LOUNGE (377 Yazoo Ave., tel. 601/627−4421) and RED'S (395 Sunflower Ave., tel. 601/627−3166).

[DELTA BLUES MUSEUM]

Crammed into the town's Carnegie Public Library, this museum is a must for blues fans. Following the music's rise from the Mississippi backwaters to international acclaim, it displays photos, bios, books, records, and some more unusual items, including the sign from the Three Forks store in Greenwood (*see below*); a guitar (named, as always, Lucille) donated by B.B. King; a life-size wax figure of Muddy Waters; and ZZ Top's Muddywood guitar, made from timber taken from Waters's childhood home on Stovall Plantation. The museum, set up with funds donated by ZZ Top and the National Endowment for the Humanities Trust, opened in 1979; there are plans for expansion. *114 Delta Ave., tel. 601/627−6820, http://www.clarksdale.com/blusmuse.htm. Admission free. Open weekdays 9−5.*

KING OF THE DELTA BLUES

Guitarist and vocalist Robert Johnson was born Robert Leroy Dodds in Hazlehurst, 35 miles south of Jackson, on May 8, 1911. (He took the name Johnson at

17, when he discovered the identity of his father.) He died at 27, and his legacy rests almost solely on a batch of about 40 songs he recorded over four days in 1936 and '37. Johnson's legend began to grow when Elmore James cut his "Dust My Broom" and Junior Parker had a hit with his "Sweet Home Chicago" after World War II. But it was Columbia's 1961 release of the *King of the Delta Blues Singers* compilation that catapulted Johnson's name to mythical status in rock circles. Eric Clapton made his vinyl singing debut with Johnson's "Ramblin' on My Mind" on the 1966 *Bluesbreakers* album, and two years later, with Cream, he recorded the first of several versions of Johnson's "Crossroads Blues." The Rolling Stones included "Love in Vain" on their 1969 album, *Let It Bleed,* and had a go with another Johnson song, "Stop Breaking Down," on 1972's *Exile on Main Street.*

G. T. THOMAS HOSPITAL (RIVERSIDE HOTEL)

Injured in an auto wreck on Highway 61 in September 1937, Bessie Smith was brought to G. T. Thomas Hospital but died soon after. Blues folklore holds that it was a whites-only establishment and turned away her ambulance—Edward Albee even wrote a play about it, *The Death of Bessie Smith*—but Thomas was actually a black hospital.

In 1944 the hospital was converted into a hotel. Sonny Boy Williamson II and Ike Turner later stayed—Turner wrote "Rocket 88" here—and their names can still be seen in the register. John F. Kennedy, Jr. stayed here on a blues-landmarks trip around the Delta. *615 Sunflower Ave., tel. 601/624–9163. Rooms: $40.*

Chess Records/courtesy of Jim O'Neal Collection

Sonny Boy Williamson II

[STACKHOUSE RECORDS]

Another essential stop for a blues fan touring the Delta, Stackhouse is crammed full of rare recordings and such blues paraphernalia as voodoo charms. It's also an unbeatable source of local knowledge: Delta maps featuring all the definitive landmarks are available, and staff are pleased to give the latest information on gigs and hard-to-find juke joints. The store is owned by archivist and all-around approachable guy Jim O'Neal (one of the founders of *Living Blues* magazine). He also runs the Rooster Blues label, which records local artists like Lonnie Pitchford. *232 Sunflower Ave., tel. 601/627–2209.*

STOVALL PLANTATION

As a child in the '20s, McKinley Morganfield grew up in a small cabin on this isolated plantation outside Clarksdale; his love of playing in the dirt earned him the nickname Muddy Waters. In his early 20s, he drove a tractor for a living, brewed moonshine, and played the guitar at Stovall's makeshift juke joint. Following a visit to the Delta by government-sponsored musicologist Alan Lomax, Waters cut his first record—for the Library of Congress. Looking for commercial success, he left in 1943 for Chicago, where he made his name with pioneering urban blues songs like "Rolling Stone," "I'm Ready," and "Mannish Boy."

Despite countless twisters over the years, Waters's dilapidated cabin is still in existence. It stood here, with notices warning that a

Muddy Waters

"big nasty mojo" would be laid on trespassers, until May 1996, when it was disassembled to begin a five-year world tour sponsored by the House of Blues chain. After being exhibited at blues festivals and other events, the restored cabin will be returned to the plantation, where its site is currently marked with a monument. *Oakhurst Ave. at Stovall Rd., 7 mi NW of downtown.*

WADE'S BARBERSHOP

At his old-fashioned barbershop, Wade Walton cuts hair while singing a mean blues. In the '50s Sonny Boy Williamson II used to drop in here en route to Helena, Arkansas, to get spruced for his *King Biscuit Time* radio show. Walton, who can even pick out a tune on his straight-edge razor, was once a member of Ike Turner's Kings of Rhythm and has recorded an album, *The Blues of Wade Walton. 317 Issaquena Ave., tel. 601/624–6067.*

DOWN TO THE CROSSROADS

Sometime around 1930 Robert Johnson met the devil at the junction of highways 61 and 49, near Clarksdale, and sold his soul in exchange for guitar lessons. Or so says the blues lore, spread by rivals when Johnson turned up after a few years away with the spellbinding technique evident in songs like "Rambling on My Mind" and "Love in Vain." The crossroads story is, in fact, an old legend, previously applied to another performer, Tommy Johnson (no relation), who it was claimed had gone down to the crossroads to meet Legba, a devious African god, who retuned his guitar and taught him how to play afresh.

Drew

Two of the Staple Singers—Cleotha and Pervis—were born here in the mid-'30s. Members of the veteran group perform at an annual festival held in the town's Staples Park every June. Drew, 30 miles south of Clarksdale on Highway 49, is also home to the **MUSIC MART** (161 N. Main St., tel. 601/745–6576), a record store stocked with a wide range of blues recordings.

Greenville

Greenville is the busiest river port in the state and the largest Mississippi Delta town. One of the Delta's best-known current-day blues artists, Booba Barnes, is based here, and the annual Delta Blues Festival, held the third Saturday in September, is one of the largest local music events.

Valerie Wilmer/courtesy of Jim O'Neal Collection

On April 21, 1927 the Mississippi River burst through a newly built levee a few miles north of here at Mount Landing. A 20-foot-high wave swept across the cotton fields, flooding surrounding towns and leaving Greenville under water for 10 weeks. The incident inspired a number of blues songs, including Bessie Smith's "Back Water Blues," Charley Patton's "High Water Everywhere," and Memphis Minnie's "When the Levee Breaks," famously covered by Led Zeppelin on their fourth album (and carelessly credited on the original vinyl disc to "Memphis"). Since then engineers have forced the Mississippi to flow 6 miles west of town, around a lake left after the levee break.

Greenville's Booba Barnes

EATINGDRINKINGDANCINGSHOPPINGPLAYINGSLEEPING

Greenville's nightlife is more rough and raucous than that of smaller, laid-back Clarksdale, but there are a few juke joints along Nelson Street. One long-running blues club is **PERRY'S FLOWING FOUNTAIN** (816 Nelson St., tel. 601/335–9836), which Little Milton sang about in the early '60s. The legendary **DOE'S EAT PLACE** (502 Nelson St., tel. 601/334–3315), home of the state's biggest and best ribs, is well worth a visit.

Greenwood

In 1938, a year after his last recording session, Robert Johnson died an agonizing death. Explanations vary, but the leading theory is that he was poisoned with strychnine-laced whiskey, administered by the husband of a woman he had been flirting with at a party at Greenwood's long-gone Three Forks store.

Greenwood, 50 miles south of Clarksdale on Highway 49E, is encircled by some of the best cropland in the Delta and remains one of the South's major cotton markets. It's also the 1926 birthplace of Eddie Jones, a.k.a. Guitar Slim, whose 1954 R&B smash, "The Things That I Used to Do," has become an R&B standard. Another Greenwood native is soul singer Betty Everett (born 1939), whose "You're No Good" and "It's in His Kiss" were big hits for Linda Ronstadt and Cher, respectively.

Holly Ridge

NEW JERUSALEM CHURCH

Mythologized and much-covered blues singer Charley Patton (1887–1934) spent his life in and around the Delta; he is buried here under a headstone donated in 1991 by former Creedence Clearwater Revival vocalist John Fogerty. *Hwy. 82, 7 mi W of Indianola.*

Holly Springs

GRACELAND TOO

This town in the north of the state, 30 miles from Oxford, is home to one of the South's more unlikely attractions: a bizarre Graceland tribute known as Graceland Too. In their two-story, white-columned villa just off the graceful, tree-lined courthouse square, Paul Macleod and his son, Elvis Aron Presley Macleod, have made a shrine to the king of rock & roll. Graceland Too is crammed full of Elvisy ephemera—busts, cardboard cutouts, license plates, T-shirts, magazines open at relevant articles—and every bit of wall space is covered with photos, posters, postcards, and cuttings. Graceland Too only recently opened to the public, and the Macleods are trying to do some structural work to make the house look a bit more like the Graceland up in Memphis. *Randolph St. at Cholson St., tel. 601/252–7954. Admission: $5. Open daily.*

Indianola

Indianola, 60 miles south of Clarksdale, has two claims to fame: America's largest catfish processing plant and B.B. King. Born in nearby Itta Bena, King grew up here in the '30s and heard his first blues at **CLUB EBONY** (404 Hannah St., tel. 601/887–9915); he now plays an outdoor gig every June in Fletcher Park. His palm print is just about visible on the sidewalk at the corner of 2nd and Church streets, and the signposts along B.B. King Road are popular photo stops.

Jackson

Although it's Mississippi's capital and largest city, Jackson still has a pleasant small-town feel. In the '50s it was the home of the Rolling Stones—not Jagger, Richards, and company, but an R&B outfit called Joe Tubb and the Rolling Stones, the first group to use the name. At the time Jackson also boasted two successful indie labels, Ace Records and the blues label Trumpet; a later soul label, Malaco, produced several hits in the '60s and '70s, including Dorothy Moore's "Misty Blue" and King Floyd's "Groove Me," which had been turned down by Stax.

Jackson was celebrated in song by Nancy Sinatra and Lee Hazlewood in a 1967 single of the same name. A young Paddy McAloon, listening to the radio in the northeast of England, misheard the line "We got married in a fever, hotter than a pepper sprout" and named his band Prefab Sprout.

ACE RECORDS

Set up by former Specialty label producer Johnny Vincent in 1955, Ace musicians successfully copied the Fats Domino New Orleans sound. The label enjoyed huge '50s hits with Huey Smith and the Clowns' "Rockin' Pneumonia and the Boogie Woogie Flu" and Frankie Ford's "Sea Cruise." The distribution of the label, which also gave Joe Tex his start in the late '50s, was tied up with Veejay of Chicago. When Veejay went bust in the mid-'60s, so did Ace. *209 W. Capitol St.*

TRUMPET RECORDS

In the early '50s Sonny Boy Williamson II recorded for Trumpet Records in what is now a furniture store. Record company boss Lillian MacMurry had been searching various Delta towns in a fruitless attempt to find the singer, only to come across him by accident, hanging out at the building next door. *309 Nashville Farish St.*

McComb

The most famous native of this southern Mississippi town, 20 miles from the Louisiana border, was born Elias Bates on December 30, 1928. As a child he saw adults play a strange custom-built instrument, little more than a piece of wire stretched against a door and bridged in the middle by a stone, which they called a diddley-bow. He inverted the word to get "Bo Diddley," which he used both for his stage name and for the title of his 1955 debut single, a Top 10 R&B hit.

Bo Diddley

LYNYRD SKYNYRD CRASH SITE

Lynyrd Skynyrd's Convair 240 plane was on its way to an emergency landing at McComb on October 20, 1977, when it crashed in a swamp 8 miles from the airport and a good distance from the nearest road. A dirt track had to be cut through the undergrowth to remove the wreckage from the accident, in which singer Ronnie Van Zant and guitarist Steve Gaines were killed. There is no marker for the site. *Off Hwy. 568, near Gillsburg.*

LAST FAIR DEAL GONE DOWN—TWICE?

Robert Johnson's grave is almost as controversial as his death. According to his death certificate, the guitarist is buried outside the clapboard Mount Zion Church (Leflore Co. Rd. 511, off Hwy. 7), 18 miles north of Morgan City, where Columbia Records recently paid for an imposing monument inscribed with some of his lyrics. However, some say that shortly after his burial at Mount Zion, Johnson's sister had his body moved to Quito's Payne Baptist Church (Leflore Co. Rd. 512W, off Hwy. 7, SW of Greenwood). The headstone in Quito was installed in the early '90s by a rock group called the Tombstones, who'd read about the controversy in *Living Blues* magazine.

Oxford

Set amid rolling hills on the edge of the Holly Springs National Forest, wealthy Oxford, with its pristine town square, coffeehouses, and mansion homes, is a long way from the Delta—if not in distance, then certainly in spirit. The setting for many of William Faulkner's novels, it's also home to the University of Mississippi, "Ole Miss." In 1962 a bitter conflict erupted on campus when a black student, James Meredith, tried to enroll; he eventually had to be smuggled in by troops. At his graduation ceremony, Meredith wore a button proclaiming NEVER, the slogan of the state's segregationist governor, turned upside down. This image stuck with Bob Dylan, whose "Oxford Town" includes the line "never going down to Oxford Town." The university, now home to the world's largest blues archive, has recently instituted an annual conference for the study of the life and works of Elvis Aron Presley.

THE BLUES ARCHIVE

The world's most extensive blues archive comprises 5,200 LPs, 7,500 singles (including thousands of rare blues 78s), and B.B. King's personal record collection, which he amassed during his days as a Memphis DJ. There are also thousands of books and magazines, many donated by Jim O'Neal, a founder of *Living Blues* magazine, which the university now produces. Although the public can visit the archive and listen to its holdings, the facility is intended mainly for researchers; visitors should book an appointment. *Farley Hall, University of Mississippi, Grove Loop, tel. 601/232–7753. Open weekdays 8–5, weekends by appointment.*

Parchman

PARCHMAN FARM

Although Mose Allison, arguably the only well-known *white* Delta blues singer, sang the line "I'm sitting down here on Parchman Farm, ain't never done no man no harm," he was never an inmate of Mississippi's largest prison. A number of other bluesmen did end up doing a stretch here, however. Son House, the sizzling singer who was a protegé of Charley Patton's and a teacher of Robert Johnson's, shot a man at a party near Lyon in 1928 and served 18 months of a 15-year sentence. Bukka White wrote "Parchman Farm Blues" while serving time for manslaughter and in 1939 recorded for the Library of Congress, a feat that won him parole. If he'd been around seven years later, White could have nodded at the father of the infant king of rock & roll in the exercise yard— Vernon Presley spent some time at Parchman for forgery. In 1992 Fat Possum Records came here to record blues-singing inmate David Malone. *Off Hwy. 49W, 20 mi S of Clarksdale.*

Ruleville

[DOCKERY FARMS]

Blues buffs have traced the origins of the Delta sound to Dockery Farms, a cotton-growing settlement near the Sunflower River. In the '20s field hand Henry Sloan taught younger workmate Charley Patton how to play so-called "blue" notes. Patton, who sang about the meandering Dockery railroad on "Pea Vine Blues," became one of the first recorded blues artists (his earliest sessions date from 1929). He also used to hold the guitar above his head in concert, a gimmick later trademarked by Jimi Hendrix. *Hwy. 49W, 35 mi S of Clarksdale.*

Starkville

Starkville is best known as the site of the main campus of Mississippi State University, where in 1966 Johnny Cash was caught picking flowers at 2 AM and was thrown in the local jail for public drunkenness. Incensed at an arrest he perceived to be unjust, Cash kicked the wall of his cell and broke his left big toe.

Tupelo

Elvis Presley was born into a blue-collar neighborhood on the outskirts of this sleepy town on January 8, 1935. He lived here until age 13, when the family fled to Memphis in the middle of the night to escape debts. Tupelo's first designated Elvis Presley Day took place way back in 1956, and town authorities appear to have used the following four decades to go over the top with the dedications. Elvis's birthplace—tastefully restored, next to a peaceful chapel and a simple museum—stands on what is now Elvis Presley Drive, near Elvis Presley Park, in an area known as Elvis Presley Heights. The 850-acre Elvis Presley Lake and Campground are a few miles away. One day Tupelo will no doubt be renamed Elvisville.

MCDONALD'S

This branch has been done out as a minishrine to the cheeseburger-loving Elvis, with walls covered in mildly interesting pictures and cuttings. A Quarter Pounder with peanut butter and jelly has been inappropriately left off the menu. *372 S. Gloster St.*

MISSISSIPPI-ALABAMA FAIRGROUND

Elvis took part in his first public performance at this now run-down fairground on October 3, 1945. Entered in a fair talent contest by his head teacher at Lawhon Grammar School, Elvis sang "Old Shep" and won second prize: $5 and free admission for the day. Eleven years later, having just finished filming his first movie, *The Reno Brothers* (later renamed *Love Me Tender*), he returned to play the Mississippi-Alabama Fair and Dairy Show. Thousands lined the main street in 100° temperatures to catch a glimpse of the Tupelo-born star, and the National Guard was brought in to control the crowds. Town authorities designated the day, September 26, Elvis Presley Day. Elvis's stage show was still unrestrained in those days, and as he started singing "Don't Be Cruel," hysterical fans invaded the stage and tore the rhinestone buttons from his shirt. He performed here again the following year at a benefit concert for the restoration of his birthplace. *Mulberry Alley, off W. Main St.*

[ELVIS PRESLEY BIRTHPLACE, MUSEUM, & CHAPEL]

Elvis Aron Presley and his stillborn twin brother, Jesse Garon, were born in this tiny "shotgun shack"—so named because a shotgun bullet could pass from the front through to the back—on January 8, 1935. The house was built by Vernon Presley for $180, and it takes only a few minutes to look around its two rooms: the kitchen and the bedroom where Elvis was born. None of the furniture is original; the only things Elvis would recognize are the wooden doors and floors, the fireplace, and the family photo used on the front cover of his 1971 *Elvis Country* LP.

In a separate building behind the house is a small museum featuring stuff Elvis donated for posterity: a mike used at his last recording session, motorcycle boots, and a Las Vegas jumpsuit. Next to the museum is a chapel built with donations from various sources,

Elvis Presley's first home

including the First Assembly of God Church (909 Berry St.), the first he attended. The chapel pews and windows bear inscriptions from family and friends, including manager Colonel Tom Parker. *306 Elvis Presley Dr., tel. 601/841–1245. Admission: $1 (birthplace), $4 (museum), chapel free. Open Mon.–Sat. 9–5, Sun. 1–5.*

TUPELO HARDWARE COMPANY

Elvis bought his first guitar from this old-fashioned general store, which looks untouched since the January 1946 day when he walked out with the instrument. Legend has it that Elvis wanted a gun, but that mom Gladys preferred a guitar. *114 W. Main St., tel. 601/842–4637.*

Vicksburg

Natives of the Delta's southernmost town, on Highway 61 at the confluence of the Mississippi and Yazoo rivers, say the word *jazz* originated here in the '20s, coined to describe the playing of local drummer Chaz (or Jazz) Washington. Etymological evidence suggests they're fooling themselves, but the Yazoo did lend its name to the '80s British electropop duo of Alison Moyet and Vince Clarke, a group known in the United States as Yaz.

Willie Dixon, the city's most famous musician (born July 1, 1915), wrote poetry as well as the lyrics to Muddy Waters's "Hoochie Coochie Man" and "Little Red Rooster." During World War II Dixon won a famous court case asserting his right to be designated a conscientious objector. He later became an amateur boxing champion (often sparring with Joe Louis) and then moved to Chicago to produce Muddy Waters and play bass for Chuck Berry. Never one to be modest about his status, Dixon called his autobiography *I Am the Blues.*

NORTH CAROLINA

A bridgehead between the nation's capital and the sleepy South, North Carolina encompasses everything from the "research triangle" of Raleigh, Durham, and Chapel Hill to poor, rural areas along its Appalachian western border. Of late it's been gaining a reputation for producing such fiery indie bands as Superchunk and Archers of Loaf.

These '90s groups aren't the state's first musical contribution. Clyde McPhatter, lead singer of the original Drifters in the mid-'50s, was born in Durham in 1933. Later Drifter Ben E. King was born Benjamin Earl Nelson in Henderson in 1938. Some well-known blues singers also come from the state, such as Sonny Terry, born in 1911 in Greensboro (where Jesse Jackson earned his reputation in the early '60s), and Wadesboro-born Blind Boy Fuller (1907), who worked with Terry in the '40s.

Courtesy of UNC Southern Folklife Collection

Brownie McGhee plays with Greensboro's Sonny Terry

Chapel Hill

Since the late '80s, a slew of loud punk bands have followed Superchunk (whose Mac and Laura also run the Merge label) out of this college-dominated suburb of Durham and onto the airwaves of college radio. It's also where brothers Mike and David Connell, who went to school at the University of North Carolina, formed their namesake band, the Connells, in 1984.

Chapel Hill was the 1911 birthplace of Floyd Council, a Blind Boy Fuller–style blues performer who left little in the way of a legacy except for his name: It provided half the inspiration for Pink Floyd's name. (The *Pink* bit came from South Carolina bluesman Pinkney Anderson.)

Cat's Cradle (*see below*) is Chapel Hill's best spot for live rock, though **Local 506** (506 W. Franklin St., tel. 919/942–5506), a smaller affair, also puts on up-and-coming area bands. **The Cave** (452. W Franklin St., tel. 919/968–9038) is a tiny hangout with an eclectic roster of blues and roots. **School Kids Records** (144 E. Franklin St., tel. 919/929–7766) is a good general record store with lots of local music.

Chapel Hill's Archers of Loaf

CAT'S CRADLE

The best indie venue in town, Cat's Cradle is where Superchunk, Archers of Loaf, Small, Dillon Fence, Polvo, Spatula, Ben Folds Five, and other local bands made their name. The club also pulls in the top touring acts. *206 W. Franklin St., tel. 919/967 –9053.*

Durham

Tobacco-manufacturing Durham, home of Duke University, has a rich black heritage and was a popular meeting place for blues singers in the '20s and '30s. Sonny Terry, who lost each of his eyes in separate accidents five years apart, met Blind Boy Fuller while busking downtown in 1934. Before long they teamed up with the Rev. Gary Davis, who was also blind. Davis later moved to the Bronx, where he taught Ry Cooder how to play slide guitar. Blues impresario John Hammond came to Durham in 1938 looking to book Blind Boy Fuller for his Carnegie Hall Spirituals to Swing show, only to find that the guitarist was in jail for attempting to murder his wife.

Fort Bragg

Link Wray, one of the first guitarists to explore the sonic possibilities of the electric guitar, was born here as Lincoln Wray on May 2, 1930. In the '50s he polished his guitar playing while recovering from TB in the hospital. His most influential record, "Rumble," a growling number meant to evoke the violence of a razor fight, is perhaps the only instrumental ever to be banned from the radio. In 1994 Wray experienced a bit of a revival after he was included on the *Pulp Fiction* soundtrack.

Joni Mitchell appeared regularly at the Fort Bragg army base in the mid-'60s, and "Beat of Black Wings" from 1988's *Chalk Mark in a Rain Storm* tells the story of being hassled by a Vietnam veteran, "Killer Kyle," after a gig here.

Winston-Salem

The doo-wopping Five Royales came out of the Winston-Salem area in the early '50s and recorded some of the best-known R&B hits of the era for Cincinnati's King Records. Their originals include "Think" (later covered by James Brown and Aretha Franklin) and "Dedicated to the One I Love" (the Shirelles, the Mamas and the Papas).

R.E.M. recorded their first records, the single "Radio Free Europe" (1981) and the EP *Chronic Town* (1982), here at the Drive-In Studios, a facility set up by Mitch Easter, later of Let's Active, in his parents' garage. Other groups that took advantage of this most garage of garage-band studios include Chris Stamey and Pylon.

TENNESSEE

Few states can match Tennessee's influence on the shape of rock & roll. Rockabilly, soul, country, and urban blues all owe a major debt to Memphis or to Nashville or to both. Given this vibrant musical heritage, it seems almost inevitable that many of rock's early greats—Jerry Lee Lewis, Roy Orbison, and, of course, Elvis himself—cut their first tracks in the state's enormously influential studios. And then there's Jack Daniels, the whiskey, made in the hamlet of Lynchburg, that has provided the inspiration for many a gig and studio session.

Tennessee Songs

Joan Baez, "Brand New Tennessee Waltz" (1971)
Charlie Daniels Band, "Tennessee Blues" (1977)
Joe Ely, "Tennessee's Not the State I'm In" (1977)
Rosanne Cash, "Tennessee Flat Top Box" (1987)
Arrested Development, "Tennessee" (1992)
Manic Street Preachers, "Tennessee" (1992)

Hendersonville

Spread along the shores of Old Hickory Lake, Hendersonville is packed with churches and the homes of country stars. Tour buses come out regularly from Nashville, 20 miles away, so fans can drool over the enclosed compounds of Barbara Mandrell, Billy Ray Cyrus, Johnny Cash, and so on. Roy Orbison once made his home here too, but the town held tragedy for him. On June 7, 1965, his wife, Claudette, fell off her motorbike during a lakeside ride and was crushed by a truck. Then, in September of 1968, while Orbison was touring England, his two sons died in a fire at his home after playing with gasoline.

Knoxville

The hometown of the University of Tennessee is perhaps best known among music historians as the place where Hank Williams, Sr. *may* have died. On New Year's Eve, 1952, Williams was being chauffeured to a gig in Canton, Ohio. En route he fell unconscious and was taken to Knoxville's Andrew Johnson Hotel. A doctor was called, and although Williams had been drinking, two shots of morphine were administered. Hotel porters carried him back to the car at around 11 PM; by the time he reached Oak Hill,

Hank Williams, Sr., center, in healthier days

West Virginia, it was clear that country's top performer was not sleeping but dead. Country buffs still argue over whether or not Hank was already deceased by the time the car pulled into Knoxville. The hotel has since been converted into offices, housing the local education board, a TV station, and other businesses.

Lynchburg

JACK DANIELS DISTILLERY

Lynchburg—a village 70 miles southeast of Nashville, with a population of 361—is home to the quintessential rock & roll spirit: A bottle of Jack Daniels has been featured on more than a few album covers and T-shirt designs. The distillery, dating back to 1866, is the oldest in the country, but sadly, Moore County is dry, so visitors can't sample any of the famous sourmash whiskey after taking in the free hour-long tour. *Hwy. 55, tel. 615/759–6180. Open daily 8–4.*

Jim Brady/courtesy of Jack Daniels Distillery

Jack Daniels Distillery

Memphis

I MET A GIN-SOAKED BARROOM QUEEN IN MEMPHIS—THE ROLLING STONES, "HONKY TONK WOMEN"

Memphis is much more than just Elvis Presley. The only large city in the Delta region, the city stands at a natural crossroads, with the Appalachians to the east, New Orleans to the south, St. Louis and Chicago to the north, and Texas to the west. Those who passed through left the legacy of their regional music styles: blues, jazz, country, and hillbilly folk. This enviable musical heritage extends back to the turn of the century, when the Memphis music scene belonged to crude vaudeville versions of blues tunes played by makeshift ensembles known as jug bands. During the '40s the city's sound underwent a revolutionary change when an upbeat jazz influence, coupled with electrical amplification, helped create rhythm & blues.

This pioneering Memphis R&B sound in turn influenced the sound of Sun Records, responsible for, among other things, introducing Elvis Presley to the world in the '50s. Presley's hybrid of blues and country—the combination that became known as rockabilly—encouraged the likes of Jerry Lee Lewis, Roy Orbison, Johnny Cash, Charlie Rich, and Carl Perkins to come to Sun. In the early '60s, at the newly formed Stax Records across town, black and white musicians played together, despite heavy segregation. Stax artists like Wilson Pickett and Otis Redding shaped a new form of R&B—soul—and Stax became the most successful label in the South. A decade later, nearby Hi Records reaped similar kudos and sales with Al Green, *the* soul superstar of the time.

Memphis went through a rough patch in the '70s, both musically and financially, as businesses left for the suburbs and the wrecking ball flattened most of Beale Street. But since the mid-'80s, the city has been spending money. Much of downtown has been smartened up; Beale Street, with its museums and nightclubs, is thriving, even if it does resemble a giant blues theme park; Elvis Presley's Graceland draws three-quarters of a million visitors a year; and almost always a music festival of some kind, like the Blues Music Week in October, is going on. A small-but-healthy indie scene ensures that Memphis does not remain rooted in the past, and bands are lining up to use such studios as

Easley and the rejuvenated Sun. In short, the city, now a major tourist destination, is a not-to-be-missed stop for music fans.

Some Memphis Songs

Chuck Berry, "Memphis Tennessee" (1959)
Duane Eddy, "Night Train to Memphis" (1960)
Lonnie Mack, "Memphis" (1963)
Bob Dylan, "Stuck Inside of Mobile with the Memphis Blues Again" (1966)
Chuck Berry, "Back to Memphis" (1967)
King Curtis, "Memphis Soul Stew" (1967)
Muddy Waters, "Going Back to Memphis" (1967)
John Martyn, "Going Down to Memphis" (1968)
Paul Revere and the Raiders, "Going to Memphis" (1968)
Neil Diamond, "Memphis Street" (1969)
Them, "Memphis Lady" (1970)
Mott the Hoople, "All the Way from Memphis" (1973)
Paul Butterfield, "Living in Memphis" (1981)
John Fogerty, "Big Train from Memphis" (1985)
George Thorogood and the Destroyers, "Memphis Marie" (1985)
The Cult, "Memphis Hip Shake" (1987)
Marc Cohn, "Walking in Memphis" (1991)
The Pixies, "Letter to Memphis" (1991)

Beale Street and Downtown

Around the turn of the century, black workers who had moved up from the Delta to work unloading cotton off Mississippi riverboats began moving into the inexpensive townhouses along Beale Street, on the south edge of downtown. By the '20s Beale had developed into the prime black social center of the mid-South. The city's black businesses were segregated into surrounding side streets, and all manner of vaudeville theaters, clubs, juke joints, and gambling houses had sprung up. By day guitarists would busk along Beale, while at night the area swung to a sophisticated big-band kind of blues, closer in spirit to Dixieland than the Delta.

During the Depression, Beale Street's glory faded. It had a brief revival after World War II—more and more musicians from the Mississippi Delta were settling in the city or passing through on the way to St. Louis, Chicago, or other northern cities—but it was stifled in the '50s when a police crackdown on the street's renowned vice closed the clubs. The riots that followed the assassination of Dr. Martin Luther King, Jr. and the recession of the '70s saw most of the area flattened, with only a handful of venues and businesses surviving.

Recent massive reconstruction has made Beale a thriving nightlife center once again. Local opinion is divided, however: Some claim the new Beale, with its cobblestones, sandblasted facades, rebuilt "Victorian" buildings, and neat signage, is a travesty. Others point to the success of the music-theme museums and to the teeming crowds buzzing around clubs like B.B. King's and the Rum Boogie Cafe.

Jerry Lee Lewis has developed a habit of dropping in, allegedly uninvited, to Beale Street clubs to "challenge" whoever's playing to a jam. For the most part, however, the dozen or so nightclubs within this four-block stretch put on traditional urban blues and R&B for a mixture of tourists and fashionable locals. Slick and professional, the clubs also double as reasonably priced restaurants at lunchtime and early evening. For a more down-home feel, it's better to try somewhere that's *not* advertised on the tourist brochures; the **UNNAMED JOINT** below Earnestine and Hazel's Sundry Store (531 S. Main St., off Beale St.), for instance, puts on a worthy "Kickin' Saturday Live Blues" night.

Until he died in 1993, Clarence "Pops" Davis stood outside **ALFRED'S** (197 Beale St., tel. 901/525–3711) greeting patrons with a patter that went something like "W. C. Handy, he's a personal friend of mine…Elvis, he's a personal friend of mine…gimme a dollar." Gary Hardy and the Sun Studio Trio, a rock & roll covers band led by the current owner of the Sun studios, play here regularly. Since opening in 1991, **B.B. KING'S BLUES CLUB** (143 Beale St., tel. 901/524–5464) has become the street's most famous club, thanks to its proprietor. When he drops in to play the 650-seat venue, half a dozen times a year, the cover charge takes a fivefold hike from the usual $5. The club serves a menu of Cajun-style food, while the inevitable B.B. gift shop is next door.

The letters from the original STAX sign at the demolished studio (*see below*) take pride of place above the stage at the **RUM BOOGIE CAFE** (182 Beale St., tel. 901/528–0150), joined by guitars donated by Albert Collins, the Black Crowes, and others. Acts here play traditionalist R&B. Larger than most of the street's clubs, **KING'S PALACE CAFE** (162 Beale St., tel. 901/521–1851) offers up "championship gumbo" backed by blues more commercial and contemporary than what's on at the other joints.

If you ever wondered about the charms mentioned in Muddy Waters' "Hoochie Coochie Man," visit **A. SCHWAB'S DRY GOODS STORE** (163 Beale St., tel. 901/523–9782) and take a look at some John the Conqueror root—a mandrake named for the mythical figure who tore off the Devil's arm and whipped his butt with it. Virtually unchanged in appearance since opening in 1876, the oldest store on Beale claims "If you can't find it at Schwab's, you're better off without it," but that assumes you do feel a need for 99¢ Mississippi Slim Jim ties, grossly oversize clothes, and a specialty line of voodoo powders.

Courtesy of Center for Southern Folklore

B.B. King in his WDIA days

Courtesy of Center for Southern Folklore

THE BEALE STREET BLUES BOY

B.B. King (born Riley King in Itta Bena, Mississippi, in 1925) arrived in Memphis in the late '40s and soon began appearing at local amateur shows as part of the Beale Streeters, a loose gathering that included Johnny Ace, Junior Parker, and Bobby Bland. A local radio slot on WDIA soon followed, and Riley began calling himself the Beale Street

Blues Boy—B.B. for short—before cutting the guitar-flash blues records like "Three O'Clock Blues" and "Sweet Little Angel" that made his reputation. A presence in the city for over half a century, he now owns a tourist-oriented club on Beale Street.

ARCADE RESTAURANT

This stylish soul-food restaurant was the setting for numerous scenes in Jim Jarmusch's film *Mystery Train,* named for the last song Elvis recorded for Sun, in which Elvis's ghost appears before a group of tourists (one of whom is played by Joe Strummer). Opened in 1919, the Arcade is reputedly Memphis's oldest surviving eatery; it now stands on a near-desolate street just off Beale that's slowly inching its way back to life. *540 S. Main St., tel. 901/526—5757. Open daily 11—9.*

BEALE STREET BLUES MUSEUM

Based downstairs in the renovated Old Daisy Theater, one of the few Beale Street buildings that has stood here all century, this museum does a reasonable, if detached, job of telling the street's music history. There are plenty of obscure photos, vintage posters, and personal belongings, along with displays on Ethel Waters, Victoria Spivey, and other often-overlooked female blues singers. *329 Beale St., tel. 901/527—6008. Admission: $5. Open Mon.—Sat. 11—5.*

[CENTER FOR SOUTHERN FOLKLORE]

Although it deals with all aspects of Southern culture, this museum—based in what was Lansky's clothing store, where Elvis Presley got his duds throughout the '50s—provides the best in-depth background to Delta blues and rockabilly in Memphis. Special exhibitions change regularly, and the walls are always covered with archive photos, obscure record sleeves, and above-average biographies. Opened in 1989 and run on a nonprofit basis, the center also contains a gift shop selling books about blues, plus CD compilations of various regional musical styles. There's also a small performance space where septuagenarian blues pianist Mose Vinson, once a janitor at Sun Records, plays every Friday and Saturday

Mose Vinson at his piano

while enthusiastically explaining the basics of his boogie-woogie style. *130 Beale St., tel. 901/525—3655. Open Mon.—Sat. 9—5:30, Sun. 1—5:30.*

W. C. HANDY HOME

W. C. Handy's name is plastered around town with almost as much abandon as that of Elvis. Handy was the leader of one of the South's most successful black dance bands during the early part of the century and—as tourist brochures love to tell you—is commonly cited as the "Father of the Blues." All he really did, however, was take an existing sound and modify it for white ears.

Born in Alabama, Handy first heard Delta-style blues in Mississippi in 1903 and soon began incorporating elements of that sound in his music. His first big hit in this vein was 1911's "Memphis Blues," originally written as a campaign song for a local politician. Handy then opened a very successful publishing company at 392 Beale Street and wrote hit after hit, including "Beale Street Blues" and "St. Louis Blues," which, before rock came along, was the most-recorded song published in the United States. (For a while, lesser songwriters made a mint by adding the word *blues* to the title of hundreds of barely suitable songs for fashionable effect.)

This tiny shotgun shack was Handy's home between 1908 and 1912, but not on Beale Street—it originally stood a few miles south, at 659 Jeanette Place, and was transported here during Memphis's mid-'80s museum-opening craze. Inside are original furniture, photos, and sheet music, and a staff that does its best to make Handy live up to his reputation. *352 Beale St.; for info, call Heritage Tours at tel. 901/527–3427. Admission: $2. Open Mon.–Sat. 10–6, Sun. 1–5.*

MEMPHIS MUSIC HALL OF FAME

This compact museum does a fair job of explaining how Memphis became a major recording center. Dotted throughout are pictures and well-researched bios of Hall of Famers, whose ranks include Elvis Presley, Jerry Lee Lewis, Johnny Cash, Otis Redding, and Isaac Hayes. Among the mementos are a Jerry Lee Lewis piano and a Booker T organ, while Rufus Thomas's white cape and hot pants and Isaac Hayes's exotic costumes show where Prince got a lot of his ideas. Listening posts give a chance to hear some of the sounds that made Memphis famous. *97 S. 2nd St., tel. 901/525–4007. Admission: $5. Open Sun.–Thurs. 10–6, Fri.–Sat. 10–9.*

NATIONAL CIVIL RIGHTS MUSEUM

On April 4, 1968, Dr. Martin Luther King, Jr., was assassinated while standing on the balcony of this building, then the Lorraine Motel. King regularly patronized this black-owned business, as did musicians from nearby Stax Records, who would hang out by the pool when the studio's lack of air-conditioning became too unbearable. After the motel closed in the '80s, the museum was built into the framework of the building, preserving King's room, No. 306, as it was on the day he died. *450 Mulberry St., tel. 901/521–9699. Admission: $5. Open Mon. and Wed.–Sat. 10–6, Sun. 1–6.*

WHBQ RADIO

WHBQ, one of the city's key stations in the '50s, was based in the now-defunct Hotel Chisca, south of Beale. The station's best-known DJ, the manic Dewey Phillips, hosted the "Red Hot and Blue" show, essential listening for Memphis's first generation of rock & roll aspirants. On July 7, 1954, Sun Records' Sam Phillips handed Dewey (no relation) a test pressing of Elvis's first single, "That's All Right (Mama)." The DJ was so impressed he yelled, "Degawwhhh, it's a hit, it's a cotton pickin' hit!" right on air. Within minutes the switchboard was jammed, and he began playing the track over and over while desperately trying to get Elvis in for an interview. Eventually the singer was found at a local cinema and whisked into the studio.

Once Presley became a star, Dewey Phillips began calling everybody, including himself, Elvis—he'd even call up Atlantic Records VP Jerry Wexler and say, "Hi Elvis, this is Elvis." When Wexler and co-executive Ahmet Ertegun popped into the station one day in 1956 to plug records, Dewey told listeners he had a "couple of Yankee record thieves" with him. But after the show, he took the pair to meet Presley at a now-demolished club, where they unsuccessfully tried to buy out the future King's contract from Sun. Atlantic offered $30,000, which they could barely afford, but lost out to RCA, which bid an extra $10,000. Elvis didn't sing at the club that night, but Ertegun got up and did an impromptu version of Muddy Waters's "Hoochie Coochie Man," which won over a skeptical Dewey Phillips to Atlantic's cause and convinced him to play the label's New York records on WHBQ. Now based in the suburbs, the station features sports and talk, having abandoned music after DJ Rick Dees assaulted the pop world with his 1976 single, "Disco Duck." *S. Main and Linden Sts.*

East of Downtown

Roads sweep east from downtown past boarded up shops, housing projects, and empty lots before reaching smart suburban homes and flourishing strip malls. Nearer downtown are numerous former residences of Elvis Presley, most of them demolished; farther out are Ardent and the reborn Sun Records studios.

LET'S PLAY HOUSE

After moving from Tupelo in 1948, Elvis Presley, his parents, Gladys and Vernon, and grandmother Minnie May lived at several addresses in this humdrum part of town, until sufficient royalties realized the Graceland purchase in 1957.

572 POPLAR AVENUE. A once-elegant mansion converted into tiny apartments, now demolished, was the Presleys' first Memphis home. All 16 families who lived at No. 572 shared one bathroom and kitchen.

370 WASHINGTON STREET. After a year the Presleys lived here briefly in summer 1949, just a few hundred yards from their first address. It too is now demolished.

185 WINCHESTER STREET, NO. 327 LAUDERDALE COURTS. A quarter-mile west of Washington Street is the earliest surviving Elvis address in Memphis, a housing project for low-income families—Vernon had just lost his job at a local paint factory. The Presleys stayed here from September 1949 until they were evicted in January 1953, their income having been discovered to be above the allowed limit.

698 SAFARANS STREET. A Presley address for a few months in early 1953, this housing project has been torn down.

462 ALABAMA STREET. The family rented this apartment near Lauderdale Courts for $50 a month from April 1953 through fall 1954. The Alabama Street block, now replaced by a slip road, was a considerable step up from previous residences. It was while living here that Elvis wandered into Sun Records to cut a birthday record for his mother.

2414 LAMAR AVENUE. For the first time in Memphis, the Presleys were able to rent a *house,* thanks to the money coming in from Sun Records. While living here, 4 miles southeast of downtown, Elvis made his television debut (March 5, 1955) on the Louisiana Hayride. The site is now part of an industrial complex.

1414 GETWELL ROAD. From summer 1955 to May 1956, the family rented this house, now replaced by an auto-parts store. Elvis's busy touring schedule prevented him from spending much time here.

1034 AUDUBON DRIVE. Elvis bought this white three-bedroom bungalow for $40,000 *cash* in May 1956. Gladys hung out her wash to dry, much to her neighbors' disgust, though that probably wasn't as unsightly as the pink Cadillac that her son brought home that summer. The following March Elvis decided his superstar status warranted a suitable residence, and they moved to Graceland.

AMERICAN SOUND STUDIO

In the late '60s, American was one of the top studios in the country. Founded by Seymour Rosenberg, Charlie Rich's manager, and by Chips Moman, who had built the Stax studio, American got some of the South's best musicians—including Bobby Womack—to work here as session players. From November 1967 to the end of 1970, it placed 120 songs in the Top 20. Hits included Sandy Posey's "Born a Woman," James and Bobby Purify's "Shake a Tail Feather," and Dusty Springfield's *Dusty in Memphis* album. For the Box Tops' "The Letter," the biggest-selling single of 1967 and 1968, Moman's production technique was simply to tell 16-year-old singer Alex Chilton to say "aeroplane," not "airplane."

Elvis Presley came here in January 1969—after a 12-year absence from Memphis studios—to record such career-reviving material as "Suspicious Minds," "Kentucky Rain," and "In the Ghetto." During these sessions Moman complained that Elvis was singing terribly. "When I told him he was off pitch," he told *Mojo*'s Barney Hoskyns, "his whole entourage would nearly faint." Moman, who had the word *Memphis* tattooed on his right arm, briefly took American to Atlanta before going on to produce Johnny Cash and Waylon Jennings in Nashville. The studio has since been demolished and replaced by an auto-parts store. *827 Thomas St., at Chelsea St.*

ARDENT

Before this smart suburban studio moved to its current location in 1971, it shifted from one ad hoc address to another, settling in at 1457 National Avenue for five years at the end of the '60s. In those days Stax would send musicians over to Ardent when their space was booked up, which is how Isaac Hayes ended up cutting his massive-selling *Hot Buttered Soul*—often touted as the epitome of Stax's technique—at Ardent. A band, led by ex–Box Tops singer Alex Chilton, came here to record their first album; unhappy with the name they were using—Ice Water—they wandered outside, spotted the Big Star supermarket opposite (since demolished), and realized their search was over. The studio, started by Federal Express founder Fred Smith in 1971, is now run by former Big Star drummer Jody Stephens. ZZ Top's *Eliminator* (1983), the Replacements' *Pleased to Meet Me* (1987), and R.E.M.'s *Green* (1988) were all recorded here. Visitors during the '90s have included the Bar-Kays, the Gin Blossoms, Primal Scream, and locals Big Ass Truck, who have been signed by Rounder. *2000 Madison Ave., tel. 901/725–0855.*

HUMES HIGH SCHOOL

Elvis Presley attended this now run-down school from 1949 until graduating in June 1953. That April he gave his first Memphis stage appearance, singing Johnny Lair's "Keep Them Cold Icy Fingers Off of Me" at a school show. He won first prize, naturally, and for an encore did Teresa Brewer's "Till I Waltz Again with You." During Elvis Presley Memorial Week, held every August to mark the anniversary of his death, pupils take visitors on guided tours of the school, relating stories of Elvis and classmates Red and Sonny West. *659 N. Manassas St.*

SHANGRI-LA

Besides the rare singles and latest releases, this quirky record store is home to an alternative record label (the roster includes the local Grifters) and a shrine to '70s tack. You'll find such delights as a Kiss board game, Partridge Family lunchbox, and Mork from Ork radio. *1916 Madison Ave., tel. 901/274–1916. Open daily noon–7.*

[SUN RECORDS]

The studio that launched the careers of Elvis Presley, Johnny Cash, Jerry Lee Lewis, Roy Orbison, Carl Perkins, and Charlie Rich had a modest start. In January 1950, local DJ Sam Phillips opened it as the Memphis Recording Service, making most of its money by letting people cut their own discs for $4. Just about the only recording space in town, it began to be used by out-of-town record companies—L.A.'s Modern label and Chess from Chicago—for recording local blues artists, including B.B. King and Howlin' Wolf, which gave Phillips the capital to organize his own sessions. In 1951 he produced Jackie Brenston's "Rocket 88," with Ike Turner on piano, and leased the master to Chess; it topped the R&B charts, was covered by Bill Haley, and is now cited by many rock historians as the first rock & roll record.

With extra cash, Phillips started his own label, Sun, in 1952. Rufus Thomas's "Bear Cat" (a thinly disguised riposte to Willie Mae Thornton's "Hound Dog") was the label's first hit, in 1953. Then came Elvis, whose five Sun singles in 1954 and 1955 spurred Phillips to build his roster of rockabilly acts, resulting in recordings by Carl Perkins ("Blue Suede Shoes," the first record to top the pop, country, and R&B charts), Johnny Cash ("I Walk the Line"), Jerry Lee Lewis ("Whole Lotta Shakin' Goin' On"), and Roy Orbison ("Ooby Dooby").

On December 4, 1956, Elvis Presley, by then at RCA, brought a showgirl he'd met during an engagement in Vegas to have a look around the studio. Perkins was in the middle of cutting a song at the time; Lewis was on piano, and Cash was hanging out in the control room. The four buddies got talking, started jamming, and Phillips kept the tapes running. The "Million Dollar Quartet" (or trio, since Cash's performance is undetectable) became one of the most talked-about sessions of the '50s, but it was not until March 1990 that RCA was finally able to sort out the legal complexities and release the resulting double album.

Things slowed down in the latter part of the decade, not helped by Jerry Lee Lewis's marriage scandal. Phillips closed the studio in December 1959 when the lease ran out, and he moved operations

Carl Perkins, one of Sun's rockabilly stars

to the Sam Phillips Recording Service (at 639 Madison Avenue, and still operated by his sons). The original Sun space was not restored to recording until Memphis musician Gary Hardy took over in 1987. U2 cut a number of tracks for 1988's *Rattle and Hum* at the son of Sun, supervised by "Cowboy" Jack Clement, Phillips's assistant from the old days.

Recording is now done at night, and by day there are "tours" of the tiny 18-by-30-foot space. The two-track mono recorder that Phillips used is still there, as is the mike that Presley crooned into. Next door the Sun Studio Café dishes up soul food. During the '50s, when it was known as Ma Taylor's Diner, Elvis signed part of his RCA contract while chomping his way through a cheeseburger here. *706 Union Ave., tel. 901/ 521–0664.*

<hr>

ROCK & ROLL NO. 1

In the summer of 1953, Elvis Presley parked his Ford pickup truck outside Sun and paid $4 to cut a record as a birthday present for his mom. Asked by recording supervisor Marion Keisker what kind of singer he was, Elvis replied, "I sing all kinds," but admitted that he sounded a little bit hillbilly. For the disc he sang the Inkspots' "My Happiness" and "That's When Your Heartaches Begin," accompanying himself on acoustic guitar.

In one version of the events that followed—the story is mired in controversy—Keisker thought his voice was unusual and managed to get a portion of the

demo onto tape, which she played to Sam Phillips when he returned. She also made a note for herself: "Good ballad singer, hold." Phillips was impressed but said the boy needed a lot of grooming. On Friday, January 4, 1954, Elvis returned for another $4 disc, cutting "Casual Love Affair" and "I'll Never Stand in Your Way" in front of a lukewarm Phillips.

A few months later, Phillips received a demo of a song called "Without You," recorded in Nashville by an unknown black singer whom Phillips tried to contact to no avail. As a last resort, Keisker suggested Presley, whom they then called at home. Legend has it that Elvis ran the half-mile from his house at 462 Alabama Street to Sun before Phillips had hung up the phone, but the session was not a success.

Phillips persevered and arranged for Elvis to visit the 21-year-old guitarist Scotty Moore. At Moore's house they went through a selection of R&B, country, and popular stuff by Eddy Arnold, Hank Snow, and Billy Eckstine. They were joined by a neighbor, bassist Bill Black, who was impressed neither by the racket they were making nor by Elvis's greased-up hair and matching pink shirt and slacks. Black nonetheless agreed to join them at Sun for an audition, where they tried the tearjerker "I Love You Because" and the more uptempo "Trying to Get to You."

During a break Elvis grabbed his guitar and began messing around with Arthur Crudup's "That's All Right (Mama)," and soon he, Black, and Moore were jamming. Phillips was amazed and, sensing a potential hit, taped the performance. As one of the musicians pointed out in less than polite language, Elvis sounded like he was black. Not that this dissuaded Phillips, who coupled "That's All Right (Mama)" with Bill Monroe's "Blue Moon of Kentucky"—a daring combination of an R&B song and a white hillbilly number—and released it as a single. He sent a copy to Dewey Phillips at WHBQ, and Elvis had himself a hit—the first "white" rock & roll record.

Elvis's first recording studio, Sun Records

TALIESYN BALLROOM

Now the site of a Taco Bell restaurant, this spot held the venue where the Sex Pistols played the second gig of their farcical 1978 U.S. tour. They didn't quite live up to their fearsome reputation, but that didn't stop the Memphis Police Department from giving the following warning at a press conference: "Memphis is a clean city, we will not tolerate any...simulated sex on stage. They can be nude if they like. They can spit or even vomit. No laws against that, but there must be no lewd or indecent behavior." Sid Vicious was in top form, indulging in a bit of self-mutilation with a knife and boasting to a local journalist that he wanted to be like Iggy and die before he was 30, only to be informed that Iggy was both still alive and over 30. *1477 Union Ave.*

South Memphis

All roads lead to Elvis Presley Boulevard, a stretch of Highway 51 that leads in turn to Graceland. Presley's final residence and resting place is one of the true rock shrines, but the boulevard is awash with loads of businesses trying to get a cut of the nostalgia dollar. Elsewhere on the south side are the church of soul great (and now Reverend) Al Green and the empty lot that marks the site of the Stax Studio.

EATINGDRINKINGDANCINGSHOPPINGPLAYINGSLEEPING

Best of the Elvisy establishments is the **WILSON WORLD MOTEL** (3677 Elvis Presley Blvd., tel. 901/332–1000 or 800/WILSONS), across the road from Graceland, which offers the chance to get deep into the Elvis experience with rooms featuring a 24-hour Elvis Channel. You'll pay around $60 a night.

EASLEY RECORDING

In 1995 the city's premier alternative studio played host to Sonic Youth. Feeling a need to offload the band's legacy, the fellows came here toying with the idea of changing their name to Washing Machine, but used it for the album title instead. Offering some of the best rates in the city, Easley has long been popular with local acts. Big names from out of town who have recently recorded here include the Jon Spencer Blues Explosion and Pavement (studio owner Doug Easley engineered *Wowee Zowee* and played pedal steel on some tracks). *2272 Deadrick St., tel. 901/323–5407.*

FULL GOSPEL TABERNACLE

Soul fans, visiting musicians, tourists, and the actually religious drop in to this suburban church a few miles south of Graceland to catch the world's most soulful

Reverend Al Green of the Full Gospel Tabernacle

preacher, the Reverend Al Green. The former Mr. Soul got religion big time in 1977, when a girlfriend threw a pan of hot grits over him. He now tells his congregation, "Don't come here with a solemn look on your face. We're here to have church." Sunday services start at 11 AM, but as the Reverend Al is in big demand to preach around the country, he isn't here every week. He's also a popular choice for weddings—there's a two-year wait. *787 Hale Rd., off Hwy. 51, Whitehaven, tel. 901/396–9192.*

[GRACELAND]

Put simply, Graceland—tacky, sentimental, and way over the top—is irresistible. There's no typical visitor among the hordes who make their way to the home where Elvis Presley lived for 20 years and finally checked out in 1977. Members of a leather-jacketed rock band on tour making jokes about drug consumption, a Southern Baptist church party focusing on the man's god-fearing side, a tourist from some far-flung part of the planet wondering what the hell's going on, or even perhaps a truly dedicated Elvis fan—in all, around 750,000 people drop in every year. It's all part of the fun of visiting Graceland, and while the tour guides inside the house don't touch on his wilder activities, they're not entirely schmaltzy about the whole deal either.

The antebellum-style mansion was built in 1939 on what was then open farmland for the Toof newspaper family, one of whom was named Grace (hence Graceland). Elvis bought it in 1957 at age 22 for $100,000, and although he didn't spend that much time here until quitting Hollywood in 1969, he set the place up as a kind of adult playground. Friends and hangers-on—the "Memphis mafia"—would drop by for pistol-shooting sessions, games of pool, marathon TV watching, karate workouts (Elvis was an eighth-grade black belt), or

Courtesy of Graceland

Home of the King

a big dinner. Not everyone waited for an invitation: Bruce Springsteen was escorted from the premises by security guards on April 29, 1976, after jumping a fence, and Jerry Lee Lewis was arrested on November 23, 1976, when he turned up at four in the morning, waving a Derringer pistol, demanding to be let in.

The fun was all over within the year. At around 9 AM on August 16, 1977, Elvis was found dead in his bathroom from coronary arrhythmia at 42. It's not known for certain whether the king passed away on the throne or on the floor. Some 75,000 grieving fans gathered outside the house for an impromptu remembrance service, and flowers were sent to Graceland from around the world. Elvis Presley Memorial Week, held each year to mark the anniversary of his death, continues to be the busiest time of the year, followed by his birthday, January 8.

It's not possible to just walk in and buy the $9 ticket. Instead, shuttle buses depart from the mall opposite, driving past the Wall of Love—covered with tens of thousands of loving inscriptions—and through the wrought-iron gates, which have a cool design incorporating a pair of guitar-playing Elvises and a batch of musical notes. The tours make the mansion seem surprisingly small; only seven of the 19 rooms are open, and the bathroom where he died is absolutely out of bounds. On the ground floor is the Living Room, with its mirrors, stained glass, and profusion of peacocks (symbol of eternal life, and Elvis's favorite bird); next door is the Music Room, with the piano where he sang gospel songs. The tour naturally heads for the kitchen; in its heyday, it was ruled by three staff cooks, one of whom was always on duty—Elvis would wake up ready for a breakfast of burnt bacon at 4 PM and was often in the mood for a cheeseburger or a huge, deep-fried peanut-butter-and-banana sandwich (a model of which sits on the stove).

In the basement are the Pool Room and the TV Room, with its tasteful navy-and-lemon color scheme. Here Elvis would watch three programs simultaneously—an idea he got from Lyndon Johnson. The top downstairs sight, however, is the Jungle Room, which has tropical effects, woodcarvings, and a waterfall. Elvis designed it himself to rekindle memories of his favorite place, Hawaii, and it was also a home away from home for his whiskey-sipping pet chimp, Chatter. The 1976 album *Moody Blue,* his last, was recorded in the Jungle Room using a mobile recording truck that pulled up outside.

Out in the garden is the Trophy Room, formerly Elvis's game room, with rows of tall glass cabinets displaying autographed copies of his five Sun singles; his army uniform; a white, flared Las Vegas suit with a wing collar; a gold lamé suit; his gun collection; the FBI Narcotics badge he managed to scam off of Richard Nixon; and all 111 gold LPs. Tours end in the Meditation Garden, where Elvis, his parents, and his paternal grandmother, Minnie Mae Presley, are buried; more than a few tears are shed.

Directly across the boulevard is Graceland Plaza, the commercial wing of the well-marketed multimillion-dollar Elvis industry. The attractions include a car museum (with the pink jeep he used in *Fun in Acapulco*), the Sincerely Elvis mini museum (with its 22-minute video, *Walk a Mile in My Shoes*), and two jet planes (*Lisa Marie* and *Hound Dog II*). There are also a couple of '50s-style diners, along with numerous gift shops that sell a mildly disappointing array of Elvis periphera. *3764 Elvis Presley Blvd. (Hwy. 51), tel. 800/238–2000 or 901/332–3322. Admission: $17; house only, $9; individual areas, $5 each. Open daily 7:30–6 (closed Tues. Nov.–Feb.).*

The Meditation Garden

HI RECORDS/ROYAL RECORDING

The label that gave the world the sophisticated, smoochy soul of Al Green was based in this converted movie theater around the corner from Stax Records. Hi began in 1956, but it wasn't until Willie Mitchell became head of A&R in the late '60s that the label did remarkable work. Mitchell met Arkansan Al(bert) Green(e) in Midland, Texas, and asked him back to Memphis "to become a star." Using former Stax drummer Al Jackson, Jr. and three Hodges brothers—Teenie, Charles, and Leroy—on guitar, organ, and bass, Mitchell cultivated an intense moody sound. Described as "deep soul," the sound was perfected on Green's series of million-sellers: "Let's Stay Together," "I'm Still in Love with You," "Tired of Being Alone," and so on. Hi closed in 1977, but the studio, now known as Royal Recording, is still open and run by Mitchell. Recent success has come from Scottish teeny-poppers Wet Wet Wet, blues artist Johnny Mayo, Syl Johnson, Krystof (the Polish Elvis), and rappers 201. *1320 S. Lauderdale St., tel. 901/774−7720.*

[STAX RECORDS]

In the '60s and early '70s Stax defined the sound of Southern soul with a catalog that featured Wilson Pickett, Isaac Hayes, Sam and Dave, and Booker T. and the MG's, plus Otis Redding on its Volt subsidiary.

Courtesy of Stax/Fantasy, Inc.

Headquarters was a disused movie theater, the Capitol, in a rough neighborhood about a mile south of Beale Street. Owners Jim Stewart ("ST") and sister Estelle Axton ("AX") brought in guitarist Chips Moman to rebuild the place. He ripped out the seats, built a control room on the stage, hung home-made drapes on the walls to help the acoustics, placed an echo chamber in the toilets, and began developing the Stax sound. The candy stand in the lobby was converted into a record store, giving the label a doorstep indicator of public tastes. When work was finished, they emblazoned the cinema awning with the title SOULSVILLE U.S.A., a Southern retort to the HITSVILLE U.S.A. banner that hung outside Motown's studio in Detroit.

Stax began developing its sound around a tightly knit mixed-race house band, the Mar-Keys, who later developed into the MG's (Memphis Group), featuring Booker T. Jones on organ, with Steve Cropper on guitar, Donald "Duck" Dunn on bass, and drummer Al Jackson, Jr. In 1965 the label found its

The Stax marquee

definitive sound—punchy horns, tight rhythms, suggestive lyrics—with Wilson Pickett's "In the Midnight Hour," Sam and Dave's "Hold On, I'm Comin'," and Otis Redding's *Otis Blue* album, cut in 24 hours that July. More standards poured out over the next few years, including Eddie Floyd's "Knock on Wood" and Redding's "Sittin' on the Dock of the Bay," recorded three days before he died, in a plane crash on December 10, 1967.

The following April, Dr. Martin Luther King, Jr. was assassinated at the nearby Lorraine Motel, where many Stax musicians stayed when in town. During the subsequent riots, the

Stax studio was one of the places where protestors grouped, and a cordon of Memphis's finest surrounded the building after rumors that white musicians such as Dunn and Cropper were going to be attacked by their black coworkers. Nevertheless, the hits continued, Isaac Hayes's triple-platinum *Hot Buttered Soul* and *Shaft* among them.

In the early '70s, success went to Stax's head. Bizarre signing decisions were made, and in January 1976 the label went bust. Berkeley, California–based Fantasy Records, home of the Stax-influenced Creedence Clearwater Revival, bought the rights to the back catalog and kept the Memphis sound alive for a new generation of soul fans, but in the '80s Soulsville U.S.A. was torn down. The site is now overgrown with weeds, a commemorative plaque the only reminder of the its past. Somewhere in the city, however, some of the studio's fittings are in storage, and they may eventually find a home in one of Memphis's ever-growing number of museums, visitor centers, and parks. *926 E. McLemore Ave.*

Nashville

There's thirteen hundred and fifty-two guitar pickers in Nashville—Lovin' Spoonful, "Nashville Cats"

Nashville loves to call itself "Music City U.S.A." and backs the claim up by an impressive statistic: There are more businesses connected with the music industry—publishers, managers, agents, attorneys, studios, and record companies, not to mention souvenir shops—here than in any other U.S. city, Los Angeles and New York included. The obvious disclaimer, however, is that the vast majority of these concerns are devoted exclusively to country.

Indeed, neither country music nor Nashville, for that matter, has been the same since the evening in 1927 when George Hay declared on Nashville's WSM station: "For the past hour we have been listening to music taken largely from the grand opera, but from now on we will present the *Grand Ole Opry.*" That was the cue for the start of America's longest-running country-music program and the origin of a multimillion-dollar empire that now comprises a record label, a TNN cable-television station, an ultraluxury hotel, and more.

The Nashville music business really got going during the postwar prosperity of the '50s, when the city emerged as the logical regional base for the music industry. Though its location was handy for tapping the hillbilly talent of the Appalachians, Nashville wasn't then as country-oriented as it is now. The Excello label recorded blues artists like Slim Harpo (the Stones covered his "I'm a King Bee," and the Yardbirds did "Got Love If You Want It"), and WLAC's 50,000-watt transmitter broadcast R&B and rockabilly on an evening show that could be picked up as far away as New York and even Iceland.

The country-music establishment soon muscled rock off the regional airwaves, however, and with a few notable exceptions (Dylan's *John Wesley Harding*, Neil Young's *Harvest*), much of the cross-fertilization between rock and country has taken place elsewhere—in L.A., Austin, or farther afield. Today Nashville's rock output remains negligible, although local band Lambchop's fusion of country and rock is well-regarded, and the loud sounds of Today Is the Day got that group signed to Amphetimine Reptile.

All this is not to say the rock fan can't have a good time in Nashville: The city may have siphoned off its worst elements to Branson, but nowhere is music as blatantly commercialized, mythologized, or folksified as here. You can play at a country & western amusement park (Opryland USA), stay at themed hotels, shop trashy stores that double as "museums," and tour neighborhoods where the stars reside. Promoters cash in with various festivals like the June "Fan Fair," the major event of the year, when country lovers get a chance to meet their idols. There are even a few significant rock & roll landmarks.

Nine About Nashville

Everly Brothers, "Nashville Blues" (1960)
Duane Eddy, "Nashville Stomp" (1963)
Lovin' Spoonful, "Nashville Cats" (1966)
The Byrds, "Nashville West" (1969)
Bob Dylan, "Nashville Skyline Rag" (1969)
Joan Baez, "Outside the Nashville Limits" (1971)
Charlie Daniels Band, "Nashville Moon" (1982)
Liz Phair, "Nashville" (1994)
Steve Earle, "South Nashville Blues" (1996)

Downtown

Broadway, marking the south end of downtown, holds most of the "authentic" honky-tonk bars—maybe a bit too authentic for those who don't fit the good ole boy image. Anecdote-laden tours of all the main music sites are widely available; if such an activity is tempting, a do-it-yourself tour is marked out by a trail of green paint on the sidewalk—maps are available from the city's visitor center.

EATING DRINKING DANCING SHOPPING PLAYING SLEEPING

The most famous Broadway bar of all (and the most sanitized—there's a souvenir stall at the rear) is **TOOTSIE'S ORCHID LOUNGE** (422 Broadway, tel. 615/726−0463), where every inch of wall is covered by photos of the Opry stars who came here to drink and then drink some more when the show was based across the street in the Ryman Auditorium. In 1996 hot rockabilly band BR5−49 completed a 36-month residency at **ROBERT'S WESTERN WORLD** (416 Broadway, tel. 615/256−7937), a former clothing store; they only made a few bucks and tips but still named their acclaimed 1996 mini-album *Live from Robert's*. A few doors away is one of the city's most popular rock nightspots, the **ACE OF CLUBS−THE DISTRICT** (114 2nd Ave. S, tel. 615/254−ACES).

Tootsie's Orchid Lounge

MAXWELL HOUSE HOTEL

This grand old hotel on the northern fringes of downtown provided the name for the coffee brand. It's also where Sean Penn proposed to Madonna, and the couple often stayed here while Penn was in Tennessee shooting *At Close Range*. *2025 Metro Center Blvd., tel. 615/259−4343 or 800/457−4460. Rooms: $130 and up.*

[RYMAN AUDITORIUM]

The Ryman was built as a tabernacle in 1892, and its fittings have barely been altered since: The gallery and wooden pews are intact, and a reverential air still permeates the joint. The *Grand Ole Opry* show moved here in 1943 and stayed until 1974, when it moved to larger, custom-built quarters in the Opryland complex, 5 miles north of town. During those three decades, the Opry managed to rack up a handful of rock milestones amid all the country.

Elvis Presley turned up for his Opry debut on October 2, 1954, worried that bluegrass star Bill Monroe would be offended by his rocking version of "Blue Moon of Kentucky." Monroe assured Elvis that it was fine, but Opry officials weren't so pleased—one told Presley he should go back to driving a truck. Elvis never played the Opry again.

In March 1968 the Byrds, who earlier that year had recruited Gram Parsons and started the West Coast country-rock movement in the process, were given a two-song slot after much lobbying by their label, Columbia. The crowd wasn't used to longhairs on their hallowed stage but seemed pleased enough with the band's version of Merle Haggard's "Sing Me Back Home." The Parsons-written "Hickory Wind" also went

Ryman Auditorium, former home of the Grand Ole Opry

down well enough, but Opry management, which ran a very tight ship, got really pissed because the (quite stoned) Byrds had reneged on an agreement to perform only country covers. Neither the Byrds nor their offshoot bands were ever invited back. However, in May 1969, the Opry was pleased to welcome Bob Dylan for an ABC special with Johnny Cash.

Three years later, Cash's contemporary, Jerry Lee Lewis, made his debut on the show under the strict proviso that there was to be "no rock & roll and no cussin'." Lewis behaved himself for the first part of the set but then launched into "Great Balls of Fire," "Whole Lotta Shakin' Goin' On," and "Good Golly Miss Molly" before announcing, "I'm a rock & rolling, country & western, rhythm & blues—singing *motherfucker!*"

After the 1974 move, the Ryman lay silent for two decades before reopening for country musicals and concerts. During the day it is still open for tours, although the displays of memorabilia—some Johnny Cash gold discs and faded photos of Opry stars—are pretty threadbare. *116 Fifth Ave., tel. 615/254−1445. Admission: $5. Open daily 8:30−4.*

Music Row and Around

Home to Nashville's music industry, Music Row lies a mile or so southwest of downtown on the other side of busy Highway 40. With the kitsch Opryland complex, this really is Country Fan Central. There's nowhere to park, and the walk isn't too appealing, but the blue-route trolley bus, usually packed with tourists ready to offload the contents of their billfold, will take you there.

There are really two very different music rows. The first spreads out for a few blocks around 16th Avenue South (Music Square East) and 17th Avenue South (Music Square West) and is the industry hub, with such major labels as Decca, RCA, Columbia, MCA, and EMI represented. The Country Music Hall of Fame is here as well. Despite the tales of peripatetic wannabes carting their demos from one record-company office to another, the area, lined with trees and villas, is surprisingly quiet.

Not so the other music row, just a block or two away on Demonbreun Street. This is where the fans come to shop, but the stores are called "museums" and charge admission to see displays of country stars' castoffs. Often more floor space is devoted to gift shops—these bits are free to get into, and more fun anyway—which can be just the place to pick up that hard-to-find Barbara Mandrell pillowcase, Randy Travis lighter, or Don Gibson pen holder.

Time's better spent a little farther north, in the labyrinthine **GREAT ESCAPE** (1925 Broadway, tel. 615/327–0646), where bin after bin of nicely priced vinyl makes for one of the best secondhand rock record stores in the nation. A few hundred yards from here is Elliston Place, Nashville's studenty-cum-slightly-bohemian enclave, with some decent stores and noncountry bars.

BLUEBIRD CAFE

Featured in River Phoenix's final movie, *The Thing Called Love,* this homey little club, 4 miles south of Music Row, has for years been where younger country artists come to attract A&R attention. Garth Brooks was signed to MCA after a stint here. In the pre-cover-charge part of the evening, names are drawn for a chance to do one number; a good reaction from the crowd guarantees a slightly better chance of making it in the competitive world of country. For the most part, however, the Bluebird stays away from the retro-rhinestone and big-hat acts, often presenting country rock and the likes of Jimmie Dale Gilmore, Mose Allison, and Janis Ian, who braved the city of 700 churches by openly discussing her homosexuality at a 1994 gig here. The occasional acoustic rock act also pops up here now and again. *4104 Hillsboro Rd., at 21st Ave. S, tel. 615/383–1461. Small cover after 9, free Sun.*

COLUMBIA STUDIO/SONY

The high-tech glass-and-steel slabs of Columbia/Sony's Nashville headquarters enclose the studio space where Gene Vincent's "Be Bop A Lula," Johnny Burnette's "Train Kept A-Rollin" (Led Zeppelin's early signature tune), most of Bob Dylan's late-'60s albums, and the *Almost Blue* country-covers LP by Elvis Costello were recorded.

Producer Owen Bradley built the studio in the early '50s, and it was known as Bradley's Quonset Hut until Columbia bought him out in 1962. Four years later, Dylan, in the middle of his acid-rock phase, arrived to make *Blonde on Blonde.* He dropped the musicians he had been working with (who later reemerged as the Band) and brought in Nashville session players. For the album's opener, "Rainy Day Women #12 & 35," Dylan wanted the sound of a rough-and-ready brass band, so he got everyone to exchange instruments and play on their back, under the table, or in other unorthodox positions. Near the end of the sessions, Dylan, searching for an epic finale, sat up all night in an amphetamine frenzy writing "Sad Eyed Lady of the Lowlands" in the studio—not, as he later claimed on *Desire,* at New York's Chelsea Hotel. One studio regular not credited on the album sleeve was janitor Kris Kristofferson, who emptied the ashtrays.

The Byrds, with Gram Parsons now in the band, came to Columbia in spring 1968 to start off *Sweetheart of the Rodeo.* With its fusion of regional styles, it would later be seen as one of the most innovative albums of the decade, even though it was the Byrds' least commercially successful work to date. It was also beset with production problems. Parsons's record company objected to his presence on the album and forced the erasure of his lead vocals, which were redone by Roger McGuinn and Chris Hillman.

Dylan was back at Columbia for his 1969 *Nashville Skyline* album, teaming up with Johnny Cash; the two had become friends after Cash wrote to *Sing Out!* magazine defending Dylan from the folkies who condemned him for going electric. They recorded several songs, but only one—"Girl from the North Country"—made it onto the album. Their "One Too Many Morn-

He walks the line

ings" was included in the documentary film *Johnny Cash, the Man and His Music.* Cash recorded here for Columbia for nearly 30 years, until 1986, when he was unexpectedly dumped from the label. *34 Music Sq. E, tel. 615/742–4321.*

COUNTRY MUSIC HALL OF FAME

This rambling but rather antiseptic museum is devoted to the story of country, from the Grand Ole Opry's early years to today's multimillion-dollar business. It's packed with biographies, costumes, videos, and movie clips of stars from Bob Wills, the Texan "King of Western Swing" in the '30s, to Garth Brooks. Much is made of Elvis Presley—the museum's most sought-out exhibit is his Cadillac, which opens to reveal a fridge, a shoe polisher, a TV, a record player, and a 24-karat gold piano—even though Nashville's country-music hierarchy conspired to ban him from the country charts up to 1971. Otherwise, country rock is poorly served. Check out displays of Gibson guitars, Gram Parsons's 1963 00-21 Martin guitar, a blue-sequined Manuel stage jacket that belonged to Chris Hillman, and the guitar and suit Steve Earle wore on the cover of *Guitar Town. Division St., 4 Music Sq. E, tel. 615/256–1639 or 800/816–7652. Admission: $8 (includes entry to RCA Studio B). Open daily 9–5.*

EXIT/IN

In the late '70s, George Jones developed a jones for cocaine and alcohol that would reportedly have put many of his L.A. rock contemporaries to shame. When his wife threw his car keys into a lake to keep him from driving off for a drink, Jones rode a lawnmower 20 miles to the nearest bar. This kind of behavior wasn't doing much for his career, and friends rallied round to get him back into the swing of things. Everything was arranged for a grand comeback at the Exit/In: Friends, industry movers, and media were out in force, but Jones wasn't together enough to finish the gig. "My friend Donald Duck is going to take over this show," he told the audience, "because Donald Duck can do what George Jones can't." Jones then sang some of his hits in a Donald Duck voice. The Exit/In still stands in the middle of Elliston Place, a very un-Nashvillean stretch of Bohemia, and puts on blues, rock, reggae, and college-circuit indie bands. *2208 Elliston Pl., tel. 615/321–4400.*

RCA STUDIO B

RCA Studio B, Nashville's oldest surviving studio, is now included in the price of a visit to the Country Music Hall of Fame, but it could easily be a nominee for rock's hall: The Everly Brothers recorded "Cathy's Clown" here, Roy Orbison did "Only the Lonely," and Elvis Presley cut "Mess of Blues." Hundreds of other classics of early rock and country, such as Dolly Parton's "Jolene," were also done here. Although no recording has taken place since 1977, plans are afoot to bring the facility back, as well as to make the current tours—which consist of a short video and a shuffle through some of the main rooms—more exciting. *Roy Acuff Pl., Music Sq. W, tel. 615/242–5167.*

Pigeon Forge

What was not so long ago a sleepy backwoods town is now a 5-mile-long strip crammed with tourists, thanks to hundreds of factory-outlet stores and Dolly Parton. Born in 1946 in the nearby rural wilderness of Locust Ridge, she became a child star by playing at various local venues and, by the age of 13, on the *Grand Ole Opry*. The day after she graduated from Sevier County High School (which has a Dolly statue out front), in the adjacent town of Sevierville, she headed for Nashville. She came back in 1985 to open a hometown commercial venture.

DOLLYWOOD

Dollywood is pure Appalachian country corn, a theme park featuring gift shops, fairground rides, gardens, craft stores, and a 5-mile trip on the *Dollywood Express* steam train. Merle Haggard, Tammy Wynette, Jerry Lee Lewis, and Carl Perkins played here for the park's 10th-birthday celebrations in summer 1995, but for the most part the live-music areas are graced by several of Parton's 11 siblings and countless cousins. The "world's only" Dolly Parton Museum is here, along with a church where she has filmed Christmas specials on the rare occasions she gets time to inspect her investment firsthand. *Dollywood La., off U.S. 441, tel. 800/365–5996. Admission: $24. Open daily 10–6.*

J.R. Rayboum/courtesy of Dollywood, Pigeon Forge, Tenn.

Dolly Parton

TEXAS

From the earliest days of rock & roll to today's alternative charts, from Buddy Holly and Roy Orbison to the Jesus Lizard and Butthole Surfers, Texas has done its own thing. Even a partial list of Texas musicians points to the diverse musical styles the state has produced. A sophisticated blues-guitar style was pioneered by T-Bone Walker (born in Linden in 1910), one of an acclaimed a line of Texas blues greats that encompasses Blind Lemon Jefferson, Clarence "Gatemouth" Brown (and his cousin, James "Widemouth" Brown), Albert Collins, Lightnin' Hopkins, Freddie King, and Johnny Guitar Watson.

Pat Graham

The Texas sound was carried on in the '60s by Johnny Winter, and the following decade by the Fabulous Thunderbirds and Stevie Ray Vaughan. Other celebrated Texans include Janis Joplin, Roky Erickson, Sly Stone, and Barry White, and then there's the Tex-Mex genre headed by Flaco Jiminez, Freddy Fender, and Doug Sahm (ex–Sir Douglas Quintet).

Rock landmarks are strewn throughout the state. Buddy Holly fans have made his hometown of Lubbock a place of pilgrimage. The state capital, Austin, believes it has the best live-music scene in the world and does in fact have something to suit everyone's

Jesus Lizard

taste—especially if it runs to hard-edged country or guitar bands. Austin also hosts the annual South by Southwest music festival, one of the country's best.

Ten for Texas

Electric Flag, "Texas" (1968)
Elton John, "Texan Love Song" (1972)
Charlie Daniels Band, "Sweetwater Texas" (1976)
Lynyrd Skynyrd, "T for Texas" (1976)
Joe Ely, "West Texas Waltz" (1978)

Alex Chilton, "Waltz Across Texas" (1980)	
Gun Club, "Texas Serenade" (1982)	
Ry Cooder, "Paris, Texas" (1985)	
Nanci Griffith, "Lone Star State of Mind" (1987)	
Michelle Shocked, "Memories of East Texas" (1988)	

Amarillo

CADILLAC RANCH

Standing out like some strange mirage by the side of the interstate, 10 Cadillacs from the late '40s to 1963 are buried in chronological order, tail fins up, in a field off the old Route 66. This oddball sight, embedded in land owned by an offbeat helium millionaire, inspired the Bruce Springsteen song "Cadillac Ranch" on *The River*. *10 mi W off I–40.*

Austin

The state capital bills itself as the "Live Music Capital of the World," a lofty statement for a Texas hill country city of just half a million. The genesis of this claim dates from the early '60s, when the hootenanny scene at Threadgill's beer joint was joined by Janis Joplin and other students from the University of Texas, and several folk and roots clubs opened around town. When Joplin and future Avalon Ballroom owner Chet Helms both left for San Francisco in the mid '60s, they forged a strong musical bond between the two cities, and in 1967 some Austin freaks opened their own psychedelic ballroom, the Vulcan Gas Company, which copied the West Coast formula of light shows, poster art, and much acid. The celebrated Armadillo World Headquarters, opening in 1970 and surviving for the rest of the decade, took up the countercultural mantle after the Vulcan's hippie economics failed.

In the '70s Austin also became the focus for a new breed of country-rock crossover artists (invariably described as "outlaw country" or "cosmic cowboy" music), led by disillusioned Nashville songwriters Willie Nelson, Jerry Jeff Walker, and Michael Martin Murphy. They were joined mid-decade by the Lubbock contingent of Joe Ely, Butch Hancock, and

Bruce Dye/Trance Syndicate Records

Ed Hall

Jimmie Dale Gilmore, all of whom still keep a high profile in the city. Antone's, a still-thriving blues club, opened and mounted as house bands the revivalist Fabulous Thunderbirds and the Cobras (featuring Stevie Ray Vaughan).

In the late '70s University of Texas students started to make their mark around the punk scene at Raul's, and bands like the Violators and the Big Boys achieved regional recognition. As the '80s progressed, the focus of young Austin bands shifted and was dubbed (by disgruntled punks) the "New Sincerity" movement. Meanwhile, an underground culture was developing, and by the early '90s Austin's laidback twentysomething lifestyle served as the premise for a big-screen indie hit, Richard Linklater's 1991 film *Slacker*.

With a music scene bolstered by the PBS television show *Austin City Limits* and the South by Southwest festival, Austin has more than 50 active venues, many of which clump together on the East 6th Street strip downtown. The eclectic scene produces hundreds of bands in genres ranging from tejano to psychedelic noise. Keep an eye out for country singers Wayne Hancock and Toni Price, singer-songwriter Lucinda Williams, and bands like Starfish, Ed Hall, and Sixteen Deluxe.

SOUTH BY SOUTHWEST

What started in March 1987 as a spinoff of New York's now-defunct New Music Seminar has developed into perhaps the most important get-together on the music-industry calendar. Even though the South by Southwest festival gets bigger every year—on its 10th anniversary, in 1996, it featured 600 acts on 40 stages over four nights—it still aims to satisfy both fans and industry bigwigs. SXSW (as it's usually called) maintains its focus on unsigned bands and caters to industry newcomers through its how-to seminars. Around 40% of the bands come from the region, although past festivals have helped launch such out-of-towners as Green Day, Veruca Salt, Lisa Loeb, and the Gin Blossoms. SXSW also showcases big names (Willie Nelson, Johnny Cash, Iggy Pop, Jello Biafra) and introduces international acts like the U.K.'s Bush, Bettie Serveert of the Netherlands, Ireland's Saw Doctors, and Russia's Limpopo.

SXSW takes place in mid-March. Admission to all gigs and seminars costs around $200 if you register about six months before; the walkup rate is double that. The real bargain is a wristband (around $40) that provides entry to all gigs. The event has been so successful that spinoffs have sprung up in Portland, Oregon (North by Northwest) and Toronto (North by Northeast); Austin now also hosts a SXSW Film Festival and a SXSW Multimedia Festival, both around the same time as the music bash. For more info contact SXSW HEADQUARTERS (tel. 512/467–7979) or check it out online at http://sxsw.com/sxsw.

Around Downtown

Heralded in some quarters as the ultimate live-music experience, the East 6th Street strip is, in reality, overly commercial and boozy, with shots bars and discos coming and going all the time. Although Steamboat 1874 and the excellent Emo's (*see both below*) are certainly worth your time, it's best not to limit yourself exclusively to this street—many other great venues are scattered throughout downtown and the rest of the city.

EATING DRINKING DANCING SHOPPING PLAYING SLEEPING

The **AUSTIN MUSIC HALL** (208 Nueces St., at 3rd St., tel. 512/263–4146), the city's main midsize venue, occupies a likable '30s Art Deco building; since 1994, it's hosted everyone from Dylan to the Offspring. The **ELECTRIC LOUNGE** (302 Bowie St., tel. 512/476–FUSE) offers a wide range of acts, from psychedelia to spoken word and performance art. After it burned down in 1993, the place was kept going in a tent while rebuilding in order to satisfy the regulars.

ARMADILLO WORLD HEADQUARTERS (AWHQ)

It's coming up on two decades since Austin's most celebrated club closed, but Armadillo logos today remain behind many bar counters, and you can still buy the T-shirts at Threadgill's. Started in July 1970 in an old armory at the back of an ice rink, the club acquired its name from a creature drawn on the wall by a local artist, Jim Franklin, just before

Self at the Electric Lounge

it opened. The armadillo continued to pop up on concert posters (one getting it on with the state capitol, another smoking a massive joint) and on murals inside the club (appearing out of the blood-splattered chest of Freddie King, who cut a live album here). Local freaks became so attached to the 'dillo that they launched a campaign to get the university football team to change its name to the Armadillos from the less-inspired Longhorns.

The AWHQ picked up from where the pioneering Vulcan Gas Company (*see below*) left off, but was better run and had a beer licence to help make up for losses at the door. What really made the 1,500-person club stand out from others in the city—and indeed the country—was the sheer diversity of acts. Ballet and boogie rock might show up on the same bill, alongside touring artists as different as Ravi Shankar, Earl Scruggs, and Bruce Springsteen. Other regular visitors were Commander Cody and His Lost Planet Airmen, who did a live album here, and Asleep at the Wheel, who relocated to Austin from California mainly because they loved playing this boozy venue so much. As co-owner Eddie Wilson says, "Hell, we wanted string quartets in [even if] it was bizarre to see grannies and bikers in the same hall on the same night." (Wilson was a regular MC. His finest moment came in 1972 when a crowd's undemonstrative response to his announcement of an upcoming gig by Willie Nelson provoked him to retort, "Hell, he's just the Bob Dylan of country music, you hippie assholes.")

With some clever PR, the Armadillo came to be seen as a kind of countercultural laboratory at work in the center of Texas, but by the mid-'70s a clutch of new clubs that could operate on smaller profit margins began to provide competition. The big names of progressive country had moved on, and by the late '70s new scenes were developing, most notably punk. The Armadillo did begin to book new-wave bands—Elvis Costello, the Ramones—but became too unprofitable and closed on New Year's Eve 1980, with a bill featuring Austin hillbilly icon Kenneth Threadgill. The next day, Eddie Wilson reopened Threadgill's restaurant (*see below*). *525½ Barton Springs Rd.*

DRISKILL HOTEL

This grand downtown hotel, built in 1876 by a Victorian cotton baron, is a favorite watering hole of Kinky "Big Dick" Friedman. Friedman made his name in the mid-'70s leading a band called the Texas Jewboys, which was known for such songs as "They Ain't Making Jews Like Jesus Anymore." He recently eased off recording to write whodunits about a Texas detective who lives in Greenwich Village and is called...Kinky Friedman.

The **TEXAS WALK OF STARS**—more than 60 stars embedded in the sidewalk along East 6th and Trinity streets in tribute to famous Texans—starts at the Driskill, and it's here that you'll find most of the musical honorees, including Willie Nelson, Janis Joplin, Kenneth Threadgill, and Bob Wills. Buddy Holly is farther down Trinity Street alongside L.B.J., George Foreman, Larry Hagman, Joan Crawford, and Steve Martin.

L7's Donita Sparks surfs the crowd at Emo's

During SXSW the large Brazos Street stage is erected next to the front door of the hotel, making the Driskill the best place—though not the quietest—to stay during the festival. It's nearly always the first hotel to get booked up. The evening shows are free, and more than 10,000 have squeezed onto the block to see such headliners as Matthew Sweet and Iggy Pop. *604 Brazos St., at E. 6th St., tel. 512/474–5911. Rooms: $150–$200.*

EMO'S

Since May 1992 Eric "Emo" Hartman's club has provided the 6th Street area with a first-class alternative venue. Cover is just $2 even for the likes of the Afghan Whigs, Urge Overkill, and Throwing Muses, and pints of Sam Adams go for $1.50. The formula seems to please the clientele, seemingly a nightly casting call for *Slacker.* The club has two stages; the main one bears a mural of such famous Texan ne'er-do-wells as David Koresh, Lee Harvey Oswald, and Charles Whitman. Besides touring indie bands, Emo's presents new Austin groups like Gomez, Noodle, Jesus Christ Superfly, Sincola, and Chain Drive. Emo's hit the headlines during SXSW 1994 when Ric Rubin's American Recordings booked new signee Johnny Cash to play a showcase here. *603 Red River St., tel. 477–EGOS.*

LA ZONA ROSA

This kitschy downtown venue—think loud murals and the name spelled out in car hub-caps on a chain-link fence outside—specializes in tejano music and singer-songwriters. Some of the big local names to have appeared here are Lucinda Williams, Jimmie Dale Gilmore, and Sarah Elizabeth Campbell. Sundays there's a gospel brunch; Tuesday is Bummer Night, when local songwriters compete to come up with the saddest and/or cheesiest song. *4th and Rio Grande Sts., tel. 512/472–9075.*

LIBERTY LUNCH

In 1976 a rudimentary space that had in previous lives been a lumberyard and a restaurant began presenting live music. For years the club was in limbo, its lot earmarked for new municipal offices, and not until 1993 were the owners able to remodel it into a cavernous space that now holds 1,000, with roll-up walls that allow fans to see bands in a patio setting in summer. Although the emphasis is on alternative touring bands, virtually

Chavez at Liberty Lunch during SXSW

everyone has played here, from Dolly Parton and Nirvana to Joe Ely and Bjork. Ian Moore, Starfish, and many other locals also got a start here. *405 W. 2nd St., tel. 512/477–0461.*

LUBBOCK OR LEAVE IT

Butch Hancock, who founded the Flatlanders with Joe Ely and Jimmie Dale Gilmore in Lubbock around 1970, owns this friendly little downtown store. The influential country band made only one record, *More a Legend Than a Band,* released in 1972 as an 8-track only, and then Hancock moved to Austin. He has continued to perform and write some notable songs; "Tennessee's Not the State I'm In" and "She Never Spoke Spanish to Me" appeared on Ely's debut solo album in 1977. Soon after, Hancock set up his own Rainlight label, but to date his albums—including the *Live in Australia* co-effort with Gilmore—have achieved more critical acclaim than commercial success.

Lubbock or Leave It stocks CDs and tapes and West Texas photography, posters, jewelry, and barbecue sauces. There's also a gallery of Hancock's landscape paintings (he gave up live performance to concentrate on art in the early '80s), and to the rear is a performance space where Hancock usually gets together some buddies during SXSW. *406 Brazos St., tel. 512/478–1688. Open Mon. 10–4, Tues.–Fri. 11–6, Sat. noon–6.*

STEAMBOAT 1874

The longest-running rock club on the carpetbagging 6th Street strip has a strong reputation for indie and blues acts, as exemplified by resident band Mr. Rocket Baby. Other locals to have played this pleasant bar space include the Arc Angels, Six Is Nine, Little Sister, and Radio Thieves. One of the big hits during SXSW 1995 was a gig here by Presidents of the United States of America (or POT USA, as they get called down here). *403 E. 6th St., tel. 512/478–2913.*

STEVIE RAY VAUGHAN STATUE

R&B boogie-rock guitarist Stevie Ray Vaughan made his name in the mid-'70s playing at Antone's and other Austin clubs with the Nightcrawlers and the Cobras. Killed in a 1990 helicopter accident, he is commemorated by a life-size statue in Shoreline Park, across Town Lake from downtown and close to the First Street Bridge. During summer there are frequent outdoor music events in the surrounding park, called Auditorium Shores. *Off Riverside Dr. at S. 1st St.*

VULCAN GAS COMPANY

By 1967 California's influence was grabbing hold of the Austin rock scene, and a collective of sorts hastily opened this downtown venue, a primitive place with few amenities other than a great psychedelic light show. It was never able to get a beer license, although, with hallucinogens and marijuana sold openly, this wasn't an issue for many gig goers. The 13th Floor Elevators performed regularly; so did Johnny Winter, who came to national attention and a Columbia contract thanks to a *Rolling Stone* review of a gig here. The club lasted less than three years, however, largely as a result of the absence of bar takings and a campaign by the local establishment and press, who didn't like the sight of drug-addled hippies wandering around downtown. *316 Congress Ave.*

The Drag

The Drag—the stretch of Guadalupe Street that runs along the west mall of the University of Texas between 21st and 26th streets—is dominated by bookshops, fast-food emporia, and other receptacles of student dollars, as well as trinket stalls and a gaggle of panhandlers. Richard Linklater used the area as a setting for many scenes in *Slacker*.

EATINGDRINKINGDANCINGSHOPPINGPLAYINGSLEEPING

INNER SANCTUM (504 W. 24th St., tel. 512/472−9459) was the first place in the city to stock punk records, and in the late '70s it hosted record-launch parties for many of the bands that came out of the scene at Raul's (*see below*). These days, however, the best source for new and alternative sounds is **SOUND EXCHANGE** (21st and Guadalupe Sts., tel. 512/476−2274), which has held events for the Butthole Surfers, the Skatenigs, Sixteen Deluxe, and many others in recent years. There's also a big branch of **TOWER** (2402 Guadalupe St., tel. 512/478−5711), with a good selection of CDs by local artists. Farther along is **HALF PRICE BOOKS, RECORDS, AND MAGS** (3110 Guadalupe St., tel. 512/451−4463), where the J.F.K. conspiracy scene from *Slacker* was filmed.

ANTONE'S

What's often cited in blues circles as the best club in the South opened in July 1975 at 141 East 6th Street with a five-night stand by Clinton Chenier. Muddy Waters, Willie Dixon, and Albert King came soon after. Resident bands included the Cobras, featuring Paul Ray and Stevie Ray Vaughan, and the Fabulous Thunderbirds, whose Jimmie Vaughan still plays here regularly.

This big log cabin is the third location (there was a place downtown at the turn of the '80s, but high rents forced the club out), and it's nothing fancy inside. Weekends usually see big-name blues acts play, including local Angela Strehli, while country, zydeco, and other roots music is represented during the week. Across the street is **ANTONE'S RECORD STORE** (2928 Guadalupe St., tel. 512/322−0660), which stocks recordings by the club's three labels (specializing in blues, country, or Texas rock). *2915 Guadalupe St., tel. 512/474−5314, http://www.antones.com.*

THE HOLE IN THE WALL

This venue puts on mostly new regional guitar bands, but its unpretentious atmosphere drags in big names from time to time, such as Mike Mills and Michael Stipe of R.E.M., who came to jam after a September 1995 show at the South Park Meadows. During a recent SXSW festival Mojo Nixon was onstage here doing his "Don Henley Must Die" ditty when the ex-Eagle himself popped out of the crowd. *2538 Guadalupe St., tel. 512/472−5599.*

RAUL'S

Starting in January 1978, in the wake of the Sex Pistols' farcical jaunt through Texas, an unassuming Mexican bar underwent a radical change in genre. A Pistols-inspired punk combo, the Violators, persuaded bar manager Joseph Gonzalez Jr. to give them and the Skunks a gig and managed to pull in a reasonably sized crowd, so Gonzalez let them play each week. It wasn't for several months, however, that Raul's went supersonic and began attracting media attention.

On September 19, 1978, situationist-art punks called the Huns made their stage debut on the same night that the local police decided to fabricate a noise complaint against the venue. Phil Tolstead, singer for the Huns, spotted a cop in the crowd and started shouting abuse at him. The cop jumped onstage, and the two got into a scuffle, which widened to include the crowd and more cops. Eventually the singer, four fans, and a club bouncer (who was trying to break things up) were arrested. This was Austin's first punk "riot," and it made front-page news. The Huns became local heroes of sorts, a rash of new bands appeared, and Raul's became the hub of Austin's punk scene.

That scene lasted only three years, but in that time two live albums were released, and the Standing Waves, the Next, the Re•Cords, and many others got their first gigs here. Raul's is now the Texas Showdown Saloon, a turd-brown dive that, despite offering cheap beer, doesn't even get students. *2610 Guadalupe St., tel. 512/472–2010.*

AUSTIN CITY LIMITS

This music showcase, concentrating on progressive country, has been broadcast on PBS for over 20 years. Shows are taped by the local KLRU TV station, usually in fall, in the Communications B building on the UT campus. There are around 400 free tickets for each taping, which get snapped up fast. Call KLRU (tel. 512/ 471–4811) for details, or write to Austin City Limits (Communications Building B, University of Texas, Austin, TX 78712).

UNIVERSITY OF TEXAS (UT)

The 50,000 students of the University of Texas have always had a strong cultural influence on Austin. At the start of the '60s, young UT musicians would travel out to Threadgill's to jam with old-timers; the best known of this bunch was Janis Joplin, whose casual appearance and attitude so stirred up the preppies, jocks, and frat boys that they voted her "ugliest man on campus" in 1962. She left the following January without graduating. After leaving the Velvet Underground in the early '70s, Sterling Morrison earned a Ph.D. in medieval literature here and was a part-time teaching assistant. His degree must have come in handy a short time later, when he worked as a tugboat skipper in Houston.

Dominating the campus is the skinny library tower. "The Ballad of Charles Whitman," by UT graduate Kinky Friedman, tells the story of a man who killed several people after going on a random shooting spree in the mid-'60s from the top of this building. When Friedman performed the comedic number at the Armadillo, there was stunned silence. Elvis Costello's "Psycho," the B side of "Sweet Dreams," recounts the Whitman saga from the perspective of the shooter.

In the UT Union Building is the long-running **CACTUS CAFÉ** (tel. 512/471–8228, http://www.utexas.edu/student/txunion/amuse/cactus/cactus.html), where all the top names in roots, country rock, and folk have played. *Guadalupe St. between 21st and 26th Sts.*

Elsewhere Around Town

BROKEN SPOKE

This old-style wooden dance hall on the south side of town opened in 1964 and has resisted change ever since. Just inside the front door is a down-home eatery selling what it claims is the finest chicken-fried steak in the city; off to the left is a small museum with items donated by stars who have played here, Dolly Parton, Kris Kristof-ferson, Willie Nelson, and George Strait among them. Disciples of Billy Ray Cyrus should be warned that line dancing is HATED here and positively discouraged. Instead you're invited to two-step to Don Walser, Derailers, Alvin Crow, and the best Texas has to offer. During SXSW 1993, Jimmie Dale Gilmore hosted an all-nighter with a re-formed Flat-landers, Lucinda Williams, and many others. (If you get hooked on the old-time atmo-sphere and top country music here, **GRUENE HALL** [1281 Gruene Rd., Gruene village, New Braunfels, tel. 210/606–1281] is another great atmosphere-soaked place to visit. Stuck out in the hill country halfway between Austin and San Antonio, it's the oldest dance hall Texas, dating from the 1870s.) *3201 S. Lamar Blvd., tel. 512/442–6189.*

CONTINENTAL CLUB

In existence since 1957, the Continental—where the bar scene from *Slacker* was filmed—is another old-style venue that doesn't seem to have had a refit of any sort: A smiling Elvis portrait beams down from behind the stage, and along the walls are tacky murals that attempt to depict Venice or some such city. In the '80s, when Mark Pratz (now at Liberty Lunch) was doing the booking, the club put on new guitar bands and rockabilly, but the current program focuses heavily on roots, blues, and country. Junior Brown, wielding a custom-made "Guit Steel" (a Telecaster and lap steel all in one body) and described as "Hendrix goes country," played on Sundays in the early '90s before hit-ting it big. These days Tuesday nights are the domain of Austin vocal star Toni Price. The **AUSTIN MOTEL** (tel. 512/441–1157), more or less directly opposite, has provided rest-ing quarters for musicians over the decades; basic rooms come cheap, at around $45. *1315 S. Congress Ave., tel. 512/441–2444.*

Toni Price plays the Continental

THE BEACH (CROWN AND ANCHOR PUB)

The postpunk, so-called New Sincerity movement centered on the Beach, which opened in 1983 in what had been a folk club and ice-cream parlor. Strumming bands like the Dharma Bums, Texas Instruments, True Believers, and Zeitgeist were happy to take up this moniker and played loud new music not dissimilar to the early R.E.M. The New Sincerity bands dominated a 1995 MTV show on the Austin scene. That program also included a performance by Daniel Johnston. Brought up in nearby rural San Marcos, he arrived in town around late 1984 and began handing out home-recorded tapes of his lo-fi songs. Lots of bands at the Beach covered his compositions, and he's become something of a cult figure. The Beach closed in the late '80s, another victim of the raising of the Texas drinking age to 21. It's now called the Crown and Anchor and does not currently put on live rock bands. *2911 San Jacinto Blvd., tel. 512/322–9168.*

[THREADGILL'S]

Threadgill's restaurant, a 15-minute drive from downtown, would be an essential stop just for its huge portions of great Southern food at bargain prices, but it's also the place where the Austin music scene started. It was opened as a gas station and beer joint in 1933 by local character Kenneth Threadgill, who sang and yodeled in the Jimmie Rodgers tradition. He got the first post-Prohibition liquor license in Travis County that year, and soon hillbilly jam sessions packed the place a couple nights a week.

In the early '60s student folkies from UT came out to listen to and play along with the old-timers. These students included Powell St. John, who went on to play with Mother Earth; music writer Bill Malone; future rock promoter (and Big Brother and the Holding Company manager) Chet Helms; and Janis Joplin, who also worked here as a waitress in 1962. The jam sessions continued until 1974, when Threadgill, by then a cult figure, closed the place and took time out to play at festivals and clubs throughout the country.

On New Year's Day 1981, Eddie Wilson, founder of the Armadillo World Headquarters, reopened Threadgill's the day after his beloved AWHQ closed. He added extra seating and reestablished Wednesday music nights. Jimmie Dale Gilmore led the house band for a while before handing over the baton to Champ Hood; both play on a live CD recorded here in 1991.

The place gets jammed on Wednesday "Sittin' Singin' 'n Supper" sessions, but it's is worth a visit anytime. In the back porch are pics of Janis Joplin, and at the end of the parking lot is a two-story banquet facility (visits by arrangement only) with a museum devoted mostly to Texan memorabilia, with a couple of display cases devoted to Threadgill and local music festivals. The memory of Kenneth Threadgill is kept alive with the Austin Musicians Appreciation Supper, held here on his birthday, September 12. *6416 N. Lamar Blvd., tel. 512/451–5440.*

VICTORY GRILL

For four decades the stretch of East 11th Street that runs from the present site of I–35 to Rosewood Avenue was the center of black social life in Austin. The most enduring of the neighborhood's clubs is the Victory, which opened around 1945 and recently reopened after a fire caused its closure for a few years in the early '90s. An early visitor to the club was Bobby "Blue" Bland, who sang (and won) talent contests here regularly in the late '40s, while some of the big names who came through in its '60s heyday were B.B. King, Clarence "Gatemouth" Brown, and James Brown. The Victory continues to put on local blues acts. *1104 E. 11th St., tel. 512/477–6770.*

Beaumont

This conservative oil town near the Gulf of Mexico and the Louisiana state line is the hometown of albino guitarist Johnny Winter, of whom blues discographer Charles Shaar Murray has said, "He may not be the best white guitar player in the world, but he sure as hell is the whitest." The Big Bopper, born J. P. Richardson in Sabine Pass on October 29, 1932, is buried at the **FOREST LAWN MEMORIAL PARK** (4955 Pine St., tel. 409/892–5912); he died in the same Iowa plane crash that killed Buddy Holly.

Dallas

Dallas (commonly grouped with Fort Worth as the Metroplex) may be best known for oil, Kennedy's assassination, and that soap opera, but the city has loads of new guitar bands. Although overshadowed by smaller Austin, Dallas has produced the Toadies, Hagfish, Deep Blue Something, Little Green Men, and Tripping Daisy, which has threatened to make it biggish for the past couple of years.

It is also the birthplace of several big names. Marvin Lee Aday (born September 27, 1947) purportedly got his nickname—Meat Loaf—at an early age: He weighed over 200 pounds by the time he was 14. Sly Stone (born Sylvester Stewart, March 15, 1944), Stephen Stills (January 3, 1945), and Stevie Ray Vaughan (October 2, 1954) also were in Dallas, and members of the longtime tour-circuit favorite Reverend Horton Heat are also natives. A more recent product of the city is Lisa Loeb, who graduated from the chichi, all-girls Hockaday School in 1986 before heading for Brown University.

Hagfish, the catch of the day

EATINGDRINKINGDANCINGSHOPPINGPLAYINGSLEEPING

The place to see live music is definitely the Deep Ellum neighborhood, east of downtown just past the Central Expressway. In the '20s and '30s this was the city's main nightlife zone for blacks and had many juke joints. Today its warehouses have been transformed into brightly painted galleries, innovative restaurants, fancy stores, and several good rock and dance clubs.

The **ORBIT ROOM** (2809 Commerce St., tel. 214/748–5399) was opened by the same people who run Emo's in Austin and Houston; touring punk and alternative bands like the Melvins and Green Day appear, as well as such surprise guests as Johnny Cash. **TREES** (2707 Elm St., tel. 214/748–5009) holds 1,000, has a balcony, and gets an impressive list of bands, recently including the Cramps, Rancid, 311, and Alanis Morissette. **BILLY BOB'S** (2520 Rodeo Plaza, tel. 817/624–7117), out in the Stockyards in Fort Worth, claims to be the biggest honky-tonk in the world; it brings in the top country stars each weekend and puts on pro-rodeo events. For records, check out **BILLS** (8118 Spring Valley Rd., tel. 214/234–1496), with over a million discs in stock plus loads of collectibles.

LONGHORN BALLROOM

This big red barnlike arena, once run by Jack Ruby, was built in the late '40s and still pulls in reasonably big names on weekends. It's an intentionally gaudy place, with Texas gewgaws and portraits of country giants hanging on the walls, and must have been an odd setting for the Sex Pistols, who played their fifth U.S. date here, in January 1978. As usual, all the attention was on Sid Vicious, who had written GIMME A FIX on his chest and had only one string working on his guitar. Helen Killer, a punk who had traveled from L.A. especially to attack Vicious, got onstage and head-butted the Pistols' bassist. Vicious carried on playing regardless, of course, and when his head stopped bleeding, he broke a bottle on his chest to get more blood. *1027 S. Industrial Blvd., tel. 214/421–6262.*

ST. MARKS SCHOOL OF TEXAS

Steve Miller formed his first band, the Marksmen, while attending this all-boys private school. A fellow pupil and band member was Boz Scaggs. The pair enrolled at the University of Wisconsin and then went to San Francisco, where the Steve Miller Blues Band was formed in late 1966. *10600 Preston Rd., tel. 214/363–6491.*

STEVIE RAY VAUGHAN'S GRAVE

Blues-rock guitarist Vaughan was born in Dallas but made his reputation gigging around Austin in the '70s. In 1983 he played on David Bowie's *Let's Dance* and went on to work with other big names, including Eric Clapton. His own band, Double Trouble, achieved only moderate commercial success, with four studio albums just nudging their way into the Top 40. However, an album by the Vaughans (with fellow Austin club vet and brother Jimmie) called *Family Style,* released after Stevie's death in a 1990 helicopter crash, went to No. 7 in the *Billboard* charts. A compilation of his work went Top 10 the following year. *Laurel Land Memorial Park, 6000 S. Thornton Fwy., tel. 214/371–1336.*

Curt Doughty

Reverend Horton Heat, rockabilly gods from Dallas

El Paso

This binational sprawl of 2 million people—on the Mexican side of the border, it's called Ciudad Juarez—has inspired a number of songs, including Marty Robbins' country ballad about "the west country town of El Paso" and Kinky Friedman and the Texas Jewboys' "I'm Just an Asshole from El Paso" (a retort to Merle Haggard's "Okie from Muskogee").

On a less amusing note, in 1983 Def Leppard lead singer Joe Elliott called El Paso "the place with all those greasy Mexicans," a remark that got him banned from local airwaves until he apologized. Johnny Cash also ran into trouble here: In October 1965 he was arrested at the El Paso airport when 688 Dexedrine and 475 Equinil pills were found stuffed into a cheap guitar he'd picked up in Mexico; he received a 30-day suspended sentence on drug charges.

Houston

HI EVERYBODY. I'M ARCHIE BELL AND THE DRELLS OF HOUSTON, TEXAS. WE DON'T ONLY SING, WE DANCE JUST AS GOOD AS WE WANT—ARCHIE BELL AND THE DRELLS, "TIGHTEN UP"

Before he joined the Beatles, Ringo Starr considered moving to this city rich in black musical tradition because his hero, blues singer Lightnin' Hopkins, lived and busked here in the late '50s. Amos Milburn was born in Houston (1927), cut his R&B standard "Chicken Shack Boogie" (1948), and died here (1980). It is also the birthplace of Johnny Guitar Watson (February 3, 1935), Leon Haywood (February 11, 1942), and Billy Preston (September 9, 1946).

In the '50s Houston was home to one of America's most successful independent R&B labels, Duke/Peacock. Started in 1949 as Peacock by Don Robey and run out of his Bronze Peacock nightclub, it got its full name after he bought out the defunct Memphis Duke label in 1953. Duke/Peacock released Willie Mae Thornton's original "Hound Dog," as well as much by Bobby "Blue" Bland.

Following the British invasion of the mid-'60s, Doug Sahm formed Houston's leading guitar group, the Sir Douglas Quintet, named in deference to the vogue for anything British. A couple years later, Mayo Thompson formed the original Red Crayola, which quickly sank into oblivion but was re-formed by Thompson 10 years later in London as a kind of Britpunk supergroup, with the Raincoats' Gina Birch on bass, the Swell Maps' Epic Soundtracks on drums, and X-Ray Spex's Lora Logic on sax.

The nation's fourth-largest city sprawls and then sprawls some more, but the two best neighborhoods for music—the Heights and Montrose—lie within the I-610 loop. The latter has lots of cool gay clubs and Emo's, a punk joint. For a city of its size, Houston has produced few major bands but locals like Poor Dumb Bastards, the all-grrrl Manhole, and the blurring-noise combo Blueprint are worth checking out.

CITY AUDITORIUM (JESSE H. JONES HALL)

Ballad-singing R&B heartthrob Johnny Ace blew his brains out in a game of Russian roulette backstage on December 23, 1954; he died the following day. Some reports claim that he was trying to impress a girl sitting on his lap at the time. The hall, now renamed, houses the Houston Symphony Orchestra. *615 Louisiana St, tel. 713/227–3974.*

EMO'S

This tiny venue in the Montrose district opened in December 1989 as an "alternative lounge," with new music blaring out over the speakers. After a successful first year, owner Eric "Emo" Hartman decided to throw a thank-you anniversary party and brought in Killdozer to play. Locals demanded more live music, and since then many now-giant bands, including Hole, have played here. *2700 Albany St, tel. 713/523–8503.*

GOLD STAR STUDIOS (SUGAR HILL)

Huey Meaux ran his Crazy Cajun, Tribe, and Teardrop labels out of Gold Star Studios. He recorded so-called swamp-pop, like Rod Bernard's "This Should Go on Forever"; what came to be known as Tex-Mex, with Baldemar Huerta (a.k.a. Freddy Fender); the Sir Douglas Quintet ("She's About a Mover" was recorded here); and Doug Sahm when he went solo. Meaux also recorded much of the Duke/Peacock label's output, as well as such Texas blues artists as the ill-fated Johnny Ace, Johnny Winter, and T-Bone Walker. After a spell in jail in the '70s for conspiracy to violate the Mann Act (taking minors across state borders for unscrupulous purposes), Meaux returned to the music biz in 1975 with Freddy Fender's No. 1 "Before the Next Teardrop Falls." He also turned up as a DJ on David Byrne's *True Stories,* enjoying a surprise '80s hit with "My Toot Toot." The studio is now called Sugar Hill, and Meaux apparently is still found at the controls. *5626 Brock St, tel. 713/926–4431.*

Lubbock

Bible Belt Lubbock, home to Texas Tech University, is the largest city in the Texas Panhandle and makes its money from oil and ranching. It's best known, of course, as the hometown of Buddy Holly. The singer was born here, lived here for most of his life, and is buried here. A statue of him is the town's top tourist attraction, and he is celebrated every first week in September with a Budfest. Advance details for Holly fans are gladly given by Bill Griggs at the **BUDDY HOLLY MEMORIAL SOCIETY** (Box 6123, Lubbock, TX 79493). The **LUBBOCK CHAMBER OF COMMERCE** (1120 14th St., tel. 806/763-4666) produces a leaflet to all the Holly sights.

BUDDY HOLLY GRAVE

The singer's headstone is inscribed with a Fender guitar and uses the real spelling of his name, Holley. *City of Lubbock Cemetery, 2011 E. 34th St., tel. 806/767-2270.*

BUDDY HOLLY RECREATION AREA

The city dedicated this landscaped park to its most famous export, and it's especially popular with fans because the big sign gives a handy photo opportunity. *N. University Ave., 4 mi from downtown.*

BUDDY HOLLY STATUE

This 8½-foot-tall bronze statue was unveiled in 1979. A walk of fame spreads out from its base, with plaques honoring other local musicians, such as the Crickets, Roy Orbison, Joe Ely, and Waylon Jennings, who had his own Lubbock radio show when he was 12. *8th St. and Ave. Q.*

J.T. HUTCHINSON JUNIOR HIGH SCHOOL

Holly was performing here with friend Bob Montgomery before they hit their teens, and the school has various mementoes on display. *3102 Canton Ave.*

KDAV RADIO (KRFE)

Holly and his friend and earliest jamming partner Bob Montgomery did a weekly music show from these studios in 1953. The place is still standing, though nowadays the call letters are KRFE. The current occupants are usually pretty good at giving studio tours on weekdays if advance notice is given. *6602 Martin Luther King, Jr., Dr. (formerly Quirt St.), tel. 806/745-1197.*

TABERNACLE BAPTIST CHURCH

A telegram from Elvis Presley was read at Buddy Holly's funeral, held in here in February 1959. Phil Everly was one of the pallbearers. A portion of Holly's royalties still go toward the church's upkeep. *1911 34th St.*

HOLLY HOMES

Charles Hardin Holley (he dropped the e in Holley when he started recording) came into the world in at 1911 6TH STREET on September 7, 1936; the home was moved to a different site in the mid '70s, and the precise location, despite inquiries by Holly fans, is still not known. The Holley family struggled from rented house to rented house in the Lubbock area, moving on average around once a year; the home at 1305 37TH STREET, where Buddy and the folks were living when "That'll Be The Day" climbed the charts in 1957, is still standing and occupied. Peggy Sue (Backham) was matron of honor when Buddy Holly married Puerto Rican Maria Elena Santiago in 1958; the wedding took place at 1606 39TH STREET, then the family home, and the couple lived there for a short time before moving to New York.

Port Arthur

This no-frills blue-collar port city—showing the signs of wear after oil fortunes dived—was the birthplace of Janis Joplin on January 19, 1943. She didn't hang around long, leaving for the University of Texas and then California.

MUSEUM OF THE
GULF COAST

Bart Bragg, Criccio Studio, Port Arthur, TX

The musical-heritage section of the museum's flashily curated "American Pop Culture" exhibit (there's a similar one devoted to sports stars) is dedicated to musicians, songwriters, and producers from southeast Texas and southwest Louisiana. Honorees include the Big Bopper, Clarence "Gatemouth" Brown, Clifton Chenier, George Jones, Tex Ritter, and the Winter brothers (Edgar and Johnny). You'll find snappy interactive audiovisual displays, biographical details,

Janis on display at the Museum of the Gulf Coast

and lots of memorabilia. An extensive display on Port Arthur's own Janis Joplin has, not surprisingly, been given pride of place: There's a giant rotating gold disc surrounded by a montage made of a Nudie suit, paintings from high school and her California days, gold records, and lots of personal items and papers donated by her family. *700 Procter St., tel. 409/982–7000. Admission: $3.50. Open Mon.–Sat. 9–5, Sun. 1–5.*

San Antonio

Steeped in history, San Antonio is probably the most popular tourist destination in Texas, but city authorities could probably have done without some Brit travelers—namely, Messrs. Osbourne and Vicious.

THE ALAMO

After Ozzy Osbourne's wife hid his clothes to keep him from going out boozing, he put on one of her dresses and went to explore the city. In an inebriated state, he relieved himself up against a wall, only to find it was the Alamo—in Texas, the most hallowed of ground—where Davy Crockett, Jim Bowie, and 187 other Texan martyrs died while defending the mission against the Mexican army. The local police were not pleased. No. Ozzy was banned from performing in the city and charged with being drunk in public and pissing on an important piece of state heritage. *300 Alamo Plaza, tel. 210/225–1391. Admission free. Open Mon.–Sat. 9–6:30, Sun. 10–6:30.*

BLUE BONNET HOTEL

Robert Johnson only had two recording sessions. The first—with "Crossroads Blues," "Terraplane Blues," and "Come on in My Kitchen," among others—is said to have been conducted for ARC Records on November 23, 1936, in a temporary studio in the Blue Bonnet Hotel. However, as with all things related to Johnson, blues buffs have been arguing over whether the session was here or in the swankier Gunter (now the Gunter Sheraton, at 205 East Houston Street). Most seem to vote for the Blue Bonnet, which was torn down in the late '80s; the lot became part of a landscaped downtown space. *St. Mary's St. at Pecan St.*

RANDY'S RODEO

The Sex Pistols played the most sensational show of their short U.S. tour at this ballroom in January 1978. As soon as the show started, the rowdy Texans (many of them country-music good ole boys who resented "their" venue being used for such purposes) threw anything they could find at the band—hot dogs, burgers, popcorn—and the sheriff got hit in the head with a bottle of Jack Daniels. Sid diplomatically calmed everyone down by yelling, "You cowboys are all a bunch of fucking faggots." Now called Randy's

Ballroom, the venue also derives some income from bingo sessions. *1534 Bandera Rd., tel. 210/434–6266.*

Wink

Built in two years after the '30s oil boom, Wink is now nearly deserted. Roy Orbison grew up here in the '40s and early '50s and escaped as soon as he could. The street where he lived is now renamed Roy Orbison Avenue, but his house is gone. Shortly after the singer died in 1988, the mayor tried to get a $30,000 statue erected; only $500 was donated, however, with many locals claiming not to know who "The Big O" was. Wink now hosts an annual Orbison festival the second Saturday in June, with sounda-like and lookalike contests.

ROY ORBISON MUSEUM

A cut-out of Orbison stands by the door of this "museum," which could kindly be said to lack funding. The people at City Hall can let you in during office hours, and with advance notice, a volunteer will give a talk on Orbison. *205 E. Hendricks Blvd., City Hall tel. 915/527–3441.*

THE MID WEST

Chicago, the nation's third-largest city, power base of the urban blues, and a major force in indie rock during the '90s, manages to dominate Illinois economically, culturally, and musically. East St. Louis, tucked into the southwest corner of the state, has also had an illustrious tradition of blues, jazz, and R&B. And of course Illinois also holds Aurora, home of Wayne and Garth.

Chicago

Popular music owes a great deal to Chicago, which took the blues sound born in the Mississippi Delta and shaped it into a potent form of rock & roll. When Muddy Waters and Howlin' Wolf moved to the city in the '40s—soon to be joined by Otis Rush, Buddy Guy, and other southern bluesmen—they played the rough-and-tumble bars of the South Side. In order to be heard above the bar noise, they soon amplified their acoustic Delta sound with electric guitars, bass, and drums—a setup that became the instrumental backbone of Chess Records' blues recordings. When Chuck Berry and Bo Diddley joined the label, they borrowed the guitar-bass-drums arrangement and so established the model for what is still the most popular lineup for a rock & roll band.

Beyond blues, Chicago also had an active gospel scene (Mahalia Jackson lived here) and played a major role in the rise of soul in the early '60s with records like Fontella Bass's "Rescue Me" and Gene Chandler's "Duke of Earl." Chicago soul had a more adult reputation than that coming out of nearby Detroit. It was personified by Curtis Mayfield and the Impressions, whose '60s hits—a run that included "I'm So Proud," "People Get Ready," and "Keep on Pushing"—are identifiable by their sweet vocals, soaring harmonies, and distinctive guitar, which was often praised by Jimi Hendrix.

In the mid-'60s, the first Chicago guitar groups appeared in the form of the Shadows of Knight (their only national hit was a reworking of Them's "Gloria" in 1966) and the Buckinghams. With the '70s the city became synonymous with the schmoozy AOR kings Chicago Transit Authority (later renamed Chicago). Post-punk, however, the music scene altered radically, becoming much more prolific and decidedly hardcore. The '80s saw the establishment of house music, played in the city's predominantly black and gay nightclubs, and the Wax Trax label's first releases in 1980 supported an industrial dance movement headed by Ministry and Front 242. Two years later Steve Albini (now a top producer) started his influential noisemongering with Big Black, named—and we've come full circle—for a river in the Mississippi Delta.

The '90s indie scene has been headed by the Smashing Pumpkins, Liz Phair, and Urge Overkill; other bands waiting to emerge include Sabalon Glitz, the Smoking Popes, and Red Red Meat. The city's tradition of strong indie labels is carried on by Kranky, Thrill Jockey, Minty Fresh, and the powerhouse concern of Touch and Go Records, which has put out work by the Butthole Surfers, Killdozer, and Urge Overkill, among many others.

Chicago 16

Robert Johnson, "Sweet Home Chicago" (1937)
Paul Butterfield Blues Band, "Born in Chicago" (1966)

Dr. West's Medicine Show and Junk Band, "The Eggplant That Ate Chicago" (1966)
Isaac Hayes, "Going to Chicago Blues" (1968)
The Fugs, "Chicago" (1969)
Scott Walker, "Thanks for Chicago, Mr. James" (1970)
Crosby, Stills, Nash and Young, "Chicago" (1971)
The Doobie Brothers, "Chicago" (1971)
The Bee Gees, "Living in Chicago" (1973)
ZZ Top, "Jesus Just Left Chicago" (1973)
Joe Stampley, "The Sheik of Chicago" (1976)
Chicago, "Take Me Back to Chicago" (1977)
Robert Fripp, "Chicago" (1979)
Joe Jackson, "Showtime in Chicago" (1988)
Ten Years After, "Goin' to Chicago" (1989)
The Fall, "Chicago Now" (1990)

Around the Loop

Lying just to the south of the Chicago River, the city's central business district is called the Loop, after the tracks of the elevated trains—the El—that encircle its core. Hectic during the day, especially at lunch, the area isn't all that exciting at night. West of the Loop is Grant Park, where the Chicago Blues Festival is held every year.

BISMARCK THEATER AND HOTEL

This grand, if somewhat faded, Loop hotel attracted the top British bands of the early '80s—New Order, the Cure, and Echo and the Bunnymen. One night, a few numbers into a Frankie Goes to Hollywood gig, the frenetic dancing caused the floor to collapse—all that was holding the crowd from falling into the basement was thick carpeting. The management felt that canceling the gig could cause a riot, so they hauled people away from the abyss, put a barrier around the hole, and sent the band back to play, with the crowd 75 feet back from the stage. Recent gigs have included Tori Amos and King Crimson. *171 W. Randolph St., tel. 312/236−0123.*

BUDDY GUY'S LEGENDS

One of the most successful of the second batch of Chicago's blues performers, Louisiana-born guitarist Buddy Guy hit the city's blues clubs in 1957 and went on to

The scene at Buddy's

have a career that included a successful 20-year partnership with harmonica-player and singer Junior Wells and a support slot on a Rolling Stones European tour. Although never a major recording artist (for a long time Guy didn't even have a label in the United States, relying on distribution through British and French companies), he was always held in high esteem on the blues circuit.

In 1989 Guy opened this fair-size club, whose back wall has a huge mural that features such Chi-town blues legends as Muddy Waters, Howlin' Wolf, and Little Walter. Personal contacts in the music world have allowed the hands-on owner to book some big names: Eric Clapton did a four-night run in 1994, and Otis Rush, still based in Chicago, appears frequently. At other times Legends gets the best local and national touring blues acts. *754 S. Wabash St., behind the Hilton, tel. 312/427–0333.*

CHICAGO BLUES ARCHIVE

The collection here includes thousands of blues recordings and hundreds of books, magazines, and photos, as well as some hand-written music and lyrics by Howlin' Wolf and instruments belonging to some of the city's finest blues practitioners. *400 S. State St., tel. 312/542–7279. Admission free. Open Mon. 9–7; Tues. and Thurs. 11–5; Wed., Fri., and Sat. 9–5; Sun. 1–5.*

WHERE'S THE BLUES MUSEUM?

While Memphis has been busy turning its downtown into what's more or less a blues theme park, Chicago has yet to come up with a lasting dedication to its greatest musical claim to fame. However, several organizations are attempting to get the funding to put something together. The most likely to succeed seems to be the Blues Heaven Foundation, which in 1994 bought the former Chess Studios and hopes to have some kind of exhibitions there. Chicago-born singer Lou Rawls has set up the not-for-profit Tobacco Road Inc., which plans to turn an old movie house into a recording facility, library, and museum on the South Side.

PETRILLO BAND SHELL

In Grant Park, near where the Yippies were flattened by the cops at the Democratic National Convention in 1968 (*see box*), there was another youth-versus-the-forces-of-Mayor-Daley battle three years later when Sly and the Family Stone's failure to turn up for a concert at the Petrillo Band Shell sparked a riot. The band shell is now the center of activities for the annual three-day **CHICAGO BLUES FESTIVAL** (tel. 312/744–0573), which usually takes place over the first weekend of June; all the best local talent is joined by big names like Chuck Berry and B.B. King. *Grant Park, near E. Jackson and Columbus Drs.*

THE 1968 DEMOCRATIC NATIONAL CONVENTION

The Youth International Party (the Yippies), led by Abbie Hoffman and Jerry Rubin, organized a massive antiwar Festival of Life to coincide with the August 1968 Democratic National Convention, held in Chicago. Their plan was to attract kids with a free rock festival, encourage them to march through the streets smoking dope, and then nominate a hog as a presidential candidate. Things didn't go very smoothly, however. Mayor Richard Daley, a Democratic boss, promised that his police force would stop the march; antiwar bands such as the Fugs and Country Joe and the Fish pulled out when the situation began to look heavy; and the Yippie leaders got into fights about everything, down to whether the presidential hog should be cute or ugly.

The Yippies managed to get a free show going in Lincoln Park, on the north side of the city, featuring the MC5 and a solo gig by the Fugs' Ed Sanders, but Daley ordered the area to be cleared by nightfall. A thousand cops turned up and ripped down tents and sprayed tear gas, while Allen Ginsberg ridiculously tried to calm the crowd by suggesting they all hum a mantra.

Later in the week, around 10,000 assembled in Grant Park and tried to march on the Convention. The marchers got no farther than the part of the park opposite the Hilton Hotel, where the police, in front of the world's TV news crews, beat the

hell out of anyone they could get their hands on. By the end of the convention, over 1,000 were injured and more than 600 had been arrested, including Rubin, Hoffman, Black Panther leader Bobby Seale, and folkie Phil Ochs. Many were moved by the sheer violence of the occasion, including Hunter S. Thompson, who was in attendance. Ochs wrote the song "William Butler Yeats Visits Lincoln Park and Escapes Unscathed" and used the image of a gravestone that read PHIL OCHS. BORN EL PASO, TEXAS, 1940. DIED CHICAGO, ILLINOIS, 1968 for the cover of his *Rehearsals for Retirement* album. The Fugs recorded a song, simply called "Chicago," with the refrain "May you sleep in peace, Mayor Daley."

Near North

The stretch of Michigan Avenue north of the river is known as the Magnificent Mile for its expensive department stores and hotels. The streets running off Michigan also get into the hunt for tourist dollars with a gamut of theme restaurants, some with a rock feel.

EATING DRINKING DANCING SHOPPING *PLAYING* SLEEPING

A Near North **McDonald's** (600 N. Clark St., tel. 312/664–7940) has been decked out in rock & roll memorabilia—heavy on Elvis, James Dean, and the Beatles, whose white plaster-cast statues take pride of place inside a glass cabinet. Theme restaurants are thick on the ground around here—the Hard Rock Cafe, Planet Hollywood, an Al Capone restaurant, and Ed Debevic's, a '50s-style diner, are neighbors, as is a massive new branch of the **House of Blues** (300 N. State St., tel. 312/527–2583), which opened in fall '96; besides a large restaurant, the HoB includes a 1,500-seat concert venue and 400-room hotel.

ASTOR TOWERS HOTEL

The Beatles' last U.S. tour, in 1966, had a very different beginning from the mass hysteria at New York's JFK airport that marked their American debut in 1964. At a televised press conference held at Chicago's Astor Towers on August 11, John Lennon was grilled over an interview with London's *Evening Standard* several months earlier, in which he was quoted as saying, "Christianity will go, it will shrink and will vanish—we're more popular than Jesus now. I don't know which will go first, rock & roll or Christianity."

The Beatles' people felt that the situation had to be defused (there were bonfires going on throughout the Bible Belt using Beatles records as fuel, and some reports say the tour was almost canceled), so at this press conference Lennon apologized for his earlier remarks, saying, "I'm sorry I opened my mouth. I'm not anti-God, anti-Christ, or anti-religion. I wouldn't knock it. I didn't mean we were greater or better." The setting of this act of diplomacy has now been converted into an apartment building. *1340 N. Astor St.*

CHICAGO RECORDING COMPANY

What was the original *Playboy* studio now houses the city's largest recording concern, where in the past two years limos have disgorged Pearl Jam, the Smashing Pumpkins, R. Kelly, and Michael Jackson. *232 E. Ohio St., tel. 312/822–9332.*

Brooke Williams

The Smashing Pumpkins' D'Arcy

PEACE MUSEUM

The first American museum exclusively devoted to promoting nonviolence through the arts opened at a previous downtown location in 1981. While curating an exhibit called "Give Peace a Chance" (which also featured items relating to John Lennon, Woody Guthrie, Stevie Wonder, Bob Dylan, and others), the museum asked U2 to supply some lyrics from *War*. The band liked the idea of the museum so much that they visited in 1983, learned of a previous exhibit about Hiroshima entitled "The Unforgettable Fire," and named their 1984 album after it. *314 W. Institute Place, 1st Floor, tel. 312/440–1860.*

North Side

Chicago gets more exciting the more time you spend in its northern neighborhoods. The four major areas of note are Lincoln Park, Wrigleyville, Wicker Park, and Uptown. The Lincoln Park neighborhood, inland from the park of the same name, is centered on three main drags—Lincoln, Clark, and Halsted—each with relatively good record, book, and clothing stores. Wrigley Field, the grand old baseball park, has given its name to Wrigleyville, north of Lincoln Park. Uptown, a mile farther north at the junction of North Broadway and West Lawrence, is more run-down than the other neighborhoods but has two major concert halls and a few quirky hangouts.

Brad Miller

Liz Phair

Wicker Park, just over a mile west of Lincoln Park, is the current trendy zone, with clubs, bars, cafés, and stores to suit alternative needs. It's also known as Guyville, a nickname bestowed by Chris Holmes of the Chicago band Sabalon Glitz to describe the boyish scene here. The term was featured famously in the title of Liz Phair's breakthrough 1994 album, *Exile in Guyville*. Before that Urge Overkill used the name for "Goodbye to Guyville" on the 1993 EP *Stull*.

EATING DRINKING DANCING SHOPPING PLAYING SLEEPING

Two of the city's best-known, if rather touristy, blues clubs are in Lincoln Park on Halsted. **B.L.U.E.S.** (2519 Halsted St., tel. 312/528–1012) has been going for more than two decades, during which time Sunnyland Slim and all the local big names have appeared. Across the street, the more basic **KINGSTON MINES** (2548 Halsted St., tel. 312/477–4646) attracts rock stars like Mick Jagger and Bob Dylan when they're in town. The Byrds' James (later Jim, then Roger) McGuinn learned to play guitar at Lincoln Park's **OLD TOWN SCHOOL OF FOLK MUSIC** (909 W. Armitage Ave., tel. 312/

525−7793) in the late '50s; the still-active folk center now offers good gigs at least once a week.

In Wrigleyville, just a ball's throw from the Cubs' home, the **CUBBY BEAR** (1059 W. Addison St., tel. 312/327−1662) has a very boozy atmosphere; the club generally hosts a more mainstream kind of rock but also books an eclectic range of big names from Johnny Cash to Ali Farka Toure.

Wicker Park is in many ways typical of a scene taking over a cheap-rent area. There are still thrift shops and vacant lots, but the busy intersection of Damen, North, and Milwaukee, about 2 miles northwest of the Loop, now has the best conglomeration of bars, cafés, venues, and record stores in the city. The **RED DOG** (1958 W. North Ave., tel. 312/278−1009) has cutting-edge funk and acid jazz. The **BOP SHOP** (1807 W. Division St., tel. 312/235−3232) puts on top-notch jazz. Record stores are headed up by Wax Trax (*see below*) and **QUAKER GOES DEAF** (1937 W. North Ave., tel. 312/252−9334), which offers CDs for around $10 and is good for alternative rock. There's also a branch of London-based **RECKLESS RECORDS** (2055 W. North Ave., tel. 312/235−3727), with new and used CDs and vinyl.

ARAGON BALLROOM

Built in 1926, this fine old Uptown theater, with little Spanish castles painted onto the balconies and twinkling lights on the ceiling, was for years the prime place for touring big bands. In the late '60s it started putting on psychedelic bands but lagged behind the Kinetic Playground (*see below*), which had a comprehensive program each week. By 1970 the Aragon was able to attract bands of the caliber of the Grateful Dead, Ten Years After, and Country Joe and the Fish, and by mid-decade it was putting on the likes of the Stooges, Black Sabbath, and Aerosmith, as well as Rock 'n' Wrestling shows. More recently the venue has presented as varied a bunch as Dwight Yoakam, the Black Crowes, Liz Phair, and Nirvana, as well as lots of Latino pop and rock acts. *1106 W. Lawrence Ave., tel. 312/561−9500.*

DAYS INN

During the '90s this Lincoln Park establishment has become the motel of choice for most of the bands playing the Metro and Riviera. Past occupants include the Red Hot Chili Peppers, Soul Asylum, Nirvana, and Offspring, reportedly one of the very few to trash the rooms. Featuring free continental breakfast, served at the enlightened time of noon, and a coin-op laundry, the motel is perfect for touring bands. The Mekons expressed their appreciation—they sang that the Days Inn "is a very nice place to stay when you're stuck in Chicago with nothing to do all day." *646 W. Diversey Pkwy., at N. Clark St. and N. Broadway, tel. 312/525−7010. Rooms: $75.*

DELILAH'S

At this dark North Side dive's Black Sunday events, the DJ is (touring permitting) Urge Overkill's Blackie Onassis, who has been able to pull in such guest DJs as Liz Phair. The bar has become a favorite place for visiting bands to hang. *2771 N. Lincoln Ave., tel. 312/472−2771.*

DOUBLE DOOR

Opened in June 1994, this hub of the Wicker Park night scene has been able to book big names thanks to its tie-ins with the Metro (*see below*). Liz Phair has played several times, and the Shoes taped a live CD here in December 1994. During a four-night run to aid local charities, the Smashing Pumpkins played their first live shows of 1995 here, unveiling 23 new songs, the bulk of that year's *Mellon Collie and the Infinite Sadness* double CD. *1572 N. Milwaukee Ave., tel. 312/489−3160.*

GREEN MILL COCKTAIL LOUNGE

During Prohibition, this beautiful turn-of-the-century bar was run by Machine Gun John McGurn; Al Capone was a regular. The owners keep a great scrapbook that chronicles that era and the prime jazz acts that have performed over the decades. Rock bands perform rarely—although Jeff Buckley did have a recent gig—but you can catch top-quality jazz, often national acts, and soak up a bit of the history of Chicago's underbelly. *4802 N. Broadway, tel. 312/878-5552.*

KINETIC PLAYGROUND

Chicago's premier psychedelic ballroom opened relatively late in the era, on Easter 1968. Originally called the Electric Theater, it was renamed the Kinetic Playground after a lawsuit was brought by the Electric Circus in New York. Shows very much copied the San Francisco formula, mixing the best rock bands from the West Coast and Britain (the Byrds, Fleetwood Mac, the Who) with traditional blues artists, of whom the city had a wealth (Muddy Waters, Howlin' Wolf, B.B. King). A bad fire in 1970 brought an end to the venue's psychedelic era; it's now part of a roller rink complex. *4812 N. Clark St..*

Marty Perez

LOUNGE AX

One of the hippest alternative clubs in the city, this basic Lincoln Park venue holds only around 400 but gets in top acts like Steve Albini's Shellac. It's also a favorite hangout of longtime scenester Cynthia Plaster Caster, leader of the supergroupies who spent much of the '60s making casts of rock stars' penises. For several years the bar been battling with neighbors over noise levels, and in 1996 the club released a compilation on Touch and Go to raise cash for legal fees (and to finance a move, if it comes to that); called

Lounge Ax

Lounge Ax Defense and Relocation, the CD includes contributions from Sebadoh, Tortoise, and Yo La Tengo. *2438 N. Lincoln Ave., tel. 312/525-6620.*

[THE METRO]

Joe Shanahan and Joe Prino took over a floor of this old warehouse and former nightclub next to Wrigley Field in 1982, booking R.E.M. as their first band. Today the club occupies the entire building. The top floor holds offices and the Top Note Theater, used mainly for band rehearsals. Guns N' Roses used the space for six months prior to the release of *Appetite for Destruction*—they left L.A. to get away from the drug scene, but met with limited success. Soul Asylum has also rehearsed in the theater, and the Smoking Popes shot their first video here. In the basement is the Smart Bar, decked out in industrial style, which plays techno and other dance music all week. In the early days Al Jourgensen would bring down the latest Ministry, My Life with the Thrill Kill Kult, and other Wax Trax band mixes straight from the Chicago studio to see how they went down with the crowd.

The real attraction, however, is the main room, the Metro. It holds around 1,100, is wide enough to ensure great sight lines, and has good sound. Firmly established as the city's leading venue for nonarena acts, the Metro is where the Smashing Pumpkins and other local bands like Material Issue and Eleventh Day Dream had early shows, often as support acts. Liz Phair saw a ghost here once and wrote about it for *Great Chicago Stories*, a book to which some of the city's main personalities contributed. No less an authority than Iggy Pop names the Metro as one of his favorite venues.

Over the past decade, everyone from James Brown to Faith No More has played here, and a number of bands have appeared under assumed names, including Pearl Jam, Hole, and the Black Crowes. The Smashing Pumpkins came thinly disguised as the Turnips but didn't fool many—the doors closed with a line stretching around the block. At ♀'s 1993 show, he played for over three hours, refusing to stop even when the management put on the house lights after two hours.

The Metro also has a reputation for getting the best breaking European bands. At a New Order gig in June 1983, the air-conditioning wasn't working, and the place got so hot that some of the band's computer equipment melted, forcing them to perform an acoustic version of "Blue Monday." Oasis's set at an October 1994 gig—basically all of the debut album plus a nine-minute version of "I Am the Walrus"—was caught on tape and released by Epic as a promotional CD. *3730 N. Clark St., tel. 312/549–0203.*

Marty Perez

Pavement at the Metro

RIVIERA

Another of Uptown's elegant concert venues, the Riviera, with a nice dark interior and comfortable seats and boxes, was originally a movie theater but has been putting on rock shows since the '70s. At the end of that decade, Elvis Costello opened here for Tom Petty, while more recent visitors have included Jane's Addiction, Veruca Salt, and the Orb. *4746 N. Racine St., tel. 312/275–6800.*

SHAKE RATTLE AND READ

Since 1986 local musicos and bands on tour have been hanging out at Ric Addy's cavern of pop culture. Besides stocking thousands of cult paperbacks and some collectible discs, the shop holds an amazing number of back-issue rock and style magazines, including *Hit Parader, Crawdaddy, Downbeat, Eye,* lots of underground stuff, and the British weeklies *New Music Express, Melody Maker,* and *Sounds. 4812 N. Broadway, tel. 312/334–5311.*

SHARON'S HILLBILLY HEAVEN

Time has stood still in this must-see Uptown dive bar that has an unreconstructed Appalachian feel and Confederate flags on the wall. The drinks are cheap, and the jukebox is stocked with—and only with—country classics. Dwight Yoakam shot the video for "Guitars and Cadillacs" here, and on a recent tour he stipulated that he would play in Chicago only at the Aragon, which is across the street, so that he could have the post-gig party at Sharon's. And he doesn't even drink. *1113 W. Lawrence Ave.*

UPTOWN THEATER

The second-largest custom-built theater in the country (after Radio City Music Hall in New York), the Uptown served as a vaudeville venue for decades before hosting rock gigs in the late '70s and early '80s. Among those who performed here are Prince (who opened for Rick James), Bob Marley, and the Grateful Dead—the last band to play at the theater before it closed in 1984. Since then it's been used as a film set—for *Backdraft* and *Home Alone II*—although locals who remember concerts here hope that the city's most beautiful old theater will someday host them again. *4814 N. Broadway.*

WAX TRAX

In 1978 Dannie Flesher and Jim Nash opened a Chicago branch of their four-year-old Denver record store on the 2400 block of North Lincoln Avenue. The store became something of a landmark, and parts of *Pretty in Pink* and various videos (including Teenage Fanclub's "The Concept") were filmed on site.

In 1980 the Wax Trax label appeared and almost immediately established itself at the vanguard of the emerging industrial-dance scene, releasing groundbreaking early discs by Ministry, My Life With The Thrill Kill Kult, Front 242, and KMFDM. Ministry's Al Jourgensen practically became the in-house producer, recording and mixing many Wax Trax acts at the studios of **CHICAGO TRAX** (now at 3347 N. Halsted St., tel. 612/525–6565), including such Ministry side projects as the Revolting Cocks, 1000 Homo DJs, and Lard.

With most of its bands signing up with major labels, Wax Trax hit financial problems in the early '90s and was sold to TVT, which revived the imprint in 1995 with a three-CD box set of various artists. The store, with bins of industrial sounds, imports, and used product, recently moved to trendy Wicker Park. However, with the death in 1995 of cofounder Jim Nash, Wax Trax's future remains uncertain. *1653 N. Damen Ave., tel. 312/862–2124.*

WRIGLEY FIELD

In May 1971, Peter Cetera, lead singer of Chicago, got beaten up at a Cubs/Dodgers game at this beautiful old ivy-covered ballpark by good old boys who objected to the length of his hair. He needed some surgery and lost a few teeth. *1060 W. Addison St., tel. 312/831–CUBS.*

The South and West Sides

The South Side technically starts just below the El tracks of the Loop, but the area begins in earnest farther south, in the predominantly African-American neighborhoods where Muddy Waters, Howlin' Wolf, and Otis Rush first got noticed. There are still a number of important blues clubs in the area. The West Side, renowned for its many Frank Lloyd Wright–designed buildings, also has a few items of musical interest.

The largest and most commercial South Side club is the **CHECKERBOARD LOUNGE** (423 E. 43rd St., tel. 312/624–3240), where Magic Slim and the Teardrops are regulars. There's a more cozy, neighborhood feel at **CUDDLE INN** (5317 S. Ashland Ave., tel. 312/778–1999).

[CHESS STUDIOS]

Phil and Leonard Chess, Polish immigrants who owned a local nightclub, started a small label called Aristocrat in 1947. The brothers soon began producing records to appeal to the increasing number of black Southerners who were moving north, particularly from the Mississippi Delta. In 1950 the label, renamed Chess, settled in to studios at 2120 South Michigan Avenue, where an impressive roster of blues artists—Howlin' Wolf, Elmore James, Muddy Waters, and John Lee Hooker—began to record.

Chess also served the growing market for rock & roll with doo-wop records like the Moonglows' "Sincerely" and with such hard rockers as Dale Hawkins's "Suzy Q," one of the first rock records with a "modern" electric-guitar sound, courtesy of James Burton. Chuck Berry, early rock & roll's most prolific songwriter, enlisted many of Chess's finest blues musicians to back him on what is still one of rock's most covered back catalogs, including "Roll Over Beethoven," "Rock & Roll Music," "Sweet Little Sixteen," "The Promised Land," and "Johnny B. Goode." Another great success came from Bo Diddley, whose namesake single introduced his much-copied shuffle rhythm.

The Rolling Stones visited the studios in June 1964—Mick Jagger had written to this address in the '50s to get records mail-ordered to him in England—and Willie Dixon, Muddy Waters, and Chuck Berry dropped in to see the toasts of British R&B. The Stones returned to the studio in May 1965 to record, starting work on "Satisfaction" and the U.K. EP *5 By 5*,

Courtesy of Jim O'Neal Collection

The ultimate Chicago blues showdown

for which they did an instrumental called "2120 South Michigan Avenue." Muddy Waters, to the Stones' astonishment, carried in their bags. (The Chess brothers liked to have their artists use their free time constructively; Waters would often paint Leonard Chess's house when he wasn't recording.)

In the mid-'60s, Chess went to pieces, weakened by Chuck Berry's imprisonments and unable to come to grips with soul. The label moved out of the Michigan Avenue studios in 1967, folding when Leonard Chess died in 1975, shortly after being bought out by tape manufacturer GTR, which got rid of the blues catalog, deeming it passé.

In early 1994, the Blues Heaven Foundation—founded by Willie Dixon, who wrote blues songs like "Spoonful" and "Back Door Man"—used its funds and a big donation from John Mellencamp to purchase the building and open offices inside. The foundation hopes to get several projects going: a royalty-recovery program for artists who wrote big hits but didn't get the cash they were entitled to; an educational program for schools; and a small blues and R&B museum. *2120 S. Michigan Ave, tel. 312/808—1286.*

COMISKEY PARK

On July 12, 1979, local DJ Steve Dahl, who claimed that disco had cost him his radio job, arranged a huge record-smashing session, the Disco Demolition Derby, at a White Sox/Tigers double-header. Those who brought a disco record for destruction got in for 98¢, and between games the crowd smashed tens of thousands of discs, skimming them like Frisbees across the ballpark. White Sox officials and the cops weren't so hot on such behavior, and a riot started, with antidiscoites tearing up the turf; the second game of the day had to be canceled.

In earlier times, boogie-woogie piano-playing, Rock & Roll Hall of Fame inductee Jimmy Yancey (1898—1951) had a job on the ground staff. He started in 1925 and kept his job for 25 years, even after his recording career kicked off in 1938. The original Comiskey Park was demolished in 1990 and replaced with the adjacent New Comiskey. *324 W. 35th. St.*

MAXWELL STREET MARKET

John Lee Hooker filmed his scene in the *Blues Brothers* movie at this long-established street market, where, in the '40s and '50s, blues players who had just arrived in town would busk on the weekends. Aretha Franklin did her spot for the film, singing "Think," at **NATE'S DELICATESSEN** (807 W. Maxwell St., tel. 312/421—9396), a favorite neighborhood deli. While the market is no longer the shopping extravaganza—cum—cultural experience it once was, the vendors still show up on summer Sunday mornings, when some quality blues can still be heard. *W. Maxwell St. at S. Halsted St.*

VEE JAY RECORDS

One of Chicago's biggest labels in the '50s and '60s, black-owned Vee Jay was formed in 1953 by Vivien and Jimmy (hence the name) Carter Bracken and became a prototype for Berry Gordy's outfit in Detroit a decade later. Despite hits from Jimmy Reed, John Lee Hooker, Betty Everett, the Dells ("Oh What a Night"), Jerry Butler ("For Your Precious Love"), the Four Seasons, and Gene Chandler (the chart-topping "Duke of Earl"), the label went bankrupt in 1964... shortly after releasing the Beatles' first U.S. single, "Please Please Me" and crediting it to "The Beatles." *1449 S. Michigan Ave.*

[THE WAREHOUSE]

The club that gave its name to the term *house music* started in the late '70s. In the early '80s, transplanted New York City DJ Frankie Knuckles developed the mix of electro-Teutonic rock and high-BPM (beats per minute) soul that would shake the world's dance floors and influence rock and pop acts from Primal Scream to

John Lee Hooker

Madonna. The club holds only about 600, still plays house music, and attracts a pre-dominantly gay, black crowd. *1800 S. Michigan Ave.*

MUDDY WATERS GRAVE

Muddy Waters (born McKinley Morganfield) moved to Chicago's South Side in 1943 and died in the city on April 30, 1983, at the age of 68. The grave is out in the south-western neighborhood of Worth. *Restvale Cemetery, 117th Ave. at Laramie Ave., tel. 708/385–3506.*

East St. Louis

This largely African-American city, just across the Mississippi River from St. Louis, has been a major source of black music since the '20s. Miles Davis grew up here. It's also where Ike and Tina Turner started out in the mid-'50s; they recorded medium-size hits for New York's Sue records, like the unprophetic "It's Gonna Work Out Fine" (1961), before moving to L.A. in 1962. Michael Stipe was raised in the suburbs and wrote the track "Just a Touch," from R.E.M.'s *Life's Rich Pageant*, about the city.

COSMOPOLITAN CLUB

Chuck Berry, as part of the Sir John's Trio, started out playing this club in the early '50s. He almost decided to quit rock & roll to become a painter/decorator when he earned $450 for painting the club—more than he got for performing in it. *17th St. at Bond St.*

Evanston

Northwestern University is based here, 30 minutes north of Chicago. Journalism student Steve Albini had a punk show on the college's radio station, WNUR, until he locked himself in the studio one evening and played Wagner continuously. He later produced the six-song *Strange I...* for N.U. students Nathan Katruud (National "Nash" Kato) and Ed Roeser ("Eddie" King Roeser) of Urge Overkill and released the EP on his own Ruth-less label.

Northwestern alums Urge Overkill

Brad Miller

EATINGDRINKINGDANCINGSHOPPINGPLAYINGSLEEPING

VINTAGE VINYL (925 Davis St., tel. 708/328–2899) is loaded with new and used CDs and vinyl. It's especially good for new singles and claims to get European imports within seven days of their release. A past customer was a teenage Eddie Vedder, who hung out here before moving with his family to San Diego.

INDIANA WANTS ME/LORD, I CAN'T GO BACK THERE—R. DEAN TAYLOR, "INDIANA WANTS ME"

Outside Indiana's few cities and college towns, a conservative air pervades. In 1964, when the allegedly rude lyrics of "Louie, Louie" were threatening to subvert the nation's youth, it was the politicians of Indiana, acting on a complaint from a concerned Indianapolis resident, who led the charge to ban the song. The governor at the time, one Matthew Welsh, took it upon himself to find the words pornographic, and he lobbied, extremely successfully, to get the state's radio stations to stop playing the tune. Today it's still one of those Midwest places that record executives bear in mind when a band comes up with artwork that may not get stocked in stores.

Besides Michael Jackson, famous Indianans include James Dean, and Axl Rose and Izzy Stradlin of Guns N' Roses. John(ny) (Cougar) Mellencamp was born and still lives in Freetown, a small town in the south of the state. Alumni of Indiana University at Bloomington include Booker T. Jones (of the Stax house band, the MG's), who was studying here when "Green Onions" hit the charts in 1962. John Strohm of Veb-Deluxe (formerly with the Blake Babies and the Lemonheads) and Lisa Germano, who records on 4 AD, are Bloomington natives.

Fairmount

Morrissey filmed the video for his 1988 "Suedehead" single at the grave of his hero, James Dean, in Park Cemetery, 2 miles west of the screen idol's hometown of Fairmount. The **FAIRMOUNT HISTORICAL MUSEUM** (203 E. Washington St., tel. 317/948–4555) holds some information on him, and **REBEL REBEL** (425 N. Main St., tel. 317/948–3336) stocks much Dean memorabilia.

Gary

The only major city on the state's narrow share of the Lake Michigan shore, Gary gave birth to America's most successful family act, the Jackson Five. Their first disc, the unsuccessful "I'm a Big Boy Now" b/w "You've Changed," was issued on a local label, Steeltown, in 1968. That year the singing brothers won Amateur Night at the Apollo in Harlem, after which soul singer Bobby Taylor recommended them to Motown. The Jacksons started recording for Berry Gordy's label in 1969, and soon after the company moved them to L.A. Gary may no longer have the Jacksons, but city officials announced plans in 1995 to build a Jacksons theme park.

MICHAEL JACKSON RESIDENCE, 1958–71

Michael Jackson and his siblings—there were nine kids in all—grew up in this cramped, two-bedroom clapboard house, appropriately situated on Jackson Street. The Jacksons' 1989 album, *2300 Jackson Street,* commemorated this childhood home.

Joe Jackson, the boys' father, played guitar in a covers band, the Falcons, but he wouldn't let the kids use the instrument; a gallant Tito would sneak some practice whenever pop was out. Once his offspring began displaying their talent, however, Jackson senior would make them rehearse for a couple of hours after doing their homework. If Michael or any of the brothers missed a rehearsal or a dance step, Joe beat them.

In the early '60s, Jackie, Tito, and Jermaine formed a singing group, refusing at first to allow the younger Marlon and Michael to take part. But once it became apparent that Michael had great potential, he was invited in—to play the bongos. Michael took over as lead singer when the Jackson Five (the name was suggested by a neighbor) began entering local talent shows, covering Motown and James Brown songs. *2300 Jackson St., at 23rd Ave.*

MR. LUCKY'S LOUNGE

Michael Jackson had his professional debut at the age of six at this club in 1964. There were holes drilled in the walls between the men's and women's bathrooms, and Michael's father, worried about the effect this would have on the boy's development, at first refused to allow him to perform here. *1100 Grant St., tel. 219/885–9095.*

Indianapolis

Although sprawling Indianapolis is the 12th-ranked U.S. city in terms of population, it's not nearly as high on the list of those with rock & roll connections. Until the '50s it did have one of the region's best jazz scenes, centered on Indiana Avenue, where the Ink Spots and Wes Montgomery started out. The jazz days faded after an interstate was driven through this area of downtown, but a healthy number of venues still offer live jazz.

CHATTERBOX TAVERN

This small, friendly neighborhood bar, in a century-old building near downtown, is the essential stop for jazz. Decorated with Christmas lights, weirdo sculptures, and Indy 500 stuff, the club encourages musicians to sit in anytime for music ranging from traditional to free-form. Next to the bar is a refrigerator bearing the autographs of Lou Rawls, Don Henley, John Hiatt, Wynton Marsalis, and the Count Basie Band—just some of the jazz and rock greats who have played here. *435 Massachusetts Ave., tel. 317/636–0584.*

MARKET SQUARE ARENA

On June 26, 1977—manager Colonel Tom Parker's 68th birthday—Elvis Presley gave his final performance; within two months he was dead. A couple of pictures in the lobby of this 18,000-seat downtown venue commemorate the Last Concert, but nowadays it's best known as the home of the NBA's Pacers. *300 E. Market St., tel. 317/639–2112.*

SLIPPERY NOODLE INN

Indiana's oldest bar, open since 1850, was originally a boarding house used by railroad travelers. Until the end of the Civil War, escaped slaves traveling north on the Underground Railroad also hid in the basement. During Prohibition, much of the city's whiskey supply was made in the same basement and associates of the gangster John Dillinger (who is buried in the Crown Hill Cemetery here) hung out upstairs. There are still a few bullet holes around to prove it.

The Slippery Noodle is now the best no-frills venue in downtown Indy for bluesy rock, and its intrigu-

At the Slippery Noodle

ing history helps attract musicians normally far too big to play either of its two rooms. Those who have come to jam and nose around include Gregg Allman, Stephen Stills, Mick Fleetwood, John Mayall, and Harry Connick, Jr. *372 S. Meridian St., tel. 317/631 – 6968.*

Lafayette

William (Axl) Rose was born here on February 6, 1962, followed two months later by his eventual Guns N' Roses bandmate Jeff Isabelle, who became Izzy Stradlin. Axl got his moniker from the name of an early band he was in. Also from Lafayette is the late Shannon Hoon, the former lead singer of Blind Melon. None of the three made it to Purdue University, whose 36,000-student campus dominates the west side of town.

Terre Haute

In the early '60s, Chuck Berry served time in the federal penitentiary in this out-of-the-way western Indiana town for transporting a 14-year-old girl, Janice Escalanti, across the Missouri state line for alleged immoral purposes. Berry was originally given five years, but he appealed, defended himself in court at the retrial, and had his sentence reduced to two years.

One of rock's most-mourned tragedies—the plane crash that killed Buddy Holly, the Big Bopper, and Ritchie Valens—happened in February 1959, near the town of Clear Lake, Iowa. The forested Great Plains state, stuck between the Mississippi and Missouri rivers, is also celebrated for its movie stars: John Wayne was born in Winterset, and in *Star Trek IV: The Voyage Home,* James T. Kirk admits that Iowa, not outer space, is his home.

Centerville

41° N, 93° W

Iowa inspired one of the most intriguing songs by the British proto-grunge band Wire. Bassist Graham Lewis, looking out the plane window while traveling from L.A. to New York, was so impressed by the mapmaking skills of America's cartographers that he dedicated a song to them, the 1979 single "Map Reference 41°N 93°W." The coordinates, which identify the center of gravity of the North American landmass, come out in the middle of the Iowa countryside between Albia and Chariton, near the appropriately named Centerville.

Clear Lake

SURF BALLROOM

Buddy Holly, the Big Bopper, and Ritchie Valens played their last gig before 1,500 fans in this north Iowa town, halfway between Minneapolis and Des Moines, on February 2, 1959. En route to their next gig, their plane crashed and all aboard were killed. The ballroom resolutely refuses to change its period decor and now hosts an annual Buddy Holly tribute to mark the February anniversary. *460 N. Shore Dr., tel. 515/357–6151.*

Courtesy of the Surf Ballroom

The Surf Ballroom today

Des Moines

VETERANS MEMORIAL AUDITORIUM

During their extensive 1981–82 U.S. tour, Ozzy Osbourne's Blizzard of Oz erected a big catapult onstage; the idea was that fans would hurl up bits of offal and stuff, which would then be fired back into the crowd. As the tour progressed, fans thought up weirder and weirder things to throw, but on January 20, 1982, the ultimate offering was made: a stunned bat. Osbourne, thinking it was a rubber toy, tried to bite off its head and got a shock when the bat bit back. He had to be hospitalized to rule out rabies. *833 5th Ave., tel. 515/242–2946.*

Mason City
BUDDY HOLLY CRASH SITE

Buddy Holly, the Big Bopper, and Ritchie Valens were killed early in the morning on February 3, 1959, when their Beechcraft Bonanza plane crashed in the snow about 8 miles northwest of the Mason City airport. The performers had just played in Clear Lake (*see above*) and were in a hurry to get Moorhead, Minnesota, scene of their next gig. Holly wanted to get his suit cleaned, Valens wanted a haircut, and the Big Bopper wanted some "sleep." J. P. Richardson, the Bopper, was particularly unlucky—he had agreed to go on the plane at the last minute, taking the place of Holly's bass player, the future country star Waylon Jennings. The backing musicians, who had traveled in a separate plane, decreed that the Moorhead show had to go on, and it did, later that day, with the rest of the Crickets plus Dion and the Belmonts.

Holly's death has been seen by some as an early rock & roll nemesis; in his 1971 chart-topper, "American Pie," warbler Don McLean proclaimed it "the day the music died." At the time, some members of the American press treated the demise of the Bopper and Valens as the bigger loss: They were considered rising stars, while Holly was dismissed as passé.

Twenty-one years after the fatal crash, the sheriff of Cerro Gordo County found what turned out to be Holly's glasses while walking in a field. A memorial marks the spot where the plane came to a halt after skidding 200 yards across a cornfield; it's about half a mile west of Gull Avenue, and not that easy to find. *Gull Ave. at 315th St., off S28.*

Kansas is best recognized in rock circles for its namesake AOR band, who reached the Top 20 in early 1977 with "Carry on Wayward Son." However, the state was also the setting for the timeless 1939 musical *The Wizard of Oz,* which has had a surprising influence on rock. Ozzy Osbourne adapted the title for his band, Blizzard of Ozz. Elton John named his top-selling 1973 album *Goodbye Yellow Brick Road,* and Captain Beefheart appropriated the image for his earlier track "Yellow Brick Road." David Bowie so liked the melody of "Somewhere Over the Rainbow" that he incorporated it into his 1972 single "Starman," and in 1974 America hit the Top 10 with "Tin Man." Sidney Lumet's all-black, late '70s version of the film, retitled *The Wiz* and set in New York, starred Michael Jackson, Diana Ross, and other Motown stalwarts.

Lawrence

This liberal and artsy town, 50 miles west of Kansas City, is home to the bluegrass-grunge band Paw and to William S. Burroughs, who has been feted by many of rock's finest, including Kurt Cobain and the Disposable Heroes of Hiphoprisy. The liveliest local venue for new music is the **BOTTLENECK** (737 New Hampshire St., tel. 913/841–5483), which gets in the best indie bands on the college circuit.

Leavenworth

Melissa Etheridge grew up in sleepy Leavenworth (about an hour northwest of Kansas City), where most people seem to work for Hallmark. She received her first acclaim at 11 when she sang a self-penned song at a talent show held at the Leavenworth Plaza shopping mall. The town held a Melissa Etheridge Day in November 1994, when she returned to play her high-school auditorium.

Wichita

AND THE WICHITA LINEMAN IS STILL ON THE LINE—GLEN CAMPBELL, "WICHITA LINEMAN"

Glen Campbell's Jimmy Webb–written 1968 hit, "Wichita Lineman," with its Rickenbacker intro, swirling strings, and evocation of endless sun-soaked highways, has emerged in recent years as a highly name-droppable cult favorite, beloved of artists as diverse as Nick Cave and Oasis. Around the same time, Bob Dylan cut the more frivolous "Yea! Heavy and a Bottle of Bread," later included on *The Basement Tapes,* in which he's "headin' out for Wichita in a pile of fruit."

The huge lakeland state of Michigan—or, to be precise, Detroit and the neighboring college town of Ann Arbor—has provided three significant musical genres: Motown, the proto-punk sound of the MC5 and the Stooges, and a techno-dance beat that borrowed heavily from German electronic outfits.

Ann Arbor

A 40-minute drive west of Detroit, Ann Arbor, the home of the University of Michigan campus, is crammed with bookstores, record shops, sidewalk cafés, and delis. In the late '60s, Bob Seger made early appearances at college bars and the MC5 and the Stooges lived here under the tutelage of radical poet John Sinclair. The Laughing Hyenas, perennial indie hopefuls, formed here in 1984. Today the local scene is wildly eclectic, ranging from all types of roots music to the much-touted (in Ann Arbor, at least) Restroom Poets to self-proclaimed "retard-rockers" the Monarchs.

EATINGDRINKINGDANCINGSHOPPINGPLAYINGSLEEPING

The **ANN ARBOR BLUES AND JAZZ FESTIVAL** (tel. 313/665—4755) featured some terrific bills in the early '70s; revived as a two-day event in 1992, it now manages to get an interesting lineup each September. There are live performances at Gallup Park and in the wonderful Art Deco **MICHIGAN THEATER** (603 E. Liberty St., tel. 313/668—8480), a good place to check out anytime for cheap movies and local-band nights.

DISCOUNT RECORDS (300 S. State St., tel. 313/665—3679), a long-running downtown record store, has employed many musicians over the years, including local boy Iggy Pop in the mid-'60s. The **BLIND PIG** (208 S. 1st St., tel. 313/996—8555) is an ever-popular indie club where both Nirvana and Pearl Jam played on early tours. **RICK'S AMERICAN CAFÉ** (611 Church St., tel. 313/996—8555) hosts some touring bands. The **BIRD OF PARADISE** (207 S. Ashley Ave., tel. 313/662—8310) pulls in top jazz names. Look for club listings in the free monthly *Current,* and tune in to **WCBN** (88.3 FM) for an eclectic choice of programming.

THE ARK

One of the Midwest's most respected roots-music clubs was founded as a coffee bar by five local churches in 1965. While another church-led coffeehouse, the Canterbury (*see below*), went for singer-songwriters, the Ark concentrated on traditional ballads and Celtic and Cajun styles. When the Canterbury closed in the early '70s, the Ark broadened its focus, and since then everyone in the folk world has played here, including Richard Thompson, Mary Chapin Carpenter, the Bothy Band, and Clannad.

Originally set up in a home at 1421 Hill Street, the Ark moved to a big wooden cabin at 637½ South Main Street in 1984, and 11 years later, to its current downtown space. The venue, which holds 500, is now run by a nonprofit educational organization that also books the long-running Ann Arbor Folk Festival, a one-day event held each January at the university's Hill Auditorium. Headliners have included John Prine, Taj Mahal, Donovan, Lyle Lovett, Nanci Griffith, and Richie Havens. They also book the three-day summertime Frog Island Festival, heavy on New Orleans jazz and world music, held in nearby Ypsilanti. *316 S. Main St., tel. 313/761−1451.*

CANTERBURY HOUSE

In operation between 1965 and 1972, this cozy coffee bar was set up by the Episcopal Student Organization under the auspices of the local clergy. During the daytime the alcohol-free venue would host religious meetings, while at night there were bands. The MC5 played several times, and out-of-towners included Janis Joplin, Joni Mitchell, and Neil Young, who recorded his 1969 U.K. single "Sugar Mountain" at a gig here. The venue is now an Armenian restaurant. *328 Maynard St.*

COACHVILLE MOBILE PARK

This trailer park in Ypsilanti, a likable little blue-collar sibling of Ann Arbor, was where James Jewel Osterberg grew up. In 1964, at 16, he started drumming with a local band, the Iguanas, and soon moved on to the Prime Movers, where he took up his nickname—Iggy after the Iguanas, and Pop after a legendary local druggie. After some time in Chicago, he returned to Michigan and in 1967 formed the Psychedelic Stooges. *3423 Carpenter Rd., Ypsilanti.*

Chris Cuffaro/Virgin Records

The inimitable Iggy Pop

PIONEER HIGH SCHOOL

This contender for the nation's top rock & roll high school was attended by Iggy Pop, most of the Stooges, all of the Rationals, Bob Seger, Deon Jackson—who had an R&B hit in 1966 with "Love Makes the World Go Round"—and Bill Kirchen of Commander Cody and His Lost Planet Airmen. For good creative measure, it also boasts documentary filmmakers Ken and Rick Burns of *Civil War* fame. *601 W. Stadium Blvd.*

SCHOOLKIDS RECORDS

Although it hasn't grown quite as big as Borders Books, which also originated in Ann Arbor, Schoolkids' is one of the country's major independent music retailers. Going since 1974, the company set up its own label in 1992, recording mostly local bands. Releases have come from the poppy Kiss Me Screaming, ex-Rational Scott Morgan, and an eclectic roster of rockabilly, jazz, and blues acts, including some compilations from Ann Arbor Blues and Jazz Festivals. Three retail outlets flourish on East Liberty Street. The main store stocks mainstream rock and is also good for blues, R&B, and jazz. The walls are covered with pictures of those who have done in-store performances—Iggy Pop (several times), the Misfits, Stevie Ray Vaughan, Sonic Youth, and Hüsker Dü, among them. There's also a comprehensive indie, techno, and alternative store, and Michael Nyman is a big fan of the classical unit. *523 E. Liberty St., tel. 313/994−8031 or 800/445−2361, http//www.schoolkids.com.*

John Sinclair—music journalist, poet, radical activist, and mentor and manager of the MC5—became a cause célèbre in the late '60s. He founded the White Panthers, a Yippie/SDS–like social-activist group that adopted a 10-point program to, among other things, "smoke dope and fuck in the streets"—a threat that the police took seriously.

In January 1967, cops raided the Artists' and Writers' Workshop in downtown Detroit and arrested Sinclair and 56 others on drug charges. Sinclair was charged with possessing two joints of marijuana and sentenced to 10 years in prison. The music world rallied round: A two-night benefit, the first of several consciousness-raising fundraisers, was held in January 1970 at the Grande Ballroom. In the lineup were the MC5, the Stooges, SRC, UP, Scorpion, Commander Cody, the Bob Seger System, the Amboy Dukes, Mitch Ryder and the Detroit Wheels, the Rationals, and Brownsville Station.

John Lennon and Yoko Ono, wearing "Free John Now" T-shirts, appeared at a December 1971 benefit at Ann Arbor's Crisler Arena and performed four songs, including "Luck of the Irish" and one called "Ten for Two," a commentary on the stupidity of Sinclair's sentence. Also on the bill were Stevie Wonder, Commander Cody, Phil Ochs, and Bob Seger. Black Panther Bobby Seale was a speaker, along with Jerry Rubin and Allen Gins-

John Sinclair reads at Schoolkids' Records

berg, in what was dubbed a "political Woodstock." Sinclair was finally released at the end of the year, after about two years inside. He went on to serve as creative director of the Ann Arbor Blues and Jazz Festival for several years, and now lives in New Orleans, where he performs regularly with his band, the Blues Scholars.

STOOGES MANOR

Thanks to a big advance from Elektra, the Stooges were able to rent a large house that they referred to as Stooges Manor—a name they particularly liked to use in front of other local musicians with less salubrious digs. A mention of the Manor also became customary when chatting up women, and band members kept a collection of their female visitors' panties stapled to the kitchen countertop. The fun lasted for a couple of years before the group split up in 1977; a bank now occupies the spot. *Corner of Packard and Eisenhower Sts.*

STOOGES "MUSEUM"

A completely bogus story, complete with a mock-up photo, appeared in Detroit's *Motorbooty* magazine and started a rumor that this house on the edge of the U of M campus holds a private collection of Iggy memorabilia, including wax models of all the Stooges. The joke has endured—thanks to locals playing along with it. The house was actually the headquarters of the White Panther Party, headed by John Sinclair, who managed the MC5 for a time. Members of that band, plus some Stooges, lived or crashed here and in the other Panther houses at 1510 and 1522 Hill Street. The "museum" is now in the hands of a housing co-operative. *1520 Hill St.*

Iggy Pop saw the Velvet Underground for the first time on this downtown campus in April 1967. He claimed the gig changed his life and made him want to be a rock & roll star. Danny Field, an executive for Elektra records who was later instrumental in signing the Stooges, saw the MC5 at a show in the campus' Union Ballroom in September 1968; the band picked up its first recording contract a week later. George Frayne taught in the Arts School in the late '60s and formed Commander Cody and His Lost Planet Airmen here. Madonna won a dance scholarship to the School of Music and enrolled in fall 1976. She stayed for about a year and waited tables at the Blue Frogge, now Rick's American Café (*see above*).

Bay City

Scottish impresario Tam Paton, desperately looking for a name for his group, stuck a pin in a map of the Unites States. It landed at Bay City, Michigan—a nice enough little town 80 miles northwest of Detroit on the shores of Lake Huron, with big mansions and an even bigger Dow petrochemical plant—and the Bay City Rollers were born. The city is the literal birthplace of Madonna Louise Ciccone, who was born in Mercy Hospital on August 16, 1958, to a family that eventually had four boys and four girls. The Ciccones were in Bay City visiting Madonna's French-Canadian maternal grandmother, to whom the singer indirectly owes her name—Madonna was named for her mother, born Madonna Fortin. Although baby Madonna was brought back to the family home in Pontiac, Michigan, after a few days, the politicians of Bay City planned to honor her with the keys to the city in the mid-'80s. They withdrew the invite after nude photos, taken during her early years as an artist's model, appeared in *Playboy* and *Penthouse*.

Detroit

DON'T FORGET THE MOTOR CITY!—MARTHA AND THE VANDELLAS, "DANCING IN THE STREET"

The Motown sound didn't simply appear from nowhere. During the '40s and '50s, Detroit had a reputation for top late-night bars and clubs, with appearances by acts like John Lee Hooker, Sam Cooke, LaVern Baker, and Hank Ballard. Despite the lively scene, however, there were few local labels; Chess set up outposts in the late '50s with the Anna and Check-Mate labels, but they failed to make much of an impression. Then Berry Gordy, a Detroit songwriter who had written several hits for local ex–Golden Gloves boxer and singing sensation Jackie Wilson, became aware of the void in the market, so he borrowed a few hundred bucks and set up Motown.

While Gordy's roster of labels was busy conquering the world in the '60s, other local soul and R&B labels appeared. Golden World/Ric-Tic, which Gordy eventually bought out, recorded Edwin Starr, and Revilot had the doo-wop Parliaments (featuring George Clinton). After Motown left for Los Angeles in the early '70s, the biggest local soul label was Invictus; run by the former Motown production team of Eddie Holland, Lamont Dozier, and Brian Holland, the label recorded Freda Payne and the Chairmen of the Board. Westbound, another '70s contender, had the Detroit Emeralds and Funkadelic.

Motown employed a sizable number of white staffers and even recorded some white artists (Neil Young cut some tracks in the early '60s with a band called the Mynah Birds, which also featured Rick James, but they were never released), but Detroit's white kids were into something else by the mid-'60s. As early as the summer of 1966, Detroit had a countercultural underground scene—radical magazines; a psychedelic ballroom, the Grande; bands like the MC5, Mitch Ryder and the Detroit Wheels, and the Amboy Dukes; and a spokesman in poet John Sinclair. Coming slightly later were the Stooges, the Bob Seger System, the Rationals, and the launch of *Creem* magazine by journalists Lester Bangs and Dave Marsh (among others), who were already disillusioned by the direction of *Rolling Stone*.

George Clinton, one-time doo-wop singer with Detroit's Parliaments

Brooke Williams

The late '70s saw the first vinyl experiments by producer Don Was, born Don Fagenson, of Was (Not Was), and despite some punk noises that emanated in the early '80s, the next new thing from Detroit was more influenced by Kraftwerk and other German synth bands than by Motown: Techno pioneers Derrick May, Kevin Saunderson, and Juan Atkins—along with such later arrivals as Plastikman (Richie Hawtin), from just across the river in Windsor, Canada, and Underground Resistance (Mike Banks and Jeff Mills)—had a massive influence on dance music. The city's techno clubs remained small, predominantly black affairs until 1996, when Tresor, the keynote techno club in Berlin, opened a club just off Woodward Avenue. Meanwhile, on the more mainstream side of the rock world, current local bands include the indie rockers Sponge, Sub Pop's Big Chief, ex–Was (Not Was) types Gadda Da Vida, and rappers I.C.P.

EATINGDRINKINGDANCINGSHOPPINGPLAYINGSLEEPING

For up-to-date information, pick up the free weekly *Metro Times* or hunt down a copy of the monthly *Orbit,* which always gives a good overview of the scene. The best new and touring bands play the 1,000-capacity main room of **St. Andrew's Hall** (431 E. Congress St., tel. 313/961—MELT), a stocky downtown space built originally as a Scottish benevolent society headquarters; St. Andrew's also holds Shelter, a dance club with occasional up-and-coming bands, and the Burns Room, where techno reigns. Less than a mile east, on the edge of downtown, a healthy crop of live-music venues has grown up among the warehouses of what's called Rivertown, or sometimes Bricktown. The cramped, smoky **Soup Kitchen Saloon** (1585 Franklin St., tel. 312/259—2643) always has great blues and is the premier stop. Across the river from downtown is Windsor, Canada, where the drinking age is 19; you'll find several sidewalk and patio bars, a few dance clubs, and **California's** (911 Walker Rd., tel. 519/258—1152), which always has decent indie and blues.

Other venues lie farther afield. Four miles north of the city, not far from Motown, is the gentrifying, blue-collar Polish district of Hamtramck. Besides the hard-rocking **Paycheck's Lounge** (2932 Caniff St., tel. 312/874—0254), there's **Lili's 21** (2930 Jacob St., tel. 313/875—6555), a neighborhood hangout that's seen plenty since opening in 1979; one famous tale involves the Clash, who came to do an interview with *Creem* and got so drunk on *je'ynowka* (a lethal Polish blackberry spirit) that that's about all the article talked about. Lili's has a good reputation for breaking local bands, particularly on Thursday nights, when the cover is $2 and drinks are cheap. The trendiest area in Metro Detroit has to be Royal Oak, 9 miles from downtown and stocked with alternative shops, record stores, and cafés; **METROPOLITAN MUSICAFÉ** (326 W. 4th St., tel. 810/542—1990) has live music and is worth checking out.

Detroit Tunes

Tom Jones, "Detroit City" (1967)
The MC5, "The Motor City Is Burning" (1969)
David Bowie, "Panic in Detroit" (1973)
Kiss, "Detroit Rock City" (1976)
Gil Scott Heron, "We Almost Lost Detroit" (1977)
Blondie, "Detroit 442" (1978)
Devo, "Doctor Detroit" (1983)
Alvin Lee, "Detroit Diesel" (1987)
Manic Street Preacher, "Motown Junk" (1991)

CASS TECHNICAL HIGH

Diana Ross went to this integrated arts school, renowned for its music program, as did many Motown studio-band members. It's still thought of as having one of the best high-school music departments around. *2421 2nd Ave., tel. 313/494—2605.*

CHIT CHAT LOUNGE

While Stax's house band, Booker T. and the MGs, climbed the charts with instrumentals like "Green Onions," Motown's key session players—Earl Van Dyke, Benny Benjamin, and James Jamerson—had to settle for playing jazz at this club, a brisk stroll from the studios, for a little extra cash. The Funk Brothers, as they called themselves, played on hundreds of Motown tracks but never got a credit on any album until the '70s. They eventually got to record one album themselves, but Berry Gordy insisted they be called Earl Van Dyke and the Soul Brothers (*funk* was not a Motown word), and they had to make do with instrumental versions of Motown standards rather than the driving jams they did late at night in this long-closed little joint. *8235 12th Ave.*

FLAME SHOW BAR

In 1956—at a time when Sam Cooke, LaVern Baker, and Johnnie Ray would perform here—two of Berry Gordy's sisters got the cigarette and photo concessions. Gordy, an aspiring songwriter, managed to slip in and bring tapes and lyric sheets for the singers. One night in late 1957, he heard that Jackie Wilson's manager was looking for new material. He got together with the singer, and they worked on several songs over the next two years, including "Reet Petite," "That Is Why (I Love You So)," and "I'll Be Satisfied." Gordy eventually tapped Maurice King, the leader of the house band from the club's opening night in 1950 until the early '60s, to work for Motown's artist-development department and create sensational stage shows for the Motown revues and tours. The bar is long gone. *4664 John R. St.*

FOX THEATER

Motown used to hold its Christmas revues in this 1928 theater. The acts had to play up to five shows a night all week long, and Gordy would change the bill around according to applause. It didn't matter who was the bigger recording star—if they didn't get as many cheers as a smaller act, they slipped down the bill. By the '70s the theater had slipped into being a dreary hangar with poor facilities. Then, in 1988, the Fox got a complete overhaul and now boasts a Byzantine interior with gold leaf, 300,000 glass jewels embedded in decorative figures, brass ornamentation, marble pillars, and a six-story-high lobby. These days the theater hosts the occasional concert by rock aristocracy but mostly puts on musicals and drama productions. *2211 Woodward Ave., tel. 313/567–6000.*

The Fox

GRANDE BALLROOM

In 1966, local DJ Russ Gibb visited San Francisco and was so impressed by the scene at the Fillmore and Avalon ballrooms that he decided Detroit needed some of the same. Wanting to emulate pioneering rock promoter Bill Graham, Gibb even put the slogan "Uncle Russ Presents in Detroit" on all event posters. He also used similar psychedelic flyers and posters to advertize gigs at the venue, which holds 2,000 and was built specifically as a ballroom, with lots of plaster scroll-work and no seats. By 1967 Gibb was able to book the Grateful Dead, Cream, and other hot out-of-town bands. The following year the Grande hosted Canned Heat, Big Brother and the Holding Company, Spooky Tooth, the Jimi Hendrix Experience, and Country Joe and the Fish, while the Who made a big impression in 1969.

However, the band most associated with the venue was the MC5, who did one of Gibb's earliest shows, in October 1966, and played many times subsequently, building a loyal local fan base. Two years later to the month, they recorded their debut album, *Kick Out the Jams,* live over two nights here. The title track's famed intro—"Right now it's time to…kick out the jams, motherfuckers"—didn't go down too well with Elektra executives, who dubbed out the offensive bits on later pressings. The members of the politically charged quintet, not the types to take such treatment lying down, took out ads in local magazines insulting a record chain that refused to stock their product and fought continuously over the issue with Elektra. Although the album did well, the label dropped them.

The MC5 were back in full form for a two-night benefit in January 1970 calling for the release from prison of their manager, John Sinclair. Another local band at the Sinclair benefit was the Stooges, who also made one of their first major appearances—as the Psychedelic Stooges—here in April 1968. Although their set lasted less than half an hour, they were

The MC5, Kick Out the Jams

signed up by Elektra boss Jac Holzman, who had been dragged to the show on the insistence of A&R man Danny Fields, who had himself signed the MC5 two weeks earlier. The MC5 chose the Grande to bow out on New Year's Day 1972, and the venue didn't last much longer. It now stands abandoned in a neighborhood that's gotten even tougher since the '60s. *8952 Grand River Rd., at Beverly St.*

BERRY GORDY CHILDHOOD HOME SITE

Motown founder Berry Gordy grew up here with his seven siblings. The Gordys, noted black entrepreneurs and Democratic Party activists, ran several businesses from these premises, including Berry's father's Booker T. Washington Grocery Store and a print shop where Berry worked for a while after leaving the army. Marvin Gaye and Gordy's older sister Anna lived in an upstairs apartment right after they got married in 1961. The area was redeveloped after the 1967 riots, and a medical center now stands on this site. *Farnsworth and St. Antoine Sts.*

MARINER'S CHURCH

This landmark sandstone church next to the entrance to the tunnel to Canada was where former MC5 guitarist Fred "Sonic" Smith and punk chanteuse Patti Smith married on March 1, 1980. It was also where the funeral service was held in November 1994 for Fred, who had a heart attack at age 44—a particularly harsh blow as MC5 lead singer Rob Tyner had also died of cardiac arrest just three years earlier. At the 1995 memorial service, attended by former colleagues, commemorative crosses were placed in the church and a photo of the late artists with the legend FRED "SONIC" SMITH, MUSICIAN—20TH CENTURY was displayed.

The church is also the "maritime soldier's cathedral" mentioned in folkie Gordon Lightfoot's "The Wreck of the *Edmund Fitzgerald*," a real-life tale of the crew killed when a freight ship ran aground off Michigan's Lake Superior coastline near Whitefish Point in the early '70s. *170 E. Jefferson Ave., tel. 313/259-2206.*

MICHIGAN THEATER

Iggy and the Stooges played this club in October 1973 and again the following February (the band's last performance), and both gigs were captured on the chaotic live album *Metallic KO*. At the final show, Iggy marked the occasion by rolling around on broken glass and cursing the unappreciative crowd, who replied by pelting him with eggs, bottles, and anything else at hand. The theater closed its doors soon after, and today it's one of the most surreal parking garages in the city. Walk up to the top level and you'll see that the theater's ornate decorations are still partly intact, as are tatters of the stage curtains. *Bagley and Grand River Aves.*

MICHIGAN STATE FAIRGROUNDS

At an outdoor concert here in 1961, Berry Gordy proudly presented the Miracles with their first gold disc, for "Shop Around," the record that hit No. 2 on the pop charts and sent Motown soaring past the million sales mark. Eight years later, on May 30–31, 1969, the fairgrounds were the site of the Detroit Rock & Roll Revival, a major festival promoted by Russ Gibbs and enthusiastically supported by *Creem* magazine, which had started up in the city a few months earlier. Grande Ballroom regulars like the MC5, the Stooges, and the Rationals were on the bill, along with Chuck Berry, Sun Ra, Dr. John, and Johnny Winter. *Woodward Ave. at 8 Mile Rd.*

THE MOTOWN SOUND

In the beginning, the singers on Berry Gordy's Motown label reproduced the heavy gospel sound that had shaped their musical backgrounds—lots of tambourine smashing and hand-clapping, as evident on the Marvelettes' "Please Mr. Postman" (1961) and Marvin Gaye's "Can I Get a Witness?" (1963). Then

Motown's in-house producers began placing the emphasis on arrangement, orchestration, and vocal interplay, a focus particularly evident on records like the Miracles' "Tracks of My Tears" (1965) and the Four Tops' "Reach Out, I'll Be There" (1966).

The most successful of the Motown production teams was that of Lamont Dozier and brothers Eddie and Brian Holland. The trio developed a rhythm based on the clattering mechanical beat of Detroit's assembly lines, where many of the Motown personnel had worked, and created rudimentary sound effects with chains, hammers, and planks of wood, or by stomping on floorboards. When echoes were called for, the singers were dispatched to the bathroom or attic. Holland-Dozier-Holland worked closely with a host of acts, but particularly with the Supremes. Barely out of high school when Gordy first hired them for handclap-

Courtesy of Motown Record Company, L. P., and the Four Tops

The Four Tops at Motown

ping duties, the H-D-H–produced Supremes came up with 11 No. 1 singles, including "Baby Love," "You Can't Hurry Love," and "Stop! In the Name of Love."

During the '60s Motown enjoyed more than 70 Top 10 hits, but by the end of the decade, despite the introduction of the Jackson Five, some critics felt that the label was resting on its laurels. After the operation started to move to Los Angeles in 1971, Motown's stature declined. While Marvin Gaye and Stevie Wonder forged new careers as "serious" singer-songwriters, Diana Ross worked the schmaltzy-ballad market and the Four Tops lost their way. Holland-Dozier-Holland refused to make the trip west, instead setting up their own Invictus label in Detroit.

For a while Motown was buoyed by new whiz-kid producer Norman Whitfield, who devised a powerful sound for the Temptations on early '70s hits like "Papa Was a Rolling Stone." Then Whitfield left to set up his own label and steer the career of Rose Royce, taking Motown's last "sound" with him. By the late '80s MCA had a controlling interest in Motown affairs, and in August 1993 the rich back catalogue—plus current signees Queen Latifah, Boyz II Men, and Stevie Wonder—was taken over by Polygram.

[MOTOWN]

The Hitsville U.S.A. banner still hangs outside this blue-and-white clapboard house, the last remaining Motown presence in the city where Berry Gordy built his music empire. In 1959 Gordy, an aspiring songwriter, former professional boxer, and Ford production-line worker, borrowed $700 from his family to set up a studio and record label. Although he had written "Reet Petite" and other hits for Jackie Wilson, he wasn't making much money from royalties and decided that the only way of getting a fair share was to set up his own company.

Gordy was quick to realize that although Detroit had popular local artists like Hank Ballard and Wilson and the fourth-largest black population in the country, it had no successful record companies. He founded the Tammie label, later renamed Tamla; significantly, he also set up a publishing company, Jobete (named after three of his children: *Joy*, *Berry*, and *Terry*), to keep control of the songs, and International Talent Management to supervise the careers of artists in his charge. Other labels were quickly established—Gordy, Motown, VIP, and Soul. (In Britain, records were released under the catch-all name Tamla Motown.)

Soon after his first release on Tamla—Marv Johnson's "Come to Me" in 1959—Gordy hit pay dirt, unearthing major talents like Smokey Robinson (Gordy's first signing and, with the Miracles, the source of the label's first gold record), Stevie Wonder (who released his first single at age 12), Marvin Gaye, Diana Ross and the Supremes, the Four Tops, the Temptations, and later the Jackson Five. After a couple of No. 1 singles, the Motown operation outgrew the house at 2648 Grand, and Gordy started buying up adjacent properties to house divisions of his fast-growing empire. By 1966, Motown owned eight properties along this stretch of the boulevard, between which could be seen flitting staff, session players, and recording stars at all times of the day and night.

Studio A, the "snakepit"

This golden age was not to last, however; the Motown empire moved to Los Angeles in the early '70s, and the original studios gathered dust. It wasn't until 1985 that the facility reopened, housing the nonprofit Motown Historical Museum and an education program. The key attraction is the tiny 20-by-15-foot Studio A, where the vast majority of Motown's hits were recorded. The "Snakepit," as the session players called it, was open 24 hours a day, seven days a week, from 1959 until the move to L.A. It really does look like it's been untouched for over two decades; it's crammed with many old instruments, including a Hammond B3 organ owned by studio-band leader Earl Van Dyke, a well-hammered Steinway, and assorted music stands with sheet music still on them.

Upstairs are the quarters where Berry Gordy lived between 1959 and 1961; the label's business affairs, including shipping of singles, was done from the parlor. Elsewhere in the museum, which in 1995 was expanded to incorporate the former office space at No. 2644—6 (bought in 1961 to house Jobete Publishing, the sales, billing, shipping, and PR departments), are story boards emphasizing the business acumen of Gordy and how the label grew. Displays include gold and platinum discs, album covers, and costumes—check out the sequined glove and black fedora Michael Jackson wore in the "Beat It" video.

The future looks bright for the museum. A sizable exhibition on Motown ran at the Henry Ford Museum in Dearborn through 1996, and it's planned that the artifacts—truckloads of costumes, instruments, discs, and handwritten lyrics—plus the movie theater and specially commissioned interactive displays (a mixing board and a "dance along with the Temptations" choreography class), will be moved to a site adjacent to the museum by the end of the millennium. *2468 Grand Blvd., tel. 313/875–2264. Admission: $6. Open Sun.–Mon. noon–5, Tues.–Sat. 10–5.*

NEW BETHEL BAPTIST CHURCH

During the '40s and '50s, the Rev. C. L. Franklin gained a regional reputation for his roaring gospel voice, and he and his choir were recorded by Chess and other labels. Daughter Aretha sang her first church solo here at eight, in 1950; she took lead vocals for the first time in 1956 with Chess's recording engineers sitting in the church. She did "The Day Is Past and Gone" and "14," a Clara Ward song that she was also to sing 17 years later at Ward's funeral. New Bethel is still open, and the choir commands a good reputation. *8450 C. L. Franklin Blvd., tel. 313/894–5788.*

UNITED SOUND SYSTEMS

This bright blue house next to Wayne State University holds the Motor City's second most famous studio (after Motown's Studio A, a mile up the road). In operation since 1933, it's where John Lee Hooker cut his first sides for Modern after arriving in the city in the late '40s. Smokey Robinson's Miracles made their recording debut here in fall 1957 with "Got a Job," a riposte to the Silhouettes' doo-wop hit "Get a Job."

Since the early '70s, United Sound has been owned and run by writer-producer Don Davis, who worked closely with Johnnie Taylor to score hits like "Disco Lady" and "Who's Making Love?" Another major mid-'70s success was "You Don't Have to Be a Star" by Fifth Dimension veterans Marilyn McCoo and Billy Davis, Jr. Bootsy Collins and George Clinton have been regular visitors for over 20 years, and Aretha Franklin has said that the big main studio—ideal for recording full gospel choirs—is her favorite place to record. Gold discs for her "Who's Zoomin' Who" are among those decorating the walls here. The staff is super friendly, so it might be worth calling to ask for a look around. *5840 2nd Blvd., tel. 313/832–3313.*

JACKIE WILSON GRAVE

Detroit-born Jackie Wilson, whose career took off in the late '50s when Berry Gordy wrote several hits for him, died on January 21, 1984, never having awakened from a coma after collapsing onstage in New Jersey eight and a half years earlier. He was buried in Westlawn Cemetery in Wayne, in the southwestern extremity of Metro Detroit. *31472 Michigan Ave., tel. 313/722–2530.*

SHOP AROUND

Metro Detroit has some unusual record stores, but most are way out from the center. The best neighborhood for a buying spree is Royal Oak: Repeat the Beat (520 S. Washington Ave., tel. 810/543–4310), which also has branches in Dearborn and Plymouth, is a way-cool store selling all formats. Off the Record (322 S. Main St., tel. 810/398–4436) deals in rarities. The best place for imports is Play It Again (503 S. Main St., tel. 810/542–7529).

For used records there's a massive selection at Car City Records (21918 Harper Ave., St. Clair Shores, tel. 810/775–4770). Another good place to pick up used vinyl, especially R&B, is Street Corner Music (17620 W. 13 Mile Rd., Franklin, tel. 810/644–4777). Techno and dance is well covered at Record Time (25110 Gratiot Ave., Roseville, tel. 810/775–1550), also a great source of club news.

Flint

Castigated on celluloid by Michiganer Michael Moore in *Roger and Me,* the auto-manufacturing town of Flint was where ? and the Mysterians formed in 1966 and Grand Funk Railroad got together two years later.

DAYS INN

The Who's drummer Keith Moon celebrated his 21st birthday at this motel, then part of the Holiday Inn chain, on August 23, 1968. He started drinking at 10 AM but waited until the party was getting into gear in the evening—most of the guests were dancing around in their underwear—to pick up his cake (in the shape of a drum kit—a present from drum manufacturer Premier) and begin hurling it around the room.

Moon then ran out into the parking lot, jumped into the first car he could find (a new Lincoln Continental), and released the emergency brake. The car rolled through a fence and into the hotel swimming pool, with Moon inside. He later claimed that he never thought he would drown, saying that he remembered school physics class and knew to wait until the pressure was the same inside and out before opening the door. When there was barely any air left, Moon threw open the door and swam to the surface, where he was met only by a janitor, not the cheering crowd he expected. The drummer then went back to the party, where he was greeted by an armed sheriff before slipping on some marzipan and falling, breaking a tooth.

Moon spent the night in custody with a dentist who couldn't administer anesthetic because of the level of booze in his body. The next day the sheriff put him on a plane, saying, "Sonny, don't ever dock in Flint, Michigan, again." Moon replied, "Dear boy, I wouldn't dream of it." The bill for total destruction—including a piano, paint for six cars, the Lincoln at the bottom of the pool, etc.—came close to $40,000, which he sent to the hotel with a card that read BALLS. *2207 W. Bristol Rd., tel. 313/239–4681.*

Jackson

TED NUGENT'S BOWHUNTERS' WORLD

This is the retail operation of that hunting, fishing, and generally good-living guy Ted "Cat Scratch Fever" Nugent, whose musical career kicked off in 1966 when, at 18, he formed the Amboy Dukes in Detroit. Now an elected member of the National Rifle Association's controlling committee, he also produces a bimonthly magazine, *Adventure Outdoors.* Nugent lives on a heavily guarded compound outside of town, where he and other members of the quasi-political American Bloodbrothers congregate for shooting practice. He also does a regular show on WRIF 101 in nearby Southfield. *4133 W. Michigan Ave., 90 mi W of Detroit, tel. 517/750–9060.*

Pontiac

On the northern edge of Metro Detroit, some 25 miles from the center, Pontiac is best known as the site of the impressive Silverdome, home of the Detroit Lions. There in April 1977, Led Zeppelin broke its own concert-attendance record by attracting 76,229 fans to a show that grossed over $800,000. The town was also the earliest home of Madonna—the Ciccones lived for a few years at 443 Thors Street before moving to Rochester.

Until recently downtown Pontiac had a reputation for grade-A dullness, but the area has picked up with the opening of several clubs and bars in the '90s. The most notable is **INDUSTRY** (15 Saginaw St., tel. 810/334–1999), a cavernous postindustrial dance space.

Cannon Falls

PACHYDERM DISC

Set in a rustic, out-of-the-way location, Pachyderm is one of the best-equipped studios in the Midwest. Its most famous visitors came in 1993 under the name the Simon Ritchie Band (a reference to the real name of Sid Vicious); they turned out to be Nirvana, looking for some quiet time to work on their follow-up album to *Nevermind*. The sessions, produced by Steve Albini, failed to impress Geffen executives, who thought the sound was too lo-fi and had the work substantially remixed. Other artists to record at Pachyderm include PJ Harvey, Babes in Toyland, and Soul Asylum. Cannon Falls is 50 miles southeast of Minneapolis via Highway 52. *7840 County Rd., tel. 507/263–5276.*

Duluth

Bob Dylan was born Robert Allen Zimmerman in this port town on Lake Superior on May 24, 1941, but his family soon moved to Hibbing (*see below*), some 50 miles north. In "Something There Is About You" he muses, "Thought I'd shaken the wonder and the phantoms of my youth, rainy days on the Great Lakes, walking the hills of old Duluth."

The city is the starting point of a scenic stretch of Highway 61, which hugs the cliffs for some 160 miles up to the Canadian border. In the late '80s the town received a major spruce-up, and some city councillors wanted to name a remodeled section of Highway 61 in the center of town the Bob Dylan Underpass. The proposal never had unanimous support, and the idea seemed to fade after Dylan snubbed a public function at which he was billed as a guest of honor.

The Dylan display in his hometown library

Hibbing

When Abraham and Betty Zimmerman, second-generation Russian Jews, moved to this iron-ore mining center just after World War II to set up a furniture store, with them was their four-year-old son. Robert left town practically as soon as he could, in 1959, to attend the University of Minnesota, where he changed his name to Bob Dylan.

Dylan has never had that much to say about Hibbing, although on the back cover of 1963's *The Times They Are A-Changin'* (on which there is a song about the town titled "North Country Blues"), he calls it "deserted, already dead, with its old stone courthouse decaying in the wind." In his book *Tarantula*, Dylan claimed he sold his soul to the devil to escape.

Hibbing is also the hometown of Gary Puckett (born a year after Dylan, in 1942, but raised in Union Gap,

Washington), R.E.M. drummer Bill Berry, and Angie Carlson, lead singer of tuneful indie hopefuls Grover (on Zero Hour records).

EATINGDRINKINGDANCINGSHOPPINGPLAYINGSLEEPING

DYLAN'S BOYHOOD HOME (2425 7th Ave. E) and **HIBBING HIGH SCHOOL** (800 E. 21st St.), from which Dylan graduated in 1959, still stand, but the only spot where you'll find a Dylan commemoration is at **ZIMMY'S** (531 E. Howard St., tel. 218/262–6145), a burger-and-pizza joint with lots of Dylan memorabilia on the walls.

PUBLIC LIBRARY

Hardy Dylan fans who drive up the state's ruggedly good-looking Iron Range to check out his past can head for Hibbing's main library. There's a case with newspaper clippings, photos, and school yearbooks related to Bob Dylan, but that's it. The town has made little of its Dylan connections, largely because of the singer's reluctance to donate memorabilia and personal items. One member of the Chamber of Commerce said, "He never comes back here...probably never will." *220 5th Ave. E, tel. 218/262–1038.*

Minneapolis

WELL IT'S 9TH AND HENNEPIN/ALL THE DOUGHNUTS HAVE NAMES THAT SOUND LIKE PROSTITUTES—TOM WAITS, "9TH & HENNEPIN"

According to the city's most famous recording artist, the multifaceted Prince Nelson Rogers (born June 7, 1960), "Rock N Roll Is Alive (And It Lives in Minneapolis)." This claim has a particular a ring of truth if you consider the city's musical purple patch in the early '80s—⚥ was Prince, knocking out powerful tunes, and Hüsker Dü and the Replacements were achieving critical acclaim, with Soul Asylum following in their footsteps.

Murray Bowles

Minneapolis was known in the formative years of rock & roll as a major distribution center (a role continued today by Twin City Imports, which specializes in European alternative music). The best-known area band in the '60s was the Castaways, who cut the garage anthem "Liar, Liar" but soon vanished from the public eye. In the '70s the Ramones-ish Suicide Commandos had a good run and were signed by Polygram's Blank subsidiary.

By the end of that decade, the scene began to blossom: Pete Jesperson, who worked in the Oar Folkjokeopus record store, set up the Twin/Tone label. Its greatest find was a local band called the

The Replacements' Tommy Stinson

Impediments; after some booze- and incident-ridden gigs, they changed their name to the Replacements in order to continue getting bookings. By the mid-'80s, the Reps moved to Sire for their three celebrated albums, *Let It Be, Tim,* and *Pleased to Meet Me.* Another Twin/Tone success was Babes in Toyland, who recorded their first album on the label before moving to WEA.

In 1987 a new indie operation, Amphetamine Reptile, began recording Helmet, the Cows, Tar, and dozens of others; the label also released a number of popular compilations of regional bands before being bought by Columbia. Other notable local labels include Terry Lewis and Jimmy Jam's Flyte Tyme Productions, responsible for a string of soul hits by Janet Jackson, Alexander O'Neal, Sounds of Blackness, and others. At the other end of the sound scale, Spanish Fly is a label run by Babes in Toyland drummer Lori Barbero; signees include Milk, Dumpster Juice, and Queer. And then there's K-Tel, king of compilations.

EATINGDRINKINGDANCINGSHOPPINGPLAYINGSLEEPING

Downtown, the adjoining venues First Avenue and Seventh Street Entry (*see both below*) put on a wide choice of styles. The Whittier Park neighborhood, home of the Oar Folkjokeopus record store (*see below*), is a great area to hang out; try **MUDDY WATERS** (2401 Lyndale Ave. S, tel. 612/872−2232), a coffee bar popular with local musicians. A record store worthy of a visit for new sounds is downtown's **LET IT BE** (1001 Nicollet Ave., tel. 612/339−7439), while **NORTHERN LIGHTS** (805 4th St. SE, tel. 612/331−4439; 521 W. 98th St., tel. 612/888−6774) is hot on imports. Full listings of all that's going on are covered in two free weeklies: *Twin Cities Reader* and *City Pages.*

AMPHETAMINE REPTILE RECORDS

Tom Hazelmyer, guitarist for the Twin/Tone band Halo of Flies, founded Amphetamine Reptile in 1987. The label was purchased by Columbia but remains based in Minneapolis in rather neat quarters—a former dental surgery that maintains much of its original furniture and cabinets. The well-equipped studio where many of the label's bands record (the current roster includes Gaunt, Cosmic Psychos, Screwed, Supernova, and Unsane) is in the basement. *2645 1st Ave. S, tel. 612/870−9765 (studio).*

BIG TROUBLE HOUSE, C.1982−92

For around a decade, Babes in Toyland drummer Lori Barbero lived here and became a Mother Teresa–like figure for broke band members far from home. Virtually every up-and-coming band on the indie scene—Die Kreuzen, Dinosaur Jr, Fugazi, R.E.M., etc.—saved on motel bills by crashing at this aptly named party house. Some, like Courtney Love and Stefanie Sargent (of 7 Year Bitch), stayed put for several months. A local band who rehearsed in the basement took their name from the house. Barbero moved out of the Big Trouble House in the early '90s, and it ceased to be the open establishment it once was. *1925 Colfax Ave.*

DYLAN IN DINKYTOWN

Dinkytown is the name given to the area on the east bank of the Mississippi around the 50,000-student University of Minnesota. Rife with record stores, bookshops, campus bars, and cheap cafés, it has also been the stomping grounds of a few rock & rollers—a local in the early '80s was Lori Barbero, who dropped out of the university and found fame with Babes in Toyland.

Bob Dylan enrolled at the U of M as Robert Zimmerman in 1959, but also attended only briefly. He claimed in "My Life in a Stolen Moment" that he went to college on a phony scholarship, flunked out for refusing to watch a rabbit die, and "got expelled from English class for using four-letter words in a paper describing the

English teacher." He lived at the SIGMA ALPHA MU (925 University Ave. SE) fraternity house when he first came to school but stayed little more than a month. The building has since been torn down. After moving out of the frat house, Dylan rented a room above GRAY'S CAMPUS DRUGS (329 14th Ave. SE) in 1960.

The TEN O'CLOCK SCHOLAR (416 14th Ave. SE), a student hangout and folk club, was where Dylan made his first appearances in Minneapolis. Just before he walked onstage for the first time, the organizer asked him his name. It's said that this was the first time the singer used Dylan instead of Zimmerman, although with an early repertoire heavily influenced by Depression-era folkie Woody Guthrie, it's unclear whether the name change was honoring the Welsh poet Dylan Thomas or the Western folk hero Marshall Matt Dillon. At the end of 1960, Dylan dropped out of school to journey to New Jersey, where he visited the dying Guthrie, before immersing himself in the Greenwich Village folk scene. The building has since been replaced by a Burger King.

BOMB SHELTER

Minneapolis's punk/hardcore/Oi! venue of the mid-'90s can be found in the bowels of a gun shop. Alternative impresarios Felix von Havoc and Jack Chaos provide a program of mostly local punk acts, as well as an occasional touring band. *2931 Bloomington Ave., tel. 612/821–0019.*

THE C.C. CLUB

This Whittier Park bar, across the street from Oar Folkjokeopus record store (*see below*), is Minneapolis's key music-scene drinking spot. In the '80s, when it was called C.C. Tap, members of the Replacements, Hüsker Dü, and Soul Asylum would use it as a living room. Michelle Leon, the original bassist for Babes in Toyland, rented a room upstairs in the late '80s. *2600 Lyndale Ave. S, tel. 612/ 874–7226.*

Daniel Cary

The C.C.

CENTRAL HIGH SCHOOL

Prince formed his first band in the early '70s while attending this school, where he was taught music by a former member of Ray Charles's band, pianist Jim Hamilton. Prince's group had a variety of names—Grand Central, Grand Central Station (which was already the name of a chart band), and Grand Central Corporation—and played funk courtesy of Kool and the Gang, the Ohio Players, and others. A school pal was Terry Lewis, who later founded Flyte Tyme Productions with Jimmy Jam. *3416 3rd Ave. S.*

[FIRST AVENUE AND SEVENTH STREET ENTRY]

Downtown Minneapolis's top rock venue occupies an Art Deco former Greyhound station and holds around 1,300. One of the cool things about First Avenue and its adjacent little brother, Seventh Street Entry, is that all tickets are sold through record stores, so fans don't get stung by big booking fees. The club first put on live gigs in 1970, when it was called the Depot; the opening show was Joe Cocker, then on the *Mad Dogs and Englishmen* tour. A couple of years later, it became part of the Uncle Sam's nightclub chain, then became just Sam's in the late '70s, and finally adopted its current name in 1982.

Over the past decade and a half, First Avenue has put on an eclectic roster of music ranging from Rancid and Oasis to Wynton Marsalis and Burning Spear. First Avenue was a favorite of Prince's in his earlier days: He performed here on 15 occasions and used the venue for most of the nightclub shots in *Purple Rain* (some filming was done on a set in L.A.). Babes in Toyland were signed to Warner Bros. after a show here, and Bob Mould's Sugar recorded some live tracks for the *Besides* compilation album. Such bands as Sonic Youth and the Foo Fighters now prefer to play a couple of nights here rather than doing one show in a larger, less atmospheric venue.

Seventh Street Entry, in the same building but with an entrance just around the corner, holds just 230 people and began life as the canteen for the Greyhound depot; it's now the starter stage for First Avenue. Hüsker Dü recorded *Land Speed Record* here live in 1981. More recently it has introduced English hopefuls like Elastica and Echobelly to Minneapolis audiences, and both Garbage and Son Volt chose the venue to make their first performances. *First Avenue: 701 N. 1st Ave., tel. 612/338–8388. Seventh Street Entry: 29 N. 7th St., tel. 612/332–1755.*

First Avenue

KAY BANK STUDIOS

Various studios have operated out of this Victorian theater since the late '50s, but it was in the early '80s, when the now-defunct Kay Bank was based here, that it reached its greatest fame. Hüsker Dü recorded its first single, "Statues," and its debut studio album, *Everything Falls Apart,* and various Twin/Tone bands also did stuff here. The building seems to be in constant flux, but it continues to attract music-industry P.R. and recording types. *2543 Nicollet Ave.*

THE LONGHORN BAR

For a few years in the early '80s, this former roots-music bar was transformed into a moody rock & roll joint that presented some of the hottest imports of the day (Echo and the Bunnymen, the Cure, New Order) and provided an outlet for the best new local bands. Hüsker Dü broke TV sets onstage at an early gig, and the Replacements played their first "big" gig in July 1980 in front of a few dozen people—bass player Tommy Stinson was just 13 years old. The site now serves as a parking lot for the adjacent office building. *14 S. 5th St.*

[OAR FOLKJOKEOPUS]

Open since 1973, Minneapolis's first indie store takes its name from two unlikely albums: *Oar,* the solo debut of Moby Grape's Skip Spence, and Roy Harper's *Folkjokeopus* from 1969. Most Minneapolitans just call it "Oarfolk." The city's turn-of-the-'80s punk and hardcore scene was based around the store as Twin/Tone label cofounder Pete Jesperson was then one of the managers. One of the label's first signees, the Replacements, rehearsed in the basement and handprinted the sleeves of early singles there. The cellar was also used as a crash pad by many touring hardcore and indie bands. The store is still one of the best hangouts in town (though the comfy couch and soda machine have gone to make way for more imports and collectibles) and deals mostly in alternative sounds. *2557 Lyndale Ave. S, tel. 612/872–7400.*

Oar Folkjokeopus

PAISLEY PARK

This $10 million state-of-the-art studio and headquarters, named after Prince's 1985 "Penny Lane"–ish single, opened in 1987. Besides the owner, who has recorded virtually all of his post-'87 material here, the studio has attracted a wide range of artists, R.E.M., Madonna, Bonnie Raitt, Mavis Staples, George Clinton, and Pere Ubu among them. ♀ occasionally throws the doors open to guests. On New Year's Eve 1987, 400 friends (including Miles Davis) attended a benefit for local homeless. A year later, after his shows at Minneapolis's Met Center, 500 guests were invited back to Paisley Park to see the Purple One jam with George Clinton and Mavis Staples. Otherwise, visitors are not welcome at the complex, about 30 minutes west of downtown Minneapolis; if you drive out for a look, watch for the whitewashed hospital-like building with purple window frames and other similarly colored embellishments. *7801 Audubon Rd. (take I–35 S to I–494 W to Exit 11 to Hwy. 5 into Chanhassen; Audubon will be on your right).*

REPLACEMENTS HOUSE

Replacements guitarist Bob Stinson lived with his 12-year-old, bass-playing brother, Tommy, in this house when the band formed in 1979. They rehearsed in the basement and were later photographed on the porch for the cover of the 1984 album *Let It Be.* The house looks a bit different from the album sleeve as the fire escape has since been taken down. *2215 Bryant Ave. S.*

SONS OF NORWAY HALL

The band that became Soul Asylum—then a much more garage/hardcore group called Loud Fast Rules—

Dave Pirner of Soul Asylum

made its first public appearance at a pay-to-play show at this venue in 1981. Within three years it had recorded a debut album, *Say What You Will,* for the city's Twin/Tone label. The Hall has never been a regular venue for bands, but from time to time an independent promoter may use it to put on a touring act. *1455 W. Lake St., tel. 612/827–3611.*

SOUND 80 STUDIOS

Opened in 1969, this studio attracted such big names to the cold North as the Doobie Brothers, Cat Stevens, and Bob Dylan, who recut some songs for *Blood on the Tracks* here. Sound 80's biggest 7″ success came in 1980 with "Funkytown," a hit around the globe for local sessioneers Lipps Inc. The Sound 80 name is retained by a multimedia production company that has offices in the IDS Center, downtown; the original studio on East 25th Street closed in the early '80s and has reverted to use as a warehouse. *2709 E. 25th St.*

SKYWAYS TO HEAVEN

As Bob Mould, now ensconced in central Texas, never seems to forget to remind interviewers, wintertime temperatures in Minneapolis drop well below zero. To keep everyone from freezing to death, the Skyway system was built. This climate-controlled network of first-floor corridors connects hundreds of stores and dozens of office buildings along the main pedestrian drag that is Nicollet Mall. The Replacements did a song titled "Skyways" on the 1987 *Pleased to Meet Me* album.

UPTOWN BAR

Along with First Avenue and Seventh Street Entry, the Uptown booked all the best up-and-coming bands on the alternative scene, often taking a greater chance on unknown acts. Many British bands—including Oasis, Skunk Anansie, and Silverfish—made their first appearance in the city here, while local country rockers the Jayhawks have played some lively unannounced shows here recently.

Lori Barbero worked in the kitchen for years prior to joining Babes in Toyland and showed a legendary hospitality to penniless touring bands, many of whom would end up crashing on the floor of her residence, the "Big Trouble House" (*see above*). The Uptown was also one of the first places that Kat Bjelland and Courtney Love (a short-lived member of Babes in Toyland) hung out after relocating from the West Coast. At an early Babes gig here, Barbero's late father, Jerome, came to see the band and was reportedly so shocked by the atmosphere that he tried to pull his middle-class daughter off the stage.

The Uptown has been a restaurant since the '50s and started putting on bands in the late '70s. Sadly, in spring 1996, the management decided to stop putting on bands and deal exclusively in comfort food and cheap beer. Hopefully the situation will change. *3008 Hennepin Ave. S, tel. 612/823–4719.*

Babe in Toyland Kat Bjelland

WALKER ARTS CENTER AND LORING PARK

Located on the western edge of downtown and known for its sculpture garden, this cool contemporary-arts center occasionally hosts experimental groups or the likes of Brian Eno playing and speaking. The Walker sponsored the CD-release party for Babes in Toyland's *Fontanelle* album in August 1992 in adjacent Loring Park (where Mary Tyler Moore fed the ducks in the opening credits of her sitcom), and snippets of the party were featured in their "Bruise Violet" video. The park is also the setting for the Walker's Music and Movies nights, and event with live bands and showings of classic films held on Tuesdays during summer. *Vineland Pl., tel. 612/374–3701.*

St. Paul

A 10-minute drive from its twin city of Minneapolis, St. Paul likes to think of itself as the more venerable and cultured of the pair. It's where F. Scott Fitzgerald was born, where Hüsker Dü played their first gig (at the long-gone Ron's Randolph Bar), and where Vixen formed in 1981.

Bob Mould in Hüsker Dü

EATING DRINKING DANCING SHOPPING PLAYING SLEEPING

The music scene here pales in comparison to its neighbor, although the **BLUES SALOON** (601 Western Ave. N, tel. 612/228–9959), north of downtown, is the best blues club in the Twin Cities area and attracts many nationally known artists.

CIVIC CENTER

Springsteen opened his *Born in the U.S.A.* tour here in June 1984 and used the venue again that July to shoot the "Dancing in the Dark" video, during which he picked actress Courtney Cox (now of *Friends*) out of the audience of extras at the invitation-only concert.

Prince sold out five nights at this 18,000-seat venue at Christmas of the same year. Minnesota governor Randy Perpich designated the period "Prince Days," amid opposition from Christian groups who objected to the Purple One's apparent lustfulness. *143 4th St. W, tel. 612/224–7403.*

Missouri is dominated musically by its two main cities: St. Louis, home base of Chuck Berry, and jazz-rich Kansas City. The southern part of the state is taken up by the picturesque Ozark Mountains, which gave their name to a now largely forgotten '70s country-rock outfit, the Ozark Mountain Daredevils. The mountain region is also home to the voraciously marketed town of Branson, now virtually a country-music theme park, full of "family entertainment" theaters with MOR acts like Tony "Tie a Yellow Ribbon" Orlando, Jim "Spiders and Snakes" Stafford, and the Osmonds.

Kansas City

Revered in jazz circles, Kansas City straddles two states—Kansas and Missouri—with the more lively parts in the latter. During Prohibition the city "Boss" Pendergast turned a blind eye to the alcohol ban, with the result that jazz clubs flourished—more than 50 in the area around 18th and Vine alone. After Pendergast was sent to the state pen in the late '30s, many of the venues closed. Soon, however, the blues-powered big-band sound of Count Basie and the bebop innovation of Charlie Parker took hold in long-gone clubs like the Sunset or the Eblon Theater.

Blues shouter Joe Turner, born in KC in 1911, also started making a name for himself in local blues bars during Prohibition. In 1938 he and pianist Pete Johnson cut the acclaimed "Roll 'Em Pete," and in the '50s the singer joined New York's Atlantic Records, for which he recorded the original version of "Shake, Rattle and Roll" in 1954. Bill Haley sanitized the song for the pop market by removing the lewd line "over the hill and way down underneath."

At the start of the '50s, a duo of 18-year-old songwriters, Jerry Leiber and Mike Stoller, wrote one of their first hits, "K.C. Lovin'," performed by Little Willie Littlefield. Wilbert Harrison reconstituted the song into its now better-known form, "Kansas City," which hit the top of the charts in 1959 and was covered by the Beatles on *Beatles for Sale*. Since then the city has made little dent in the rock charts. Current hopefuls include the noisy Season to Risk and Grither and the pop-punk Go Kart.

EATING DRINKING DANCING SHOPPING *PLAYING* SLEEPING

The city recently revamped the 18th and Vine Historic District, and various projects, including a jazz-and-blues museum, are on the drawing board. The **MUTUAL MUSICIANS' FOUNDATION** (1823 Highland Ave., tel. 816/421−9297) occupies the former African-American musicians union hall, now a National Historic Landmark; rowdy jam sessions held every Friday and Saturday night are open to the public. Westport, south of downtown, has the best bars and clubs; **Hurricane** (4048 Broadway, tel. 816/753−0884) is the top indie spot. The area's roster of great used-record stores is headed by **Recycled Sounds** (Westport Rd. at Main St., tel. 816/531−4890).

Kansas City Six

Jim Jackson, "Jim Jackson's Kansas City Blues" (1927)
Wilbert Harrison, "Kansas City" (1959)

Furry Lewis, "Going to Kansas City" (1961)
Procol Harum, "The Devil Came from Kansas" (1969)
Gene Clark, "Kansas City Southern" (1977)
Van Morrison, "Eternal Kansas City" (1977)

St. Louis

A river city on the far eastern edge of the state, just south of where the Missouri flows into the Mississippi, St. Louis is still America's second-busiest inland port. It also boasts what is reputedly the world's largest brewery, the Budweiser- and Michelob-producing Anheuser-Busch. Halfway between Memphis and Chicago, St. Louis was a convenient stopping-off point for black workers leaving the South, as was the city of East St. Louis (*see above*), directly across the river in Illinois. In the '50s these settlers helped develop a local R&B style, epitomized by Albert King, which was much copied in the '60s by guitar-heavy British blues groups like Free. The city's greatest rock legacy, however, is Chuck Berry, arguably rock's first great singer-songwriter, who moved to St. Louis as a baby.

Chuck Berry

EATING DRINKING DANCING SHOPPING PLAYING SLEEPING

Although it seems to have dried up as a source of talent, St. Louis still has a great tradition for nightlife, with several key pockets throughout the city. Downtown's cleaned-up Laclede's Landing historic district has a number of live-rock venues, most notably Mississippi Nights (*see below*). The cobblestone streets and redbrick buildings of Soulard, in the southern part of town, are home to half a dozen unpretentious, low-cover bars that put on live blues on the weekends. The one not to miss is the **1860 HARD SHELL CAFÉ AND BAR** (1860 S. 9th St., tel. 314/231–1860), where a lively crowd dances to good-quality soul, blues, R&B, and Cajunish bands. University (or "U") City, over on the west side, holds predictably collegiate hangouts and stores, as well as some great inexpensive restaurants and the landmark Blueberry Hill (*see below*).

Some St. Louis Songs

Chuck Berry, "St. Louis Blues" (1965)	
Chuck Berry, "You Came a Long Way from St. Louis" (1965)	
The Easybeats, "St. Louis" (1969)	
Flamin' Groovies, "St. Louis Blues" (1976)	
Arlo Guthrie, "St. Louis Tickle" (1978)	

CHUCK BERRY BOYHOOD HOME

An infant Charles Edward Berry moved with his family to this home on Goode Avenue from San Jose, California, where he was born on October 18, 1926. The Berrys stayed here for two years before moving to a house on Labadie, but Chuck liked the name Goode enough to use it for his most famous character, Johnny B. Goode. Despite the song's praise of a country boy's guitar technique, it was actually dedicated to his piano player, Johnnie Johnson. *2520 Goode Ave.*

[BLUEBERRY HILL AND WALK OF FAME]

Since 1972 owners Joe and Linda Edwards have gradually converted their Victorian warehouse into a venue with many callings: nightclub, restaurant, record store, brewery (of Rock & Roll beer), and concert hall. Blueberry Hill is jammed full of rock & roll memorabilia, including the guitar on which Chuck Berry supposedly composed "Johnny B. Goode." *Cashbox* magazine has described the jukebox as the best in America, with selections taken from the Edwardses' collection of 30,000 singles. Outside is the St. Louis Walk of Fame, with some 40 stars honoring such local talents as Berry, Miles Davis, William Burroughs, Josephine Baker, and Tina Turner. *6504 Delmar Blvd., tel. 314/727–0880.*

Memorabilia at Blueberry Hill

MISSISSIPPI NIGHTS

Nirvana played here shortly after the Guns N' Roses incident at the Riverport Amphitheater (*see below*) and joked about staging a riot of its own. Kurt Cobain invited hundreds of stagedivers onto the stage, which got so packed that the venue's owners called the cops. Eventually Krist Novoselic intervened and won over the police, and the management allowed the band extra time to finish the set. The venue, in the restored Laclede's Landing sector of downtown, consistently books the best touring bands and puts on top blues acts. *914 N. 1st St., tel. 314/421–3853.*

RIVERPORT AMPHITHEATER

Frustrated over security's failure to deal with a camera-wielding fan at a July 1991 Guns N' Roses gig, Axl Rose waded into the crowd and did the job himself. Things turned ugly after Rose, who was dragged back onstage by a roadie, announced that the gig had just ended. In the riot that followed, more than 50 people were hurt, 15 were arrested, and $200,000 worth of damage was done to the venue and the band's equipment. The band blamed the supposedly lax security; nevertheless, a warrant was issued for Rose's arrest on charges of inciting a riot. With a possible one-year sentence hanging over his head, the singer has since kept away from Missouri. *14141 Riverport Dr., Maryland Heights, 14 mi. N.W. of downtown, tel. 314/298–9944.*

JAIL HOUSE ROCK

Chuck Berry: prolific songwriter, exponent of the famous duck walk, rock & roll riff king—and regular troublemaker. The teenage Berry was sent to reform school after committing two robberies and holding up a motorist with a gun. In 1961 he went to prison for three years for violation of the Mann Act, which made it a felony for a man to cross a state line with a woman with whom he intended to commit an immoral act; the prosecution claimed the 14-year-old girl he was with was an El Paso prostitute. In 1979 he was jailed again, this time for evading $100,000 in taxes. Berry was never idle in jail. While serving time in the early '60s, he wrote "No Particular Place to Go" and began "Promised Land," for which he needed a road map to get the geography right—the guards thought he was plotting an escape.

Wentzville

BERRY PARK

Chuck Berry lives a hermetic existence in this complex, once planned as a rival to Disneyland. When he opened Berry Park in May 1961, it featured miniature golf, a swimming pool, and a children's zoo but was dogged with bad luck and an absentee landlord who was incarcerated in various penal institutions. Big-name acts were meant to headline at the park, but the promoter never booked them, a situation that eventually led disgruntled ticket-holders to riot.

Berry soon closed the place down and has used it ever since as a private retreat. He doesn't take kindly to visitors, invited or not. When the band assembled by Keith Richards for the movie *Hail Hail Rock & Roll* (some of which was filmed here) turned up to rehearse, Berry billed them for using his guitars. When English journalist Andy Bull, researching his book *Coast to Coast,* knocked at Berry Park, the door was answered by a mysterious figure, face obscured by the screen-door mesh, who curtly asked him what he wanted. Taken aback, Bull fumbled for an answer and then blurted out that he'd just like to shake Chuck Berry's hand. A hand appeared, shook Bull's, and then slammed the door shut. *Buckner Rd., 35 mi W of St. Louis on I–70.*

NEBRASKA

When rock artists have a tale of woe to tell or want a metaphor for how the American Dream has turned sour, they look to Nebraska for a vivid illustration. In 1982 Bruce Springsteen, influenced by Terence Malick's *Badlands*—a fictionalized account of Charlie Starkweather's Nebraskan killing spree, which claimed 10 people in eight days—surprised all by releasing a dark acoustic LP recorded on four-track, simply entitled *Nebraska*. This follow-up to the massively successful *River* was Springsteen's testimony to the despair of the Reagan years. The unrelenting gloominess of the album, epitomized by the title track and "Johnny 99," spilled over onto the cover, a beautiful, stark photo of a byway somewhere in the nether reaches of the state. Steve Earle on *The Hard Way* and Richard Marx on his "Hazard" single are among other songwriters who have used Nebraska to symbolize the woes of unemployment and broken promises.

Alliance

It's 300 very flat miles through cornfields from Lincoln to the scenic part of Nebraska, the rocky, craggy Panhandle. The city of Scottsbluff, the area's main commercial center, is the birthplace of Eagles and Poco bassist Randy Meisner, born March 8, 1947. In Alliance, 50 miles farther up U.S. 385N, stands Nebraska's finest tourist attraction, Carhenge.

CARHENGE

This rough copy of the standing stones of Stonehenge is made of old gray-painted Chevys, Cadillacs, and Plymouths and set in a cornfield. Most visitors see it as a humorous piece of pop art, but state bureaucrats, who once tried to pull it down, thought it was

Druids in Nebraska?

Courtesy of the Friends of Carhenge

an eyesore, and a few fundamentalist Christians are convinced it's a Satanic shrine. Nevertheless, it's on the cover a recent Steely Dan greatest-hits collection. *U.S. 385N, 2 mi N of Alliance, tel. 308/762–1520 for info.*

Omaha

A metro area of almost half a million people, with not too much to show for itself but a string of big malls, Omaha has produced few names familiar to the music fan other than Tubes frontman Fee Waybill (born John Waldo in 1950) and rappers 311, who got together here in 1990. The city has been mentioned by various artists throughout the years, including Bob Dylan, who claimed in the goofy "I Shall Be Free No. 10" that he was going to ride into Omaha and out to the golf course, where he would "carry *The New York Times,* shoot a few holes, blow their minds."

Moby Grape's 1967 single "Omaha," an exuberant psychedelic roller-coaster ride, bore no resemblance in tempo to its distinctly suburban inspiration. In 1994 another West Coast band, Counting Crows, inserted a laid-back track, also entitled "Omaha," onto their debut album; this time there was a direct reference to the place, a rather apt refrain of "Omaha, somewhere in middle America."

OMAHA CIVIC AUDITORIUM

When the Rolling Stones came to town on their first U.S. tour, the band was met at the airport by Omaha's finest and whisked into town, escorted by a dozen police bikes with sirens wailing—a bit of an overreaction, considering that only a few hundred turned out to see the group play. Some 13 years later, on June 19, 1977, a full house of 15,000 saw one of Elvis Presley's final shows. Along with material from a concert in Rapid City, South Dakota, two days later, tape from this performance comprises the 1977 album imaginatively called *Elvis in Concert. 1804 Capitol Ave., tel. 402/444–4750.*

Lincoln

Lincoln is laid out on a grid, with north–south streets numbered and east–west thoroughfares lettered. It's fairly difficult to get confused, although that didn't stop Allen Ginsberg calling his poem about O Street "Zero Street." Worth checking out in this surprisingly likable college town is the **Zoo Bar** (136 N. 14th St., tel. 402/435–8754), which frequently attracts big-name blues acts on their way between Chicago and Kansas City; it was voted the Blues Foundation club of the year in 1993. In a different dimension is **Rock & Roll Runza** (210 W. 14th St., tel. 402/474–2030), mildly famous for its roller-skating waitresses, '50s jukebox, and greasy burgers.

In some quarters it still hasn't sunk in that the Erieside city of Cleveland was awarded the Rock and Roll Hall of Fame. The city hasn't even produced as many hits as Cincinnati, the birthplace of King Records, and some of its smaller neighbors—Kent and Akron—have pumped out almost as many acts of any note. However, now that the hall is up and running, there's no doubt that Cleveland has risen to the occasion, and it's also a good home base for further rock & roll excursions to Cincinnati, or to Detroit, Chicago, or the Andy Warhol Museum in Pittsburgh.

Akron

I WENT BACK TO OHIO/BUT MY CITY WAS GONE—THE PRETENDERS, "MY CITY WAS GONE"

The early '70s were the most significant musical years in the world rubber capital, 35 miles southeast of Cleveland. Devo started out here in 1972, and the following year Chrissie Hynde departed for Europe, where she would later form the Pretenders. Another key '70s Akron band was Tin Huey.

THE BANK

In 1975 and 1976, this atmospheric former bank office was Akron's equivalent to the Pirate's Cove in Cleveland. Devo persuaded the owners to put on a punk night once a week, and such emerging Cleveland bands as Pere Ubu and the Dead Boys would play regularly. The club closed in the early '90s, and the area is being redeveloped for a new minor-league stadium. *Main and Exchange Sts.*

RUBBER BOWL

In August 1972, a Jefferson Airplane gig at this wonderfully named 40,000-seat venue ended in a riot after a bomb threat disrupted proceedings. Frustrated fans threw bricks at cops, who responded by squirting tear gas all over the place. When band members objected to the heavy-handed treatment, Jack Casady was arrested, Grace Slick was maced, and Paul Kantner's head kissed the concrete floor. These days rock shows are infrequent, and the venue is most often used for college football. *George Washington and Triplet Blvds., tel. 330/978−1272.*

Cincinnati

Although sometimes dubbed "Censornati" for the city authorities' record of clamping down on pieces of art and performance that don't fit in with their family values, this metropolis on the Ohio River, directly across from Kentucky, is by no means all doom and gloom. The types who support censoring are usually well indoors at night, and there are quirky little scenes around downtown, Mount Adams (directly to the east), and studenty Corryville, a quick ride uphill.

In earlier years, the city was a hub of R&B activity. Local label King Records plowed a revolutionary path in both country and R&B, particularly through the work of James Brown. The Isley Brothers grew up here and sang in a local church choir before going to New York in the mid-'50s. Bootsy Collins spent his childhood here and later played guitar on James Brown's "Sex Machine" at the King studios. The McCoys' Rick Derringer lived here for a while and wrote "Hang on Sloopy," now the official state song. For information on local blues and R&B history, check out the award-winning book *Going to Cincinnati* (1993, University of Illinois Press) by local musician Steve Tracey. In modern times the city is best known for being the home base of the Afghan Whigs (originally from nearby Hamilton), whose success dispatched a gaggle of A&R hunting expeditions to Cincy, with bands like the Wolverton Brothers, Throneberry, and the Ass Ponys eventually picking up contracts.

EATING DRINKING DANCING SHOPPING PLAYING SLEEPING

I.R.S. recording artists Over the Rhine take their name from the emerging nightlife district on the north edge of downtown, where there are a few bars pumping out jazz, blues, and acoustic rock, as well as a couple of dance places. Bars of a similar bent can be found in nearby Mount Adams, an attractive hilltop community a mile from downtown; two to try are **BLIND LEMON** (936 Hatch St., tel. 216/241–3885), a dark bar with music most nights and a bonfire on Saturday, and the **PAVILION** (949 Pavilion St., tel. 216/721–7272), which has a great terrace with views of the city.

For indie and metal fans, the place to go is Vine Street in Corryville, 2 miles north of the city center. Here on one block you can find a rock & roll laundry called Sudsy's (*see below*), numerous other bars, cheap eats, and clothing stores. Also here is **BOGART'S** (2621 Vine St., tel. 513/281–8400), where U2 played way back in spring 1981 and the Afghan Whigs continued to gig long after they became nationally known. On either side of Bogart's are two of Cincy's best record stores, **WIZARD** (2629 Vine St., tel. 513/961–6196) and **MOLE'S RECORD EXCHANGE** (2615 Vine St., tel. 513/861–6291).

CROSLEY FIELD

At the 1970 Cincinnati Pop Festival, Iggy Pop leapt into the audience and walked on their upstretched hands. He's therefore attributed with starting the stagediving and body-surfing crazes in one fell swoop. The venue was ripped down soon after and replaced by Riverfront Stadium, the downtown home of the Bengals and the Reds.

KING RECORDS

One of the most successful independent labels of the '50s and early '60s, Cincinnati's King was unique in that it made inroads into both black and hillbilly music. The label was started in 1945 by local record-store owner Syd Nathan, one of the first in the city to run a racially integrated business.

Much of King's success was due to Nathan's business sense, not his less-than-keen musical ear: On hearing a demo of "Please Please Please," James Brown's debut King single, which would eventually go gold, Nathan is said to have called it a piece of shit and temporarily fired company executive Ralph Bass for signing the singer. Brown went on to be the label's greatest star; at the height of his fame, in the mid-'60s, he kept an office here and wrote part of "Papa's Got a Brand New Bag" on site. King was also responsible for recording Hank Ballard's original version of "The Twist" and featured top-selling R&B acts like Earl Bostic, Bullmoose Jackson, and blues guitarist Albert King, plus such hillbilly favorites as the Delmore Brothers and Cowboy Copas.

King was a tightly run and remarkably self-sufficient organization. Everything was taken care of at the five-building headquarters, from recording through pressing, label printing, packaging, and shipping. Nathan also set up a publishing company, Lois Music (named after his wife), and oversaw a number of subsidiary labels, including DeLuxe, Federal, Bethlehem, and Queen. Not one to do things by halves, Nathan had a black-topped desk shaped like a record. After his death, in 1968, King employees were gathered to listen to a farewell greeting the late owner had recorded on vinyl in the studios. The plant closed in 1971, and the rights were eventually bought out by the Nashville company Gusto.

The five buildings are currently leased to a dairy company, but the studio space is still structurally intact. A group of local music enthusiasts and politicians has drawn up plans to buy the buildings and turn them into a museum dedicated to the city's musical history, as well as a recording studio for local teenagers. Requests for information and any offers of help can be addressed to the King Records Museum Project (c/o Joseph Gorman, 1429 Cedar Ave., Cincinnati, OH 45224, tel. 513/541–9078). The site is in the Evanston neighborhood, about a 10-minute drive from downtown. *1540 Brewster Ave. Take I–71N to Dana exit, turn left on Dana Ave., go about 1 mi, cross Montgomery, go left on Woodburn, then right onto Brewster (which runs parallel to I–71).*

10 Regal King Size

Jimmy Witherspoon, "No Rollin' Blues, (1949)
The Dominoes, "Sixty Minute Man" (1951)
Boyd Bennett and the Rockets, "Seventeen" (1955)
Platters, "Only You" (1955)
James Brown, "Please Please Please" (1956)
Bill Doggett, "Honky Tonk" (1956)
Little Willie John, "Fever" (1956)
The Five Royales, "Dedicated to the One I Love" (1957)
Hank Ballard, "Finger Poppin' Time" (1960)
Freddy King, "Hideaway" (1961)

RIVERBEND MUSIC CENTER

Jesus Lizard lead singer David Yow was fined $327 for "disorderly conduct…and exposing his private parts" after his stage act at the Cincy leg of the Lollapalooza tour, held at this amphitheater on July 18, 1995. Yow, who has brought the captain out onstage before, stripped naked, played with his member, and pretended to stick his microphone up his butt. Local cops sent a message to Yow to desist. The singer put his clothes back on but devoted much of the rest of the performance to slagging off authorities in the city of "Censornati." The cops had had enough by then and gave him a ride to the station after the band left the stage. During Hole's set, later in the day, Courtney Love told the crowd about what had happened, called for Yow's release, and flashed her own bits, which apparently did not draw the same attention from the cops. *Kellogg and Sutton Aves., Anderson Township, 20 min. from downtown, tel. 513/232–6220.*

Brad Miller

Jesus Lizard

RIVERFRONT COLISEUM

At a Who gig on December 3, 1979, 11 people died and scores more were injured when there was a mass rush to get to unreserved seating near the front of this auditorium. The incident led to enquiries that effectively spelled the end of "festival" seating at enclosed venues. In 1981 a Coliseum show ended a mammoth worldwide tour for Bruce Springsteen; it was the last time Steve Van Zandt appeared with the E Street Band. *Mehring Way at New Central Bridge.*

[SUDSY MALONE'S ROCK & ROLL LAUNDRY AND BAR]

Since opening in the mid-'80s, this laundromat-cum-bar-cum-venue has been putting on the best regional rock bands, as well as a strong selection of touring indie/alternative bands. Acts play the large, dark, Celtic-flavored room seven nights a week, and the cover charge is usually waived if you bring in two loads of laundry. Cincinnati bands the Afghan Whigs, Throneberry, and the Ass Ponys all started out here. Whigs singer Greg Dulli told journalists he got barred from the place for throwing a load of beer bottles into the washing machine and selecting full spin; this event seems to have gone unnoticed by those Sudsy's staff members asked about it. *2626 Vine St., tel. 513/751–9011 (bar) or 513/751–2300 (laundry). Bar open to 2:30 AM, laundry open 7 AM–12:30 AM.*

Cleveland

HELLO, CLEVELAND... ROCK & ROLL!—SPINAL TAP WAR CRY

The Rock and Roll Hall of Fame is here and not in some other city because Cleveland had the balls to put up the money. For a city to pin its hopes and much of its economic aspirations on a building dedicated to rock & roll is somewhat absurd, but it's working. The $65 million the city pumped into the Hall of Fame was a signal for other developers to follow suit. If Howard the Duck came here today, he'd find it hard to make the putdown of "the armpit of the nation" stick. Likewise, only the ignorant refer to it as the "Mistake on the Lake," although the incident that made Cleveland the whipping post of every comedian and columnist since the '70s—the polluted Cuyahoga River catching fire—is still somewhat fondly recalled by locals as proof that Cleveland has character.

Besides having the bucks ready, the city owes the presence of the museum within its borders to Alan Freed, the early '50s Cleveland DJ who is widely credited with popularizing the term *rock & roll* and was instrumental in jolting a staid music industry into believing that rootsy R&B could develop mass appeal. However, the city wasn't very supportive of rock & roll in those days. In 1956 it invoked a '30s law barring kids from dancing in public unless accompanied by an adult. At the height of the Brit invasion, the city introduced a "Beatles Ban" on teenybop groups so that teenage girls would not be subverted. Whether this had an effect on the city's music scene is debatable, but little came out of Cleveland in the two decades after Freed left for New York except for a few Brit-inspired pop acts and the Outsiders, one-hit wonders with "Time Won't Let Me" in 1965.

By the early '70s some papers and magazines labeled Cleveland the "next Liverpool" on the paltry evidence of such local bands as the Raspberries and Blue Ash from nearby Youngstown. But by mid-decade, a more innovative noise was coming out of dive bars like the Viking and the Pirate's Cove: the sounds of Pere Ubu and Devo, who often came up to the city from Kent. Others to emerge from the Cleveland area in the '70s were Joe Walsh and the Michael Stanley Band, and the tiny indie label Cleveland International Records was where Meat Loaf's *Bat Out of Hell* first got released in 1977. Metal ruled during the '80s, but with local indie and punk bands around the end of the decade, things swung. The big name to emerge from the city has been Trent Reznor of Nine Inch Nails; others include Filter, Dink, Sons of Elvis, Craw, and Cobra Verde.

Record companies had earmarked Cleveland as a key pilot city for new sounds as early as the '50s, and it still is today—Mike Shea of the Cleveland-based *Alternative Press*

NIN's Trent Reznor

Anastasia Pantsios

magazine puts this down to the fact that "if New York and L.A. are the only cities where a band is hot, they won't last. If they're liked in Cleveland and the Midwest, the band will be around for a while." The city supports innovative radio, with a batch of great college stations that aren't afraid to experiment. Clevelanders also spend more money per capita on discs than residents of just about any other city, which means there's always a healthy stock of secondhand bargains around.

EATINGDRINKINGDANCINGSHOPPINGPLAYINGSLEEPING

Cleveland's nightlife has always been a tad better than average. To check out the latest details, grab the excellent *Free Times* or the *Scene* magazine, free from bins and venues. Besides the venues written up below—including Agora Ballroom, Euclid Tavern, Peabody's Down Under (listed under Pirate's Cove), Phantasy, and Wilbert's—here are other established joints that are worth checking out:

CLEVELAND CAFÉ (11901 Berea Rd., just N of I-90 at W. 117th St., tel. 216/941–9144) has cover bands galore—including imitators of Metallica, Kiss, U2, and Aerosmith. **CLUB ISABELLA** (2025 University Hospitals Dr., University Circle, tel. 216/229–1177) serves up quality late-night jazz and Italian food. The **GROG SHOP** (1765 Coventry Rd., tel. 216/321–5588) is a small indie and alternative club with occasional police hassles. **THE WHISKY** (1575 Merwin Ave., tel. 216/522–1575) is a huge dance club on the downtown side of the Flats; a range of sounds and themes are available each week. The **ODEON CONCERT CLUB** (1295 Old River Rd., the Flats, tel. 216/574–2525) is a new, well-planned venue that's been successful at attracting most of the best touring acts since it opened in 1995.

Downtown Cleveland

BLOW IT UP, BLOW IT UP/BLOW IT UP BEFORE JOHNNY ROTTEN GETS IN—THOMAS JEFFERSON SLAVE APARTMENTS, "ROCK 'N ROLL HALL OF FAME"

Although squillions of bucks have been thrown at downtown Cleveland, it still hasn't achieved a coherent pleasantness. It's hard to escape the glib sales tie-ins that downtown businesses have come up with to get some of the spinoff dollars from the arrival of the Rock and Roll Hall of Fame—there's as much Hall of Fame product on sale as that of the resurgent baseballing Indians.

The "Rock Hall," as Clevelanders have taken to calling it, cuts an angular figure right by the lake, downhill and a little off the beaten path from the core of downtown, which revolves around Terminal Tower, two floors of mall and plenty more of offices. On the other side of the tower, toward the river, is the Warehouse District, still to realize its potential as an artsy enclave, although Wilbert's menu of blues and roots music is a good start. Directly downhill from here is the Flats—what the tourist brochures try to tell you is nightlife nirvana; it isn't, but check out what bands are on at the Odeon and Peabody's Down Under.

CLEVELAND CONVENTION CENTER

The convention center has subsumed two key venues in the story of Cleveland rock, though relatively few concerts take place in them these days. The larger of the two, the Public Auditorium (or Public Hall), was where the Beatles played to a packed house of 10,000 on September 15, 1964. They were ordered offstage to let hysterical fans calm down. The mayor soon put a halt on Brit invaders—the "Beatles Ban," as the local papers called it—after a young female fan fell from a balcony at a Stones concert. It was not until 1966 that a teen-oriented band, this time the Dave Clark 5, was allowed to play this hall.

Only a glorified partition running the width of the stage separates the auditorium from the comfortable, rather ornate 3,000-seat Music Hall, which had the grip on most major performances around the turn of the '70s. Music would bleed through from here into the Public Hall and annoy theater aficionados. Those who played here included the Doors (right after Morrison's arrest in Miami, so he didn't do anything profane), the Jimi Hendrix Experience (their only Cleveland show), the Who, John Mellencamp, and U2; nowadays, it's a good setting for the likes of Lyle Lovett. *E. 6th St., between St. Clair and Lakeside Aves., tel. 206/348–2229.*

COMFORT INN

Elvis Presley stayed here in the '50s, the Rolling Stones in the '60s, but it was Led Zeppelin who made a real mark on the place, then called Swingo's Hotel, by throwing food out their room windows and blaming it on Elton John. Although the place has been cleaned up quite a bit by the current franchise, it's by far the least expensive place to stay in downtown Cleveland. *1800 Euclid Ave., tel. 216/861–0001. Rooms: $60.*

CUYAHOGA RIVER

The Cuyahoga River, which weaves and snakes crazily through the valley separating the Flats and the Ohio City neighborhood, caught fire in 1969, inspiring arch-sardonicist Randy Newman to write "Burn on Big River." Caused by petroleum-soaked timber getting caught under the stanchions of a bridge, the "fire" only lasted for five minutes and was out by the time the fire boats arrived. Nonetheless, the incident lives on in Cleveland legend, and even Michael Stipe had something to mumble about it on the track "Cuyahoga" on R.E.M.'s *Life's Rich Pageant.*

MUNICIPAL STADIUM

This massive stadium, built in 1931 on the shores of Lake Erie, was the setting for the September 2, 1995, concert to celebrate the opening of the Rock and Roll Hall of Fame, just a few hundred yards away. The seven-hour televised event brought together some of the hall's inductees—Bob Dylan, Chuck Berry, Aretha Franklin, and Al Green—and mixed them up with some newer acts, such as Slash, Alice in Chains, Melissa Etheridge, and the Gin Blossoms.

The stadium has played host to many of the biggest names since the mid-'60s, including the Beatles, the Rolling Stones, Crosby, Stills, Nash and Young (who pulled in over

90,000 for one of their reunion shows), Michael Jackson, and U2. However, the Indians moved out after the 1994 season, the Browns—incidentally, Elvis Presley's favorite football team—left for Baltimore, and the lakefront stadium is going to be replaced by a new facility before the turn of the millennium. *1085 W. 3rd St.*

PIRATE'S COVE (PEABODY'S DOWN UNDER)

The Flats is Cleveland's much-hyped entertainment district. Just downhill from Public Square, it's a zone of bars, chain restaurants, and nightclubs patronized by those who

favor much hair spray, department-store eau de cologne, and tight clothes. It flashes, beats, and oozes rehashed '80s disco well into the night. Back in 1975, though, things were a little different. Cleveland was having an economic hemorrhage, and this area, once the heart of its shipping and manufacturing base, was one of the quietest places in the Midwest at night, save for the fumes from a few remaining industrial plants. During the week the bars did little trade except for the odd foreign sailor coming in off a freighter. One such bar, occupying part of John D. Rockefeller's first warehouse, was the Pirate's Cove.

In late summer 1976, after the Viking Saloon (*see below*) burned down, members of Pere Ubu persuaded the Cove's owner to let them play one night for the door takings. It proved a good move for both parties, starting an almost yearlong series of Thursday-night gigs featuring the Ubus playing with local and touring groups from the emerging new-wave scene. Akron's Devo and Tin Huey played, as did 15-60-75 from Kent, plus the Styrene Money Band, the Pagans, the Waitresses, and Human Switchboard.

Pere Ubu's David Thomas at Pirate's Cove

In winter, with icy winds zipping off Lake Erie, the place would get so cold that burst pipes were a regular occurrence. One night it got so bad that the 50 or so customers who had braved the weather stood on chairs to keep warm. The live version of "Thirty Seconds over Tokyo" that appeared on the Ubus' first live album was recorded on a cassette recorder at one of the Thursday-night gigs. Another Thursday two French music journalists came up to Pere Ubu after a set and told the band that they had just invented new wave.

After the Ubu entourage left, the Cove continued to put on punk acts. Currently called Peabody's Down Under, it still is a good bet for seeing decent alternative bands, with some established names like the Afghan Whigs preferring to do two nights in these cramped surrounds rather than one show at a larger venue. *1059 Old River Rd., the Flats, tel. 216/241–0792.*

PROSPECT MUSIC

In business since 1941 and now the only downtown music-instrument store, Prospect may not be the best-stocked outlet in the city, but it is worth popping in for a look at the autograph book, which contains dedications from Jimi Hendrix and many others. *738 Prospect Ave., tel. 216/621–5409.*

RECORD RENDEZVOUS

The record store where the term *rock & roll* was supposedly coined closed in the mid-'80s and is now a sports concern. Former owner Leo Mintz was the first in town to stock the music that introduced white kids to black R&B music—mostly records from Chess,

Atlantic, Roulette, and other indie labels. In 1951 he became friends with a new DJ in town, one Alan Freed, and persuaded him to switch formats from classical music to the type of new sounds he was selling. They packaged the music into a lively show and used the term *rock & roll* to describe the sound. Both Mintz and Freed were keen to establish that they thought of the term first (Freed even owned the copyright on the word for a short time), but others say it just came out of general shop talk. In any case, the words *rock & roll* had long been used as slang in blues circles to describe sexual congress. *300 Prospect Ave. SE.*

[ROCK AND ROLL HALL OF FAME AND MUSEUM]

In 1983 the Rock and Roll Hall of Fame Foundation was set up in New York by industry movers, including Atlantic Records' Ahmet Ertegun and Jann Wenner of *Rolling Stone*, as a not-for-profit organization that would recognize the pioneers and major talents of the rock world and build a commemorative hall of fame and archive. They planned to locate that building among the record-industry offices of New York City, but in 1984 veteran West Coast rock promoter Bill Graham suggested it might be better to house the hall elsewhere.

In early 1986 *USA Today* ran a massive spread speculating on where the hall should be located and asked readers to register their opinions through a telephone poll. That was all Cleveland needed. Local radio and newspapers took up the campaign, and Clevelanders phoned and phoned and phoned the newspaper, achieving an overwhelming victory with 110,315 votes. Second-place Memphis got only 7,268. A promised financial package sealed the decision for Cleveland, and the city was named as the site for the Hall of Fame that May.

Hal Stata/courtesy of Rock and Roll Hall of Fame and Museum

The leather suit from the 1968 comeback special

The foundation quickly commissioned I. M. Pei (also responsible for the 1988 Louvre extension) as architect, and plans were drawn up for a $26 million building in the Public Square. Then things bogged down—fundraising in Cleveland was slow, and some foundation members still considered New York the appropriate home. In 1990, after much negotiation, a new, larger site on the waterfront was chosen, and the cost rose to what some estimates say was close to $90 million. The ground-breaking ceremony—with Pete Townshend and Chuck Berry undertaking some manual labor—took place in June 1993. Dennis Barrie, who made his name at the Contemporary Arts Center in Cincinnati, was appointed director, and Jim Henke, a former *Rolling Stone* music editor, was named chief curator.

The decision to fork out big bucks on a landmark building seems to have paid off. The Hall of Fame is set to define the city's skyline just as the Gateway Arch has done for St. Louis or the Space Needle for Seattle. Before he started designing, Pei, born in 1917, attended a rock gig for the first time and sampled the landmarks and bars of Memphis and New Orleans. The result of his research is a bold geometric form, with a 162-foot-high tower anchoring cantilevered offshoots, including one of Pei's trademark glass pyramids (as at the Louvre). For the grand opening, on September 2, 1995, the city was swamped with the limos of rock's rich and famous and the crowds drawn for a weekend of festivities that included a huge concert in the nearby Municipal Stadium (*see above*) and an aerial blessing from the Flying Elvises.

The price of Pei's art is that most of the exhibitions lie below ground, in the Ahmet Ertegun Exhibition Hall, which holds only 1,500 visitors at a time, causing long lines on the weekend. The collection is still very much in a state of transition. Two years before opening, the hall had virtually nothing except a lot of promises, but it has managed to pull together an impressive range of stuff.

The first thing you come across in the big subterranean hall is a movie theater that shows two films: *Mystery Train,* looking at the roots of rock & roll, and *Kick Out the Jams,* a series of often funny interviews (none more so than Steve Tyler discussing his role in the GNP of Peru). Then it's on to the various displays, which include Early Influences, four huge storyboards covering the likes of Howlin' Wolf, Jimmie Rodgers, Professor Longhair, and Bessie Smith; the Beat Goes On, with four touch screens (they could use a lot more) that allow you to trace your favorite band back to its earliest influences; Don't Knock the Rock, a fairly weak look at those who've attacked rock, from J. Edgar Hoover to Tipper Gore to Bob Dole's recent attacks on rap lyrics; U Got the Look, a display of costumes, of which Bootsy Collins's outfits are the show stealer; and Rockin' All Over the World, on eight cities and times that have had a major influence on rock, from Memphis rockabilly and blues (1948–49) to Seattle grunge (1985–95).

Individual displays cover the Rolling Stones, the Allman Brothers, Elvis (featuring some rare items on loan from Graceland), and others. Elsewhere in the basement is another movie theater, this one showing a film on songwriting; a huge collection of drumsticks; Janis Joplin's Porsche, repainted with its original psychedelic livery; and several obligatory guitars (the more smashed the better, judging by the donations from Pete Townshend and Mike McCready).

Above ground, Pei's airy pyramid has the feel of a modern-art gallery. Hanging above the lobby, which holds a pricey record and gift store, are three Trabant cars that were once part of a U2 stage set. At the top of each stairwell is a case full of paraphernalia relating to specific artists or genres—U2, Neil Young, the Byrds, etc. Gracing the walls are black-and-white portraits of key artists by such photographers as Annie Leibovitz. The second floor has a look at the importance of radio DJs, a re-creation of Sam Phillips's Memphis Recording Service/Sun Records studio, a bank of three dozen TVs playing rock videos, and a couple of display cases devoted to rock magazines. The next floor is taken up

Piet van Lier/courtesy of Rock and Roll Hall of Fame and Museum

Cars dangle in the Rock Hall lobby

by a café and a huge inflatable teacher from Pink Floyd's *The Wall* tour that growls at a huge decibel level every five minutes. The fourth floor has the main theater, where the movie *Rock Is,* examining the impact of rock on culture and society, is shown.

The top two floors are devoted to the inductees. The fifth floor is the Hall of Fame lobby, where video screens constantly show the induction ceremonies held each year. To qualify for selection, an artist must have released a record at least 25 years prior to the date of nomination. The floor also holds a working studio where interviews can be broadcast to radio stations around the world. A narrow staircase leads to the Hall of Fame itself, a somber place where screens the size and quality of Powerbooks flicker images of the inductees, with their autographs etched in the glass alongside. A music-free zone, the

Hall of Fame Inductees

Performers

The Allman Brothers Band
The Animals
LaVern Baker
Hank Ballard
The Band
The Beach Boys
The Beatles
Chuck Berry*
Bobby "Blue" Bland
Booker T. and the MG's
David Bowie
James Brown*
Ruth Brown
The Byrds
Johnny Cash
Ray Charles*
The Coasters
Eddie Cochran
Sam Cooke*
Cream
Creedence Clearwater Revival
Bobby Darin
Bo Diddley
Dion
Fats Domino*
The Doors
The Drifters
Bob Dylan
Duane Eddy
The Everly Brothers*
The Four Seasons
The Four Tops
Aretha Franklin
Marvin Gaye
The Grateful Dead
Al Green
Bill Haley
The Jimi Hendrix Experience
Buddy Holly*
John Lee Hooker
The Impressions
The Isley Brothers
Etta James
Jefferson Airplane
Elton John
Janis Joplin

B.B. King
The Kinks
Gladys Knight and the Pips
Led Zeppelin
John Lennon
Jerry Lee Lewis*
Little Richard*
Little Willie John*
Frankie Lymon and the
Teenagers
Bob Marley
Martha and the Vandellas
Clyde McPhatter
Van Morrison
Ricky Nelson
Roy Orbison
Carl Perkins
Wilson Pickett
Pink Floyd
The Platters
Elvis Presley*
Otis Redding
Jimmy Reed
Smokey Robinson
The Rolling Stones
Sam and Dave
The Shirelles
Simon and Garfunkel
Sly and the Family Stone
Rod Stewart
The Supremes
The Temptations
Ike and Tina Turner
Joe Turner
The Velvet Underground
Muddy Waters
The Who
Jackie Wilson
Stevie Wonder
The Yardbirds
Neil Young
Frank Zappa

Nonperformers

Paul Ackerman
Dave Bartholomew
Ralph Bass

Leonard Chess
Dick Clark
Tom Donahue
Ahmet Ertegun
Leo Fender
Alan Freed*
Milt Gabler
Gerry Goffin and Carole King
Berry Gordy, Jr.
Bill Graham
Holland, Dozier, and Holland
Jerry Leiber and Mike Stoller
Johnny Otis
Sam Phillips*
Doc Pomus
Phil Spector
Jerry Wexler

Early Influences

Louis Armstrong
Charlie Christian
Willie Dixon
Woody Guthrie
The Ink Spots
Elmore James
Robert Johnson*
Louis Jordan
Leadbelly
The Orioles
Les Paul
Ma Rainey
Professor Longhair
Jimmie Rodgers*
Pete Seeger
Bessie Smith
The Soul Stirrers
T-Bone Walker
Dinah Washington
Hank Williams
Howlin' Wolf
Jimmy Yancy*

Lifetime Achievement

John Hammond*
Nesuhi Ertegun

* original inductees, 1986

hall seems more like a memorial than a celebration and stands out from the frivolity of much of the rest of the building.

What's really going to make the hall a place of pilgrimage for rock buffs will be the work of the education department, due to come on line in late 1996. Besides temporary exhibits, this department will develop special events, including lectures by leading writers, songwriters, and filmmakers. A series celebrating the hall's inductees kicked off in April 1996, and since then Roger McGuinn, Jerry Wexler, Ray Davies, Levon Helm, and others have participated in question-and-answer sessions. The Oral History and Archives project aims to be a hub for popular-music scholarship, with banks of taped interviews, a fully stocked library, and online computer access. The department also foresees organizing field trips to the places where it all happened, from Memphis to Liverpool.

The hall hopes to attract a million visitors a year. It gets particularly busy on the weekends, when you have to book a time to visit. Since at busy times it's hard to get near the interactive screens—one of the real high points—it's worth trying to get here midweek. For a comprehensive tour, plan on spending a full day. *1 Key Plaza, North Coast Harbor, tel. 800/493–ROLL; advance tickets in Europe, tel. 01444/811047; http://rockhall. com. Admission: $11.50. Open summer Mon. and Tues. 10–5:30, Wed.–Sun. 10–9; rest of year, Tues. and Thurs.–Sun. 10–5:30, Wed. 10–9.*

TERMINAL TOWER

Rising 708 feet, or 52 stories, above Public Square in the heart of downtown, this 1930 tower provided the name for Pere Ubu's 1985 compilation album. Back in the '80s, there wasn't much but decay to see from the 42nd-floor observation deck, but today it provides good views of the Rock and Roll Hall of Fame and all the other big-money building schemes around town.

VIKING SALOON

This downtown college hangout, which burned down in 1976, often gets mentioned in the same breath as the New York venue Max's Kansas City. The link between the two was Viking mainstays Pere Ubu and the Dead Boys, both of whom achieved a wider audience by playing at the New York club and appearing on its compilation LP.

The pre-Ubu bands Cinderella Backstreet and Rocket from the Tombs both gigged here. The latter's debut, in December 1974 at the "Special Extermination Night," also featured two other left-field Cleveland acts, the Mirrors and the Electric Eels, in a show that's said to have kick-started Cleveland's underground scene. When RFTT broke up in summer '75, it

Stiv Bators of the Dead Boys

Anastasia Pantsios

spawned the Dead Boys, whose Stiv Bators took to the stage here one night stark naked. Pere Ubu made its debut performance on New Year's Eve 1976, doing a mix of tongue-in-cheek, riff-filled versions of Stooges, Velvet Underground, and garage-rock covers. Ubu vocalist David Thomas also worked part-time at the door around this time. *E. 21st St. and Chester Ave.*

WILBERT'S

This likable blues and roots venue in downtown's emerging Warehouse District also serves fine Southwestern food. Although it only opened in the early '90s, Wilbert's has established itself thanks to the booking policies of owner and blues enthusiast Mike Miller. Among those to have played here include John Mayall, Mick Taylor, Otis Rush, and C. J. Chenier. To show he was serious about promoting top-class blues and roots music in the city, Miller gave Robert Lockwood, Jr. a regular slot. Lockwood, the stepson of Robert Johnson, thought to be the only living person to have taken guitar lessons from that most legendary of blues legends, moved to Cleveland in 1960 and was a major influence on B.B. King. Now in his 80s, Lockwood also regularly plays over on the West Side at **BROTHERS LOUNGE** (11609 Detroit Ave., tel. 216/226–3560). Many Clevelanders want to see him enrolled in the Hall of Fame. *1360 W. 9th St., tel. 216/771–2583.*

WJW RADIO

Having worked at various small stations throughout Ohio, Alan Freed came to Cleveland in 1950 and began working for a TV station before picking up regular work at WJW radio, an AM station with a powerful transmitter that reached a large part of the state. Freed signed on to play classical music but then became friendly with Leo Mintz, owner of the town's Record Rendezvous store, who persuaded him that his future lay in playing rough, danceable R&B, a black music style that was finding a following among the city's white youth.

In 1951 Freed went to the station bosses, got the go-ahead for a youth-oriented show, and then almost got fired—not for scrapping the station play list, but for playing records by black artists. Listeners supported him, however, and he was given a free hand on the late-night shift—the Moondog Shift, as he called it. Soon he'd christened himself the Moondog and was whooping and screaming in between records, swigging whiskey on air, pounding telephone books with his fists to beef up the beat, talking to an imaginary studio dog, and referring to his listeners as Moondoggers or Moon Puppies.

The *Moondog Rock and Roll Party* initially attracted a black audience (most of whom thought this screaming disc jockey with jivelike vocals was himself black), but whites soon picked it up, especially after the press brought the music to national attention following the riot at Freed's showcase gig at the Cleveland Arena in 1952 (*see below*). He became one of the first DJs in the country to play records from the Chess and King labels—what *Billboard* up to 1949 had called race music—for a white, teenage audience. He is forever associated in rock legend with popularizing the term *rock & roll,* a hip and clever way of making the black-sounding rhythm and blues appeal to a multiracial audience.

Having put Cleveland on the map as a premier city for record companies to pilot new sounds, Freed left for a job at New York's WINS in 1954. There he continued championing R&B until money troubles and the payola scandal ruined his career; he died in 1965. WJW is no longer based in the city, but there's a plaque outside the building, and one of the current residents is *Scene,* the longest-running music-and-arts free weekly in the country, which celebrated its 25th year in 1995. *One Playhouse Square Building, 1375 Euclid Ave.*

East Side

The main route east out of downtown, Euclid Avenue passes the former Cleveland Arena and the Agora Ballroom. After 5 miles everything gets green around University Circle—an area of parks, cultural institutions, medical foundations, and the grungy little

Euclid Tavern, a supremely sweaty little joint with some of the best alternative and progressive blues bills in town.

EATINGDRINKINGDANCINGSHOPPINGPLAYINGSLEEPING

Just beyond the Euclid Tavern (*see below*) is Cleveland Heights, a studenty, alternative
scene where **RECORD REVOLUTION** (1832 Coventry Rd., tel. 216/321–7661) stocks
lots of new and used alternative and jazz albums, plus T-shirts and other indie and Dead-
head wear; sometime Pere Ubu drummer Scott Krauss is often behind the counter.
Down the street is the **GROG SHOP** (1765 Coventry Rd., tel. 216/321–5588), a small,
youthful bar with alternative bands.

AGORA BALLROOM, 1967–84

Renowned as the venue that broke the likes of Springsteen and Bowie in the Midwest, the
Agora started out in 1966 as a student joint near Case Western Reserve University. The
following year it moved to East 24th Street, where it began booking some of the best local
bands of the day: the James Gang, Damnation of Adam Blessing, Glass Harp, and numerous psychedelic acts. Pop was a mainstay of the club, and the Raspberries, the most successful Cleveland band to come out of this scene, were signed to Capitol in 1972.

By the early '70s, the Agora (thanks to tie-ins with WMMS FM, *Scene* listings magazine,
and the Belkin Productions promotion company) developed a grip on the local scene
that lasted well into the '80s and spawned a number of Agora franchises throughout the
region. Any new act coming through Cleveland, particularly a British one like Bowie or
Bad Company, played here.

The Agora largely ignored the alternative scene that was blossoming in northeast Ohio
in the mid-'70s, though for a while its basement, known as the Mistake Club, provided a
space for new local bands. Devo and Pere Ubu shared a spring residency in 1976 with
Akron's Tin Huey; tracks on both of Ubu's live albums were recorded here on a reel-to-
reel machine.

Later in the decade, the main room hosted the likes of the Clash, Talking Heads, and
XTC. The Sex Pistols were slated to play here, but problems over visas prevented their

Pere Ubu backstage at the Agora in 1978

appearance. Springsteen broadcast live from here in 1978 to mark the 10th anniversary of WMMS, and U2 played on their first two major U.S. tours, in April and December 1981. The Plasmatics caused a bit of a stir in 1981 when Wendy O'Williams hit the stage dressed in shaving foam (and maybe bikini bottoms); as the night went, on the foam dripped off. The gig, filmed by a local TV station, was captured on a hard-to-find bootleg video.

The Agora burned down in 1984, and as Anastasia Pantsios of Cleveland's *Free Times* wrote, "no single club so completely dominated the market again." Its current site is in midtown (*see below*). *1730 E. 24th St., at St. Clair Ave.*

CLEVELAND ARENA

Nine months after he began his R&B show on WJW, Alan Freed felt the time was right to whip up the emerging scene with a big live event. He assembled a lineup that included the Dominoes, Tiny Grimes and His Highlanders, Danny Cobb, and Varetta Dillard for a show to take place at this hockey rink on Friday, March 21, 1952. A day before the gig, some 2,000 of the 13,000 tickets were unsold, so on the eve of the show Freed enthusiastically promoted what he called the Moondog Coronation Ball over the air. Some 10,000 young people, most of them black, turned up for the extra tickets. As soon as the first act, Paul Williams and His Hucklebuckers, hit the stage, a massive crowd broke down the doors, and the police were kept busy for the remainder of the evening.

The media accused Freed of deliberately overselling the show, with some papers calling for him to be dumped in jail. The most vociferous criticism came from the city's black newspaper, the *Cleveland Call and Post*, whose editorial denounced the music as "gut bucket blues," referred to the "weed-smoking elements that crashed the doors," and accused Freed of building his act on a "foundation of immorality, vulgar suggestion, and hidden indecency." Proving that all publicity is good publicity, Freed's radio show got syndicated throughout the Northeast and Midwest, and his concerts became better managed and more popular. He assembled a 23-piece orchestra to back the musicians, and regularly included the Cleveland-based quintet the Moonglows—a band he managed himself—as well as the Drifters, Joe Turner, and Fats Domino.

These later packages also featured Clevelander Screamin' Jay Hawkins, who had earlier boxed in a local Golden Gloves contest in this arena and was noted for stage props that included coffins, voodoo insignia, and a skull called Henry. The Moondog tours catapulted Hawkins to the crest of his career in 1957, when he appeared in the *Mister Rock and Roll* movie that starred Alan Freed. Hawkins's role as an African bush warrior with a bone through his nose angered the NAACP, however, which got the film company to cut parts out and even lobbied the National Casket Association to stop supplying the coffins for his stage act. After that Hawkins had to be content with dragging his act around Europe, until he got a role in the 1977 movie *American Hot Wax*, also about Alan Freed, in which he played a similar role.

The Cleveland Arena also hosted a 1972 fund-raiser for George McGovern's presidential campaign featuring James Taylor and Paul Simon, soon after the latter's split with Art Garfunkel. The building is now gone, and the local Red Cross headquarters is here. *3717 Euclid Ave.*

DROME RECORD STORE

John Thompson (a.k.a. Johnny Dromette) opened Cleveland's first punk record store—originally known as Hideo's Discodrome—in the mid-'70s. The shop at 12417 Cedar Road soon became the center of a buzzing scene, doubling as a performance space where film screenings, spoken-word evenings, and parties took place and where the Pagans and Devo both played. Dromette released some Pagans singles on his own Drome label, and, in spare moments, part-time employee David Thomas packaged his

Pere Ubu records and helped put together the fanzine *CLE*. The store moved to 11800 Detroit Road on the west side and then to 1290 Euclid Avenue before closing in 1980 after a bad fire. Dromette still runs his Infodrome organization out of L.A. *Infodrome, email idrome@hollywood.cinenet.net.*

EUCLID TAVERN

Alternative Press called this little venue 5 miles east of downtown the consistently best indie club in the city. Monday and Wednesday are usually given over to unsigned touring bands, and Saturday has been the long-term residence of the veteran Mr. Stress Blues Band. It's also the place to catch 15-60-75 when it comes to town. The frill-free tavern has a long, dark main room with a battered metal ceiling and a games area in the rear; it was used as a setting in the otherwise forgettable 1987 film *Light of Day,* starring Michael J. Fox and Joan Jett, with Trent Reznor as an extra. *11629 Euclid Ave., University Circle, tel. 216/229–7788.*

Cleveland's own Craw at the Euclid

MIDTOWN RECORDING STUDIO

Soon after leaving school, Trent Reznor got a job here, and part of the deal was that he could use the studio when it wasn't booked. These were the circumstances under which the first Nine Inch Nails album was recorded. Artists on his Nothing Records label, such as Marilyn Manson, have also done some work here, though local rap bands are the main customers these days, along with LeVert, the O'Jays, and other soul acts. *2108 Payne Ave., tel. 216/861–7232.*

THE PLAZA

For more than a decade starting in the early '70s, this blond brick apartment building was home to most of Pere Ubu and a smattering of other musicians, photographers, artists, and writers. The apartments were owned by Allen Ravenstine (who played synthesizer on some early Ubu releases), and Ubu precursor Rocket from the Tombs, the Electric Eels, and other bands rehearsed in the basement. Onetime resident David Thomas reckoned the six-story block was built by 19th-century industrialists to house their girlfriends—the fountain in the courtyard was heart-shaped. Ravenstine sold the Plaza in the mid-'80s, but it's still a popular address for arty types. *Prospect Ave. at 32nd St.*

SUMA RECORDING

For the past three decades, this studio east of the city, known as the Cleveland Recording Company from 1934 until a name change in 1977, has been the area's foremost rock recording facility. Grand Funk Railroad, the James Gang, and many other regional acts have recorded here, and other visitors throughout the years have included Fleetwood Mac, Stephen Stills, Lenny Kravitz, Donny Osmond, and the British indie band Gene. It's most associated with Pere Ubu—the band's David Thomas is a particular fan of the place—who have recorded here from sessions in 1975 up to the *Ray Gun Suitcase* album 20 years later. *5706 Vroman Rd., Painesville, 30 mi E of downtown, tel. 216/951-3955.*

WHK AUDITORIUM AND AGORA BALLROOM, 1986-PRESENT

This faded Art Deco theater, once known as the WHK Auditorium, was used for live radio broadcasts in the '50s, as well as a number of concerts, including the Rolling Stones' first appearance in the city, the following decade. During spring and summer of 1977, the then underused venue was picked out by local record store owner Johnny Dromette to host the Disastodrome series of punk shows, which featured Chi-Pig, Destroy All Monsters, Devo, Pere Ubu, the Styrene Money Band, and the Suicide Commandos. Parts of the Devo and Ubu sets later popped up as live tracks. The WHK decal is still faintly embedded on the theater's east wall; the call letters will be familiar to Beatles fans from the front cover of *Sgt Pepper*, where they are stitched onto the shirt of a doll.

Mother Love Bone in 1989

The Agora Ballroom moved in here after a fire at its former premises, and tried to enliven its image. Although the club has attracted many great names to the new larger premises, it has never quite attained the status of its former location. *5000 Euclid Ave., tel. 216/881-6911.*

West Side

Cleveland's west side starts across the Cuyahoga River with the Flats' west bank, an area that isn't as developed (yet) as the downtown portion of the Flats. Ohio City, the area directly beyond the Flats, is in some parts hip and in other parts rough, although there are a few decent bars and cafés. It's also homebase for *Alternative Press* (6516 Detroit Ave., tel. 216/631−1212) magazine. A mile or so farther along the waterfront is more comfortable Lakewood, the prime area of interest for record shoppers.

EATINGDRINKINGDANCINGSHOPPINGPLAYINGSLEEPING

TRILOGY (2325 Elm St., tel. 216/241−4007), one of the top clubs in the Flats, plays dance music in an old foundry; Saturdays see underground house, and Sundays bring a very popular techno night. In Ohio City, the **BRILLO PAD** (6418 Detroit Ave., tel. 216/961−0440) stocks a great range of drinks and has dance music in its cramped basement. Good microbrewed ales are on tap at the **GREAT LAKES BREWING COMPANY** (2516 Market St., tel. 216/771−4404). One of the best hangouts on the west side is the **RED STAR CAFÉ** (11604 Detroit Ave., tel. 216/521−7827), which keeps late hours and is in among some of the best secondhand clothes and thrift stores in the city.

CHRIS' WARPED RECORDS (13383 Madison Ave., Lakewood, tel. 216/521−4981), owned by Chris Andrews (formerly of local hardcore band the Spudmonsters), has good stocks of metal, punk, and alternative sounds. Next door is **CHAIN LINK ADDICTION** (13385 Madison Ave., tel. 216/221−0014), known not so much for its slim CD selection as for it's chic accessories and piercing services; there's an east-side branch next to the Euclid Tavern. **PLATTERPUSS** (15601 Detroit Ave., Lakewood, tel. 216/531−6743), good for new bands and secondhand albums, also stocks a weird range of imports and collectibles (Jesus Jones is a speciality). **MY GENERATION** (25947 Detroit Ave., Westlake, tel. 216/871−5586) stocks all formats and tastes. **ROYAL GARDEN RECORDS** (23812 Lorain Rd., Fairview Park, tel. 216/779−4450) has well over 100,000 pieces of vinyl in stock—jazz, blues, pop, classical, and polka—including many 78s. They can even convert your turntable to 78 rpm.

PHANTASY NITE CLUB

This former discotheque, run by the Defrasia family for years, has three stages and is the largest club on the west side. A popular local new-wave band, the Pagans, played here in the early '80s, as did the Adults, the Exotic Birds, and System 56; since then it's seen Elvis Costello, the Pogues, Soul Asylum, and Trent Reznor. Two other venues are in the same complex: The Subterranean Symposium continues to put on lesser-known acts, but there hasn't been a show in years at the Phantasy Theater, where Ministry, Hüsker Dü, the Smithereens, and the Ramones all once played. *11802 Detroit Ave., Lakewood, tel. 216/228−6300.*

Ger Burgman

LOST IN XANADU

In one of the more beloved scenes from Rob Reiner's cult rockumentary *This Is Spinal Tap,* the band leaves the green room of a Cleveland club only to wander its backstage corridors, unable to find their way to the waiting crowd. Shouting, "Hello Cleveland! Rock & roll!," they burst through a final door, thinking it leads to the stage, only to find the bowels of the hall. Tapheads hoping to visit the Xanadu Star Theater may be shocked to discover that the club was entirely fictional.

Derek Smalls, "kind of like lukewarm water"

Columbus

By far the least visually attractive of Ohio's triumvirate of "C" cities, the state capital was picked by some, including *The New York Times,* to take over where Seattle left off in the early '90s. It hasn't really lived up to expectations, but thanks to good coverage from the Cleveland-based *Alternative Press,* Gaunt, Thomas Jefferson Slave Apartments, New Bomb Turks, Scrawl, and other such bands have built dedicated followings.

EATINGDRINKINGDANCINGSHOPPINGPLAYINGSLEEPING

Members of Thomas Jefferson Slave Apartments, Gaunt, and New Bomb Turks have worked behind the counter at **USED KIDS RECORDS** (1992 N. High St., tel. 614/294–3833), Columbus's punk and alternative superstore.

HOLIDAY INN CITY CENTER

This hotel was the site of Elvis Costello's infamous racist outburst during an argument with members of Stephen Stills's backing band in March 1979. Costello, who also had taken a swipe at Stills's cocaine addiction and troubled career, began to insult the U.S. music scene. When Bonnie Bramlett, one of Stills's band, drew parallels between Costello's sound and that of American R&B, the pub-rock singer-turned-punk announced that Ray Charles was a "blind, ignorant nigger" and James Brown another "dumb nigger." The debate ended in a rumble after Bramlett punched Costello. Elvis, who was involved in the Rock Against Racism concert series in the U.K. at the time, explained later that he had said the most outrageous things he could think of to end the argument. Incredibly, the incident didn't seem to mar his career. *175 E. Town St., tel. 614/221–3281.*

Dayton

Favored by market-research companies because of its absolute normalness, this city 45 miles north of Cincinnati produced several big names during the early days of rock and R&B. The Ohio Players, who had such hits in the '70s as "Skin Tight," were formed way

Guided By Voices

back in 1959 as the Ohio Untouchables. More recently Dayton has become known as the hometown of Braniac, the veteran low-fi band Guided by Voices, and of the Breeders' Deal sisters, Kim and Kelley, who were busted for various drugs here in 1994. Kim's 1995 project, the Amps, produced an album that she told *Melody Maker* was "kind of Dayton-centered cos I was just trapped there—the police, the fucking lawyers, and court dates. It was awful, it was as cold as hell." Tipp City, 20 miles north of Dayton, provided the name for the First Amps' single.

EATINGDRINKINGDANCINGSHOPPINGPLAYINGSLEEPING

The best Dayton spot for blues and jazz during the past quarter of a century has been **GILLY'S** (132 S. Jefferson St., tel. 513/228–8414), where B.B. King, Wynton Marsalis, and Clarence "Gatemouth" Brown have all appeared.

Kent

*THIS SUMMER I HEAR THE DRUMMING/FOUR DEAD IN OHIO—*CROSBY, STILLS, NASH AND YOUNG, "OHIO"

This college town, half an hour's drive out of Cleveland and best known as the place where the National Guard shot four students, was where 15-60-75 and the Waitresses emerged in the '70s. Devo also used the town as a stepping-stone. The latest band to come out of Kent is Capitol signee Dink.

JBS

This club, still putting on a fine list of touring indie bands in its two rooms, opened its doors in 1966. The James Gang had a two-year residency from 1969 and were signed by MCA, while a year or so later the Raspberries were signed here to Capitol. By the mid-'70s, the Kent scene was just as lively as Ann Arbor's had been a few years earlier, what with Devo, Glass Harp, and 15-60-75 pulling in the fans. A healthy number of live-music venues existed until 1975, when six of them were mysteriously wiped out by fires. Jbs was the only one to rebuild.

A 1978 incident that still leaves many northeast Ohioans rubbing their heads: Jerry Wexler, A&R head at Atlantic, came to Jbs and met Bob Kidney, the singer and songwriter

Anastasia Pantsios

Devo

for Kent's 15-60-75—"the Numbers Band," most people call it—whose fusion of R&B jazz licks and Joy Division mystique commands a loyal following in the region. Wexler said he was on a tight schedule and didn't have time to check out Kidney's band, and instead went into the other room to watch new-wavers Tin Huey, whom he subsequently signed. The Numbers Band still plays here every weekend, and although the band members (who include saxophonist and keyboard player Terry Hynde, brother of the chief Pretender) are all around 50, there's still hope that though they've been going since 1970, nationwide recognition isn't far away. *244 N. Water St., tel. 216/678–2774.*

KENT STATE UNIVERSITY

The fatal shooting by the National Guard of four students at a demonstration protesting the U.S. bombing of Cambodia on May 4, 1970, inspired several songs. First to express his disgust was Neil Young, who wrote "Ohio" immediately upon hearing the news; Crosby, Stills, Nash and Young recorded the single, which was rush-released and came out just eight days after the killings. The incident is also mentioned in Marvin Gaye's "What's Going On." Mike Love wrote the Beach Boys' "Student Demonstration Time" ("four martyrs earned the new degree—the Bachelor of Bullets"). Singer-songwriter Holly Near's reflections appear in "It Could Have Been Me."

One Kent State student who was there that day was Chrissie Hynde; another witness was Joe Walsh, who formed the James Gang here in 1969 and in the '80s paid for a monument to the dead. Other alumni include members of Devo, who performed their first gig here in late 1973.

OKLAHOMA

Oklahoma's oil boom in the '20s gave way to the awful deprivations of the '30s, when the exodus of families from the dust bowl to California prompted scores of sympathetic songs from Woody Guthrie, as well as John Steinbeck's 1939 novel, *Grapes of Wrath.* The latter's hero, Tom Joad, was revived by Bruce Springsteen for the title of his reflective 1995 album, *The Ghost of Tom Joad.* Since dust-bowl days, Oklahomans have

been the butt of jokes about "Okies," which led country singer Merle Haggard to declare his pride in being an "Okie from Muskogee," even though he was from Bakersfield, California. (Actually, his parents were forced to leave their east Oklahoma farm in the early '30s.)

The state, best known for the 1943 Rodgers and Hammerstein musical, *Oklahoma!,* has produced a few notable performers: R&B pioneer Lowell Fulson, born March 31, 1921, played in local bands under the name Tulsa Red. Mannford's Lee Hazlewood (born July 9, 1929)

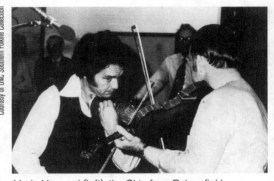

Merle Haggard (left), the Okie from Bakersfield

produced Duane Eddy and collaborated with Nancy Sinatra. The soporific J. J. Cale, born Jean-Jacques Cale in Oklahoma City on December 5, 1938, named his 1974 album *Okie.* Soul singer Ted Taylor, whose "Rambling Rose" was covered by the MC5 on *Kick Out the Jams,* was born in Ocmulgee on February 16, 1934.

Oklahoma City

The state capital—"oh so pretty," according to Bobby Troup's "Route 66"—is also home to the Flaming Lips, wayward druggy experimentalists turned MTV favorites, who formed here in 1984. The Black Crowes were the first band to play the city after the Murrah Federal Building was bombed in 1995, and they donated all proceeds to relief-work charities. The Butthole Surfers' 1996 release, *Oklahoma!,* provoked some criticism until the band informed the media that they were genuinely big fans of Rogers and Hammerstein.

Tulsa

Full of wondrous Art Deco architecture and religious fervor, Tulsa is most musically famous for the Bacharach-David song "24 Hours from Tulsa," which Gene Pitney took to the upper reaches of the charts in late 1963. Neither composer Bacharach nor lyricist David had ever been to Tulsa—they just liked the romance of the setting. The early '80s hard-funk outfit the Gap Band took its name from the first letters of three Tulsa streets where the band members grew up: Greenwood, Archer, and Pine.

CAIN'S BALLROOM

The Sex Pistols played their sixth and penultimate U.S. gig at this shabby 700-seat ballroom on January 11, 1978, and were picketed by a Baptist preacher. Cain's was once home to Bob Wills and the Texas Playboys, who in the '40s and '50s broadcast their daily *Western Swing* radio show on KVOO from here. The walls are full of pictures of Willis and Hank Williams, but not of the Pistols. *423 N. Main St., tel. 918/584–2309.*

SOUTH DAKOTA

South Dakota is a land rich with Wild West legend—stamping ground of Wild Bill Hickok, General Custer, and Crazy Horse—and a spiritual home for Native Americans. Two areas of the state, the Badlands and the Black Hills, have caught the imagination of two of rock's biggest songwriters, among others.

Bob Dylan has twice visited South Dakota in song. The 1963 track "The Ballad of Hollis Brown" tells the story of the murder of seven people on a South Dakota farm and contains the haunting refrain, "Somewhere in the distance there's seven new people born." Seven years later, on "Day of the Locusts," he sings of escaping a stressful honorary degree ceremony at Princeton University, New Jersey, by fleeing to the Black Hills of Dakota, "glad to get out of there alive."

For Paul McCartney the "black mining hills of South Dakota" were a convenient location for "a young boy named Rocky Raccoon," the hero of the loopy cowboy tale of the same name on 1968's "White Album." Meanwhile Liz Phair states her intention to "get drunk and fuck some cows" on her 1995 track "South Dakota."

Custer

CRAZY HORSE MEMORIAL

Sixteen miles southwest of Rushmore, near the town of Custer, work continues on a massive sculpture of the Lakota military strategist who defeated General Custer at Little Bighorn; when completed, sometime next century, it will be even bigger than the presidents' tribute. Crazy Horse is also familiar as the name adopted by Neil Young for his most regularly used backing band. On the *Weld* tour, he used a huge backdrop of the Lakota leader in battle stance at every gig. *U.S. 16–385, tel. 605/673–4681. Admission $15 per vehicle or $6 per adult. Open daily 8 AM–dark.*

Robb DeWall

Crazy Horse in progress

Keystone

MT. RUSHMORE NATIONAL MEMORIAL

A few miles west of the small town of Keystone and some 25 miles southwest of Rapid City stands the huge Mt. Rushmore National Monument, sculptor Gutzon Borglum's granite carvings of presidents Washington, (Theodore) Roosevelt, Jefferson, and Lincoln. Deep Purple used a pastiche of the structure, with members of the band taking the place of the politicians, for the cover of the *Deep Purple in Rock* album. *U.S. 16, tel. 605/574–2523. Admission free. Open daily.*

WISCONSIN

A land of farms and forests, beer and cheese, Wisconsin was also the scene of two of rock's most infamous aircraft crashes: those that took the lives of Otis Redding in 1967 and Stevie Ray Vaughan 23 years later. The state's two most interesting stops are its biggest city, Milwaukee, and the college town of Madison.

East Troy

In August 1990, after playing a set at the Alpine Valley Music Theater, Stevie Ray Vaughan and three members of Eric Clapton's band died when their helicopter crashed into a mountainside at the Alpine Valley Ski Resort, a few miles away. There is no marker for the crash site, which is near the top of the ski lift. *Co. Hwy. D, 5 mi from East Troy, which is 40 mi SW of Milwaukee, tel. 414/642–7374.*

Madison

Downtown Madison, which occupies a narrow isthmus between two lakes, is the home of the University of Wisconsin—and one of the prettiest cities in the country. It certainly got the okay from the normally irascible Henry Rollins, who in his book, *Get in the Van,* seems to be happy only when he's drinking java in one of State Street's many coffeehouses.

CAFÉ MONTMARTRE

At this favorite hangout of Madison music types, including Butch Vig and Garbage, the owners painted the walls pink to coincide with that band's official album-release bash in mid-1995. *127 E. Mifflin St., tel. 608/255–5900.*

Madison's Killdozer

OTIS REDDING CRASH SITE

At 3:28 on the afternoon of December 10, 1967, the plane carrying 26-year-old Otis Redding from Cleveland to a gig in Madison crashed in heavy fog and fell into Lake Monona. Otis and nearly all his backing band, the Bar-Kays, died, although trumpeter Ben Cauley survived. There is a memorial to the soul singer by the lake in Law Park on John Nolan Drive, just out of downtown.

SMART STUDIOS

The studio was founded in the mid-'80s by Steve Marker, who began recording locals Killdozer and area punk bands, plus TAD and Paw. Soon U2, Depeche Mode, Nine Inch Nails, and House of Pain were getting tracks remixed here. In the early '90s, Butch Vig, a studio co-owner, made his name producing breakthrough albums for Nirvana, the Smashing Pumpkins, and Soul Asylum. In 1994 Marker, Vig, producer Duke Erikson, and singer Shirley Manson formed the band Garbage. *1254 E. Washington Ave., tel. 608/257–9400.*

Milwaukee

The state's best-known city, Milwaukee, is home to Miller, Pabst, and scores of other breweries and was also the inspiration for the standard "What Made Milwaukee Famous," which gave Jerry Lee Lewis a country hit in 1968 and took Rod Stewart to the U.K. Top 10 in 1974. The Violent Femmes are the most famous hometown band, followed by thrash rockers Die Kreuzen.

MECCA AUDITORIUM

At a November '95 concert, in front of more than 5,000 fans, Green Day lead singer Billy Joe Armstrong was arrested by police for waving his penis around in public, then released on $150 bail. *500 W. Kilbourn Ave., tel. 414/271–4000.*

ORIENTAL THEATER

One afternoon in 1981, Chrissie Hynde of the Pretenders noticed a band of local musicians jamming outside this theater. Impressed by their racket, she asked them to open that night's show for her band. They were the Violent Femmes, still the most famous rock export of Milwaukee. *2230 N. Farwell Ave., tel. 414/276–8711.*

THE
WEST

I WAS STANDING ON A CORNER IN WINSLOW, ARIZONA—THE EAGLES, "TAKE IT EASY"

Home of the Grand Canyon and the O.K. Corral, Arizona is now more silicon and New Age than Old West. The state has turned out groups like the Meat Puppets and the Gin Blossoms, as well as jazz bassist Charles Mingus, the subject of Joni Mitchell's 1979 album *Mingus*. Its cities have had their fair share of lyrical mentions: Jimmy Webb's much-covered "By the Time I Get to Phoenix" and the Tucson appearances in the Beatles "Get Back" and Paul Simon's "Under African Skies" leap to mind. Trace the fast-disappearing Route 66 through Flagstaff (don't forget Winona), or head straight for Arizona's capital.

Phoenix

Sun-scorched Phoenix, zooming up out of the desert, offers little besides interminable shopping malls and suburban houses. When Glen Campbell, Isaac Hayes, and Nick

Jodie Foster's Army

Cave finally got here, they couldn't have had much fun. Those who took a route out of Phoenix to international success include Alice Cooper (born in Detroit but reared in Arizona), Stevie Nicks, and the Tubes.

The '80s were productive years for the city, with the emergence of the punky Meat Puppets and JFA (Jodie Foster's Army), the rootsy Green on Red and Giant Sand, the experimental Sun City Girls, and the big-selling Gin Blossoms. Today's crop of bands includes the dreamy Six String Malfunction and the angsty Beats the Hell Out of Me; the live-music scene, however, is erratic and supports few decent venues.

AUDIO-VIDEO RECORDERS OF ARIZONA

Duane Eddy recorded 12 Top 40 hits at this studio in the '50s and '60s, including "Peter Gunn," "Rebel Rouser," and "Because They're Young." Eddy got all the credit for the banal but ever-hummable tunes, but the echoey atmospheric sound that characterized them was actually the work of producer Lee Hazelwood, who later worked with Gram Parsons and Nancy Sinatra. Eddy's engineer, Floyd Ramsey, retired in 1991, and the studio moved up to 3830 North 7th Street; the original site now houses offices. *3703 N. 7th St.*

SUN DEVIL STADIUM

U2's *Joshua Tree* tour wrapped up at this college football stadium on December 19 and 20, 1987. The two shows were featured in the band's concert film, *Rattle and Hum,* whose filming Bono described as like *Apocalypse Now* but without the helicopters. The Rolling Stones caught Sun Devil Stadium on film six years earlier in *Let's Spend the Night Together. Arizona State University, Tempe.*

VETERANS MEMORIAL COLISEUM

Before the Doors played here in November 1968, the *Phoenix Gazette* dubbed them "possibly the most controversial group in the world." Morrison, perhaps not wanting to disappoint the 10,000-strong crowd, threw things from the stage, swore, denigrated President-elect Nixon, and made rude gestures. The cops prepared for a full-scale riot, but only sporadic fighting broke out, and a mere seven people were arrested. Morrison escaped any rap. *1826 W. McDowell St., 602/258–6711.*

VIP CLUB

Alice Cooper was a member of the Spiders, the VIP's mid-'60s house band. The group formed in 1964 at local Cortez High School, where Alice (then plain Vince Furnier) and pals played Beatles and Stones covers under the name the Earwigs. As the Spiders, they dressed entirely in black and used a giant web as a stage prop. A few years later they were replaced at the VIP by an early version of the Tubes. *4133 N. 7th St., tel. 602/788–7000.*

Los Angeles and San Francisco ensure that there are a wider range of rock & roll sights in California than in any other state. Both metro areas have produced musical movements that capture a particular freewheeling West Coast attitude: From the sunny anti-establishment psychedelia of the Haight-Ashbury to the nihilism of Orange county punk, the Golden State has always been on the edge.

California 10

Beach Boys, "California Girls" (1965)
The Mamas and the Papas, "California Dreaming" (1966)
Led Zeppelin, "Going to California" (1971)
The Move, "California Man" (1972)
Albert Hammond, "It Never Rains in Southern California" (1973)
Eagles, "Hotel California" (1976)
Ramones, "California Sun" (1977)
Sweet, "California Nights" (1978)
Dead Kennedys, "California Über Alles" (1982)
L.L. Cool J, "Going Back to Cali" (1988)

Altamont

[ALTAMONT SPEEDWAY]

On December 6, 1969, less than five months after Woodstock, a one-day festival at Altamont Speedway provided a dark reminder of how things can go all wrong. The event was planned as a free concert in Golden Gate Park by the Rolling Stones, who hoped it would help mitigate bad publicity over the high ticket prices of their U.S. shows. City authorities agreed to allow park access as long as the concert was announced no more than 24 hours in advance. The Stones, however, eager to get good press, spilled the beans two weeks beforehand, and the authorities withdrew permission, saying they couldn't cope with the expected crowds. Several options for other venues fell through, and it wasn't until the day before the concert that Altamont was picked.

Local Hells Angels, who were willing to work for beer and drugs, were hired to provide security—a decision that led to mayhem. Skirmishes had already broken out between the crowd and drunken Angels when Santana kicked off the event. During Jefferson Airplane's set, Marty Balin jumped into the crowd to help a kid who was being beaten up by some Angels, and the singer was knocked unconscious. After the Stones came on, the fists really began flying. Jagger pleaded for order, but it was too late. During "Under My Thumb," an 18-year-old from Berkeley, Meredith Hunter, pulled a gun and was knifed to death by an Angel as the band played on. *17001 Midway Rd. (35 mi east of Bay Area on I–580, between Livermore and Tracy).*

Berkeley

Home to the massive flagship campus of the University of California, Berkeley is still best known for the antiwar, antiestablishment protests of the '60s, an era when the town also played host to a radical folk and psychedelic scene and to famed LSD chemist Owsley Stanley, who pumped out millions of doses from his "factory" on Virginia Street. A local independent label, Fantasy, scored big in the late '60s with Creedance Clearwater Revival; Journey cut *Escape* at the studio, still operating at 10th and Parker streets.

In the '80s the town embraced the rebellious element of the punk movement, and local bands like Psycotic Pineapple played such venues as the Keystone, the Longbranch, and the Berkeley Square. Berkeley also provided a postgrunge antidote with Green Day and Rancid, both of which emerged from the scene at 924 Gilman (*see below*) to sell millions.

Ralph Granich

Psycotic Pineapple in front of the Keystone

EATINGDRINKINGDANCINGSHOPPINGPLAYINGSLEEPING

With its legions of coffee bars and student joints, Berkeley is a fun place to hang. Activity centers on the first five blocks of Telegraph Avenue, which runs south from the campus into Oakland and is generally a better bet for shopping than Haight-Ashbury, across the bay. You'll find a chaotic and colorful potpourri of cafés, book and record stores, buskers, clothing emporia, panhandlers, and gawking tourists, along with an army of street vendors hawking a mix of '60s and '90s countercultural items, jewelry, and political pamphlets.

You can bust the credit limit on your plastic at Telegraph's great record stores. **AMOEBA MUSIC** (2455 Telegraph Ave., tel. 510/549–1125) has over 30,000 CDs and 100,000 used LPs; the range of 7" singles is great. **RASPUTIN'S** (2350 Telegraph Ave., tel. 510/848–9005) has the largest selection of rock music in Berkeley. **LEOPOLD'S** (2518 Durant Ave., just east of Telegraph, tel. 510/848–2015) is best for hip-hop and funk. A few doors down, there's a branch of **TOWER RECORDS** (2510 Durant Ave., tel. 510/841–0101).

Other worthwhile record stores in the area include **MOD LANG** (2136 University Ave., tel. 510/486–1850), a small shop that's good for U.K. imports and dance music. **DOWN HOME MUSIC** (10341 San Pablo Ave., tel. 510/525–2129), in neighboring El Cerrito, is affiliated with the Arhoolie Records label; it stocks an amazing collection of blues, folk, jazz, world, roots, and country recordings.

Not surprisingly, Berkeley's live-music scene is driven by student tastes, although 924 Gilman (*see below*) attracts a more punky proletarian crowd. **BERKELEY SQUARE** (1333 University Ave., tel. 510/841–6555) is a sweaty alternative club with a high-school skater-rat crowd, though its heyday was back in the hardcore early '80s. Local bands play **BISON BREWING** (2598 Telegraph Ave., tel. 510/841–7734) several nights a week. The smoke- and alcohol-free **FREIGHT AND SALVAGE** (1111 Addison Way, tel. 510/548–1761) is a long-running folk club that presents everything from singer-songwriters to Celtic roots music.

Rancid—East Bay punks

BESERKELEY RECORDS

When the popular local band Earth Quake got dropped by A&M in the early '70s, their manager, Matthew King Kaufman, set up an independent label that went on to sign the Rubinoos and Greg Kihn. However, the act most associated with Beserkeley was Jonathan Richman and the Modern Lovers, whose lead singer virtually lived at the company's offices—aspirationally known as Home of the Hits—for several years. The house is now a private residence. *1199 Spruce St.*

JABBERWOCK

In the early '60s, the long-gone Jabberwock was a major stop on the folk circuit. Country Joe McDonald, a local boy who had an apartment upstairs, played here many times between 1965 and 1967 with the Fish (the band took its name from a Chairman Mao quote: "Revolutionaries move through the people like the fish through the sea"). *2901 Telegraph Ave.*

METALLICA HOUSE

In early 1983 members of Metallica found an ideal new bassist in Cliff Burton, of the San Fran rockers Trauma. Burton liked Metallica's sound but refused to join the band in L.A., so James Hetfield, Lars Ulrich, and Dave Mustaine relocated to this house just north of Berkeley. It became band HQ for the better part of the decade. *3140 Carlson Blvd., El Cerrito.*

924 GILMAN

This no-frills club, housed in a formerly abandoned warehouse in the unstudenty end of town, has been a daytime hangout and all-ages venue for East Bay punks since 1987. Operation Ivy, made up of students from nearby Albany High School, was one of the first bands to make its mark here; members Tim Armstrong and Matt Freeman went on to form Rancid. Contemporaries in the 924 scene were Crimpshine, Neurosis, Mr. T Experience, and Green Day. The habitués of 924 were not so welcoming to one older-generation punk, the Dead Kennedys' Jello Biafra: At a Fixtures gig in 1994, he was attacked by slam dancers who yelled "Sellout rock star—kick him!" as they broke both his legs and delivered head wounds. *924 Gilman St., tel. 510/525–9926.*

Pat Graham

Billie Joe of Green Day

UNIVERSITY OF CALIFORNIA AT BERKELEY

Cal, as the Berkeley campus is commonly known, counts among its alumni rock critic Greil Marcus, Police drummer Stewart Copeland, and Jann Wenner, who wrote rock reviews for the *Daily Cal,* the student paper, before dropping out to start *Rolling Stone.* The most famous Cal venue is the Greek Theater, an open-air amphitheater that hosted the Doobie Brothers' last live show in 1982, but the school's halls and dorms have also staged thousands of gigs over the years. The infamous Barrington Hall—an anarchic student co-op closed down in the early '90s after one too many acid-fueled party guests leaped from the fifth-story roof—hosted any number of punk bands, including the Dead Kennedys and Rancid precursors Operation Ivy.

Joshua Tree

The vast, silent landscape of the Mojave Desert, occupying much of south-central California, has provided an awesome setting for many rock videos—among them the Rollins Band's "Liar"—and album covers. The stunning Joshua Tree area has most associations with rock & roll. Dotted with the weird gnarled trees for which it's named, Joshua Tree marks the transition between high and low desert and since the '60s has been a favorite getaway spot for L.A.-based musicians. Daniel Lanois keeps a studio just outside town, and surf-guitar vet Dick Dale lives in nearby Twenty-Nine Palms. Dutch photographer and director Anton Corbijn has also been a regular visitor. His most famous Mojave piece is probably the front cover of U2's *Joshua Tree.* He also snapped the reclusive Don Van Vliet (a.k.a. Captain Beefheart, who spent many years living out here) for the front of 1980's *Ice Cream for Crow* album.

[JOSHUA TREE INN]

Late on the night of September 17, 1973, Gram Parsons was found in a comatose state by friends in Room 8 of this motel. The former Byrd and Flying Burrito Brother was taken to the Hi-Desert Hospital in nearby Yucca Valley, where he was pronounced dead. The autopsy report gave the cause of death as "drug toxicity, days, due to multiple drug use, weeks."

Parsons was not the only celebrated guest in the '70s; others who came to stay at the Joshua Tree included Keith Richards (a good friend of Parsons's), various former Byrds and Burrito Brothers, and John Belushi, who came to work on scripts with other members of the *Saturday Night Live* team. Just another old desert roadhouse then, it has since been souped up into a cozy B&B that attracts a considerable number of Parsons fans each year. The owners keep a small library of cuttings and books about the singer, and guests who stay in Room 8 get to sign a book of tributes to Parsons, which include one from the Lemonheads' Evan Dando, who came down for a week in June 1993. If staying in Room 8 seems too freaky, then Room 9, where Emmylou Harris stayed several times, may be a better choice. *61259 Twentynine Palms Hwy., tel. 619/366–1188 or 800/366–1444. Rooms (with breakfast): $90.*

[JOSHUA TREE NATIONAL PARK]

At the July 1973 funeral of former Byrd Clarence White, killed by a drunk driver while loading gear into a truck outside an L.A. club, Gram Parsons told his friend Phil Kaufman what he wanted done in the event of his death. Three months later, Parsons was dead, so Kaufman borrowed a hearse, went to LAX (where the body was awaiting transportation to New Orleans), and conned the airport police into believing the burial plans had changed. Kaufman and Parsons's friend Michael Martin—both in a stupor of drugs and drink—then drove out to Joshua Tree National Monument to give Parsons the cremation he'd requested. They took the body to Cap Rock—a heap of huge rounded boulders where Parsons would often smoke himself silly and contemplate such pressing matters as flying saucers and the stability of the San Andreas Fault—then split open the casket, doused the body with gasoline, and threw on a match. Parsons's remains were found by park rangers the next morning. No record was kept of the actual location of the cremation, but many Parsons fans have taken it to be a blackened concrete slab at the back of the rock pile, and have etched dedications into it. Kaufman (who was arrested but released after agreeing to pay $750 for the casket) has said he doesn't believe he and Martin went so far from the road and puts the charred rocks down to someone's barbecue. *Tel. 619/367–7511. Admission: $5 per vehicle.*

Los Angeles

SOMETIMES I FEEL LIKE MY ONLY FRIEND/IS THE CITY I LIVE IN/THE CITY OF ANGELS—RED HOT CHILI PEPPERS, "UNDER THE BRIDGE"

Scattered throughout this giant metropolitan sprawl are venues, bars, studios, and hangouts that have been named, celebrated, and immortalized by artists since the earliest days of rock. Most of the major labels—Geffen, Elektra, MCA, Capitol, A&M, RCA—have their headquarters here, as do such influential independents as SST, Epitaph, Alias, and Death Row. All the industry's major players—managers, lawyers, producers, and svengalis—live or keep a presence here. The city has also drawn at some time or other nearly every band bent on world domination (the Beatles, the Stones, Led Zeppelin, Nirvana) and nurtured such home-grown talent as the Beach Boys, the Doors, and many rap artists.

It all started when Capitol Records, seeing what the place had done for the movie industry, set up in Hollywood in 1942 and began drawing in talent from all over the United

States. By the mid-'50s, the label was scoring big hits, and other companies had followed Capitol west: MGM was recording Hank Williams, ABC Paramount had Ray Charles, and RCA signed Elvis Presley. At the end of the decade the Warner Bros. film company set up a recording arm to capitalize on the teen market and signed up the Everly Brothers. However, none of these acts were based in L.A. Even the city's successful independent labels used mainly imported talent. By the early '60s there were hundreds of rock and pop artists living in L.A., but the city was still producing very few sounds of its own.

That changed in 1963 with the surf scene created by Dick Dale, Jan and Dean, and America's first self-sufficient rock & roll band: the Beach Boys. Further inspiration came via the folk scene. The L.A. folksingers, though, were more concerned with making music and having fun than with changing the world, so they added a dance beat and gave birth to a new sound, folk-rock, epitomized locally by the Byrds and such imitators as Love and Buffalo Springfield. The Doors, meanwhile, based their sound on the blues, enriched by Ray Manzarek's powerful organ. Less chart-oriented but with a huge cult following was a freaky pair of high school friends: the prolific Frank Zappa and Captain Beefheart.

Things turned sour at the end of the '60s, and a reflective tone came to the fore, particularly in the work of singer-songwriters like Neil Young, Stephen Stills, Joni Mitchell, and Jackson Browne. The music also took on a sweet country tone inspired by Gram Parsons's stint with the Byrds on the 1968 LP *Sweetheart of the Rodeo*. By 1977, however, the big L.A. acts had opted for a crystal-clear production sound, and the Eagles and Fleetwood Mac had, in *Hotel California* and *Rumours*, respectively, delivered the ultimate statements in designer-lifestyle, L.A.-based corporate rock.

Black Flag

A reaction to the L.A. music establishment was soon to come: Punk bands like Black Flag, the Germs, the Dils, and the Weirdos built and sustained sizeable followings, but as the punk scene lost its fizzle on both sides of the Atlantic, new-wave acts took over Los Angeles's alternative scene. These, however, either failed to make much impression or, like the Go-Go's and the Bangles, plowed an increasingly mainstream furrow. Loud guitars and theatrics came to rule '80s L.A., with camped-up metal bands like Poison, Van Halen, and Guns N' Roses taking up punk's in-your-face attitude.

If the advent of punk had annoyed the L.A. rock establishment, then '90s gangsta rap caused even more fretting. The major labels, unsure of how to deal with a style born on the streets of South Central, were eager to rake in the profits nonetheless. After Ice-T's insistence on releasing *Cop Killer* got him dropped by Columbia, West Coast rappers started to set up their own labels to avoid corporate censorship; the most successful of these ventures is Dr. Dre's Death Row Records, based in the well-to-do university district of Westwood. The search for a grunge alternative netted another indie success story of the '90s when Hollywood-based Epitaph scored what's said to be the biggest-selling nonmajor-label album: 1994's *Smash,* by Orange County's Offspring, which sold some 7 million copies.

EATINGDRINKINGDANCINGSHOPPINGPLAYINGSLEEPING

The top way for a music fan to see L.A. is on a rock tour led by the **MAGICAL HISTORY TOUR** (tel. 310/392–1500), although they currently accept group reservations only. The same organization also conducts L.A. Nighthawks, a crawl of all the best gigs in town.

An L.A. 20

The Beatles, "Blue Jay Way" (1967)
Richard Harris, "MacArthur Park" (1968)
Flying Burrito Brothers, "Sin City" (1969)
Stooges, "L.A. Blues" (1970)
Doors, "L.A. Woman" (1971)
Canned Heat, "Long Way from L.A." (1972)
Patti Smith, "Redondo Beach" (1975)
Van Morrison, "Venice USA" (1978)
Tom Petty, "Century City" (1979)
X, "Los Angeles" (1980)
Cheech and Chong, "Born in East L.A." (1984)
Red Hot Chili Peppers, "Out in L.A." (1984)
The Fall, "L.A." (1985)
Joe Ely, "Letter to L.A." (1987)
Grateful Dead, "West L.A. Fadeaway" (1987)
Frank Black, "Los Angeles" (1993)
Sheryl Crow, "All I Wanna Do" (1994)
Liz Phair, "dogs of l.a." (1994)
Everclear, "Santa Monica" (1995)
Mike Watt, "Drove Up from Pedro" (1995)

Downtown L.A. and South

Nighttime starts early here—office workers check out as early as 3 PM to get onto the freeways—but the entertainment options aren't that hot. **AL'S BAR** (305 S. Hewitt St., tel. 213/687–3558 or 213/625–9703), a dark, smoky dive set among the warehouses and artists' lofts on the edge of Little Tokyo, has been putting on everything from punk to folk to spoken word for more than 15 years.

SAM COOKE DEATH SITE

With a live LP in the Top 30, Sam Cooke was in L.A. partying when he met 22-year-old Elisa Boyer at a club on December 11, 1964. They drove to South Central and registered at the Hacienda Motel as Mr. and Mrs. Cooke. Later, Boyer fled the room, taking with her most of Cooke's clothing. The singer, wearing one shoe and a jacket, broke into the motel's office, where he thought she was hiding; instead, he found Bertha Franklin, the manager, who shot him three times with a .22 and then, as the autopsy revealed, hit him with a stick. Boyer claimed that Cooke had forced her into the motel room and that she'd escaped, taking his clothes for safety, when he went to the bathroom. The low-rent motel, now known as the Webb, stills stands in this rundown part of town. Cooke is buried at Glendale's **Forest Lawn Cemetery** (1712 S. Glendale Ave.). *9137 S. Figueroa St., South Central.*

MARVIN GAYE DEATH SITE

In early 1984 Marvin Gaye returned to L.A. from Belgium and moved in with his parents in the plush two-story home he had bought for them. Drugs, a divorce from Anna Gordy (daughter of Motown founder Berry), the end of another brief marriage, his split with Motown, and a nightmare tax bill all combined to mess him up, and friends were concerned about his threats to commit suicide. On April 1, 1984, the day before his 45th birthday, he got into an argument with his father, a retired minister. In the course of the fight, Gaye senior produced a .38 and pumped two fatal shots into his son's body. The autopsy revealed the heavy extent of the soul star's cocaine addiction. His father, who claimed self-defense, was found guilty of involuntary manslaughter. *2101 S. Gramercy Pl., Crenshaw.*

MORRISON HOTEL

When the Doors came here to take the front-cover photo for the *Morrison Hotel* LP, the hotel's owner told them to get lost; they sneaked back and got the shot anyway. Drop by for a look, but this shabby joint is not a place to stay. The greasy spoon pictured on the back of the album—the Hard Rock Café, no less—was at 300 East 5th Street but is currently boarded up. *1246 S. Hope St.*

SHRINE AUDITORIUM

Now used for film sets—Michael Jackson's hair caught fire during a Pepsi commercial shoot here—this was an important venue in the psychedelic days. Hendrix, the Dead, and Country Joe all played here in 1968. It's also used for Grammy and Oscar ceremonies and for Shriner events. *University of Southern California, 32nd and S. Figueroa Sts.*

U2 VIDEO SHOOT

In March 1987, just before taking off on the *Joshua Tree* tour, U2 set up on a rooftop above a liquor store in this washed-up part of downtown. With camera crews atop nearby buildings and overhead in a helicopter, they began shooting the video for "Where the Streets Have No Name." At first the band lip-synched, but after a local radio station mentioned what was going on, a crowd of a thousand or so turned up, packed the sidewalks, and spilled over onto the street. Bono and company went into a short set until the L.A.P.D. came along and pulled the plug. *7th and Main Sts.*

KAREN CARPENTER, CHANTEUSE AND SUPER

Downey, 10 miles southeast of downtown L.A., is the sleepy town to which Karen and Richard Carpenter's family moved from Connecticut in 1963. When royalties started pouring in during the '70s, the siblings invested in a pair of still-standing apartment blocks named after two of their favorite compositions: We've Only Just Begun, at 8345 5th Street, and Close to You, at 8356 5th Street.

On February 4, 1983, Karen was taken to the Downey Community Hospital, where she died from heart failure, brought on (according to the autopsy) "by chemical imbalances associated with anorexia nervosa," at age 32. She is buried at nearby **Forest Lawn Cemetery** (4471 Lincoln Ave., Cypress, tel. 714/828–3131), where Eddie Cochran's grave is also to be found, in an ornate crypt inscribed with the dedication A STAR ON EARTH—A STAR IN HEAVEN.

Hollywood

"Hollywood" isn't in Hollywood anymore: The film companies relocated over the hills years ago, and many of the famous recording studios have been replaced by strip malls or vacant lots. The Capitol Records tower is one of the country's most visual rock landmarks, however, and the area's somewhat creepy feel at night shouldn't put you off coming for gigs.

EATINGDRINKINGDANCINGSHOPPINGPLAYINGSLEEPING

Besides Club Lingerie (*see below*), check out the **Anti-Club** (4658 Melrose Ave., tel. 213/661–3913 or 213/667–9762 after 7:30 PM), a lively all-ages venue that has put on an adventurous blend of underground bands since the early '80s; among those who played here on their on the way up are L7, Primus, the Red Hot Chili Peppers, the Rollins Band, and Dwight Yoakam. **Dragonfly** (6510 Santa Monica Blvd., between Highland and Vine Sts., tel. 213/466–6111), an excellent no-frills venue, has live music most nights and a garden-patio escape zone.

If you get a hankering for a grand slam, head over to the **Rock & Roll Denny's** (7373 Sunset Blvd., tel 213/876–6660), so called for the countless rock bands who eat or have eaten here; other than the preponderance of leather and spandex, it doesn't look any different from the other three billion branches of the chain. **Lucy's El Adobe Restaurant** (5536 Melrose Ave., tel. 213/462–9421) is a family-run Mex place frequented by rock stars, many of whose photos line the walls.

If you've got dollars to drop on musical instruments, there are dozens of shops around the giant Guitar Center (*see below*). The **Rock Shop** (6666 Hollywood Blvd., tel. 213/466–7276) is packed with T-shirts, posters, and buttons, with an emphasis on metal. The area around Los Feliz and Vermont Avenue, toward Griffith Park, has a number of cool book, record, and clothing stores. **Rockaway** (2390 N. Glendale Blvd., tel. 213/644–3232) in East Hollywood stocks a huge selection of used CDs.

Hollywood and Vinyl

Kool and the Gang, "Hollywood Swingin' " (1974)
Runaways, "Hollywood" (1977)
Ronnie Spector, "Say Goodbye to Hollywood" (1977)
Bob Seger and the Silver Bullet Band, "Hollywood Nights" (1978)
Holger Czukay, "Hollywood Symphony" (1980)
Go-Betweens, "Before Hollywood" (1982)
Black Flag, "Hollywood Diary" (1984)
Red Hot Chili Peppers, "Hollywood" (1988)
Public Enemy, "Burn Hollywood Burn" (1990)
Menswear, "Hollywood Girl" (1995)

[CAPITOL RECORDS]

This is the essence of Hollywood—a bizarre building that's kitschy and cool at the same time. The 13-floor cylindrical tower, erected in 1956, looks like a stack of records, an idea said to have come from two of the label's mainstays, Nat King Cole and songwriter

Johnny Mercer. To add to the tackiness quotient, the "stylus" on top of the building continuously blinks out H-O-L-L-Y-W-O-O-D in Morse code. The gold discs of Capitol artists from Frank Sinatra to the Beastie Boys are lined up in the foyer, the only area open to the public, but the Walk of Fame (*see below*) runs right past the building, and some of the label's most famous performers—Steve Miller, Bob Seger, Tina Turner, John Lennon, Gene Vincent, and Duran Duran—have their stars embedded in the sidewalk outside. *1750 N. Vine St., tel. 213/462–6252.*

Capitol Records

THE STUDIO SYSTEM

Besides Capitol Records, a number of other labels have (or once had) studios in Hollywood.

A&M RECORDS (1416 North La Brea). Herb Alpert and Jerry Moss established this label in 1962. Before the company was sold to PolyGram in the late '80s, A&M was a huge independent with a roster that included the Police, Bryan Adams, and Janet Jackson. The building itself has some history: It was once Charlie Chaplin's studio, and in 1985 "We Are the World" was recorded here.

GOLD STAR STUDIO. Phil Spector created the Wall of Sound—a production technique evident in "Be My Baby" (Ronettes) and "You've Lost That Lovin' Feelin' " (the Righteous Brothers)—at this studio at Santa Monica and Vine. The site has housed a minimall since the studio burned in the mid-'80s.

RCA RECORDS (6363 Sunset Blvd.). The Rolling Stones recorded "Paint It Black" and other hits at RCA, which also hosted Monkees' sessions and some '70s appearances by Elvis Presley. In 1988 RCA was bought out by BMG.

SUNSET SOUND RECORDERS (6650 Sunset Blvd.). In 1966 the Doors cut the whole of their first album here in little over a week. The Rolling Stones *Beggars Banquet* and Prince's *Purple Rain* were also done here.

CLUB LINGERIE

There's been drinking and dancing going on at this venue since the '30s. Eddie Cochran played here in the '50s, when it was called the Red Velvet, as did the Righteous Brothers the following decade. In the '70s it was a soul club, with Motown (which had its offices just down the way) providing many of the top acts, including Stevie Wonder. Today Club Lingerie is one of the best places in L.A. to catch indie and alternative bands. This reputation rests on the eclectic booking policy of Brendan Mullen, who made his name by putting on punk bands at the short-lived Masque club (*see below*). Recent years have seen shows by the Cramps, the Replacements, Guns N' Roses, the Red Hot Chili Peppers, and Nirvana, as well as blues and avant-garde jazz combos. Sellouts are common, so it's best to turn up early. *6507 Sunset Blvd., tel. 213/466–8557.*

DARBY CRASH DEATH SITE

Darby Crash (a.k.a. Jan Paul Beahm), the amphetamine-and-booze–fueled lead singer of the Germs, who was featured at length in the punk documentary *The Decline of Western Civilization,* died in this one-story house on December 7, 1980, from a preplanned heroin overdose. His demise didn't grab the same media attention as other punk deaths of the period (Ian Curtis of Joy Division and the Ruts' Malcolm Owen) because the next day John Lennon was shot. Crash is buried at the **HOLY CROSS CEMETERY** (5835 Slauson Ave., tel. 213/776–1855) in Culver City. *137 N. Fuller Ave.*

GRIFFITH OBSERVATORY

This copper-domed observatory has been featured on album covers (the Byrds' 1970 *Untitled*) and in movies (most famously, *Rebel Without a Cause*, thus the statue of James Dean on-site). The Laserium presents laser shows set to the music of Pink Floyd, U2, and such. *2800 E. Observatory Ave., Griffith Park (entrance on Los Feliz Blvd.), tel. 213/664–1191.*

[GUITAR CENTER AND ROCK WALK]

The Strip is overloaded with musical-instrument stores, most of which would probably fit into the enormous Guitar Center, which stocks a vast range of rock-related instruments. Since 1985, the store has followed the Hollywood logic that where there's a sidewalk, there should be a walk of fame, so palm prints of some 50 artists are embedded in concrete near the entrance. *7425 W. Sunset Blvd., tel. 213/874–1060.*

HOLLYWOOD BOWL

On August 23, 1964, the Beatles became the first pop band to appear under this big white shell, set in a large natural amphitheater. The show was taped by Capitol, but the label was disappointed with the results, so the recording went unreleased until 1977. A similar episode befell the Doors' mini-LP and video, *Live at the Hollywood Bowl*, which didn't come out until 1987. The bowl primarily presents symphonic music. *2301 N. Highland Ave., at Cahuenga Terrace, tel. 213/850–2000.*

HOLLYWOOD HAWAIIAN HOTEL GRACE (PRINCESS APARTMENTS)

Fleetwood Mac was staying in this hotel in February 1971 when guitarist Jeremy Spencer popped out to buy a pack of cigarettes. On the way to the store he met members of the Children of God cult, joined up on the spot, and that was the last the band saw of him for a couple of years. Spencer had always been religious; he even had a Bible sewn into his jacket. Of course, he also used to do Elvis impersonations where he sang "hunka hunka love" with a dildo hanging out of his trousers. *1801 Grace Ave., tel. 213/462–4011.*

HOLLYWOOD PALLADIUM

Built in the '40s, this 5,000-capacity theater has of late put on a strong lineup of such bands as Belly, Faith No More, and Archers of Loaf. At a 1995 Hole gig, newly signed recording artist Mary Lou Lord came backstage to join in the partying. Courtney Love, who says Lord built a career out of having once given Kurt Cobain a blow job, would have none of it. Still in her stage outfit, a baby-doll slip, the barefoot Love chased Lord out of the theater and down Sunset Boulevard, followed by cheering fans. *6215 Sunset Blvd., tel. 213/962–7600.*

LANDMARK HOTEL (HIGHLAND GARDENS MOTEL)

On Friday, October 2, 1970, after completing a recording session for *Pearl* and going to Barney's Beanery for drinks with her Full Tilt Boogie Band, 27-year-old Janis Joplin went back to this motel, then a favorite of rock stars who wanted to be close to Hollywood's drug dealers. Not until Sunday evening was her body discovered in Room 105. The coroner's report listed the cause of death as "acute heroin-morphine intoxication" due to "injection of overdose." Joplin took a hit of pure heroin that was perhaps 10 times as strong as her usual dose; she is thought to have died more or less instantly. The funeral service was held at Westwood Village Mortuary on October 7, and six days later her ashes were scattered from a plane off the coast of Marin County. The few unfinished bits and pieces of *Pearl* were filled in, and the album—along with her version of Kris Kristofferson's "Me and Bobby McGee"—hit the top of the charts. Joplin's death was the second in a trio of big rock fatalities within the space of a year: Jimi Hendrix had died in London barely two weeks before, and Jim Morrison was found dead in a Paris bathtub the following July. *7047 Franklin Ave., tel. 213/850-0536. Rooms: $50-$90.*

Courtney Love, Hollywood Palladium troublemaker

THE MASQUE

L.A.'s punk scene originated in this large space in the bowels of a theater in 1977, when the established Sunset Strip venues were ignoring bands like the Germs, Social Distortion, X, and the (pre-pop) Go-Go's. Just six months after it opened, the club was closed for violations of the fire code; it reopened nearby on Santa Monica Boulevard but after a few months was again forced to shut down for the same reason. The Masque's founder, Brendan Mullen, is now the booker for Club Lingerie. *Cherokee Ave. at Hollywood Blvd., behind Ritz Theater.*

MOTION PICTURE COORDINATION OFFICE

This agency produces a daily list of what's being shot around the city, including music videos. *6922 Hollywood Blvd., Suite 602, tel. 213/485-5324. Open weekdays 9-5.*

RODNEY BINGENHEIMER'S ENGLISH DISCO

Hollywood's rock & roll gossips are still eager to recall the days of this long-defunct club, which opened in 1972 and soon established itself as the epicenter of Sunset Boulevard's pill-popping, cross-dressing, groupie-fucking glam-rock period. A hangout for mostly English acts, such as Slade, T Rex, and David Bowie, the place was a wild scene (as documented by, among others, Danny Sugerman in *Wonderland Avenue*), with hordes of young women punching and kicking to get to the likes of the Sweet. Proprietor Bingenheimer took his responsibilities as lord of the manor seriously: As Kim Fowley told *Mojo* magazine, "Rodney fucked movie-star bitches you wouldn't believe. He fucked so many that in his early 20s he had a stroke. Allegedly Led Zeppelin paid the bill...because he had no insurance." Worried about the potentially libelous nature of such a quote, a *Mojo* editor phoned Bingenheimer asking for verification, to which the man known as the Mayor of Sunset Strip replied, "No, that's complete bollocks. It was in my 30s." *7561 Sunset Blvd.*

SPOTLIGHT TATTOO

One of the best tattoo parlors in L.A., this is where Flea from the Red Hot Chili Peppers gets his work done. *5859 Melrose Ave., tel. 213/871–1084.*

HOLLYWOOD WALK OF FAME

This tour-bus magnet, started in 1958, emanates from the junction of Hollywood Boulevard and Vine Street. It runs along Hollywood from Gower Street to La Brea Avenue, and along Vine from Yucca Street (where the Capitol Records tower stands) to Sunset Boulevard. A full list of all the stars on the walk is available from the HOLLYWOOD CHAMBER OF COMMERCE (6541 Hollywood Blvd., tel. 213/461–4213).

Tim Perry

There are about 50 stars dedicated to modern musicians, including: Chuck Berry (1777 Vine St.); John Lennon (1750 Vine St.); the Beach Boys (1500 Vine St.); Elvis Presley (6777 Hollywood Blvd.); and Jimi Hendrix (6627 Hollywood Blvd.). In December 1994 Doris Day's star (6278 Hollywood Blvd.) was amended by a punk fan to read Green Day.

Sunset Strip

Sunset Boulevard snakes for some 20 miles from downtown L.A. to the sea, but some of the world's most celebrated rock venues are concentrated along the mile-long Sunset Strip, which runs west from Crescent Heights to Doheny Drive. Don't expect anything too raucous, however: Significantly higher on the social scale than neighboring Hollywood, the Strip serves the corporate side of the record industry, with clubs that showcase their new acts, private clubs that host their parties, dozens of huge billboards that advertise their artists, and a couple of CD supermarkets to sell their wares. That's not to say the Strip's not fun—there are a half-dozen gigs each night, rock-associated eateries galore, and famous rock hotels where you too can lay your head.

EATING DRINKING DANCING SHOPPING PLAYING SLEEPING

It's hard to beat staying near the Strip on a visit to L.A. Besides such famous rock palaces as the Chateau Marmont and the Hyatt (*see below*), there's **LE MONTROSE** (900 Hammond St., tel. 310/855–1115 or 800/776–0666), an excellent choice in a quiet residential area favored by stars wanting a peaceful time within a two-minute walk of the Roxy and the Whisky. Also fashionable with bands and record execs is the **MONDRIAN HOTEL** (8440 W. Sunset Blvd., tel. 213/650–8999), with friezes and murals in the Dutch artist's distinctive style splashed around the exterior walls.

TOWER (8801 W. Sunset Blvd., tel. 310/657–7300) and **VIRGIN** (8000 W. Sunset Blvd., tel. 213/650–8666) both have big stores here. The SST Superstore (*see below*) stocks all of the label's catalogue, and **RECORD SURPLUS** (8913 W. Sunset Blvd., tel. 310/659–9994) has a reasonable selection of used music in all formats. Zappa advised people to eat here on the track "Suzi Creamcheese," and **BEN FRANKS** (8585 W. Sunset Blvd., tel. 310/652–8808) still serves great diner food 24 hours day. **SUNSET STRIP TATTOO** (8418 Sunset Blvd., tel. 213/650–6530), patronized by Axl Rose, is one of a number of such parlors in the area.

CHATEAU MARMONT

Shielded from the traffic by tall trees, this big white luxury hotel resembles a Norman castle and has long been popular with the rock and film aristocracy. Stars who have come here for some privacy, away from hangers-on and gawking tourists, include Mick Jagger, Bob Dylan, Janis Joplin, John Lennon and Yoko Ono, Rod Stewart, and Evan Dando. In 1964 Barry Mann and Cynthia Weill, two of the Brill Building's most prodigious songwriters, installed a piano in Room 2H and knocked out "You've Lost That Lovin' Feelin'," which became a megahit for the Righteous Brothers.

Many of rock's finest have gorged themselves on all manner of excess at the Marmont: The hotel was a favorite stop for Led Zeppelin, who are said to have attempted some matchmaking between a groupie and a Great Dane they found wandering the grounds. Jim Morrison injured his back while hanging off a drainpipe outside his room, and that was after he'd had to move here because the Hyatt's usually easygoing management didn't want him swinging from *their* roof. The hotel's only casualty has been John Belushi—actor, Blues Brother, and fan of the punk band Fear—who on March 5, 1982, died at age 33 from a drug overdose in Bungalow 3. *8221 Sunset Blvd., tel. 213/656—1010 or 800/242—8328. Double room: $150—$200.*

COCONUT TEASZER

The Teaszer, daubed with garish purple paint, marks the eastern end of the Strip and has a mood midway between the punk clubs of Hollywood to the east and the rock palaces west on the Strip. There's been music here since the '60s, and in recent years it's been an important place for new bands to break into the big time: Green Day, Hole, Rage Against the Machine, Stone Temple Pilots, the Spin Doctors, and Candlebox (which was signed here by Madonna's Maverick label) all played here before the MTV Buzz Clip beckoned. The bar stocks an excellent range of (well-priced) import beers. The less frenetic Crooked Bar downstairs puts on acoustic and grunge-lite acts; with its low cover, it's one of the best places on the Strip to take it easy. *8117 Sunset Blvd., tel. 213/654—4773.*

DUKE'S TROPICANA COFFEE SHOP

The *Tropicana* in the name is a reminder of the days when, at the café's previous site, next to the Tropicana Hotel on Santa Monica Boulevard, it was the feeding station for such hotel residents as Jim Morrison, Iggy Pop, and Alice Cooper. When the Tropicana was torn down in the late '80s, Duke's moved to its current location, next to the Whisky A Go Go, and it still attracts a musical crowd for big breakfasts.

A venue called London Fog previously occupied this site. The Doors had their first gig at the club and were hired as the house band at $5 a night, $10 weekends. Their demo got them a spot on Columbia's books, but the A&R rep who came by wasn't impressed and dropped them. Soon after they were fired—a blessing really, since they went on to play the bigger, better-paying Whisky and get signed by Elektra. *8909 Sunset Blvd., tel. 310/652—3100 or 310/652—9411.*

GAZZARRI'S

Bill Gazzarri opened this club in 1963 and remained one of the larger-than-life characters on the Strip until his death in the early '90s. In 1966, when the L.A.P.D. was trying to shut down Sunset Strip clubs and rid the streets of longhairs, he spearheaded a successful campaign against overzealous city officials. Meanwhile, his club introduced such bands as the Byrds, Buffalo Springfield, and the Walker Brothers. Out of fashion for a while in the '70s, Gazzarri's began in the '80s to put on glam-metal bands with a sideshow of barely clad girlie dancers—an image documented in Penelope Spheeris's film *The Decline of Western Civilization Part II: The Metal Years.* Guns N' Roses, Metallica, Mötley Crüe, and Van Halen all played here in their early days. The club struggled on for a bit after Bill Gazzarri's death but was eventually torn down. There are rumors of a new venue opening in the now vacant lot. *9039 Sunset Blvd.*

GEFFEN RECORDS

These neat headquarters, in the style of a country villa, are home to the namesake label founded by David Geffen in the early '80s. He first got into the label business in 1970 when, as manager of Neil Young and CSN, he received a demo tape from Jackson Browne. Geffen tried to persuade Atlantic Records chief Ahmet Ertegun to sign the singer-songwriter. Despite Geffen's assurances that Browne would make him rich, Ertegun declined, saying he was already rich, and why didn't Geffen start his own label?—then he could be rich, too. Hence Asylum Records, which came to epitomize 1970s California cool with a roster that included the Eagles, Linda Ronstadt, and Tom Waits. Asylum merged with Elektra in 1973, and all was going brilliantly until the company struggled to get a foothold in the new-wave market of the late '70s, despite having a stable of by then definitely uncool singer-songwriters and country-rock types. Geffen wisely bailed out and started over on his own.

Kim Gordon of Geffen standard-bearers Sonic Youth

The first artist signed to the new Geffen label was Donna Summer, in 1980, and soon after Geffen managed to get his old buddy Neil Young away from Reprise. Unlike Elektra/Asylum, which kept faith with the acoustic set and missed out on punk, the Geffen label kept well abreast of continuing developments. One of the least likely but most significant captures was Sonic Youth, which was instrumental in persuading Nirvana to sign up in 1991. The label then threw the equivalent of a small nation's GNP at the Stone Roses and had to dispatch senior executives from L.A. to deepest Wales to make sure that the group's five-years-in-the-making *Second Coming* album would arrive before the end of 1994. The current Geffen roster also includes Aerosmith, Guns N' Roses, Hole, Weezer, Counting Crows, White Zombie, and Urge Overkill, as well as such singer-songwriter standbys as solo Don Henley and the reunited Eagles.

One artist who shouldn't expect a call is Mojo Nixon, who released a song called "Don Henley Must Die" and then had the temerity to perform it from the back of a flatbed truck outside these offices. Nixon followed with the track "Bring Me the Head of David Geffen," which appeared on promotional copies of his 1995 *Whereabouts Unknown* album. These had to be recalled after a certain music-business figure objected. *9130 Sunset Blvd., tel. 310/278–9010.*

[HOUSE OF BLUES]

Between the Mondrian and the Hyatt, two of the Strip's swankiest hotels, stands a $9 million tin shack, the third and most swish branch of the House of Blues chain started by Hard Rock Cafe cofounder Isaac Tigrett. Investors include Jim Belushi, Joe Walsh, and Dan Aykroyd. The tin stuff comes from an old cotton gin that was carted across the continent from Clarksdale, Mississippi—more precisely, from the crossroads where blues legend Robert Johnson is said to have struck his pact with the devil. The entrance is through the gift shop, but things get better after that. Blues memorabilia and folk art crams the walls of what may be the most palatial juke joint on the planet. Downstairs, the restaurant serves "international peasant fare" with a heavy Deep South/Cajun bent.

House of Blues

The nightly entertainment isn't all blues: Besides Bobby Bland, Buddy Guy, and John Mayall, the likes of Tom Jones, Waylon Jennings, Clarence Carter, Seven Mary Three, and Motörhead have played here. The Sunday gospel brunch, which features up to 70 singers, is sold out months in advance. Come show time, the bar that runs the length of the restaurant splits in half, and each side runs off on a dolly to reveal the main hall and stage. Now you begin to see where the $9 million went. *8430 Sunset Blvd., tel. 213/650–0235 or 213/650–1451; 24-hour info, tel. 213/650–0476.*

HYATT ON SUNSET (THE "RIOT HOUSE")

Previously known as the Continental Hyatt, this 250-room tower has seen the higher echelons of rock & roll depravity. In rock circles it's known as the Riot House, thanks in no small part to Led Zeppelin, whose entourage in the '70s would take over as many as six entire floors. Tales of black-magic rituals, motorcycle riding down the corridors, and roadies gang-banging groupies in tubs filled with baked beans were probably only the half of it. Then there was the furniture-destruction fetish: On one occasion in 1975, John Bonham, bored with throwing TV sets out the window, tried to heave out a piano, but it couldn't be squeezed through the frame. Things calmed down in the '80s, though Slash checked in for a while under the name Mr. Disorderly. *8401 Sunset Blvd., tel. 213/656–1234 or 800/233–1234. Rooms: $135–$180.*

RAINBOW BAR AND GRILL

Since it opened in 1973, this bar and restaurant right next to the Roxy has been pulling in rock bands, particularly Brits. Led Zeppelin often held court here, their seating area cordoned off. One night in the early '70s, John Bonham ordered 20 black Russians and downed 10 without stopping before he spotted a woman looking at him. The Zep drummer stalked over, punched her

The Rainbow

to the floor, and then quietly returned to the bar to finish the other 10 shots. On another occasion, Iggy Pop got thrown out for peeing on a plant. The interior—featured in Guns N' Roses' "November Rain" video—is smattered with framed pics of established rockers and some instruments, such as one of Eddie Van Halen's ubiquitous guitars. *9015 Sunset Blvd., tel. 310/278–4232.*

THE ROXY

This 400-capacity club was founded by a consortium of Sunset Strip players, including Elmer Valentine (owner of the Whisky), ex–Mamas and Papas producer Lou Adler, and David Geffen. On opening night, September 20, 1973, Neil Young (with Cheech and Chong opening) kicked off a four-night stand, attended by a who's who of the music biz. Other, perhaps slightly more celebrated performances in the mid-'70s included a 1976 Bob Marley gig that years later made *Rolling Stone's* list of best-ever concerts. The club also helped establish the local punk scene by staging the Ramones' first L.A. gig in 1976, as well as shows by Fear and the Germs. Recently it has concentrated more on local talent and presents the occasional bland record-company showcase; still, it does enough to maintain its reputation for presenting bands at a key time in their ascendancy, is one of the best laid-out clubs in the area, and boasts a great P.A. *9009 Sunset Blvd., tel. 310/276–2222.*

[SST SUPER STORE]

This outlet, opened in 1992 by the punk label set up by Black Flag members Greg Ginn and Chuck Dukowski in 1978, stocks assorted T-shirts and hats, as well as almost every record released by the label—on vinyl, tape, or CD—and by its imprints Cruz, Issues, and New Alliance. It's a great place to pick up some of the back catalogue, including Black Flag, Dinosaur Jr, Hüsker Dü, and the Meat Puppets. *8847 Sunset Blvd., tel. 310/652–6546.*

VIPER ROOM

It's still common to see flowers and other tributes on the sidewalk outside this slick black-walled club, part-owned by actor Johnny Depp, where River Phoenix collapsed and died in October 1993. In 1994 Johnny Cash recorded some tracks here for his *American Recordings* album. *8852 Sunset Blvd., tel. 310/358–1880.*

[WHISKY A GO GO]

The most famous venue on the Strip opened on January 11, 1964, in what had been a bank. The club soon shot to fame with the gimmick of a girl DJ playing records and dancing while suspended in a cage next to the stage, hence "go-go girl." A year later Smokey Robinson paid his respects with the Miracles' "Going to a Go-Go," and in 1967 Otis Redding recorded *In Person at the Whisky-a-Go-Go* here. All this helped the club achieve national fame, and there were soon franchised Whiskys in other cities.

Two of the house bands in the formative period were Buffalo Springfield and the Doors. The latter made their first appearance here in May 1966, and during a three-month residency they were fired several times by the nonplussed management for playing too loud and swearing. An over-the-top version of "The End" was the final straw for owner Elmer Valentine, a former Chicago cop, but by then the band had been signed by Elektra boss Jac Holzman.

By the '70s the Whisky had given up gigs and had to resort to staging theatrical productions like *The Rocky Horror Picture Show.* A colorful local eccentric, Kim Fowley, saved the day when he put on his New Wave Rock & Roll Weekend here in 1977, featuring the Weirdos, the Dils, and the Germs (led by Dottie Danger, a.k.a. Belinda Carlisle). Soon after, Elvis Costello played his first L.A. gig at the club. The '80s saw mostly hard rock—Metallica and others made their first major appearances here—and in recent years

Whisky A Go Go

the program has been widened to include such names as Melissa Etheridge and visiting indie bands. *8901 Sunset Blvd., tel. 310/652–4202.*

GUNS N' ROSES ON THE STRIP

After making their way to L.A. from parts as diverse as Lafayette, Indiana, and Stoke, England, the original members of Guns N' Roses shared an apartment in the mid '80s at 1114 North Clark Street, just around the corner from the Whisky A Go Go. Axl Rose helped pay the rent by working for a short time at the Tower Video on the corner of Sunset and Larabee, while Slash put in some time at the Centerfold News Stand at 716 North Fairfax. The band played early gigs at Gazzarri's and various other clubs along the Strip, and when the lads achieved international fame, they returned to the boulevard to shoot clips for various videos. The most ambitious of these was the $5 million "Estranged," which involved closing off part of this busy street and having surrealistic dolphins leap out of the famous billboards.

Around the West Side

While the main rock magnet on L.A.'s west side is undoubtedly the Sunset Strip, the surrounding area can also keep you busy. West Hollywood, separating Hollywood to the east and Beverly Hills to the west, has the city's largest gay community. Rainbow flags fly down the center of Santa Monica Boulevard, which, between La Cienega and Robertson, is lined with dozens of gay and lesbian clubs, cafés, and bars. When the flags give way to palm trees, you know you're in Beverly Hills, home of megastars.

Immediately west of Beverly Hills is Century City, a conglomeration of high-rise office towers built on what was once the main studio lot for 20th Century Fox. To the north, Westwood and the UCLA campus are altogether more interesting; the area's liveliest around Broxton Avenue, which has lots of studenty stores and cafés. South of Santa Monica Boulevard are the adjacent Fairfax and Melrose districts. Fairfax High School, alma mater of Phil Spector and the Red Hot Chili Peppers, marks the start of the Melrose strip, the best retail zone in the city.

Melrose is the best place for records, clothes, and jewelry, along with some good cafés. Between Fairfax and La Brea avenues, every accessory to alternative living, however defined, can be found, along with such left-field chic as Boy, X-Fuct, and Spike's Joint stores. Sunday afternoons here are kind of a catwalk for freaks: Every conceivable dress code, T-shirt logo, and hair color can be observed.

Maria Chavez/Warner Bros.

Fairfax High's Red Hot Chili Peppers

LUNA PARK (665 N. Robertson Blvd., West Hollywood, tel. 310/652–0611) puts on a mix of spoken word, rock, pop, world music, and jazz. **MOLLY MALONE'S** (575 S. Fairfax Ave., tel. 213/935–2707) has bought the full Irish ticket, with several beers from Ireland on tap, pictures of famous Irish people on the walls, and a range of quality Celtic music from traditional to rock.

At the heart of an orthodox Jewish community, **CANTER'S** (415 N. Fairfax Ave., tel. 213/651–2030) is a long-standing round-the clock deli that's seen rockers from Zappa to Slash at its formica tables; blues and rock bands play in the adjoining Kibitz Room. America's first **HARD ROCK CAFE** (8600 Beverly Blvd., tel. 213/276–7605), at the Beverley Center, has a Cadillac plunged nose down into its roof.

Throughout the west side are great record stores. In addition to Rhino Records (*see below*), there's a branch of **BLEECKER BOB'S** (7454 Melrose Ave., tel. 213/951–9111). **VINYL FETISH** (7305 Melrose Ave., tel. 213/935–1300) always has what's on the way up in punky L.A., and **NO LIFE** (7209 Santa Monica Blvd., tel. 213/845–1200) is good for indie stuff.

Many of West L.A.'s hotels have rock & roll associations. At the **BEVERLY PRESCOTT HOTEL** (1224 S. Beverwil Dr., tel. 310/277–2800), the Jerry Garcia Suite features prints and other furnishings designed by the Grateful Dead guitarist. **LE PARC** (733 N. West Knoll Dr., West Hollywood, tel. 310/855–8888 or 800/578–4837) is an all-suite property that's popular with British bands. The super-plush **SUNSET MARQUIS** (1200 N. Alta Loma Rd., tel. 310/657–1333) threw the Beastie Boys out for bad behavior in 1988, but allowed Rob Reiner to film *This is Spinal Tap* on the roof. The **RAMADA** (8585 Santa Monica Blvd., tel. 310/652–6400) stands on the site of the Tropicana Hotel, where in earlier days Iggy Pop, Tom Waits, and the Clash would check in and drink heavily. At the lower end of the scale is the **ALTA-CIENEGA MOTEL** (1005 N. La Cienega Blvd., West Hollywood, tel. 310/652–5797), where Jim Morrison crashed many a time.

BARNEY'S BEANERY

This three-room affair—comprising a loud smoky bar, a dining area with multicolored booths, and a pool room—has been here since 1920 and retains a raucous roadhouse feel. (It wasn't until the early '80s that the management took down the NO FAGS sign, a piece of decor that wasn't winning any points, this being L.A.'s foremost gay-nightlife zone.) Since the '60s, it has been a rock & roll hangout. Jim Morrison did the barfly thing here on a regular basis, and the story goes that one night Janis Joplin cracked him over the head here with a bottle of Southern Comfort. Joplin had her last drink at Barney's before returning to the Landmark Hotel and a fatal overdose. The bar stocks more than 300 beers, and the menu offers multitudinous versions of chili, hot dogs, and burgers. *8447 Santa Monica Blvd., West Hollywood, tel. 213/654–2287.*

BEVERLY HILLS HOTEL

Asylum

Welcome to the Hotel California. This grand resort hotel is the one featured on the front cover of the Eagles' multiplatinum, singles-spawning, Grammy-winning 1976 album. Famous past residents of the Pink Palace include John Lennon and Yoko Ono. Iggy Pop whittled away an advance here, annoying wealthy poolsiders with his vulgarities. Now owned by the Sultan of Brunei, the Beverly Hills reopened in 1995 after a what was reputed to be the most expensive hotel remodeling in the history of the world. *9641 Sunset Blvd., Beverly Hills, tel. 310/276–2251 or 800/283–8885. Rooms: $250.*

The Eagles, Hotel California

DOORS OFFICE

From the time they made it big until Jim Morrison's death in 1971, the Doors conducted their business affairs from the upper floor of this two-story building, now a busy coffee bar. *L.A. Woman* was recorded in a studio they rigged up on the first floor. *8512 Santa Monica Blvd.*

[RHINO RECORDS]

The country's best-known reissues label was founded in 1978 and had its roots in a secondhand-record store started by avid collectors Harold Bronson and Richard Foos. The label made an initial impact with such novelty pieces as kazoo versions of Led Zeppelin numbers, albums by local busker Wild Man Fisher produced by Frank Zappa, and "Louie, Louie" compilations. Rhino gained mainstream respect, however, by re-issuing albums by soul, blues, and jazz greats, as well as the back catalogs of such established bands as Sonic Youth. The shop, open daily, has rows of rarities and hosts some great in-store shows, often by such contemporary bands as Sebadoh and the Cowboy Junkies. The label, distributed by Capitol, is now headquartered down the road at 10635 Santa Monica Boulevard. *1720 Westwood Blvd., Westwood, tel. 310/474–8685.*

SHARON TATE/MANSON MURDERS HOUSE

A villa (since razed) set in extensive gardens just off Benedict Canyon was where members of the Manson family murdered a very pregnant Sharon Tate, coffee heiress Abigail Folger, and several others on August 9, 1969. The killings were actually a case of mistaken identity: Charles Manson's real target was Terry Melcher, owner of the house, son of Doris Day, and friend and producer of the Beach Boys. Manson had befriended Beach Boy Dennis Wilson: One night in spring 1968, Wilson came home to find his house full of people he didn't recall inviting. Just as it occurred to him that a burglary might be under way, Manson appeared and bent down to kiss Wilson's feet. The two got to chatting, and Manson ended up crashing with Wilson all that summer, costing him an estimated $100,000 for food, clothing, a wrecked car, and a gonorrhea treatment that the surfer needed after sleeping with some of the Manson Family women.

At some point, Wilson told Manson, an aspiring singer-songwriter, that Terry Melcher could secure him a recording contract. Melcher was unimpressed with Manson's warblings, however, and passed. Desperate to make contact, Manson visited the house but was told it had been rented to friends of movie director Roman Polanski. Nevertheless, four of Manson's disciples drove up late at night and killed the occupants. The cult members wrote PIG, DEATH TO THE PIGS, and the misspelled HEALTER SKELTER on the walls in blood, all references to the Beatles' *White Album,* which Manson is said to have taken as a message to start a race war. An ambiguous footnote to the tale came in 1993, when the house became a recording studio—called Pig. Nine Inch Nails recorded *Downward Spiral* here, an album with a pig theme running throughout and a track called "March of the Pigs." Trent Reznor claims he was entirely ignorant of the building's history. The house was torn down in 1994. *10050 Cielo Dr., Bel Air.*

[TROUBADOUR]

This legendary club, which in the '80s was the premier venue for metal bands, started some 35 years ago as a folk club. Roger McGuinn, Gene Clark, and David Crosby met up at the Troubadour to form the Jet Set and then the Byrds in 1964. During John Lennon's mid-'70s "lost weekend"—a 15-month binge of booze, drugs, and general boisterousness with Harry Nilsson, Keith Moon, and Ringo Starr—he went into the Troubadour one night with a sanitary napkin on his head. Few were amused, and newspapers reported that when Lennon asked a staring waitress, "Do you know who I am?" she replied, "Yeah, you're an asshole with a Kotex on his head." Another night Mr. Kotexhead got thrown out for heckling the Smothers Brothers.

The Jayhawks at the Troubadour

By then the club was on the slide. The singer-songwriters like Jackson Browne, Linda Ronstadt, various Eagles, and Neil Young who had built its reputation had moved on to bigger things, and the venue went through a lean spell that lasted well into the '80s. Owner Doug Weston gave the thumbs down to punk and new wave but hit it big with heavy and glam metal. Guns N' Roses got its first residency here in 1985 and was soon signed by Geffen. Metal still appears on the Troubadour's calendar, but indie and acoustic are also well represented. *9081 Santa Monica Blvd., West Hollywood, tel. 310/276–6168.*

UNIVERSITY OF CALIFORNIA AT LOS ANGELES

In 1964 Jim Morrison enrolled in UCLA's film school, where Francis Ford Coppola was also among the students. Here Morrison met Ray Manzarek, who had developed a reputation on campus after making several avant-garde and erotic movies. The lineup of Manzarek, Krieger, Densmore, and Morrison made its first live appearance at the college's Royce Hall in December 1965, providing improvised acoustic backing to a screening of one of Manzarek's films as an unnamed ensemble; it was not until the following year that Morrison hit on the name the Doors. Royce Hall was also the venue for an August 7, 1971, show by the Mothers of Invention, released as the *Just Another Band from L.A.* live album, and here Neil Young recorded "The Needle and the Damage Done" for the 1972 *Harvest* album. Sonic Youth's Kim Gordon, whose dad was a dean in sociology and education at the college, went to the University Elementary School here. *Westwood Plaza and Circle Dr., Westwood.*

Kelly Duane

X HOUSE

Exene Cervenka and John Doe of X lived in this house. Most of the footage featuring the band in *The Decline of Western Civilization* was shot here, as was the back cover of the *Wild Gift* album. *1118 N. Genesee Ave., West Hollywood.*

Canyons and Valleys

It's just a two-minute drive from the hustle and bustle of Hollywood to the narrow canyon roads that climb sharply up the Hollywood

Exene Cervenka and John Doe of X

hills. Since the early days of the movies, this area has provided a secluded setting for the rich and famous, and today street vendors do good trade hawking "Star Maps" that detail, with questionable accuracy, the homes of celluloid celebrities. For the most part, the big stars like to live discreetly, hidden away from the outside world, but not Madonna: When she moved into a castellated mansion on Lake Canyon Drive overlooking the Hollywood Reservoir, she had the walls painted in horizontal flame red and yellow stripes.

The area has seen many notable rock abodes over the years. Starting in the late '60s, Laurel Canyon was settled by rock musicians and immortalized on vinyl by as varied a bunch as Joni Mitchell, John Mayall, CSN, and the Doors. Intersecting the canyon is Mulholland Drive, which runs for 25 scenic miles along the crest of the Santa Monica Mountains, dividing the L.A. basin from the San Fernando Valley. The area's grand views are what have lured L.A.'s elite over the years. Those who have lived here include Arthur Lee, Steve Cropper, and Slash (before the 1994 earthquake interfered with the architecture). The road was also used for the drag-racing scenes in *Rebel Without a Cause*.

The San Fernando Valley has long been home to the big studio lots, one of which is so big it can get away with calling itself Universal City. Beyond Universal City is the North Hollywood district, once known for the sleazy strip joints along Lankershim boulevard; of late there's been a bit of a NoHo revival, with an influx of artsy cafés and performance clubs.

LAUREL CANYON

In the late '60s and the '70s, each winding lane that runs off Laurel Canyon seemed to count among its residents at least one rock & roller, including Alice Cooper, Doors drummer John Densmore, various Mamas and Papas, Roger McGuinn, and Glenn Frey. Frank Zappa had various canyon addresses before sticking to one on Woodrow Wilson Drive, where he lived from 1969 until his death in 1993. Joni Mitchell and John Mayall named albums after the canyon, and Carole King and Love used canyon houses for early album covers. Mitchell's house at 8217 Lookout Mountain Road was where one-time lover Graham Nash wrote "Our House."

BLUE JAY WAY

In 1968 George Harrison lived briefly on this leafy lane in the hills just north of the Strip. One night publicist Derek Taylor lost his way in the fog and couldn't find the Beatle's apartment. Tickled by the incident, Harrison wrote it up as "Blue Jay Way," which appeared on *Magical Mystery Tour*. The street sign is regularly removed by Beatles archivists.

FM STATION LIVE

The *FM* stands for Filthy McNasty, an Elvis Presley buddy and the club's owner (and previous owner of the Viper Room). McNasty's comfortable club promotes a range of artists from Nina Hagen and Pat Travers to local punk and metal groups. Pool tables and a huge video screen provide entertainment between bands. *11700 Victory Blvd., at Lankershim Blvd., North Hollywood, tel. 818/769-2220.*

NBC STUDIOS

Elvis Presley recorded his first comeback special here on June 27, 1968, before a live audience—the first time he'd seen one of those since a benefit in Hawaii in 1961. His manager, "Colonel" Tom Parker, wanted him to do a set composed entirely of holiday carols—the special was to be broadcast on Christmas—but the producers won out: Elvis was reunited with original bandmates Scotty Moore and D. J. Fontana, and they played familiar material, including a lengthy gospel medley, that helped reestablish Presley's credibility and launch his career in a Vegas direction. Nowadays it's possible to catch some rock performers on the *Tonight Show;* tickets for the program are available on a first-come, first-served basis. NBC offer tours of the facility for about $6. *3000 W. Alameda Ave., Burbank, tel. 213/956-5000.*

[PALOMINO]

This venue, in continuous operation since 1951, has seen all the celebrated names in country music. By the mid-'60s country-tinged bands like the Byrds and the Flying Burrito Brothers were appearing. In February 1979 Elvis Costello chose this club to unveil his first country set and recorded "Psycho," the B side of "Sweet Dreams," here live. In the '80s the Palomino championed the new breed of country from Dwight Yoakam and Steve Earle and also put on such rock bands as the Red Hot Chili Peppers. For now the club has returned to its country base, with the odd rock appearance by the likes of Arthur Lee. *6907 Lankershim Blvd., tel. 818/764-4018.*

SOUND CITY STUDIOS

Nirvana recorded *Nevermind* with producer Butch Vig at these studios in May and June 1991. Some 16 years earlier, Mick Fleetwood was scouting around for a new place to record when a producer demonstrated the sound that was achievable at the studio by playing him a track by Lindsey Buckingham and Stevie Nicks. Fleetwood chased the pair down and recorded the *Fleetwood Mac* and *Rumours* albums here. *15456 Cabrito Rd., Van Nuys, tel. 818/873-2842.*

Coastal L.A.

When SoCal-based rock stars make it big and verge on the reclusive, they buy a ranch or move to the coast. Malibu, a separate city just northwest of L.A., is synonymous with money. Bob Dylan lived here in the '70s; Brian Wilson still does, supposedly jogging daily along Trancas Beach, where he also surfed for the first time—in June 1976 at age 34, after having written $25 million worth of surfing records. Neil Young moved to Zuma Beach, just north of Malibu, in the early '70s—immortalized in the titles of his *On the Beach* and *Zuma* albums—but his two-story beach home, previously owned by F. Scott Fitzgerald, burned down during the 1978 fires.

Southeast of Malibu, Topanga Canyon shoots up from the coast into the mountains. Unlike the Hollywood hills, the canyon maintains a rural feel, as much of it belongs to the Topanga State Park. Among the musicians who hung out at a ranch here in the '60s were Eric Clapton, Neil Young, and other members of Buffalo Springfield—who were busted there in 1967 for "being at a place where it is suspected marijuana was being used."

Suicidal Tendencies

Murray Bowles

Continuing down the coast, the Santa Monica seafront marks the end of Route 66, which runs through most of L.A. as Santa Monica Boulevard. To the south is Venice, which has had a bohemian reputation since Beats hung out at its beachfront cafés in the '50s. Jim Morrison and Ray Manzarek decided to form the Doors while talking on the beach, Iggy Pop lived here for a while in 1971, and the Butthole Surfers and Suicidal Tendencies formed in the area. Although most days the beach is packed with tourists, musclemen, and in-line-skating enthusiasts, Venice at night is often a dangerous festival of lowlife; Henry Rollins's roommate Joe Cole was murdered here in 1991 by burglars.

MCCABE'S GUITAR SHOP

At night a room in this guitar shop converts into a 100-seat venue that specializes in blues and roots but also features its share of acoustic rock. The homeliest little music room in town doesn't serve alcohol—just coffee, tea, and cookies. Recent performers have included Liz Phair, Mike Watt, Butch Hancock, and Evan Dando; Henry Rollins has a spoken-word album called *Live at McCabes. 3101 Pico Blvd., Santa Monica, tel. 310/828–4403.*

JIM MORRISON MURAL

A 12- by 36-foot airbrushed mural of Jim Morrison in his more handsome prebeard period can be found on the back wall of this beauty salon. *1811 Ocean Front Walk, at 18th Pl. (on Speedway side of building), Venice.*

DENNIS WILSON DEATH SITE

Beach Boy Dennis Wilson drowned on December 28, 1983, after a heavy day's drinking and an ill-advised diving session. According to reports, he started in on the vodka early in the day and went swimming around lunchtime without a wet suit, despite the chill December waters. After coming ashore for a sandwich and more vodka, he went out again and this time didn't come back. Wilson was buried at sea—usually a federal offense, but his family received a special dispensation from Beach Boys fan Ronald Reagan. *13929 Bellagio Way, Basin C-1100, Marina Del Rey.*

Orange County

A surf-punk scene has been prospering for over a decade on the gorgeous beaches of this part of SoCal. The Vandals, Social Distortion, and Agent Orange all emerged at the turn of the '80s and were followed by Offspring, Bad Religion, and Rage Against the Machine. Supernova, Sugar Ray, and the Voodoo Glow Skulls appeared more recently.

Social Distortion

Murray Bowles

In the early '80s the local police in the town of Huntington Beach—a staunchly Republican area where most of Offspring attended high school—were so determined to eradicate the punk scene from the bars and beaches that they started classifying some bands and their fans as gangs. Suburban Costa Mesa is 6 miles south of Huntington Beach and just inland from touristy Newport Beach (where you'll find a Hard Rock Cafe and Planet Hollywood). The community is very much the nerve center of SoCal punk, with a couple of studios (the Distillery and Control World) and several venues.

EATING DRINKING DANCING SHOPPING PLAYING SLEEPING

CLUB MESA (843 W. 19th St., Costa Mesa, tel. 714/642–8448) saw locals like Offspring and Pennywise play regularly but banned punk gigs in 1995; the bar now puts on other types of rock. The **TIKI BAR** (1700 Placentia Ave., Costa Mesa, tel. 714/548–3533) still embraces punk-surf bands, as does the **LAVA ROOM** (1945 Placentia Ave., tel. 714/631–0526). **VINYL SOLUTION** (18822 Beach Blvd., Huntington Beach, tel. 714/963–1819) stocks sounds for skaters, surfers, and punks and also runs the small Vinyl Dog label.

CUCKOO'S NEST

Costa Mesa has several good venues, but it was this little dive that inspired *Rolling Stone* to report "it'll go down in history as one of the greats, along with CBGB." Before the club closed in 1985, every major L.A. punk band of the era played its stage; the space is now occupied by Zubie's Pizza Parlor. *1712 Placentia Ave.*

Mill Valley

Snuggled into the foothills of Mount Tamalpais, Mill Valley is a well-to-do professional community that's long found favor with rock types—in the '60s, Quicksilver Messenger Service had a communal base here, with neighbors like Grace Slick and Marty Balin of Jefferson Airplane. It's still a better place to hang out than, say, Sausalito, thanks to a great record store and the Sweetwater bar.

SWEETWATER

Holding a little more than 200 people, this northern California institution manages to attract big names like Sammy Hagar, Santana, and Huey Lewis, all of whom have been known to drop in and jam with whoever is playing. The bar also books a good range of offbeat gigs, such as a singing Harry Dean Stanton. Not surprisingly, it gets extremely busy, and some shows are by invitation only. *153 Throckmorton Ave., tel. 415/388–2820.*

[VILLAGE MUSIC]

One of the nation's most famous rare and used vinyl stores has been in operation for close to 30 years. With rows and rows of records, and concert posters from the '60s plastering the walls, the place seems like a museum piece. Allow several hours for a good browse. *9 E. Blithedale Ave., at Throckmorton Ave., tel. 415/338–7400.*

Monterey

[MONTEREY POP FESTIVAL]

Rock's first major festival took place here, in June 1967, with an audience of 50,000 watching the Grateful Dead, Jefferson Airplane, Janis Joplin, Otis Redding, the Byrds, the Who (in the band's first big American concert), and Jimi Hendrix (making his American debut as a solo rock star on the recommendation of Paul McCartney, whom the organizers had consulted). Monterey secured the reputations of San Francisco bands like the Airplane and the Dead at the expense of more established L.A. acts like the Beach Boys, who were supposed to headline but pulled out at the last minute, and the Byrds. Townshend and co. demolished their instruments onstage but were one-upped by Hendrix, who splashed his guitar with lighter fluid and set it on fire. For many, the highlight of the show, however, was Otis Redding, who had been invited at the last minute after the Beach Boys canceled. Following Jefferson Airplane's psychedelic light show and huge sound system, Redding and his backing band looked distinctly out of place in their green mohair suits, but despite their tinny sound, the singer won over the crowd in a big way. *Monterey County Fairgrounds, Hwy. 1 at Hwy. 68, just east of downtown.*

Novato

The Grateful Dead and other acid-popping scenesters lived at Rancho Olompali, a disused school off Highway 1, for the summer of 1966. Outside was a sign that read NO

TRESPASSING. VISITORS WILL BE EXPERIMENTED UPON. The band then lived communally in Haight-Ashbury for a couple of years before moving out to various Marin County abodes in 1968. Mickey Hart bought a ranch at 2495 South Novato Boulevard, where he used to give his horse an equine-strength dose of acid and head off into the hills with his dog, which was also tripping.

Oakland

"Welcome to Paradise," a Green Day track off *Dookie*, was supposedly about West Oakland, but not even the most brazen PR suit would have the nerve to use this a slogan for the city's tourism campaign. This blue-collar port town seems more than a bridge length away from San Francisco and bears little relationship to the neighboring college town of Berkeley. Oakland has, however, had its radical moments. It was the home of the Black Panthers, for whom the Grateful Dead played a 1971 benefit concert here, and of the Symbionese Liberation Army, best known for kidnapping Patty Hearst and mentioned in "Judy Is a Punk" on the Ramones' debut album.

Sylvester Stewart (a.k.a. Sly Stone) moved to the city in the early '60s and soon found employment with a local radio station and as a producer with Autumn Records. The Family Stone, formed in 1966, played its first gigs in Oakland bars and clubs. Others artists with links to this heavily African-American city include the Pointer Sisters (who started out in the choir of their preacher father's East Oakland Church of God), (MC) Hammer, Sheila E, and Tower of Power. Oakland has also produced local hip-hop and funk acts like Digital Underground, Oaktown 3-5-7, Tony! Toni! Toné!, and Tupac Shakur.

EATINGDRINKING**DANCING**SHOPPING**PLAYING**SLEEPING

Oakland's bars and clubs have a reputation for hard weekend partying without the self-conscious contrivances of the city across the bay. The **STORK CLUB** (380 12th St., tel. 510/444–6174) puts on challenging underground and experimental bands each Friday and Saturday. The basic, no-crap **ELI'S MILE HIGH CLUB** (3629 Martin Luther King, Jr. Blvd., tel. 510/655–6661) has been booking the best local blues acts every weekend for years. The Bay Area's top jazz venue, **YOSHI'S** (6030 Claremont Ave., tel. 510/ 652–9200), located in a Japanese

Courtesy of Eli's Mile High Club

Eli's, home of the West Coast Blues

restaurant, may soon move downtown and is worth watching out for. The **PARAMOUNT THEATER** (2025 Broadway, tel. 510/465–6400), a totally ornate '30s Art Deco palace that screens movies and stages musicals and the occasional rock concert, is one of the prettiest places to see a show in the country.

OAKLAND COLISEUM

In 1973, after two very successful promotions in Golden Gate Park (*see below*), Bill Graham moved his "Day on the Green" promotion to this 60,000-seat stadium and continued to host events, often with lavish sets. Among the wackiest of these one-day summer festivals was a 1975 show called "The British Are Coming," which featured Fleetwood Mac, Robin Trower, Peter Frampton, and others; for the event, Graham dressed the stage as a castle, complete with turrets, drawbridge, and a Union Jack backdrop. When Led Zeppelin's last U.S. show took place here two years later, John Bonham, band manager Peter Grant, and a couple others in the party beat up Graham's workers and were arrested by Oakland cops. There was a substantial out-of-court settlement.

By 1979 Graham's shows were no longer automatic sellouts; the shows came to an end with a concert dubbed "Monsters of Rock"—featuring Ted Nugent, Aerosmith, AC/DC, and Mahogany Rush—for which Graham dressed security staff as cavemen. In later years, such big acts as Springsteen, the Scorpions, and Wham! (yes!) have raised enough interest to sell the place out. In 1991 Metallica unveiled a new diamond stage formation with 12 mikes for singer James Hetfield; Lars Ulrich had a drum kit that was moved around the stage on tracks. Finally, no account of Oakland Coliseum could ignore that it was here MC Hammer got used to being in the public eye—as a batboy for the Oakland Athletics. *Tel. 510/639-7700.*

Palm Springs

The sprawling desert resort of Palm Springs has been a popular spot since the '30s, when movie stars came out here to get away from Hollywood. These days the celluloid stars have found more exclusive places, and the town does more business from retirees, the wealthy end of the gay scene, and students on spring break. Its best-known musical connection is Sonny Bono, who, until his election to Congress in 1994, served several terms as mayor. One of his proudest achievements was a ban on wearing thong bikinis on the city streets. He still owns the posh Italian restaurant that bears his name.

San Diego

The home city of Eddie Vedder, Tom Waits, and the Stone Temple Pilots is also where 17-year-old high school student Brenda Spencer shot 11 people, killing two, in January 1979. One of her statements to police, "I don't like Mondays," was the source of the title for the Boomtown Rats' 1980 No. 1 U.K. single. On a lighter note, officials at the San Diego Zoo cut short a 1966 photo session for the front cover of the Beach Boys' *Pet Sounds* album when they spotted the fun-loving bandmates pulling the ears of the goats they were posing with.

Croce's in San Diego

EATINGDRINKINGDANCINGSHOPPINGPLAYINGSLEEPING

The city has two notable and very different music clubs. The **CASBAH** (2501 Kettner Blvd., tel. 619/232-4355) opened in spring 1989 in what was a rundown Irish bar; it has hosted indie groups from around the country but is best known for breaking the bunch of bands that came out of San Diego in the mid-'90s, such as Rocket from the Crypt, Drive Like Jehu, A Miniature, Lucy's Fur Coat, and Uncle Joe. **CROCE'S** (802 5th Ave., tel. 619/233-4355), run by Jim Croce's widow, is a large club that puts on jazz and rhythm & blues every night of the week. There are also a few mementos of the singer, who died in a 1973 plane crash.

San Francisco

Although the Rock & Roll Hall of Fame cites San Francisco as one of the key places that shaped modern rock music, the city took its time getting off the mark. The Palais Royal Hotel (now the Sheraton Palace) did install America's first jukebox back in 1898, but in the '50s and early '60s the city did not have the successful record labels seen in L.A., New York, Chicago, or Memphis.

Not to say that there wasn't musical activity: By the early '60s, the musicians who would later form the backbone of all the major psychedelic-era bands were playing a thriving folk circuit. The early Bay Area bands, inspired in form by the guitar-bass-drum groups of 1964's British invasion, were lyrically influenced by Dylan. However, whereas Dylan dropped his political content by 1965, the city's bands kept their radical songs; this was particularly true of Jefferson Airplane (the most successful of the first wave of San Fran rock bands) and Berkeley's Country Joe and the Fish. Others—such as the Charlatans, Moby Grape, and Quicksilver Messenger Service—were content to get stoned and freak people out with their psychedelic light shows, while the Grateful Dead built up a following for their eco-friendly hippie mysticism after playing Ken Kesey's acid-test parties. Another key band of the era was Big Brother and the Holding Company, in reality little more than a backing band for the powerful blues roar of Janis Joplin.

At the height of the era of flower power, peace, and happiness, the business side of rock music was making advances. Rock promoters like Chet Helms and Bill Graham staged shows at various old ballrooms throughout the city, including, most significantly, the Fillmore Auditorium. By the end of 1967, following the so-called Summer of Love, the main local groups (Jefferson Airplane, the Grateful Dead, Big Brother and the Holding Company) had signed to major labels. Ludicrous sums were handed out to new bands—when Capitol signed the Steve Miller Blues Band for $750,000 in December 1967, the group

1986 Jim Marshall/Fantasy, Inc.

Creedence Clearwater Revival

had yet to make a record. The scene quickly became commercialized, with cash-in records like Scott McKenzie's "Are You Going to San Francisco?" The flower-power hippie became a cliché. Tourists flocked to the Haight-Ashbury district—where many of the bands had settled into big, low-rent Victorians—to see what all the fuss was about, and the counter-culture was promoted endlessly by *Rolling Stone* magazine, which set up here in 1967.

The second-wave San Fran bands were less political than their predecessors: the quirky Spirit, rock & roll revivalists Creedence Clearwater Revival (which by 1970 was the biggest-selling U.S. rock band ever), and the Latin-influenced Santana. As the '70s progressed, the city's rock & roll output diminished. The most intriguing native band was the deliberately uncommercial but articulate Residents, whose members kept their identities secret throughout the decade, never appearing without wearing giant eyeball masks over their heads. The '70s also saw the emergence of a solo Boz Scaggs

Jello Biafra, mayoral candidate

(after leaving the Steve Miller Band), Journey, the Doobie Brothers, and Airplane successor Jefferson Starship, but the first truly cutting-edge band to come out of the scene since the Fillmore days was the transplanted Arizona group the Tubes, which released its debut album in 1975.

San Francisco's music scene picked up with the advent of punk, which fit in neatly with the city's history of supporting rebellious commies, beats, and hippies. However, groups like the Avengers, the Offs, the Sleepers, the Mutants, and the Dils were little known outside the city—although Flipper would be counted as a major influence by bands like Nirvana in the early '90s. The best-known local punks, the provocative Dead Kennedys, issued a series of tirades against U.S. imperialism courtesy of Coloradan Eric Boucher, who renamed himself Jello Biafra and ran for mayor against Diane Feinstein; he came in a credible fourth with 10% of the vote.

The '80s saw a mixed bag of acts, from the guitar extremes of Joe Satriani, through Huey Lewis and the News, Camper Van Beethoven, World of Pooh, Chris Isaak, and Mr. Big to the rock of Metallica and Faith No More and the punky Colorfinger, which pissed a few people off with its "Kill Jerry Garcia" single. The current music scene encompasses punk, hip-hop, and rap artists, as well as bands that emphasize traditional songwriting, including the long-running American Music Club, the Red House Painters, Counting Crows, and the poppy Seven Day Diary.

San Francisco 10

John Lee Hooker, "Frisco Blues" (1963)
Eric Burdon and the Animals, "San Franciscan Nights" (1967)
The Flowerpot Men, "Let's Go to San Francisco" (1967)
Scott McKenzie, "Are You Going To San Francisco? (Be Sure to Wear Flowers in Your Hair)" (1967)
Otis Redding, "Sittin' on the Dock of the Bay" (1968)
Sly and the Family Stone, "Luv 'N' Haight" (1972)
Sammy Hagar, "Fillmore Shuffle" (1977)
Starship, "We Built This City" (1985)
808 State, "San Francisco" (1991)
Swingin' Utters, "Streets of San Francisco" (1995)

Downtown San Francisco

There's no specific center of activity in the compact downtown area, although Union Square has the city's visitor information office and the main cable-car turnaround. Ultimately this is a pretty boring part of town. East, toward the waterfront, is the busy Financial District, while west of Union Square is the Civic Center area. The city's real rock & roll diamond, the Fillmore Auditorium, is farther west, in the Fillmore/Japantown region.

EATING DRINKING DANCING SHOPPING PLAYING SLEEPING

The Great American Music Hall (*see below*) and the **WARFIELD THEATER** (982 Market St., tel. 415/775–7722) are the two main venues for rock concerts downtown. The **HARD ROCK CAFE** (1669 Van Ness St., tel. 415/885–1699), near the turnaround for the California Street cable car, has a San Francisco Wall of Fame with psychedelic-era pieces. An essential stop for record collectors, particularly of 7″ singles, is **JACK'S RECORD CELLAR** (254 Scott St., tel. 415/431–3047), which has been open since 1951 and stocks "all styles, all speeds." The Phoenix (*see below*) is *the* place to stay, but the **TRITON HOTEL** (324 Grant Ave., tel. 415/394–5000) has a suite designed by Jerry Garcia.

[AVALON BALLROOM]

What's now the Regency II movie house was, in the psychedelic late '60s, the rival ballroom to Bill Graham's productions at the Fillmore. It was run by Chet Helms, who had put on some productions with Graham; the working relationship didn't last longer than a few gigs, however, and Helms set out to find a venue where he could plug his band, Big Brother and the Holding Company. His search ended downtown at a second-floor swing ballroom built in the '30s. Although not as big as the Fillmore, it featured cool stuff like a well-sprung dance floor and lots of mirrors, drapes, and columns. Helms called his promotional organization the Family Dog and chose "May the baby Jesus shut your mouth and open your mind" as the venue's conspicuous motto.

In two and a half years after opening on April 22, 1966, Helms put on close to 500 events; almost 100 of those were Big Brother appearances, including Janis Joplin's first outing with the band in June 1966. Helms lacked Graham's business acumen, however; he let bands have massive guest lists and gave the venue over to "community" shows and fundraisers. In late 1968, concerned about the number of late-night hippie revelers on the streets, the San Francisco police refused to renew the venue's entertainment licence, thus putting an end to Helms's ballroom. *1268 Sutter St., at Van Ness Ave.*

Ken Regan/Camera 5/courtesy of Bill Graham Presents

FILLMORE AUDITORIUM

This was the first of three Bill Graham–run clubs bearing the famous Fillmore tag, a name taken from the poor and predominantly black district west of downtown where the club was located. In the early '60s this second-floor ballroom hosted the Temptations, James Brown, and Ray Charles. Its first rock show, with Jefferson Airplane, Great Society, and jazz guitarist John Handy came on December 10, 1965 and was a benefit organized by Bill Graham for the San Francisco Mime Troupe. The next month saw another benefit, this time featuring the Grateful Dead, who had just changed their name from the Warlocks. (Graham hated the new name; posters for the event had

Bill Graham

the old one in more prominent lettering.) Both benefits were sellouts, and several people saw the possibilities of making a mint out of promoting rock concerts here. First to move was Graham, who split with the Mime Troupe and started promoting gigs under the soon-to-be-ubiquitous banner of Bill Graham Presents.

The first Bill Graham Presents concert was in February 1966, with Jefferson Airplane headlining. (Jimi Hendrix opened for the band at a later Fillmore show, right after the Monterey Pop Festival in June 1967. So good was his performance that the Airplane asked if they could be *his* opening band at the following night's show.) By fall 1967 Graham was putting on shows six nights a week. That September, Cream recorded the live part of "Wheels of Fire" for their third album. The bill at the last show here, on July 4, 1968, featured Creedence Clearwater Revival, Steppenwolf, and It's a Beautiful Day.

The next day Graham moved his operation to the Fillmore West (*see below*), having had problems with the lease and mindful of the fact that after the assassination of Martin Luther King, Jr., that year, white kids were wary of venturing into what was already a tough black neighborhood. By then Graham had already established a dynasty: Over the years, 58 albums recorded at one of the Fillmores were released, and 17 went gold or beyond. He also broadened the scope of the rock world by putting on performers outside the usual sphere, like B.B. King, Otis Redding, and Ravi Shankar.

The hall became a private members' club during the '70s; in the early '80s, as the Elite Club, it presented punk bands like Black Flag and Bad Brains. Graham started promoting concerts here again in 1985, but the foundations of the big brick building were rocked by the Loma Prieta earthquake of 1989. After a multimillion-dollar retrofitting job, the Fillmore opened once again on April 27, 1994. The first to play were the Smashing Pumpkins, ironically followed soon after by Pavement, which dissed the moody Chicago group on the track "Range Life" on that year's *Crooked Rain, Crooked Rain* (an album that also featured a song called "Fillmore Jive").

Pavement

The Bill Graham Presents organization has the lease on the Fillmore, but Graham himself did not live to see the reopening: On the way to an October 1991 Huey Lewis and the News gig at the Pavilion in San Francisco, the promoter died when his private helicopter hit a power cable near Sears Point Raceway on the Marin–Sonoma county line. The crash nearly brought down the Bay Area's entire electricity supply—the city lights flickered on and off for several minutes, and the lighting rig at the Lewis gig failed for two numbers. *1805 Geary Blvd., tel. 415/346–3000.*

FILLMORE WEST

The night after his July 4, 1968, closing of the Fillmore Auditorium, Bill Graham switched over to the Carousel, a second-floor ballroom above a carpet store, which he renamed Fillmore West. With the Fillmore East up and running in New York, Graham was in a good position to attract top names and easily snapped up most of the best touring bands that came through the two cities—Led Zeppelin, the Who, the Jeff Beck Group—plus such top local bands as Santana, which had one of its first major gigs here. Within a few years, however, the big acts began playing bigger venues, such as the Oakland Coliseum, and were asking too much for shows at 2,800-capacity ballrooms like the Fillmore West to be profitable. Graham closed the place on July 4, 1971. Stadium rock had arrived.

It was during the Fillmore West's three-year run that the usually straight-laced, clipboard-wielding, in-charge-at-all-times Graham finally got dosed with acid by the Grateful Dead entourage. The band's attempts to drug the promoter had proved unsuccessful for years—it got to the point where Graham only eat unopened food or drink, nor would he kiss any of the Dead's women friends for fear they would tongue a tab into his mouth. One night a crew member came up with the idea of lacing the rims of all the soda cans in the office fridge. Graham snapped open a can, gulped it down, and ended up onstage with the Dead playing the bongos until four or five in the morning.

Before Graham won the hotly contested race to promote shows at the Carousel, several other promoters had staged big shows here: The Carousel was a favorite venue for Hells Angels parties—there was so much free beer at one shindig that it leaked down into the carpet store below. At another sellout event, police threatened to close the party down unless the Angels could stop so many people from hanging around outside; an agreement was reached whereby chapter president Sonny Barger was allowed to get in a cop car and drive up and down Market Street announcing, "This is Sonny Barger. Get the fuck off the street!" over the loudspeaker. The building is now occupied by a car showroom. *1545 Market St., at Van Ness Ave.*

GREAT AMERICAN MUSIC HALL

This former bordello was built in Victorian times and has been one of the city's premier rock venues for years. Traditional charm comes by way of frescoes, marble columns, and chandeliers. It's a particular favorite of American Music Club's Mark Eitzel, who has played solo here on several occasions. There are usually shows several nights a week, often open to all ages. *859 O'Farrell St., tel. 415/885–0750.*

Great American Music Hall

Courtesy of the Great American Music Hall

MIYAKO HOTEL

In the '60s and '70s, most of the bands who played the Fillmore Auditorium and Winterland stayed at this mid-range hotel on the border of Japantown and the Fillmore district. In 1976 most of the performers at the Last Waltz checked in here, including Bob Dylan, who rehearsed in the Osaka Room. It was also the final scene of the Sex Pistols saga. After their disastrous last gig together, at Winterland in January 1978, Johnny Rotten— who was booked into a cheap San Jose motel with a drugged-out Sid Vicious because manager Malcolm McLaren claimed they couldn't afford to all stay at the Miyako—confronted McLaren and the other two band members about some half-baked publicity scheme to visit exiled English train robber Ronnie Biggs in Rio de Janeiro. The fight split the band: McLaren, Paul Cook, and Steve Jones went to Rio, Rotten returned to London, and Sid Vicious was heading in that general direction when he OD'd on a plane to New York and had to be rushed to the hospital. *1625 Post St., tel. 415/922–3200. Rooms: $170.*

[PHOENIX HOTEL]

San Francisco's undisputed rock & roll hotel ever since it opened, in 1987, the Phoenix has been temporary home to many of the bands that play the Warfield, Slims, and the Great American Music Hall. Each guest gets a coloring book detailing the short but action-packed history of the hotel. A who's who of the indie and alternative world, from

Oasis to Snoop Doggy Dogg, have slept here, Sinead O'Connor gave her first U.S. press conference here, and John Lydon helped boost bar profits back in 1991. There's a good chance of seeing someone recognizable wandering around the central courtyard or chilling out by the pool, which has a great mosaic floor.

The Phoenix also organizes charitable events to raise money for children in the depressed Tenderloin district: Each Easter rock types (like Nirvana in 1992) hide eggs for a hunt for local kids, and every June, when the Gavin Report conference is in town, celebrities are auctioned off for a "pool toss"—it cost someone $1,000 for the privilege of chucking Eddie Vedder into the water in 1993. Adjoining the salmon-and-turquoise hotel is Miss Pearl's Jam House, a restaurant where yuppies, rastas, and rock bands mix for reggae and calypso music and Caribbean food. *601 Eddy St., tel. 415/776–1380. Rooms: $90.*

U2 FREE CONCERT SITE

November 11, 1987, provided U2 lots of (almost) free publicity. With little advance warn-ing, they parked a flatbed truck in front of a huge fountain sculpture in a plaza down by the Embarcadero and gave a free concert. Workers in the Financial District flocked to see what was going on, and a politically astute Bono declared it the "Save the Yuppie Concert," as there had been a major stock market crash some days before. Traffic came to a standstill, which inspired Bono to climb up the concrete fountain and spray-paint something like ROCK & ROLL STOP THE TRAFFIC. The mayor immediately put out a warrant for Bono's arrest, but after weeks of legal wrangling, all parties agreed that it wasn't worth arguing over, especially since a certain humbled Mr. Paul Hewson had paid to get his artwork cleaned off the next day. *Justin Herman Plaza.*

WINTERLAND

With a steep wraparound balcony and a stage in the middle of the arena, this former ice rink was once one of the most atmospheric venues in the country. It was famed for a slew of notable concerts promoted by Bill Graham, who ran the bulk of his shows here for seven years from the closure of the Fillmore West to the end of 1978. Some of Graham's coups included the Who, Bruce Springsteen (who recorded a live version of "I'm on Fire" here), and the Rolling Stones, who played a four-night run in 1972, when they were far too big for a venue that held less than 5,500. Three years later Peter Frampton recorded his megaselling *Frampton Comes Alive* here, and *The Grate-ful Dead Movie,* released in 1977, was edited together from film shot during the band's 1974 Winterland run.

Winterland may be most remembered for the final performances of two groups, the Band (*see Last Waltz box, below*) and the Sex Pistols. Supported by the Nuns and the Avengers, the English punk kings played their last show on January 14, 1978, with Sid Vicious precariously strung out on smack and interband arguments at an all-time high. The band split a few days later (*see* Miyako Hotel, *above*).

For most of the '70s this was the preferred hometown venue of the Grateful Dead. The band was a regular headliner at New Year's Eve shows, where Bill Graham would come in at midnight dressed as Father Time and breakfast would be served at dawn. On New Year's Eve 1978, supported by the Blues Brothers, the Dead played the last show held at Winterland. The rink had severe structural faults, and developers were eager to rip it down and put up apartments, which they did.

In his autobiography, *Bill Graham Presents,* Graham recalled that "nothing ever replaced Winterland. After Winterland, San Francisco changed. The communal aspect of going to gigs disappeared. Back in the '60s when it started, Winterland was the big place that nobody liked to go to. But when it closed, it was small." *Post and Steiner Sts.*

The Band's last gig, a 1976 Thanksgiving Day extravaganza at the Winterland, remains one of rock's most famous events, thanks in no small part to the documentary made by Martin Scorcese. The show started out as a low-key farewell, a kind of "the Band and friends" deal, until Winterland promoter Bill Graham got involved and let his imagination loose. Since the show happened to be slated for Thanksgiving, Graham insisted on a banquet meal, upping the cost from the usual $7 a head to $25. For the 5,400 diners, he shipped in 220 turkeys (plus 500 extra legs), 90 gallons of gravy, 400 pounds of salmon, 6,000 fresh rolls, and a truckload of other fixings. The Winterland received a $20,000 face-lift, and the stage was decked out in San Francisco Opera sets for *La Traviata* and chandeliers that had been used in *Gone with the Wind*. While dinner was served, the 40-piece Berkeley Promenade Orchestra and six professional waltzers danced.

After dinner the Band did the first set and then played backing band for the rest of the night to a wide range of acts, including their old mentor Ronnie Hawkins, Dr. John, Bobby "See You Later Alligator" Charles (his first stage appearance in 20 years), Paul Butterfield, Muddy Waters, Eric Clapton, Neil Young, Joni Mitchell, Neil Diamond (whose album Robbie Robertson was producing), Van Morrison, and Bob Dylan. For the finale the whole cast (plus Ron Wood, Ringo Starr, and Governor Jerry Brown) reassembled for "I Shall Be Released" and a lengthy version of "Don't Do It."

SoMa District

Like its role model, New York's SoHo, the district *so*uth of *Ma*rket Street is an area of imposing warehouses now turned into yuppie apartments and studios. During the '60s it provided cheap office space for *Rolling Stone,* which set up shop on the second floor of a warehouse at 746 Brannan Street. Over the past decade it's become the nerve center of the city's X-fueled dance scene, with clubs quickly opening and closing.

FORMER BILL GRAHAM PRESENTS OFFICE

In spring 1985 President Reagan's visit to a German cemetery where SS troops were buried (recalled by the Ramones on "Bonzo Goes to Bitburg") prompted promoter Bill Graham, a Jew who had escaped from Nazi Germany as a child, to take out an ad in regional papers protesting such insensitivity. Soon after the ads were published, on the morning of May 7, 1985, the offices of Bill Graham Presents—basically a big open space in a brick warehouse—were gutted by a Molotov cocktail, and a swastika was daubed on an exterior wall. The fire destroyed a museum's worth of rock memorabilia. No one was ever charged with the offense. *201 11th St.*

DNA LOUNGE

When the DNA debuted in 1985, it was virtually the only night spot in the now club-rich SoMa district. Still one of the city's best-known music-dance spots, it's been attracting cutting-edge bands since it opened, as well as bigger names, like Prince and Lenny Kravitz, looking to do a more intimate show. Counting Crows and 4 Non Blondes played some of their first headlining gigs here; nonrock performers have included reggae heavyweights Sly and Robbie and Culture, and spoken-word artists Jim Carroll and Hubert Selby, Jr. The stage is on the main floor, and a chill-out room with sofas and booths is upstairs; DJs play nightly, and there are also live acts on Friday and Saturday, when it's open until 4 AM. *375 11th St., tel. 415/626–1409.*

MIME TROUPE LOFT

This warehouse space was where Bill Graham accidentally got into concert promotion. Graham, an employee of the San Francisco Mime Troupe, was charged with fundraising. He organized a November 6, 1965, benefit gig here after the street-theater company had been heavily fined for performing (for free) in a public park without a permit. On the bill were Jefferson Airplane (which sometimes practiced in the loft), the Fugs, and Sandy Bull; Lawrence Ferlinghetti, owner of City Lights Bookstore (*see below*), read poetry to the accompaniment of the John Handy Quintet. The gig was a sellout, and Graham went looking for larger premises (*see* Fillmore Auditorium, *above*). *924 Howard St., between 5th and 6th Sts..*

SLIM'S

Boz Scaggs, who has been associated with San Francisco since his early days as a member of the Steve Miller Band, is one of the owners of this SoMa club. The interesting roster of bands it showcases focuses on acoustic, roots, and blues music and attracts many international stars. *333 11th St., between Folsom and Harrison Sts., tel. 415/621–3330.*

North Beach

In the early '50s, the tightly packed streets of the city's Italian quarter saw the birth of the Beat movement. Allen Ginsberg, Lawrence Ferlinghetti, and Jack Kerouac (who shared a pad with Neal Cassady at 29 Russell Street) came here from the East Coast, and a bohemian scene quickly grew up around North Beach's cafés and bars. Although it's getting more and more touristy, there are still a few rock dives in the area, along with some strip joints on the fringes.

EATING DRINKING DANCING SHOPPING PLAYING SLEEPING

BIMBO'S THREE SIXTY FIVE CLUB (1025 Columbus Ave., tel. 415/474–0365), a '30s-style bar venue renowned for its optical-illusion fishbowl (a girl seems to be swimming inside), has put on rock, jazz, and soul for decades; shows are only occasional, so call. In the late '50s, the best of the new-folk talent played the **PURPLE ONION** (140 Columbus Ave., tel. 415/398–8415), which today hosts a wide range of music; garage and surf sounds predominate. If you're getting sick of rock music, try **TOSCA** (242 Columbus Ave., tel. 415/391–1244), a grand old bar where the jukebox plays only opera. The city's main branch of **TOWER RECORDS** (Columbus Ave. at Bay St., tel. 415/885–0500) is near Fisherman's Wharf.

Courtesy of Bimbo's Three Sixty Five Club

CITY LIGHTS BOOKSTORE

In the late '50s and early '60s, this bookstore—along with the nearby Coexistence Bagel Shop and the Six Gallery, where Allen Ginsberg first read "Howl"—was a main hangout of the Beats. It is owned by the poet Lawrence Ferlinghetti, who, with other Beat poets, was a regular performer at the psychedelic gigs at the city's ballrooms in the late '60s. While the music section is

Bimbo's Three Sixty Five Club

disappointing, the shop's an essential stop for any thinking visitor to the city and, not surprisingly, one of the best places to pick up Beat and other poetry. Across the adja-

City Lights

cent alley, aptly named Jack Kerouac Lane, is **VESUVIO** (255 Columbus Ave., tel. 415/362–3370), a dark Beat-era bar where you can sit back and read your City Lights purchases. *261 Columbus Ave., tel. 415/362–8193.*

KMPX STUDIOS

In spring 1967, on these North Beach premises, local DJ and promoter Tom Donohue started what's said to be the world's first underground radio station. KMPX was unique in that it played non–Top 40 stuff, including lengthy album tracks and demos by local bands. The entire staff, including Donohue, went on strike in 1968 and started the still-broadcasting KSAN (95 FM). *55 Green St.*

MABUHAY GARDENS AND
ON BROADWAY

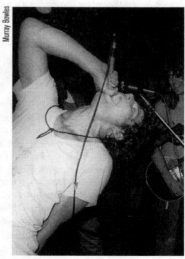

In 1976 this run-of-the-mill Filipino supper club switched its booking policy to punk, and local bands like the Nuns, the Avengers, and the Dead Kennedys soon got important early gigs. In 1978 Norman Shakey (a.k.a. Neil Young) was filming *Human Highway* and chose the club for a staged nightmare musical sequence with a long long version of "Hey Hey, My My (Into the Black)." He flew in Devo for his backing band, and after he played back the tapes, he heard a couple of the bandmembers repeating the phrase "rust never sleeps" over and over; when he called to ask what the hell they were doing, they said they'd once worked on advertising jingles and felt that one for a rust-removal product fit Young's song. The phrase became the title for his 1979 album with Crazy Horse.

Around this time Devo did a solo gig at the Mabuhay that's since become a sought-after bootleg album, *Live at Mabuhay Gardens,* with a great version of "Jocko

Scream at Mabuhay Gardens

Homo." Chris Isaak was another regular and built up a big local following long before his *Twin Peaks* warblings. Around 1980 the local punk equivalent of Bill Graham, Dirk Dirksen, started the On Broadway club in a room upstairs and put on hardcore acts—Black Flag played here over a dozen times—that found no favor with Mabuhay management. In the mid-'80s, the Mabuhay returned to its roots by featuring a famous (at least locally) Filipino Elvis impersonator. *443 Broadway.*

Haight-Ashbury

At the end of the 19th century, the area some 2 miles west of downtown that's become known as Haight-Ashbury was a quiet middle-class neighborhood. After the Depression it went downhill, however, and by the '50s Beat activists and students from nearby San Francisco State College moved here—the rent was cheap in those big, beautiful Victorian houses.

As the '60s progressed, a bohemian scene began to coalesce, fueled by doses of LSD and backed by bands like the Charlatans, Big Brother and the Holding Company, Jefferson Airplane, and the Grateful Dead. Peaceniks, dropouts, and drifters from all over the world migrated here, culminating in 1967's "Summer of Love," the heyday of the hippies. The national press caught hold of it, and onetime Haight-Ashbury resident Hunter S. Thompson wrote a memorable article, "The Hashbury is the Capital of the Hippies," for the *New York Times Magazine* in May 1967. Soon the Gray Line bus company was running tours through the neighborhood so that tourists could get a look at the flower children.

The Grateful Dead's Victorian on Ashbury

After LSD was criminalized in 1967, the area suffered an influx of harder drugs and unscrupulous dealers, and by the turn of the decade it was pretty washed up. Today it's a quietly upscale residential area, with a mix of cafés, boutiques, and the occasional artsy or ersatz-countercultural shop lining Haight Street, the main drag. The most visible elements of the old Haight are young skateboarding panhandlers, weekend hippies, and tourists, who support a trade in tie-dyed garments and New Age knickknacks.

EATINGDRINKINGDANCINGSHOPPINGPLAYINGSLEEPING

The famous intersection of Haight and Ashbury streets has gone all corporate, with a Gap on one corner and a Ben and Jerry's on another. (Upon Jerry Garcia's death in 1995, the ice cream shop couldn't sell the Cherry Garcia flavor fast enough, and tributes to the Dead head hung from every lamppost in the area.) The book, record, and head shops can be fun to browse but generally aren't as good as those on Berkeley's more freewheeling and funky Telegraph Avenue. Three decent record stores on Haight Street sell new and used product: **RECYCLED RECORDS** (1377 Haight St., tel. 415/626–4075); **RECKLESS RECORDS** (1401 Haight St., tel. 415/431–3434), the best of the three for vinyl; and **ROUGH TRADE** (1529 Haight St., tel. 415/621–4395), which boasts "hard to find music from around the world" and always has the newest British releases.

An essential stop on any San Francisco itinerary, the Haight-Ashbury district is best seen during the day, though each Friday and Saturday night for the past 10 years, the **PARK BOWL** (1855 Haight St., tel. 415/752–2366), toward Golden Gate Park, has transformed itself at the stroke of 10 PM into Rock'N'Bowl, where you can knock down pins to alternative and indie sounds. The bars of the Haight-Fillmore district, a mile east down a steep hill, are more fun. Try the postindustrial **Noc Noc** (557 Haight St., tel. 415/861−5811) and the loud **Toronado** (547 Haight St., tel. 415/863−2276).

BIG BROTHER HOUSE

In the '60s the Albin brothers, Peter and Rodney, managed this rooming house, which had been converted from a six-bedroom family home to sleep around 20 people. Low rents attracted a musical clientele, one of whom—a young Texan named Chet Helms— went on to rival Bill Graham as a concert promoter. At the end of 1964, Helms held jam sessions in the basement, charging a buck; out of these parties emerged Big Brother and the Holding Company (the players got down to two band names and couldn't choose, so they used both), featuring Peter Albin on bass. In 1966 Helms persuaded fellow Texan Janis Joplin to come up to San Francisco to join the band. The house was later ripped down and replaced by an apartment block. *1090 Page St.*

⌈ GRATEFUL DEAD HOUSE, 1966−68 ⌉

The Grateful Dead moved into this smart Victorian after Danny Rifkin, who kind of looked after their legendarily chaotic financial affairs, found a job as manager of the house. In October 1967, cops carried out a well-planned bust, nabbing all band members and girlfriends except Jerry Garcia, who was walking up the street and got tipped off by neighbors. Pigpen, who apparently never touched pot, had to be pulled off the toilet. They were jailed for six hours and released on bail, upon which they issued a press release about the harmlessness of dope and invited the media to the house to discuss the pointlessness of the police action. *710 Ashbury Ave.*

HAIGHT-ASHBURY FREE CLINIC

What is probably the nation's largest free medical concern was started in 1965 by Dr. David Smith, who wasn't a hippie but was concerned about the health and substance abuse of young people drifting into the neighborhood. His band of volunteers staffed the medical tents at all the big festivals of the late '60s, their most common task being to bring people down from bad acid trips. Bill Graham hired Free Clinic staffers to carry out a similar role at his big concerts in the '70s and '80s, and when he died in 1991 his will reportedly left a sizable donation to the HAFC. He is remembered by the Bill Graham Center for Health and Recovery, which treats alcohol and other drug dependencies.

Nirvana, Bleach

In early 1989, a flu-stricken Nirvana, on a foray down south before the release of their first album, had to call upon the services of the clinic, which at the time was running an AIDS-awareness campaign to encourage I.V. drug users to bleach their syringes. Inspired by a guy dressed up as a bleach bottle handing out flyers on Haight Street, the band decided on *Bleach* for the name of the LP. *1558 Clayton St., at Haight St., 2nd floor, tel. 415/487−5632.*

In the fall of 1968, flush with success from negotiating a big advance for *After Bathing at Baxter's,* Jefferson Airplane purchased this four-story mansion, built for a lumber baron around the turn of the century. Complete with carved banisters, lavish chandeliers, mahogany paneling, and a view onto Golden Gate Park, it was a luxurious joint. Although it was intended for business use and rehearsals, most band members ended up living here at some point during the late '60s and early '70s. It soon became a crash pad for rock glitterati like David Crosby, who stayed for ages. On January 26, 1970, Spencer Dryden and Sally Mann were married here, with a reception for 300; Dryden's ex-lover Grace Slick was maid of honor, and Paul Kantner, her partner at the time, was best man. The band sold the place for half a million bucks in 1986, and it's currently painted white, not black and gold, as it was in the '60s. *2400 Fulton St.*

Golden Gate Park

More pleasant and safer than New York's Central Park, Golden Gate Park is barely a mile wide but runs for almost 4 miles between Haight-Ashbury and the Pacific Ocean. This great slab of verdant beauty, full of botanical treasures and various museums, was a logical place for stoners to hang out when the Haight turned countercultural in the mid-'60s. Free gigs started in late 1966, and the park played host to the first Human Be-In in 1967; it's since seen dozens of rock events.

KEZAR STADIUM

Tucked into the southeast corner of the park, a short walk from Haight-Ashbury, this stadium was where the first of Bill Graham's big one-day "Day on the Green" shows took place in late May 1973. The Grateful Dead headlined, supported by New Riders of the Purple Sage and Waylon Jennings, appearing on a rock bill for the first time. When Led Zeppelin played the following month at the second "Day on the Green," the music was so loud that complaints from residents forced Graham had to shift the gigs to Oakland. He was, however, allowed to put on a benefit on March 23, 1975, to bolster the city's school funds after politicians announced that there was no money in the budget for extracurricular activities. Under the banner of SNACK (San Francisco Needs Athletics, Culture, and Kicks), he assembled a bill of Dylan and the Band, the Dead, Neil Young, and Santana, with guest appearances by Marlon Brando and other personalities from the entertainment and sporting fields. Little goes on at Kezar anymore—it seems the city still hasn't forgotten the racket made by Zeppelin.

POLO FIELD

This large amphitheater, sometimes known as the Golden Gate Park Stadium, can hold up to half a million people and was the site of the first Human Be-In on January 14, 1967, a day chosen by an astrologer. Subtitled "A Gathering of the Tribes," it was the first large countercultural gathering. Timothy Leary spoke, saying for the first time to "tune in, turn on, drop out." Allen Ginsberg led mantras, and other hippie gurus made rambling speeches. Music was supplied by the Grateful Dead, Jefferson Airplane, Quicksilver Messenger Service, Sir Douglas Quintet, and Dizzy Gillespie. Berkeley radicals from the Free Speech movement were in attendance, Hells Angels guarded the stage, and the leftish Diggers gave out free turkey sandwiches, many of which were laced with acid supplied gratis by the ubiquitous LSD chemist Owsley Stanley. The event brought mainstream media attention to the San Francisco hippie scene, and Haight-Ashbury became a magnet for tens of thousands of young transplants who heeded Leary's message.

In the early '70s, a band that had just moved from Louisiana to an apartment on East 46th Street sent a demo to Warner Bros. The label wasn't impressed and sent the tape back, addressed— as the demo had no name on it—to "The Residents," a name the band took as its own. Known for hiding their identities behind giant eyeball masks, the group received little airplay, and eventually they bought time on the city's most popular Top 40 station so their music could be heard on the airwaves. Today the band keeps a modest studio and office, downtown at 109 Minna Street, to run its record label, Ralph Records, and the Cryptic Corporation, which handles the business side of things and the Residents' CD-ROM output.

The Residents, Freak Show

Elsewhere Around San Francisco

CANDLESTICK PARK

The Beatles played their last concert on the evening of August 29, 1966, before 25,000 fans, bowing out with a version of "Long Tall Sally." The only other public appearances the four were to make were for the live telecast of "All You Need Is Love" in 1967 and the video shoot for *Let It Be* on the roof of Apple on January 30, 1969. *Off Hwy. 101 S, Candlestick exit, 5 mi S. of downtown.*

COW PALACE

This huge south-side arena was built as a cattle exhibition and rodeo space at a time when the city economy was in a nosedive. A local newspaper ran a scathing editorial saying that while there were people starving and homeless in San Francisco, a palace for cows was being built—and the name stuck. One of the first pop bands to play the Palace was the Beatles, who made their U.S. debut here in 1964; during their 30-minute set, they were pelted with jelly beans. In a 1973 appearance by the Who during the "Quadrophenia" tour, Keith Moon arrived late and proceeded to pass out during the show not once but twice. When Pete Townshend asked if there was a drummer in the crowd, an audience member came onstage and filled in for the inebriated Moon. Major acts continue to perform here. *Geneva Blvd. and Santos St., Daly City, tel. 415/469–6065.*

GOLDEN GATE BRIDGE

In May 1971 Grace Slick was racing a friend home in her Mercedes when she lost control and hit a supporting wall of this two-mile-long bridge. The ambulance crew thought she was dead, but it turned out be just a concussion. Seven years later she crashed again and was charged with drunk driving and damage to municipal property. One of the foremost theories concerning the disposition of Jerry Garcia's ashes after his cremation in 1995 was that they were scattered from the bridge; the rumor was laid to rest in April 1996 after it was revealed that Bob Weir and Garcia's widow had dispersed them in the River Ganges in India.

LET IT BE RECORDS

Way out in the Sunset neighborhood, south of Golden Gate Park, this shop specializes in Beatles collectibles, rare discs, and memorabilia. *2434 Judah St., tel. 415/681–2113.*

SANTANA MURAL

Since the '60s San Francisco has been sprucing itself up with colorful murals. "Inspire to Aspire," a huge street-corner mural of Carlos Santana painted in the mid-'80s, straddles three buildings in the Mission District, a largely Chicano neighborhood where Santana lived after moving with his family from Tijuana, Mexico. *S. Van Ness Ave. and 22nd St.*

San Rafael

Some 20 miles north of downtown San Francisco is sleepy San Rafael, a fairly ordinary little town that boasts one of Marin County's best live-music spots and one of music's most sung-about jails, San Quentin.

NEW GEORGE'S

More rock oriented than the Sweetwater in Mill Valley, New George's puts on an eclectic range of music from thrash to roots—anyone from Huey Lewis to Todd Rundgren may pop up unannounced. In the '80s and '90s, Jerry Garcia would climb onstage to jam virtually every time Los Lobos, one of his favorite bands, played here. *842 4th St., tel. 415/457–1515.*

SAN QUENTIN STATE PRISON

Johnny Cash, Johnny Cash at San Quentin

Johnny Cash played the first of several concerts at this jail overlooking San Francisco Bay on January 1, 1960; future country star Merle Haggard was in the audience, serving time for robbery. Cash returned in 1965 to cut *Johnny Cash at San Quentin.* Charles Manson also recorded a live album, *Charles Manson—Live in San Quentin,* while he was on death row; Manson is in Corcoran these days, but his songs are getting out—Nine Inch Nails, the Lemonheads, Red Kross, and GN'R have recorded covers. The prison, still open for business, is just outside San Rafael, near the west end of the Richmond–San Rafael Toll Bridge, about a 30-minute drive north of the Golden Gate Bridge.

Sausalito

Sausalito is the first Marin County community across the Golden Gate Bridge from San Francisco. As late as the '60s, it still possessed a slight bohemian edge, with bars like the Ark, the birthplace of Moby Grape, and the Trident, where Janis Joplin hung out. The Grateful Dead made the trek out to the town's heliport to practice in the mid- and late '60s. With the expansion of the marina, its now a bland yachting center.

["DOCK OF THE BAY" SITE]

Otis Redding stayed on a houseboat here in 1967 and wrote "(Sittin' on) the Dock of the Bay," which, released posthumously, was to be his biggest hit. Earlier in the '60s, several players on the folk scene—including David Crosby—lived on houseboats docked in Sausalito. *Main dock, Waldo Point.*

PLANT STUDIOS

Originally known as the Record Plant, this studio opened on Halloween 1972 with a star-studded party; John Lennon and Yoko Ono came dressed as trees. At one point Sly Stone lived on the premises, a brown wooden building in an industrial complex below the highway, and went to the lengths of having his own private entrance and bathroom built.

Among the more famous albums to have been done here are Fleetwood Mac's *Rumours,* Stevie Wonder's *The Secret Life of Plants,* and *Sports* by Huey Lewis and the News. During the mid-'90s, clients have ranged from the Breeders, Ozzy Osbourne, and David Bowie to Mariah Carey, Michael Bolton, and Harry Connick, Jr. Plan on laying out over $2,000 a day to record here. *2200 Bridgeway, tel. 415/332—6100.*

Aspen

Rock stars—Don Henley, Cher, and John Denver—have made Aspen home, and many more come to ski and whoop it up. But the most famous rock & rolling long-term resident is journalist Dr. Hunter S. Thompson, who ran for mayor in 1970 on a platform to change the town's name to Fat City and to punish *dishonest* drug dealers. He didn't lose by much. That October Thompson in *Rolling Stone*—in the first piece of gonzo political reportage he did for the magazine—that he liked the peace and quiet of Aspen because he could wander outside naked, fire his .44 magnum, and "turn up the amp to 110 decibels for a taste of 'White Rabbit.' "

EATINGDRINKINGDANCINGSHOPPINGPLAYINGSLEEPING

To get to the **WOODY CREEK TAVERN** (2858 Woody Creek Rd., tel. 202/923−4585), long a favorite of Thompson's, go 7 miles north of Aspen on Highway 82, turn right on River Road, and then take the first left. The joint still pulls in fans of the reclusive author, though nowadays he prefers the less-touristed bars of Basalt, some 30 miles away. In Aspen itself is a small branch of the **HARD ROCK CAFE** (210 S. Galena St., tel. 970/920−1666).

Denver

Thanks largely to being the only big city on the route between Chicago and the West Coast, Denver gets more than its share of top and breaking acts.

EATINGDRINKINGDANCINGSHOPPINGPLAYINGSLEEPING

Like other western cities with cold winters, Denver has gotten into the espresso and microbrewery crazes in a big way. Be sure to take ID, as the city is card-crazy. You can check out industrial-dance sounds at **WAX TRAX** (619−20 E. 13th Ave., tel. 303/860−0127), where the record chain started out before opening its more celebrated Chicago branch.

DENVER DOG

Flush with cash from promoting successful shows at San Francisco's Avalon Ballroom in the fall of 1967, the Family Dog operation thought the time was right to open a psychedelic ballroom in Denver. A lease was taken on an empty factory, and the Denver Dog's doors opened in August 1968 with a bill of Big Brother and the Holding Company and Blue Cheer. Things went well, and soon capacity crowds of 3,000 turned out for shows by the Doors and the Grateful Dead. What Family Dog didn't count on was the Denver police.

At the time, Colorado was attracting people who thought the Haight-Ashbury scene was past its prime, and a faction in the police department was determined to run the hippies out of town. Longhairs were locked up for the pettiest of offences, like blocking the sidewalk, and the Denver Dog was hassled over permits and other operational minutiae. A Dog employee filed a false-arrest suit on the most zealous policeman, a Detective

Gray, but the harassment frightened off the audience, and the venue closed barely six months after opening. Part of the space is now occupied by PTs, a strip joint. *1601 W. Evans Ave.*

HERMAN'S HIDEAWAY

This venue in the Antiques District, 2 miles south of downtown, has been putting on a varied roster of impressive names since opening in 1982. In the '90s, Phish, Blues Traveler, the Dave Matthews Band, Jane's Addiction, and the Young Dubliners have passed through. Local bands that cut their teeth here include Big Head Todd and the Monsters, Carolyn's Mother, and Furious George and the Monster Groove. *1578 S. Broadway, tel. 303/778-9916.*

THE MERCURY CAFÉ

Marilyn McGinty has been booking the most prestigious names on the alternative circuit since 1976, initially at a place on 13th Street, and since 1990 at this bar on the northeast edge of downtown. In 1995 the Mercury played host to Alanis Morissette and to the Mike Watt/ Foo Fighters/Hovercraft road tour. The café's scrapbooks reveal such past visitors as the Birthday Party, Nico, the Dead Kennedys, Black Flag (several times), and Glenn Branca, as well as Albert King and Roy Buchanan. The Mercury is open for breakfast and lunch and also puts on spoken-word performances and various offbeat shows. *2199 California St., tel. 303/294-9258.*

Marilyn (blonde at center) and Friends at the Mercury's annual Halloween bash

MILE HIGH STADIUM

The three-day Denver Pop Festival, held the last weekend of June 1969, was the last public appearance by the Jimi Hendrix Experience, a fact that wasn't exactly clear to the band—guitarist Noel Redding had to be told by a journalist that he'd been fired. *2755 W. 17th St., tel. 303/458-4848.*

[RED ROCKS AMPHITHEATER]

The most famous concert at Colorado's outdoor arena of choice, a natural amphitheater between two sandstone cliffs, took place in June 1983: Despite atrocious rain, U2 did the set that became the *Under a Blood Red Sky* video and live mini-album. Other big names have also had a rough time. When the Beatles played in 1964, they suffered from altitude sickness. In the early '70s, police used tear gas to quiet 9,000 Jethro Tull fas; pianist John Evan claimed he couldn't see his instrument for the smoke. *Red Rocks Park, Morrison, 12 mi west of Denver, tel. 303/572-4700.*

NEVADA

This sparsely populated desert state is home to Las Vegas, the gambling capital of the world and the ultimate destination for the non–rock & roll showbiz entertainer. Other major towns are few: Virginia City, where the Charlatans played some of the first-ever psychedelic gigs back in 1965, bears little resemblance to the mining town Mark Twain described in *Roughing It,* while Reno, set in the shadow of the snow-topped Sierra Nevada, describes itself as "the biggest little city in the world" but is just a tackier version of Las Vegas. To music fans, Reno is best known for Johnny Cash's "Folsom Prison Blues," in which the antihero shoots a man in Reno "just to watch him die."

Las Vegas

VIVA LAS VEGAS!–ELVIS PRESLEY, "VIVA LAS VEGAS!"

Las Vegas is 24-hours-a-day naked excess. As one stumbles bleary-eyed through the suffocating heat from one hotel-casino to the next, having lost all track of time and a regular diet, it's hard to imagine that before World War II, this was just a small railroad town on the edge of the Mojave Desert—a far cry from the city that can build a hotel modeled on the Great Pyramid, only bigger.

In lounge-singing terms, once you've headlined in Vegas, there's nowhere else to go, except back to Vegas for another season. Shows here mean megabucks for Johnny Mathis, Englebert Humperdinck, Tom Jones, and Paul Anka. Even David Lee Roth is making a handy living doing old Van Halen songs and lounge numbers at venues around town. The Hard Rock Cafe organization has opened a memorabilia-stuffed hotel-casino, and its state-of-the-art concert venue may attract more rock & rollers.

The Hard Rock Hotel and Casino

ALADDIN HOTEL

Elvis Presley married Priscilla Beaulieu in Room 363, the manager's personal suite (now the Executive suite), on May 1, 1967. Elvis had met his future bride, the daughter of a U.S. colonel, during his army stint in Germany; when Priscilla was 16, she moved to Memphis to be with him, living with Elvis's pop, Vernon, in a house behind Graceland. *3667 Las Vegas Blvd. S, tel. 702/736–0111 or 800/634–3424. Suites: $100.*

CONVENTION CENTER

In August 1964 the Beatles played their second U.S. gig in the hall that once stood on this site. Brian Epstein had banned backstage visitors, but he relented when he saw who came to call: Shirley Temple, Liberace, and Pat Boone. *3200 Paradise Rd.*

CUPID'S WEDDING CHAPEL

Axl Rose married Erin Everly (daughter of Everly Brother Don) on April 28, 1990. Even by rock & roll standards, it wasn't a long-lasting affair: He filed for divorce within 48 hours, and the marriage was annulled six months later. *827 Las Vegas Blvd. S, tel. 702/598–4444.*

FRONTIER HOTEL

Elvis Presley bombed on his Las Vegas debut in April 1956. He opened for the Freddie Martin Orchestra and comedian Shecky Green in the hotel's Venus Room (now a restaurant), but the two-week run was canceled half-way through; it wasn't until 1969 that Elvis performed again in Vegas. *3120 Las Vegas Blvd. S, tel. 702/794–8200. Rooms: $100.*

GRACELAND CHAPEL

True to its name, this chapel offers weddings that include an Elvis impersonator to serenade the newlyweds with "Love Me Tender." Jon Bon Jovi married his longtime girlfriend, Dorothea, in a spur-of-the-moment ceremony after an April 1989 gig at the L.A. Forum. After the long drive out to Vegas through the Mojave Desert, the couple first went to a casino and had themselves tattooed. Expect to pay around $200 to be hitched with all the Elvisy trimmings. *619 Las Vegas Blvd. S, tel. 702/474–6655.*

Shana Gallagher

"Elvis" and bride

HARD ROCK HOTEL AND CASINO

A giant Les Paul guitar welcomes visitors to the new Hard Rock Hotel and Casino. Billed as the world's first rock & roll hotel, it's crammed with mementos of everyone from Elvis and Bill Haley to Kurt Cobain and Eddie Vedder. The place opened to great fanfare in March 1995 with an MTV concert special featuring the Eagles, Sheryl Crow, Duran Duran, Weezer, and others, taped in the Joint, the hotel's 1,200-seat concert venue. For other big-name concerts, the concierge often holds back a few tickets to sellout shows for hotel guests. The casino features slot machines with handles shaped like guitar necks, and $5 Red Hot Chili Peppers "Give It

Away" and $100 Tom Petty "You Got Lucky" gaming chips. The Vegas Hard Rock Cafe, which has been around since 1990, is next door. *4455 Paradise Rd., tel. 702/693– 5000 or 800/HRD–ROCK. Rooms: $85–$300.*

LAS VEGAS HILTON

In 1969, after an eight-year layoff from live work, Elvis returned to performing in grand style with a four-week, 57-show residency at this huge, 3,000-room hotel, then known as the International. He stayed on the 31st-floor Imperial Suite (now known as the Elvis Presley Suite) and set new records for attendance and receipts, which he then broke all over again when he returned the following year. The shows were recorded for the Vegas part of his 1969 *From Memphis to Vegas/From Vegas to Memphis* album. When his run was over, the hotel gave him a gold belt, now on display in the trophy room at Graceland. *3000 Paradise Rd., tel. 702/732–5111. Rooms: $100 (more for Elvis suite).*

The 10 of Vegas

Elvis Presley, "Viva Las Vegas" (1964)
Darryl Hall and John Oates, "Las Vegas Turnaround" (1974)
Gram Parsons, "Ooh Las Vegas" (1974)
B-52's, "Queen of Las Vegas" (1983)
Gun Club, "The Las Vegas Story" (1984)
Was Not Was, "Wedding Vows in Las Vegas" (1988)
Cocteau Twins, "Heaven or Las Vegas" (1990)
Sheryl Crow, "Leaving Las Vegas" (1994)
dEUS, "Whose Vegas?" (1994)
Sleeper, "Vegas" (1995)

Virginia City

RED DOG SALOON

The psychedelic-rock era started as early as the summer of 1965, when a beatnik entrepreneur bought the lease on a gambling hall in this Old West mining town, 25 miles southeast of Reno. The search for a house band began and ended with the Charlatans. The Haight-Ashbury–based group is generally accepted as the first psychedelic band put together by George Hunter, a recording engineer who couldn't play an instrument and just barely sang.

For their first appearance at the Red Dog, on June 21, 1965, the players were decked out in 19th-century cowboy clothes, a look adopted by scores of bands at the end of the decade. The Charlatans also introduced some of the first psychedelic light shows, where LSD was commonly ingested by the audience. Although its recorded output was limited, the band did achieve cult status with its mildly stoned version of Leadbelly's "Ala-bama Bound." In September 1965 the Charlatans were busted for grass in California; the Red Dog's management then fired them and closed the venue, whose site today remains something of a mystery.

New Mexico, dotted with mountains, deserts, and ancient Native American sites, has seen little rock & roll activity, although Buddy Holly recorded most of his output in Clovis. Route 66, now mainly superseded by I–40, cuts across the middle of the state through motel-strip towns like Tucumcari, mentioned by Little Feat on "Willin'."

Albuquerque

HOT DOG, JUMPING FROG, ALBUQUERQUE—PREFAB SPROUT, "THE KING OF ROCK & ROLL"

David Bowie arrived in Albuquerque—New Mexico's biggest city, which sprawls alongside the Rio Grande—on the Santa Fe Superchief train to begin shooting *The Man Who Fell to Earth* in July 1975. Around the same time, Mike Judge, creator of Beavis and Butt-Head, was starting high school here; in interviews he's said that some of his colleagues in the boring 'burbs of Albuquerque were not dissimilar to his cartoon music critics/cretins.

Clovis

NORMAN PETTY STUDIOS

Born in Lubbock, Texas, Buddy Holly cut most of his massive-selling '50s hits under Norman Petty's supervision in sleepy Clovis, just inside the New Mexico state line with Texas. A year after recording Roy Orbison's debut single, "Ooby Dooby," in 1956, Petty turned his attention to Holly. A winning formula for the bespectacled singer came only after a lot of experimentation—at first Petty used a cardboard box instead of drums because he couldn't figure out how to get the right sort of amplification. Unable to decide whether to present Holly as a rough rockabilly singer or a sensitive crooner, Petty covered his bases by doing both. He targeted the solo Holly at the female market with melodious records like "Raining in My Heart" (on the Coral label) but presented Buddy Holly and the Crickets to a male audience with tough songs like "Oh Boy" (on the Brunswick label).

In the early '60s Petty enjoyed chart success with Jimmy Gilmer and the Fireballs, and he scored again in the '70s with the Babys after moving operations in 1968 to an old cinema at 206 Main Street. The original West 7th Street studio is now a mini–Holly museum (opening times vary) and hosts an annual Holly festival at the end of July. *1313 W. 7th St., tel. 505/356–6422.*

Gallup

In the early '60s, when no interviewer could get a straight answer out of Bob Dylan, he invented a story about being an orphan from Gallup to hide his middle-class Minnesotan roots. This city, basically a 10-mile strip of motels and fast-food joints, is still best known for its place on the "Route 66" lyric, in between Amarillo and Flagstaff, Arizona.

WELL I CROSSED MY OLD MAN BACK IN OREGON—STEELY DAN, "DON'T TAKE ME ALIVE"

Sandwiched in between its more populous neighbors California and Washington, Oregon can't compete in terms of rock & roll contributions. The main college town, Eugene, is of mild interest to those of a Merry Prankster or Animal House bent, while the state's only metropolis, Portland, has a healthy and very enjoyable contemporary scene.

Eugene

Set in the lush Willamette Valley, Eugene is the home of the University of Oregon, as well as the fictional Faber College in the movie *Animal House*. The surrounding area became a popular destination for hippies who wanted to get out of San Francisco when acid was made illegal in 1967. Ken Kesey (who still lives just outside town) and the Merry Pranksters settled here, and the Grateful Dead (many of whose crew members were local) played here regularly after creating a strong following during its Great Northwest Tour of winter 1968.

EATINGDRINKING**DANCING**SHOPPING**PLAYING**SLEEPING

Eugene's hippie heritage lives on in the huge annual **OREGON COUNTY FAIR** (tel. 503/343–6554), which has been staged every second week of July since the late '60s. The fair features a wide range of music, New Age seminars, and arts and crafts. Between April and December, the **SATURDAY MARKET** (8th Ave. and Oak St.) offers a scaled-down version. The best place to see performance art and such local bands as the Cherry Popping Daddies is downtown at the **WOW HALL** (291 W. 8th Ave., tel. 503/687–2746), an old union hall built by the "Wobblies" (International Workers of the World).

Portland

The City of Roses is best known in rock circles as the town that placed the song "Louie, Louie" smack bang into the national consciousness. Not one but two Portland-based bands—the Kingsmen and Paul Revere and the Raiders, who relocated here from Idaho—had hits with the song in 1963.

Between then and the end of the '80s, Portland produced few names of note, bar the Wipers and Quarterflash, who had a No. 3 hit in 1981 with "Harden My Heart." Speak to locals, however, and they'll take as much credit for the healthy state of northwestern music as Seattle. With a reputation for being more receptive to new bands, plus a greater number of all-ages venues, they have a point. Even though Nirvana, Soundgarden, and Pearl Jam all lived in the bigger city 170 miles to the north, they used to play here almost as often as in their home base.

Murray Bowles

The Wipers

In October 1995 the city's rock reputation received a further boost with the staging of the inaugural North by Northwest Music Festival. More than 300 acts from the Pacific Northwest, the Rockies, and California—ranging from hardcore and hip-hop acts through singer-songwriters—played over four nights . There are high hopes that this may become as big an annual event as Austin's South by Southwest affair.

The current crop of local artists includes Eric Matthews, the Spinanes, Gift, Everclear, and Heatmiser. Pond moved down from Alaska after a contract on the Sub Pop label beckoned. Tim Kerr Records is also based here; the eclectic indie label's releases have included Pere Ubu's 1995 album *Raygun Suitcase* and "The Priest They Called Him" by Kurt Cobain and William S. Burroughs.

EATINGDRINKINGDANCINGSHOPPINGPLAYINGSLEEPING

One of the most attractive cities of its size, quirky Portland has a generous helping of offbeat stores, museums, bars, and music venues. **POWELL'S CITY OF BOOKS** (1005 W. Burnside St., tel. 503/228—4651 or 800/878—READ), said to be the country's largest bookstore, occupies one whole block and has a great section of new, used, and discounted books on music. The most interesting record store, **LOCALS ONLY** (61 S.W. 2nd Ave., tel. 503/227—5000) specializes in local releases, with hundreds of northwest bands in stock. **CROSS ROADS MUSIC** (3130—B S.E. Hawthorne Blvd., tel. 503/232—1767) is a co-op, with more than 20 dealers selling rare vinyl and CDs under one roof.

Besides the Satyricon (*see below*), at any one time there are a dozen or so active venues in Portland, most downtown. The big downstairs room at **LA LUNA** (215 S.E. 9th Ave., tel. 503/241—5862) puts on bands, while the Living Room upstairs is a great chill-out spot. Catch local talent at **KEY LARGO** (31 N.W. 1st Ave., tel. 503/223—9919), where Robert Cray played regularly in the '80s and the Dan Reed Network and Kenny G have had residencies. **THEE O** (214 W. Burnside St., tel. 503/790—2870) is a small, kitschy joint in a space that used to be the X-Ray Café, the best venue for up-and-coming regional bands in the late '80s. The **RED SEA** (318 S.W. 3rd St., tel. 503/241—5450) puts on reggae and calypso on weekends and serves good Ethiopian food.

CRYSTAL BALLROOM

In the early '60s, during the city's fixation with all things "Louie, Louie," this vast dance hall put on all kinds of acts, including the Kingsmen and Paul Revere and the Raiders. During the psychedelic era, its revolving dance floor proved popular. The space was recently bought by local microbrew moguls, the McMenamins, who plan to open a brew-pub, wine bar, and music venue here in 1997. *1439 S.W. 14th St., at W. Burnside St.*

[NORTHWEST RECORDERS]

Two of the most famous versions of "Louie, Louie" were done at this downtown studio during the same week in 1963. Not even "Louie, Louie" 'biographer' Dave Marsh could trace who laid the track down first, but the lesser-known Kingsmen claimed a national hit over Paul Revere and the Raiders. The slurred and indecipherable vocals on the Kingmen's version were done by Jack Ely, who was ousted from the band a few days after the recording session. When the record became a success, another Kingsman had to lip-synch the much mumbled words on TV appearances; when they tried to ape the distinctive style live, it didn't go down too well. The building, no longer used as a studio, is decorated with a gold record on the front and was declared a state landmark in 1993. *415 S.W. 13th St.*

THE SATYRICON

Portland's legendary punk venue, a couple of rundown blocks north of the main Burnside drag, was where such local bands as Sweaty Nipples started out. Local gossip has

The Foo Fighters, playing publicly for the first time, at Satyricon

it that Courtney Love first saw Nirvana play here in 1989 when it was supporting a Portland band, the Dharma Bums. On March 3, 1995, the Satyricon presented the first scheduled public appearance of the Foo Fighters. *125 N.W. 6th Ave., at Davis St., tel. 503/243–2380.*

24-HOUR CHURCH OF ELVIS

Not a place for the Elvis fan without a sense of humor, this cheekily irreverent art gallery is based on offbeat artist Stephanie G. Pierce's concept that what we can't get rid of, we might as well use. A careful search reveals an Elvis tortilla chip, an Elvis shroud, a Barbie Doll room, and a shrine to the Snap-On Tools girls. The "24-hour church" tag comes from a slot machine in the window, where for a dollar you can get "married" any time of the day, receiving an Elvisy certificate and a pair of plastic rings. Visitors have included Mojo Nixon (who performed "Elvis Is Everywhere" outside the church at 1:30 AM), Z.Z. Top, Tower of Power, and Madonna (who apparently got a coin-op "marriage"). *750 S.W. Ankeny St., upstairs, tel. 503/226–3671.*

During the '90s the Emerald State has seen tens of thousands of pilgrimages to Aberdeen, the hometown of Kurt Cobain, and to Seattle, the city where he made his name. It's also the state where Jimi Hendrix was born, and a mammoth collection of his personal items will form part of the Experience Music Project, a multimillion-dollar multimedia museum due to open in Seattle in 1998.

Aberdeen

A distressed lumber and fishing town, 83 long miles southwest of Seattle at the butt end of the otherwise gorgeous Olympic Peninsula, Aberdeen is most conspicuous for trailer parks, biker bars, huge lumber trucks trundling up and down the main drag, and unemployed union members lingering outside the International Longshoremen's offices. On wet days, which are pretty frequent, it looks like the end of the earth.

Murray Bowles

Nowadays, however, the town is synonymous with Nirvana: Kurt Cobain was born in Hoquaim, 4 miles west, on February 20, 1967. His childhood years were split between Aberdeen and the small neighboring town of Montesano, where he lived for several years with his father after his parents' divorce. Future Nirvana bandmate Krist Novoselic came here with his Croatian-immigrant parents 12 years later. The Melvins, a big influence on Nirvana and Californian bands of the early '90s, plus a couple of members of the million-selling speed-metal band Metal Church, also grew up here.

MARIA'S HAIR DESIGN

Owned and still operated by Krist Novoselic's mom, this neat blue-and-purple clapboard building was where Kurt and Krist practiced with a number of different drummers back in 1986, when their band had no name. (Early Cobain/Novoselic band names included the Sell-Outs—a Creedence Clearwater Revival covers

The Melvins

band—Skid Row, Ted Ed Fred, Throat Oyster, Pen Cap Chew, Windowframe, and Bliss.) They continued to use the space from time to time, even perfecting some *Nevermind* songs here. *107 S. M St.*

THE KURT COBAIN MINI TOUR

ABERDEEN HIGH SCHOOL (414 North I St.). Cobain and Krist Novoselic attended here and after the former's death, a scholarship fund was set up by his mom, wife, and former colleagues to benefit students with artistic interests.

MORRISON RIVERFRONT PARK (Sargent Blvd.). Fans turned out for a candlelit vigil in this small park the night Cobain died. There were plans to erect a statue of him here, but family and friends quashed them.

NORTH ABERDEEN BRIDGE (Hwy. 101 S., between Aberdeen and Cosmopolis). Kurt Cobain slept out at night under this bridge (alluded to in the first line of "Something in the Way"), at a time when future bandmate Krist Novoselic had a daytime job painting it.

THE POUR HOUSE (508 E. Wishkah St., tel. 360/533-4661). Cobain was said to have played at this wooden tavern in pre-pre-pre-Nirvana days. It's still the only quarter-decent live music place in town.

Montesano

THRIFTWAY PICK RITE

Before moving up the road to Aberdeen and then on to San Francisco, most of the Melvins lived in Montesano. The hardcore trio took their name from a newspaper report about a local man named Melvin who was arrested for stealing a Christmas tree outside this supermarket. *211 Pioneer Ave. E, tel. 360/249–3420.*

Olympia

"...I WENT TO SCHOOL IN OLYMPIA/ EVERYONE'S THE SAME... WE LOOK THE SAME/WE TALK THE SAME/WE EVEN FUCK THE SAME"—HOLE, "ROCK STAR"

Pat Graham

Washington's small state capital, 60 miles south of Seattle, has had a big influence on the state's music, thanks mostly to Evergreen State College. The town saw the development of the Riot Grrl scene, and it is still home to several influential indie labels, including K records, Kill Rock Stars, and YoYo. Others with local associations include the Fleetwoods, who had a *Billboard* No. 1 in 1959 with "Mr. Blue," and Ricki Lee Jones, who was expelled from local Timberline High School.

During the '90s the pristine lawns of the high-domed State Capitol have seen rallies—Krist Novoselic spoke at some of them—in opposition to a series of "erotic music bills" that proposed jailing record-store owners who sold recordings deemed damaging to minors. One bill was passed but then vetoed; its sponsors are likely to try again.

Beat Happening's Calvin Johnson

*EATING*DRINKING*DANCING*SHOPPING*PLAYING*SLEEPING

Olympia's best source of alternative sounds, is **POSITIVELY 4TH STREET RECORDS** (208 4th Ave. W, tel. 360/786–8273). The **CAPITOL THEATER** (205 5th Ave. SE, tel.

360/754−5378), where Dave Grohl had his debut with Nirvana in late 1990, screens art films and has bands on the weekend.

EVERGREEN STATE COLLEGE

This liberal arts college has a reputation as a free-thinking institution—*Simpsons* creator Matt Groening (who names Captain Beefheart's *Trout Mask Replica* as his favorite album) is among its alumni. Sub Pop cofounder Bruce Pavitt attended between 1979 and 1983; he got involved with KAOS, the college radio station, and began to produce a fanzine called *Subterranean Pop*. One of the 'zine's contributors was Calvin Johnson, singer with Beat Happening, who went on to found K records.

Thanks to the reputation of KAOS, the college was a popular venue for gigs in the late '80s. In 1987 Kurt Cobain made his first live appearance here in a makeshift band called Brown Towel, and it was at a Halloween 1988 dorm party that he reportedly performed the ritual slaughter of his guitar for the first time. *2700 Evergreen Pkwy. NW, tel. 360/866−6000.*

Seattle

Even taking into account that every dog has its day, Seattle would not have been the bookmakers' bet for the world's liveliest musical city in the early '90s. The city had settled into being a rock & roll backwater, despite the legacies of a strong post-war blues scene (*see box below*) and native son Jimi Hendrix. In the late '70s and early '80s, however, it was one of the few cities outside California and New York to have a healthy punk-rock scene. Bands such as the Quarterfish, the Blackouts, Student Nurse, Red Dress, the Fartz, the U-Men, and Ten Minute Warning became popular fixtures at long-closed little dives like the Bird on Spring Street and the Gorilla Room and Baby O's, both on 2nd Avenue. Few of these bands made much of a mark east of the Rockies, and by the mid-'80s Seattle had a metal edge: Queensryche emerged out of neighboring Bellevue, just across Lake Washington, while Duff McKagan played in many local bands before leaving in 1985 for L.A. and Guns N' Roses.

There were, however, several independent labels pushing young local garage bands: Conrad Uno's Pop Llama label had its first release in 1982 with the poppy Young Fresh

Seattle's Jimi Hendrix mural, above the pawn shop where he bought his first guitar

Fellows, while C/Z put out *Teriyaki Asthma,* the first in a series of 10 four-song/four-band 7" EPs, which in November 1989 featured Nirvana's debut—a song called "Mexican Seafood" that later appeared on *Incesticide.* The most successful indie label of the period was Sub Pop, which released Nirvana's first album and early records by Soundgarden and Green River. (After Green River broke up, members Mark Arm and Steve Turner formed Mudhoney, while Jeff Ament and Stone Gossard played in Mother Love Bone and are now in Pearl Jam.)

By 1992 the streets of Seattle were walked by legions of youth in a uniform of grunge clothing. The band that really drew the fans was undoubtedly Nirvana; if anything, the suicide of Kurt Cobain only added to the flow. Although the Seattle scene is not as vibrant as it was five years ago, the success of Presidents of the United States of America, the Posies, Built to Spill, and others assure its continued prominance in rock circles.

Downtown

Downtown Seattle, wedged between Puget Sound and I–5, splits into several distinctive parts. Tourism Central is Pike Place Market where locals and tourists shop; the former pick up fresh seafood and veggies, the latter T-shirts, trinkets, and crafts. Just to the north is the 2nd Avenue corridor, a yet-to-be-developed part of downtown that borders the emerging Belltown neighborhood, a bit tatty around the edges but a good place to grab late-night eats in funky cafés. Running fairly parallel with 2nd Avenue is the waterfront, home to some okay fast-seafood joints and a population of panhandlers.

If Pike Place is a magnet for visitors during the day, then Pioneer Square, eight blocks south down 1st Avenue, is the place to congregate at night. It's best known for its tightly bunched collection of restored saloons—many of which date from the 1890s—that retain a historic beer-swilling feel without being too precious. Farther southeast, spreading out for a dozen blocks past the Kingdome Stadium (where the organist strikes up the refrain from "Smells Like Teen Spirit" to rouse Mariners fans), is the International District, a great place for inexpensive Southeast Asian food, particularly Vietnamese.

EATINGDRINKINGDANCINGSHOPPINGPLAYINGSLEEPING

Check out *ROCKET,* which comes out every two weeks, for info on the music scene throughout Washington and Oregon. One of the best-respected free rock papers in the country, it has been around since the mid-'80s, when one of its writers was Bruce Pavitt, in between editing the fanzine Subterranean Pop and setting up the Sub Pop label.

About a dozen bars and venues in the Pioneer Square area operate a joint program whereby $5 guarantees a not unreasonable night's entertainment at any and all of the establishments. The participating clubs offer everything from indie rock to jazz and blues. The two-room **FENIX** (2nd Ave. S at S. Jackson St., tel. 206/343–7740) puts on a mix of rock, alternative, and reggae; part-owner John Corbett, the actor of *Northern Exposure* fame, tends the bar from time to time. Just south of Pioneer Square, the **CENTRAL SALOON** (207 1st Ave. S, tel. 206/622–0209) puts on unobjectionable pub rock; during the '80s it was a key venue, with early gigs by Mudhoney, Soundgarden, Nirvana, and Alice in Chains (when they were called the Fucks).

Bo Bostruck

Central Saloon

The **MOORE THEATER** (1932 2nd Ave., tel 206/443–1744) holds 1,500 in former vaudville surrounds and has a great booking policy.

BAD ANIMALS STUDIO

This big downtown studio is where Neil Young and Pearl Jam recorded most of *Mirror Ball* and Soundgarden did *Superunknown*. Ann and Nancy Wilson of Heart are part-owners; the band made its name in Seattle as White Heart before deciding in 1970 to head back over the border to their native Canada to avoid the draft. *2212 4th Ave., tel. 206/443–4666.*

CROCODILE CAFÉ

This 188-capacity diner/bar, situated between the shabby 2nd Avenue corridor and the trendy Belltown area, has been the key grunge hangout of the '90s. Sub Pop's offices are only a few blocks away, and it usually rents the place out for its annual birthday bash. In April 1994 the label's sixth-anniversary party went ahead even though Kurt Cobain had been found dead the day before, and media lined the street outside to get sound bites.

Mad Season—consisting of Layne Stacey (Alice in Chains), Mike McCready (Pearl Jam), Barrett Martin (Screaming Trees), and blues artist Baker, whom McCready had met in a drug-rehab center—jammed here for the first time in 1994 and had such a whale of a time that they went on to release an album in 1995. *2200 2nd Ave.; music information, tel. 206/441–5611; restaurant, 206/448–2114.*

[EDGEWATER INN]

Downtown Seattle's only waterfront hotel attracts many rock & roll parties. In the '60s the rooms overlooking Elliot Bay were particularly prized because you could fish out your bedroom window. The Beatles and many other bored rock stars passed a good few hours doing this. While in town for the 1969 Pop Festival, Led Zeppelin took angling to a new level. Some of the Zep tour party hauled in a dozen or so fish and stored them in a closet with coat hangers inserted through their gills. In the ensuing orgy, one of the groupies had an intimate encounter with a half-dead fish rather than a live Zeppelin. The story quickly made its way around the rock world, with drummer John Bonham as the culprit, although tour manager Richard Cole later claimed responsibility in his auto-biography. Fishing is no longer allowed. *2411 Alaskan Way, Pier 67, tel. 206/728–7000. Rooms: $110–$170.*

MUZAK CORPORATION

This factory of easy-listening tunes was the unlikely first base of Sub Pop records. In the mid-'80s, label cofounder Bruce Pavitt got a distribution job in the YESCO warehouse (later bought by Muzak as its national headquarters), claiming it was the closest thing he could get to a music-industry job in the city at that time. Soon he got jobs for friends who played in local rock bands, such as Mark Arm (Mudhoney) and Tad Doyle (TAD). While still employed by Muzak, Pavitt compiled and released the *Sub Pop 100* album (*see* Sub Pop Records, *below*), doing all the mailings from work; record stores telephoning for extra copies were understandably confused when someone answered the phone "Muzak." Later Muzak itself got in on the grunge explosion, concocting a string version of "Smells Like Teen Spirit" that appeared on *Grunge Lite. 964 Denny Way.*

EMERALD CITY BLUES

Seattle never had an influx of black migrant workers on the scale of cities like Chicago or Detroit, but jazz and blues nevertheless enjoyed a healthy following in its late-night drinking dens. One of those who came to play the circuit in the late '40s was Ray Charles. After being orphaned the previous year, 17-year-old Ray, leaving Florida to get "as far away as the bus would take me," ended up in

Seattle for a two-year stint. He checked into a hotel in what is now the International District and soon got engagements at local clubs, including the Black and Tan Club at 1201 South Jackson Street. (The Black and Tan, like the Elks, the Rocking Chair, and other 12th Avenue clubs, has long since closed.) Around this time he changed his name from Ray Robinson, to avoid confusion with boxing's Sugar Ray, and started using heroin—a habit that took him almost two decades to kick. Another young musician then making a start in the area's clubs was Quincy Jones, who got his first break playing trumpet with an outfit called the Bumps Blackwell Junior Band.

OFF RAMP

This live-music and performance-art venue lies next to I-5 on the northeast edge of downtown and is noted for an incredibly powerful P.A.—the management used to give earplugs out before gigs. On March 1, 1991, the club hosted the debut gig of Mookie Blaylock; the band, named after the basketball star, soon changed its name (on record-company insistence) to Pearl Jam. Vedder and company returned to the Off Ramp to do a thank-you show in 1993. *109 Eastlake Ave. E, tel. 206/628–0232.*

O.K. HOTEL

This venue lies in the shade of an overpass just downhill from Pioneer Square, on the first floor of what was once a 300-room Victorian boardinghouse for sailors. Nirvana first performed "Smells Like Teen Spirit" here in April 1991 at an all-ages show. The O.K. continues to put on cutting-edge rock, as well as readings, spoken-word evenings, performance art, ambient-music nights, and experimental jazz in shabbily nice surroundings reminiscent of New York's Knitting Factory. *212 Alaskan Way, tel. 206/621–7903.*

O.K. Hotel

RKCNDY

Pronounced "rockcandy," this 500-capacity venue, which puts on mostly touring bands, was where Pearl Jam filmed its *Alive* video in 1991. It was also a popular Pearl Jam hangout before the band became too well-known. The club stands on the site of a famous breaking ground for Nirvana et al., the Motor Sports International Garage, a great club that was built into an old multistory parking garage. In a fitting gesture, Sweet 75, Krist Novoselic's new band, debuted here in March 1995. *1812 Yale Ave., tel. 206/623–6651.*

SUB POP MEGA MART

The retail arm of the Sub Pop organization offers a healthy selection of the label's back catalogue, promo pics, T-shirts, and other souvenirs. *1928 2nd Ave., tel. 206/443–0322.*

[SUB POP RECORDS]

Although not the first to release what's come to be known as a grunge record—1985's catalytic *Deep Six* compilation came out on C/Z—it is with Sub Pop that the Seattle sound of the late '80s is most closely associated. The label was set up in 1986 by Bruce Pavitt and Jonathan Poneman (a DJ at Washington State University's KCMU and a booker at the Fabulous Rainbow Tavern, a now-closed venue for local bands) who met through Soundgarden guitarist Kim Thayil.

After borrowing $40,000 to set up their business, they put out *Sub Pop 100,* a compilation with some of the hottest alternative bands at the time, including Sonic Youth and Big Black; only one band—the U-Men—was based in Seattle. Pavitt and Poneman then turned their attention to bringing local talent to national attention. Using Jack Endino's very basic Reciprocal Recording studio (*see below*), they pumped out early releases by Green River (who split into Pearl Jam and Mudhoney), Soundgarden, and Nirvana.

Plagued by thinking too big too quickly, the label had some early financial and legal kicks in the teeth, but two things saved it. The first was the Sub Pop Singles Club, a subscription-only mail-order service that generated cash in advance; in return, subscribers got limited-release 7" singles featuring the best of the regional bands, plus a long line of such out-of-towners as Dinosaur Jr, Smashing Pumpkins, Urge Overkill, the Rollins Band, and Babes in Toyland.

Sub Pop's second change in fortune wasn't as well planned. It was Pavitt and Poneman's practice not to bother with formal written contracts; the exception was Nirvana, and only because the drunken colossus Krist Novoselic went to Pavitt's apartment one night and insisted on drawing up a contract on the spot. When Nirvana moved to Geffen, the contract entitled Sub Pop to a generous cut of the band's three subsequent albums. With the extra money, the label was able to sign up bands from beyond the northwest—Afghan Whigs from Cincinnati, Boston's Sebadoh, and Velocity Girl from D.C. Sub Pop's roster continues to change, with new bands signing up and others going on to major labels, but it's still seen as one of the biggest players in the indie world. *1932 1st Ave., tel. 206/441–8441.*

Seattle Center

The 74-acre Seattle Center came to life in 1962 as the site of the World's Fair and now houses a collection of cultural exhibits, tourist attractions, and performance spaces. The keynote building is the adopted symbol of the city, the spindly, 607-foot-tall Space Needle. The complex lies some 15 blocks north of Pike Place Market, just beyond bohemian Belltown, and is linked to downtown by monorail service.

[EXPERIENCE MUSIC PROJECT]

Cleveland has the Hall of Fame, Memphis has its numerous music attractions, and sometime around 1998, Seattle, home of software giant Microsoft, will have a high-tech music exhibit (*museum* seems too old-fashioned a word). This multimillion-dollar endeavor, the dream of Microsoft cofounder Paul Allen, was going to be known as the

Jimi Hendrix Museum—Allen has amassed the world's largest private collection of Hendrix memorabilia—but it's now broadened its scope: Besides covering all facets of the northwest music scene, the Experience Music Project aims to be what Hendrix referred to as a sky church—a place where all people could come together to learn, where music could act as a cross-cultural common ground.

Although plans are still being refined, the EMP's interactive exhibits and hands-on facilities will examine how modern music began, has evolved, and is made. Items on display will include such Hendrix icons as the guitars he used at the Monterey and Woodstock festivals and the original mixing board from the Electric Lady studio in New York, as well as a smashed-up Kurt Cobain guitar, the original sheet music to "Louie, Louie," thousands of concert posters from '30s jazz events to grunge and beyond.

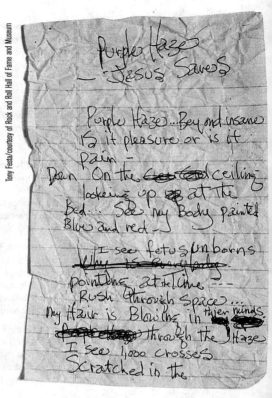

Handwritten Hendrix lyrics such as these will be displayed

Besides exhibits, EMP will include a number of other music-related facilities. A massive "Electric Library" will be stocked with all sorts of northwest recordings, common and rare, including early stuff by Ray Charles and Quincy Jones and over 3,000 Hendrix offerings. There will also be a stage that will host everything from small gigs to art films. In 1995 the project started an impressive educational outreach program that is developing state-of-the-art research facilities. *Broad St. and Denny Way, tel. 206/450–1997, fax 206/453–1985, http://www.experience.org.*

MURAL AMPHITHEATER AND INTERNATIONAL FOUNTAIN

Crowds began to gather and build little shrines near the base of the Space Needle at the Mural Amphitheater after the news of Kurt Cobain's death on Friday, April 8, 1994. By the following Sunday, as the family service took place at a nearby church, some 5,000 people gathered at the Needle heard a taped message sent by Cobain's widow, Courtney Love, in which she read out parts of his suicide note and called for the crowd to yell "Asshole!" This they did, over and over, in a combination of regret, frustration, and anger. Music by Nirvana was played over a P.A. system, and mourners began moshing in the nearby International Fountain and Flag Pavilion. Later in the evening, Love turned up to talk to the remaining fans and distributed some of her late husband's clothes. The event was marred by news the next day of a copycat suicide: A 28-year-old fan from just outside Seattle who had been to the vigil killed himself with a shotgun.

Not since San Francisco in the psychedelic late '60s has a city experienced such a pilgrimage of scenesters as Seattle did when its streets became awash in plaid shirts, cutoff denims, and Doc Martens after grunge broke big in 1991. A grim side to the Seattle rock scene has been a catalogue of rock deaths, most associated in some way with heroin, starting with Andrew Wood of Mother Love Bone in March 1990 and Stefanie Sargent of Seven Year Bitch two years later. Then in April 1994 Kurt Cobain's suicide shook the rock world, followed a few months later by the overdose of Hole bassist Kristin Pfaff.

Mia Zapata, lead singer of the Gits, was raped and murdered in the city. Her killer has still not been found, and local musicians continue to perform benefit gigs to raise funds to pay for private investigators.

The mournful and the morbid still visit the house where Cobain was found dead at 8:30 AM on April 8, 1994, by an electrician who had come to install some security devices. (The house, in the residential Madrona area, 2 miles east of downtown, is not listed here. The artist's widow, Courtney Love, still lives in the home with their daughter, Frances Bean, and has spoken at length in interviews and on the Internet about being harassed.)

At present there's still no grave site for Cobain, and his family's attempts to have a public pilgrimage place have so far failed. Soon after the death, various rumors went around about Cobain's ashes, including one that held that Love carried them around inside a teddy bear for a while. Love did plan to have his ashes interred at Evergreen Washelli Cemetery, but custodians refused, saying there were already enough visitors drawn by the graves of Bruce and Brandon Lee. Another cemetery demanded an annual payment of $100,000 to cover the extra 24-hour security they felt would be needed. In early 1996 Love reportedly took the ashes to a Buddhist monastery in upstate New York and had them ceremonially interred in a stupa. Cobain's family continues to look into placing a memorial in Olympia's Forrest Memorial Garden.

Capitol Hill

Beyond I–5 the streets ascend past residential First Hill to busy Capitol Hill, the hub of the city's gay nightlife. This area has many great cafés and stores, the best of which can be found along Broadway East and 15th Avenue East. On the area's less salubrious southern edge are a couple of key rock hangouts.

BIRDLAND

At the edge of Capitol Hill, this was the liveliest of the late-night clubs at the end of the '50s. Among the mostly black acts were the Rocking Kings, a high-school band featuring Jimi Hendrix. Rumor has it that he was fired after a gig here and beaten up by one of the other band members, who accused Hendrix of being overly familiar with his girlfriend. Soon after, in 1959, Hendrix left Seattle to join the 101st Airborne Division. *2203 Madison St. E.*

LINDA'S TAVERN

This small, dark green bar on the fringe of Capitol Hill is a hangout for local musicians and followers of Sub Pop records—label chiefs Jonathan Poneman and Bruce Pavitt are part-owners. It's said that this was one of the last places where Kurt Cobain was seen alive, sometime between checking out of a SoCal rehab clinic and being found dead. *707 E. Pine St., tel. 206/325–1220.*

MOE'S MO'ROC'N CAFÉ

Moe's might not have been around in the breaking days of grunge, but it has quickly found its place in the Seattle scene since opening on January 21, 1994. Adding further life to this street just off Capitol Hill, it attracts indie and alternative bands that are a bit too big for the Crocodile and not quite big enough to fill RCKNDY. A certain amount of cash has been poured into the joint: Wiry metal sculptures and art exhibits complement the bright green plastic seats of the café, which serves Gulf Coast food, plus

Moe's Mo'Roc'N Café

the usual espressos and desserts. In one of the bars, designated the Rose Room, cases on the walls display items that local performer Jim Rose, of the Jim Rose Sideshow Circus, has swallowed and passed through his system. While the roster of acts that has passed through here is impressive, the most remarkable gig was on June 7, 1995, when 600 people turned up for fewer than half that number of places to see Neil Young and Pearl Jam do a "secret" performance of *Mirror Ball* material for the first time. *925 E. Pike St.; music info, tel. 206/324–2406; café, 206/323–2373.*

University District and Northern Seattle

The University (or "U") District sits just beyond the 50,000-student University of Washington campus, some 4 miles north of downtown across Portage Bay. Although the area is good for shopping, it's devoid of any top venues or bars. A few miles west, beyond Woodland Park Zoo, is the fairly lively Ballard district, where by day the massive and intricate Ballard Locks are popular with tourists who come to watch salmon making their way from salt to fresh water via a huge fish ladder.

EATING DRINKING DANCING SHOPPING PLAYING SLEEPING

The main U District drag, known as "the Ave," is University Way NE between 40th and 52nd streets, a strip of thrift, clothing, book, and record stores; check out the massive selection at **CELLOPHANE SQUARE RECORDS** (1315 N.E. 42nd St., tel. 206/634–2280). At night, the Ballard area attracts people primarily to the **BALLARD FIREHOUSE** (5429 Russell Ave. NW, at N.W. Market St., tel. 206/784–3516), where interesting bands—mostly of a blues, reggae, and rootsy bent—play almost every night of the week.

JIMI HENDRIX MEMORIAL, WOODLAND PARK ZOO

Hendrix fans struggled through years of lobbying and battling bureaucratic red tape to get a memorial dedicated to their hero somewhere in Seattle; in the mid-'80s, a rather offbeat monument was unveiled in the city's zoo. Located at the African Savannah exhibit, in the southwest corner of the zoo, the monument takes the form of a large artificial rock surrounded by purple-hued shrubbery—to give that purple-haze effect—with a semipsychedelic mosaic flowing into a pond and a small plaque. It's not really worth the admission price unless you also like zoos. *5500 Phinney Ave. N, at N. 55th St., tel. 206/684–4800. Admission: $7. Open summer, daily 9:30–6; winter, daily 9:30–4.*

This small studio in the Ballard district, equipped with non-state-of-the-art eight-track equipment, is where the Seattle rock explosion can trace its vinyl roots. Jack Endino, a former navy engineer and one-time guitarist with the local noise band Skin Yard, set it up in the mid-'80s. Before the world had heard of Sub Pop, never mind Nirvana, Endino recorded (he's one of those who hate the term "produced") the 1985 compilation *Deep Six* for the C/Z label. In addition to Skin Yard, the album had tracks from Soundgarden, the Melvins, Malfunkshun, the U-Men, and Pearl Jam/Mudhoney precursor Green River. In 1987 Green River became the first band to have an EP released by Sub Pop Records, and for the next four years about half of that label's output was produced here by Endino. His portfolio included Soundgarden's 1987 *Screaming Life* EP, Mudhoney's 1988 *Superfuzz Bigmuff* (named after guitarist Steve Turner's two favorite pedals), and in 1989 the Nirvana debut *Bleach,* which the liner notes for the CD proudly proclaim was recorded for $600. The studio has had various name changes of late and is currently known as Word of Mouth. *4230 Leary Way NW.*

Curt Doughty

Steve Turner of Mudhoney

SOUND GARDEN SCULPTURE

This giant eco-sculpture—a series of 20-foot-tall steel structures arranged to catch the sound of the wind on the shore of Lake Washington—provided the name for one of Seattle's most successful bands. It's on the grounds of the National Oceanic and Atmospheric Administration Northeast. *7600 Sand Point Way NE, 3 mi northeast of University of Washington, 20-min. drive from downtown.*

Suburban Seattle

[JIMI HENDRIX GRAVE]

The most visited headstone in Greenwood Memorial Park, a flat marble stone engraved with a guitar insignia, bears the legend JAMES M. "JIMI" HENDRIX (1942—70). The grave is toward the rear of the cemetery near a big sundial; the staff is pleased to give directions. The grounds close at dusk, and police signs placed around the perimeter reinforce the message. The cemetery is in Renton, an exurb about 30 minutes from downtown Seattle with more tarmac than is necessary and a system of street naming that is far from clear; take I–405 Exit 4 and a good map. *350 Monroe Ave. NE, at N.E. 4th St., Renton, tel. 206/255–1511.*

SPANISH CASTLE

This long-closed ballroom, midway between Seattle and Tacoma, is best known for the track "Spanish Castle Magic" from Jimi Hendrix's second album, *Axis: Bold as Love.* The 2,000-capacity venue put on some of the biggest rock & roll names of the early '60s, and although Hendrix regularly attended gigs here, he never got a chance to play: There was always trouble with drunk drivers leaving the club and hot-rodding up and down Highway 99, and after a couple of fatal accidents in 1964, the authorities closed it. The building—with its pink-and-white facade, turrets, awnings, and little tower—was then demolished. The space is now a parking lot next to a Texaco gas station. *Hwy. 99, I–5 Des Moines exit.*

Tacoma

The home town of Bing Crosby is hardly one of the visual delights of the Pacific Northwest. Though substantially smaller than Seattle, 30 minutes north, Tacoma has always had a wilder and tougher reputation—stoically blue-collar, home to a big military base (even the Budweiser delivery vans roam around in camouflage colors), with air tinged by the unfragrant gases pumped out of the city's factories.

At the end of the '50s, however, Tacoma boasted the region's most popular bands—the Ventures, Wailers, Bluenotes, and Sonics—and some 30 years later it did host many grunge gigs. Apart from Bing, the town's most famous musical export has been Robert Cray, while other contemporary acts based here have included the long-running Girl Trouble, Seaweed, and Katie's Dimples.

COMMUNITY WORLD THEATER

Also remembered locally as the Community Movie Theater, this former porn cinema was a key hangout in the late '80s for embryonic local grunge bands like Malfunkshun and the Melvins; members of Hole and many other area bands also frequented the place. In 1987 Nirvana did very early show here as Skid Row, playing some original material and Creedence Clearwater Revival covers. A horrific postgig incident in summer 1987 was the inspiration for the controversial *Nevermind* track "Polly": On her way home from a show, a 14-year-old was abducted, raped, and tortured; she escaped when her captor stopped at a gas station. In the early '90s, the by then scruffy venue was sold and converted into the Templo Marantha mosque. *5441 S. M St., at S. 56th St.*

GUITAR MANIACS

This excellent musical-instrument store carries a wide stock of unusual and rare guitars. Customers have included members of Pearl Jam, who brought their buddy Neil Young along when he was playing and recording in Seattle, as well as Dinosour Jr's J Mascis and various Sonic Youth and Rolling Stones players. *752 St. Helens Ave., tel. 206/272–4741.*

STADIUM HIGH SCHOOL

Robert Cray, who was born in Georgia and lived in various places throughout the country as dictated by his father's job in the armed forces, spent his teens in Tacoma. He formed his first band, a psychedelic-rock group, while attending school here but switched to and soon mastered the blues after seeing guitarist Albert Collins play at a graduation dance in the early '70s. One of Cray's first jobs on leaving school was working for Collins's touring band. *111 N. E St., at Stadium Way, tel. 206/596–1325.*

BIBLIOGRAPHY

SELECT BIBLIOGRAPHY

The works listed below were our primary reference sources while writing this book, but we also referred to local listings in papers across the country, to *Addicted to Noise* (online at http://www.addict.com), and to a number of magazines, especially *Alternative Press, Hot Press, Melody Maker, Mojo, New Music Express, Q, Rolling Stone,* and *VOX.*

Alan, Carter. *Outside Is America: U2 in the U.S.* Winchester, MA: Faber & Faber; London: Boxtree (as *U2: Wide Awake in America*), 1992.

Amburn, Ellis. *Pearl: The Obsessions and Passions of Janis Joplin.* New York: Warner Books, 1992.

Andersen, Christopher. *Madonna, Unauthorized.* New York: Simon & Schuster, 1991.

Arnold, Gina. *Route 666: On the Road to Nirvana.* New York: St. Martin's Press, 1993.

Azerrad, Michael. *Come as You Are: The Story of Nirvana.* New York: Doubleday; London: Virgin, 1993.

Bird, Christiane. *The Jazz and Blues Lover's Guide to the U.S.* Reading, MA: Addison Wesley, 1994.

Bockris, Victor, and Gerard Malanga. *Uptight: The Velvet Underground Story.* London: Omnibus Press, 1983.

Bowler, Dave, and Bryan Dray. *Bon Jovi Runaway.* London: Boxtree, 1995.

Brown, Tony. *Jimi Hendrix: A Visual Documentary—His Life, Loves, and Music.* New York: Omnibus Press, 1992.

Bull, Andy. *Coast to Coast: A Rock Fan's U.S. Tour.* London: Black Swan, 1993.

Clayson, Alan. *Death Discs: Ashes to Smashes, An Account of Fatality in the Popular Song.* London: Gollancz, 1992.

Davis, Francis. *The Story of the Blues.* London: Secker & Warburg, 1995.

Davis, Stephen. *Hammer of the Gods: The Led Zeppelin Saga.* New York: William Morrow, 1984.

DeCurtis, Anthony, and James Henke, with Holly George-Warren, eds. *The Rolling Stone Album Guide.* Rev. ed. New York: Random House, 1992.

—————. *The Rolling Stone Illustrated History of Rock and Roll.* 3rd ed. New York: Random House, 1992.

Eden, Kevin S. *Wire: Everybody Loves a History.* Wembly, England: SAF, 1991.

Escott, Colin, with Martin Hawkins. *Good Rockin' Tonight: Sun Records and the Birth of Rock 'N' Roll.* New York: St. Martin's Press, 1992.

Fein, Art. *The L.A. Musical History Tour.* Winchester, MA: Faber & Faber, 1990.

Fong-Torres, Ben. *Hickory Wind: The Life and Times of Gram Parsons.* London: Omnibus Press, 1994.

Gaines, Steven. *Heroes and Villains: The True Story of the Beach Boys.* New York: New American Library; London: Macmillan, 1986.

George, Nelson. *Where Did Our Love Go?: The Rise and Fall of the Motown Sound.* New York: St. Martin's Press, 1985; London: Omnibus Press, 1986.

Gillett, Charlie. *The Sound of the City: The Rise of Rock and Roll.* New York: Pantheon Books, 1983.

Gimarc, George. *Punk Diary.* New York: St. Martin's Press; London: Virgin, 1994.

Gordon, Robert. *It Came from Memphis.* Winchester, MA: Faber & Faber, 1994.

Graham, Bill, and Robert Greenfield. *Bill Graham Presents: My Life Inside Rock and Out.* New York: Delta, 1993.

Gray, Marcus. *Last Gang in Town: The Story and the Myth of the Clash.* London: 4th Estate, 1990.

Grushkin, Paul. *The Art of Rock: Posters from Presley to Punk.* New York: Abbeville Press, 1987.

Guralnick, Peter. *Sweet Soul Music: Rhythm and Blues and the Southern Dream of Freedom.* New York: Harper & Row, 1986.

—————. *Lost Highway: Journeys and Arrivals of American Musicians.* New York: Vintage, 1982.

Hannusch, Jeff. *I Hear You Knockin': The Sound of New Orleans Rhythm and Blues.* Ville Platte, LA: Swallow, 1985.

Hardy, Phil, and Dave Laing. *The Faber Companion to 20th Century Popular Music.* London: Faber & Faber, 1992.

Harry, Bill. *The Ultimate Beatles Encyclopedia.* London: Virgin, 1992; New York: Hyperion, 1993.

Heylin, Clinton. *From the Velvets to the Voidoids: A Pre-Punk History for a Post-Punk World.* New York and London: Penguin, 1993.

Hirshey, Gerri. *Nowhere to Run: The Story of Soul Music.* New York: Times Books; London: Pan, 1994.

Hopkins, Jerry, and Danny Sugarman. *No One Here Gets Out Alive.* New York: Warner Books; London: Plexus, 1980.

Hoskyns, Barney. *Across the Great Divide: The Band and America.* New York: Hyperion; London: Viking, 1993.

Humphries, Patrick. *The Boy in the Bubble: A Biography of Paul Simon.* London: Sidgwick & Jackson, 1988.

Karlen, Neal. *Babes in Toyland: The Making and Selling of a Rock and Roll Band.* New York: Avon, 1995.

Kendall, Paul. *Led Zeppelin: A Visual Documentary.* New York: Omnibus Press, 1982.

Lazell, Barry, ed., with Dafydd Rees and Luke Crampton. *Rock Movers and Shakers: An A to Z of People Who Made Rock Happen.* New York: Billboard/Banson, 1989.

Marcus, Greil. *In the Fascist Bathroom: Writings on Punk 1977–1992.* London: Viking, 1993.

————. *Lipstick Traces: A Secret History of the 20th Century.* Cambridge, MA: Harvard University Press, 1989.

Marsh, Dave. *Glory Days: Bruce Springsteen in the 1980s.* New York: Pantheon; London: Sidgwick & Jackson, 1987.

————. *Louie, Louie: The History and Mythology of the World's Most Famous Rock 'n' Roll Song.* New York: Hyperion, 1993.

Morrell, Brad. *Nirvana and the Sound of Seattle.* London: Omnibus Press, 1993.

Nolan, A.M. *Rock 'n' Roll Road Trip.* New York: Pharos Books, 1992.

Palmer, Robert. *Deep Blues.* New York: Penguin, 1981.

————. *Rock and Roll: An Unruly History.* New York: Harmony Books, 1995.

Putterford, Mark. *Guns N' Roses in Their Own Words.* London: Omnibus Press, 1993.

Putterford, Mark, and Xavier Russell. *Metallica: A Visual Documentary.* London: Omnibus Press, 1992.

Raphael, Amy. *Never Mind the Bollocks: Women Rewrite Rock.* London: Virago, 1995.

Reid, Jan. *The Improbable Rise of Redneck Rock.* New York: Da Capo, 1974.

Riese, Randall. *Nashville Babylon: The Uncensored Truth and Private Lives of Country Music's Greatest Stars.* Chicago: Congdon & Weed, 1988.

Rolling Stone editors. *Neil Young: The* Rolling Stone *Files.* New York: Hyperion, 1994.

Rollins, Henry. *Get in the Van.* Los Angeles: 2.13.61, 1994.

Savage, Jon. *England's Dreaming: Anarchy, Sex Pistols, Punk Rock, and Beyond.* London: Faber & Faber, 1991; New York: St. Martin's Press, 1992.

Selvin, Joel. *Summer of Love.* New York: Dutton, 1994.

Shank, Barry. *Dissonant Identities: The Rock 'n' Roll Scene in Austin, Texas.* Hanover, NH: Wesleyan University Press, 1994.

Sinclair, John. *Guitar Army: Street Writings/Prison Writings.* New York: Rainbow, 1972.

Stanley, David E., with Frank Coffey. *The Elvis Encyclopedia.* London: Virgin, 1995.

Strong, M.C. *The Great Rock Discography.* Edinburgh: Canongate Press, 1994.

Sugerman, Danny. *The Doors: The Illustrated History.* New York: William Morrow, 1983; London: Omnibus Press, 1988.

—————. *Wonderland Avenue: Tales of Glamour and Excess.* New York: NAL/Dutton, 1990.

Sweet, Brian. *Steely Dan: Reelin' in the Years.* London: Omnibus Press, 1994.

Thomson, Elizabeth, and David Gutman, eds. *The Dylan Companion: A Collection of Essential Writing About Bob Dylan.* London: Papermac, 1990; New York: Delacorte Press, 1991.

Thompson, Dave. *Never Fade Away: The Kurt Cobain Story.* New York: St. Martin's Press; London: Pan, 1994.

Tobler, John. *This Day in Rock.* New York: Carroll & Graf; London: Carlton, 1993.

Urquhart, Sharon Colette. *Placing Elvis: A Tour Guide to the Kingdom.* New Orleans: Paper Chase Press, 1994.

Walker, Dave. *American Rock 'n' Roll Tour.* New York: Thunder's Mouth Press, 1992.

Weisbard, Eric, with Craig Marks. *Spin Alternative Record Guide.* New York: Vintage, 1995.

Welch, Chris. *Hendrix: A Biography.* New York: Omnibus Press, 1982.

Wexler, Jerry, and David Ritz. *Rhythm and Blues: A Life in American Music.* New York: Knopf, 1993; London: Jonathan Cape, 1994.

White, Charles. *The Life and Times of Little Richard.* New York: Pocket Books, 1985.

White, Timothy. *Rock Lives: Profiles and Interviews.* New York: Henry Holt & Company, 1990; London: Omnibus Press, 1991.

Woliver, Robbie. *Hoot: A 25-Year History of the Greenwich Village Music Scene.* New York: St. Martin's Press, 1986.

Wootton, Richard. *Honky Tonkin': A Travel Guide to American Music.* Charlotte, NC: East Woods Press, 1980.

INDEX

A

Abdul, Paula, *14*
Abramson, Herb, *39*
AC/DC, *31, 265*
Ace, Johnny, *129, 158*
Acuff, Roy, *81*
AD, *23*
Adams, Bryan, *247*
Adams, Johnny, *107, 110*
Adults, the, *225*
Aerosmith, *7, 8, 10, 44, 67, 169, 252, 265*
Afghan Whigs, *150, 210, 212, 297*
AGB, *110*
Agent Orange, *262*
Alabama, *80–84*
Alabama (group), *82*
Albarn, Damon, *75*
Alexander, Arthur, *82*
Alexander, Willie, *11*
Alice in Chains, *214, 294, 295*
Allison, Mose, *120, 143*
Allman Brothers Band, *36, 37, 45, 55, 58, 87, 89, 92, 98, 99*
Allman, Duane, *83, 84, 89, 97, 98, 99–100*
Allman, Gregg, *96, 97, 98, 179*
Alpert, Herb, *247*
Amboy Dukes, *185, 186, 194*
American Bandstand, *59, 61–62*
American Music Club, *267*
Amitri, Del, *58*
Amps, the, *227*
Anders, Alison, *41*
Anderson, Pinkney, *123*
Animals, the, *26, 27, 63, 85*
Anka, Paul, *83, 284*
AOR, *182*
Arc Angels, *151*
Archers of Loaf, *123, 124, 248*

Archie Bell and the Drells, *157*
Arizona, *236–237*
Arkansas, *85–86*
Armstrong, Billy Joe, *233*
Armstrong, Louis, *45, 102–103*
Armstrong, Tim, *241*
Arnold, Eddie, *135*
Aronowitz, Al, *33*
Arrested Development, *96*
Artistics, the, *69*
Asbury Jukes, *16*
Asbury, NJ, *16–18*
Asleep at the Wheel, *149*
Ass Ponys, *212*
Atlanta, GA, *95–96*
Atlantic Records, *19, 23, 39–40, 82, 83, 131*
Austin, TX, *147–155*
Autoclave, *77*
Avalon, Frankie, *59*
Avengers, the, *267, 272, 275*

B

B-52s, *92, 93, 94–95*
Babes in Toyland, *195, 197, 199, 202, 297*
Babys, the, *287*
Bad Brains, *72, 270*
Bad Company, *221*
Bad Religion, *262*
Baez, Joan, *12, 47, 54, 61, 68, 80, 106*
Baker, LaVern, *186, 188*
Baker, Susan, *71*
Balin, Marty, *238, 263*
Ballard, Hank, *186, 191, 210*
Baltimore, MD, *5–6*
Bambaataa, Afrika, *25, 51*
Band of Susans, *25*
Band, the, *22, 23, 38–39, 41, 43, 55, 56, 57, 58, 85, 101, 272, 273*
Bangles, the, *243*

Bangs, Lester, *28, 33, 186*
Bar-Kays, the, *133, 233*
Barbe, Dave, *93*
Barbero, Lori, *197, 201*
Barnes, Booba, *117*
Barooga, *10*
Bartholomew, Dave, *103, 105, 108, 109*
Bass, Fontella, *164*
Bators, Stiv, *219, 220*
Beach Boys, *19, 37, 61, 72, 228, 243, 250, 257, 263, 265*
Beacon Street Union, *8*
Beastie Boys, *23, 25, 31, 33, 39, 44, 247, 256*
Beat Happening, *292*
Beatles, the, *4, 56, 107, 167, 174, 203, 224, 236, 242, 248, 258, 279, 283, 285, 295*
"Beatles Ban," *212, 214*
Ed Sullivan Show, *41, 42, 45*
John Lennon's death, *48–49*
in New York City, *43, 52*
Beats the Hell Out of Me, *237*
Beavis and Butt-Head, *96, 287*
Beck, Jeff, *69*
Becker, Walter, *23, 52*
Bee Gees, *88, 89, 90*
Bell, Thom, *60*
Belly, *8, 13, 15, 46, 248*
Belmonts, the, *52*
Ben Folds Five, *124*
Bennett, Tony, *48, 76, 81*
Benson, George, *63*
Benton, Brook, *89*
Benton, Glen, *87*
Bernard, Rod, *158*
Bernstein, Leonard, *49*
Bernstein, Sid, *52*
Berry, Bill, *92–93, 97, 196*
Berry, Chuck, *8, 53, 59, 74, 101, 122, 164, 173, 175, 179, 190, 204, 205, 206, 214, 250*

NOTES

NOTES

THE AUTHORS

Tim Perry, the author of several *Rough Guides*, contributes to *Time Out* and other music and entertainment magazines.

Ed Glinert is a staff writer for *Private Eye* and has contributed to many newspapers and magazines, including London's *Sunday Times* and the *Manchester Evening News*.